THE END OF
ROMAN BRITAIN

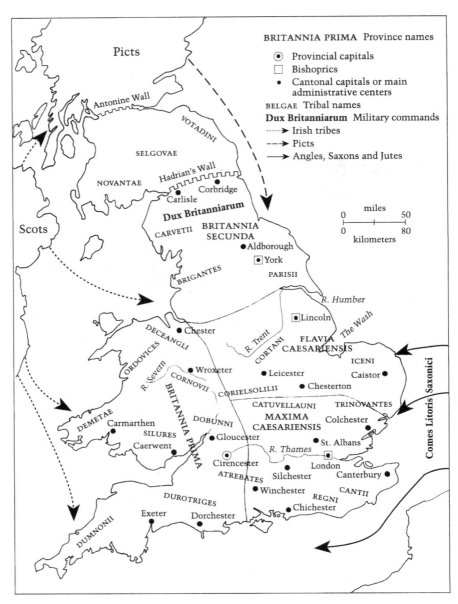

Picts

BRITANNIA PRIMA Province names

⊙ Provincial capitals
☐ Bishoprics
• Cantonal capitals or main
   administrative centers
BELGAE Tribal names
Dux Britanniarum Military commands
······▶ Irish tribes
--▶ Picts
───▶ Angles, Saxons and Jutes

Antonine Wall

VOTADINI

SELGOVAE

Hadrian's Wall

NOVANTAE

Corbridge

Carlisle

Dux Britanniarum

Scots

CARVETII

BRITANNIA
SECUNDA

miles
0   50
0   80
kilometers

•Aldborough

☐York

BRIGANTES

PARISII

R. Humber

☐Lincoln

The Wash

DECEANGLI

• Chester

R. Trent

CORTANI

FLAVIA
CAESARIENSIS

ORDOVICES

R. Severn

CORNOVII

• Wroxeter

• Leicester

ICENI

Caistor•

Comes Litoris Saxonici

CORIELSOLILII

• Chesterton

BRITANNIA PRIMA

DEMETAE

Carmarthen•

SILURES

DOBUNNI

CATUVELLAUNI

MAXIMA
CAESARIENSIS

TRINOVANTES

Colchester•

Caerwent•

•Gloucester

St. Albans•

⊙Cirencester

R. Thames

☐
London

ATREBATES

Silchester•

Canterbury•

CANTII

• Winchester

REGNI

• Chichester

DUROTRIGES

Exeter•

Dorchester•

DUMNONII

Roman Britain in the Fourth Century

The End of Roman Britain

Michael E. Jones

Cornell University Press

ITHACA AND LONDON

Cornell University Press gratefully acknowledges
a subvention from Bates College which
aided in the publication of this book.

First published 1996 by Cornell University Press.
First printing, Cornell Paperbacks, 1998.

Printed in the United States of America

Library of Congress Cataloging-in-Publication Data

Jones, Michael E. (Michael Eugene), 1952–
    The end of Roman Britain / Michael E. Jones.
        p. cm.
    Includes bibliographical references and index.
    ISBN 0-8014-2789-4 (alk. paper)
    ISBN 0-8014-8530-4 (pbk.: alk. paper)
        1. Great Britain—History—Roman period, 55 B.C.–449 A.D. 2. Rome—History—
Germanic Invasions, 3rd–6th centuries. 3. Great Britain—History—Invasions. 4.
Romans—Great Britain—History. 5. Anglo-Saxons. I. Title
DA145.J665 1996
936.1'04—dc20   95-52873

Cornell University Press strives to utilize environmentally responsible suppliers and
materials to the fullest extent possible in the publishing of its books. Such materials
include vegetable-based, low-VOC inks and acid-free papers that are also either recy-
cled, totally chlorine-free, or partly composed of nonwood fibers.

Cloth printing   10   9   8   7   6   5   4   3   2

Paperback printing   10   9   8   7   6   5   4   3   2   1

To my family

As for man, his days are as grass: as a flower of the field, so he flourisheth. For the wind passeth over it, and it is gone: and the place thereof shall know it no more.

Psalms 103: 15–16

Contents

Figures and Tables

FIGURES

TABLES

Acknowledgments

I THANK THE PUBLISHERS of two articles of mine for permission to reuse some of that material in altered form: "The Literary Evidence for Mast and Sail during the Anglo-Saxon Invasions," *Studies in Medieval and Renaissance History* 13 (1992), 33–67 (by permission of AMS Press Inc.); and "The Logistics of the Anglo-Saxon Invasions," in *Naval History: The Sixth Symposium of the U.S. Naval Academy,* copyright 1987 by Scholarly Resources Inc., used by permission of Scholarly Resources Inc.

I extend warm regards to faculty and students at the University of Texas at Austin, University College of Wales, Aberystwyth, and Bates College. Janet Meisel and P. J. Casey deserve special thanks. I am obliged to D. P. Kirby, Jeff Davies, and A. S. Esmonde Cleary, who read the manuscript and offered valuable criticisms and suggestions. Financial support for my research was provided by the Fulbright program, Social Science Research Council, and Roger C. Schmutz Fund. I gratefully acknowledge their support. The reference librarians at Bates College were always helpful. Joyce Caron patiently and promptly typed endless revisions of the manuscript. To all of these people and institutions, thank you.

M. E. J.

THE END OF
ROMAN BRITAIN

Introduction

ONE CENTRAL QUESTION has served as a lodestone throughout this book—why among all the provinces long occupied by Rome did Britain retain so slight an imprint of Roman civilization? The traditional answer has been that the Anglo-Saxons, more numerous and destructive than the other Germanic peoples of the Völkerwanderung of the fourth through sixth centuries A.D., destroyed or displaced Romano-British civilization and thereby created a virtual tabula rasa. This answer is significant, for on the assumption of a fresh beginning rest the very foundations of English national consciousness and constitutional and social identity. The liberties of Englishmen, the "Ancient Constitution," limited government, and the rights of property are seen as stretching back from the eighteenth century to the anchor of the free peasant *ceorl* and the new world formed by the Anglo-Saxon conquest.[1] The coming of the Anglo-Saxons purportedly initiated a peculiar, insular historical development. This traditional picture of the origins of England and the end of Roman Britain has always had critics. The "Germanist" theme of a fresh beginning has been balanced by a "Romanist" school stressing the significant continuity of Roman and Celtic British society into the Middle Ages. The arguments for and against continuity interweave, double, and snap at one another's tails like the zoomorphic interlace in the art of the migrations. Indeed, the historiography of Anglo-Saxon studies has been molded by this debate, a dialectic that will doubtless continue into the future.[2]

---

[1] MacDougall, *Racial Myth in English History.*
[2] Donald A. White, "Changing Views of the *Adventus Saxonum.*"

Over the last sixty years, the Germanist position has been the dominant interpretation. Recent revisionist studies, however, have eroded the edges of the traditional arguments. Many historians now accept the idea that in the west and north of England the Anglo-Saxon conquests involved a considerable annexation and assimilation of British communities, with a significant continuity of their institutions and perhaps even of their estates, rather than their extinction or expulsion. In Northumbria, the Anglo-Saxon settlement was to a great extent simply the imposition of a military elite on an ongoing British society. Even in the southeast, J. E. A. Jolliffe's venerable suspicions of continuity between Romano-British and Anglo-Saxon Kent have recently been confirmed.[3] These revisions have reduced the dimensions of the Romano-British holocaust, however, without wholly excising it from our historical interpretations. The arguments for continuity in their turn are overly dependent on logical inference rather than hard evidence. They generalize unduly from isolated facts. Attempts to demonstrate conclusively significant continuity in specific urban or rural sites have run afoul of the near archaeological invisibility of post-Roman British society and an inability to gauge accurately the longevity of use for Roman durable goods such as coinage, pottery, and glass in the post-Roman era.

There remains in recent modified Germanist interpretations an irreducible core perception that the culture of Roman Britain was destroyed primarily by the Anglo-Saxon invasions and settlements. Even allowing for a more gradual Germanization and a degree of regional continuity, the aftermath of those invasions still represented a decisive break with the past, a new chapter in the history of Britain.[4] Such a thesis is curiously anomalous when matched with current views of the transition between Roman and barbarian rule in the continental West, which involved a great degree of continuity, an "undramatic" adjustment between Roman provincials and German invaders. Moreover, the notion that the Anglo-Saxon invasions destroyed the old order and inaugurated a new one is at odds with a general intellectual paradigm that has moved away from invasion hypotheses and migrationism to emphasize cultural assimilation.[5] Although a modified version of the traditional Germanist paradigm still has

[3] Good surveys of the evidence for continuity may be found in Whittock, *Origins of England,* 60–103; Jolliffe, *Pre-Feudal England: The Jutes;* Everitt, *Continuity and Colonization.*
[4] "In what had been the wealthiest, most densely populated, and most highly civilized parts of Roman Britain, the Anglo-Saxon invasions involved the all but total destruction of the old way of life." Myres, *English Settlements,* 217. E. A. Thompson presents an unadulterated Germanist position in which "'continuity' is out of the question." *Saint Germanus of Auxerre,* 97.
[5] Goffart, *Barbarians and Romans,* 4; Rouse, *Migrations in Prehistory;* Adams et al., "Retreat from Migrationism"; Clarke, "Invasion Hypothesis."

able and learned defenders, many historians now regard its basic assumptions as vulnerable, insular, and suspect. A host of fundamental questions remain unresolved and hotly contested. Nevertheless, from the long-simmering debate a new consensus may be emerging, defined by the decisive conclusion that a significant chronological gap separates vital stages of the complex breakdown of *Romanitas* in Britain from the arrival of the Anglo-Saxons. If "de-Romanization" in Britain precedes the Anglo-Saxons, then it is not a result of Anglo-Saxon invasion and settlement.

My views place me in the anti-Germanist camp, not so much because I discount the enormous dislocations in population, economy, and society in the post-Roman era but because I disbelieve that the Anglo-Saxons were the predominant agent in the process of transformation. In the chapters that follow, I examine critically the causal link between the destruction of *Romanitas* in Britain and the direct actions of the Anglo-Saxons and explore alternative agents of that destruction. If not the Anglo-Saxon invaders, then who or what factors were primarily responsible for the ending of Roman Britain? Were the causes essentially external, part of the overall breakdown of the Roman West, or were they more localized and primarily the outcome of influences and events within Britain itself? Should we think in terms of a model of cultural change based on coercion, with the inhabitants of fifth-century Britain forced to pass grudgingly and reluctantly from the world of Roman imperium into a world of Celtic and then Anglo-Saxon tribal society and kingdoms? Should we perhaps stress choice rather than coercion and consider the possibility of the deliberate rejection of *Romanitas* by significant elements among the Britons?[6] Freed of the weight of the old invasion hypothesis, the debate over the ending of Roman Britain flows into different channels. I argue that Roman Britain was destroyed primarily because of internal failings linked to the process of Romanization and to specific problems of the economy, society, and environment. While the Anglo-Saxons were a part of the problem of security which figured significantly in the failure of *Romanitas*, they were not the major or most persistent part. In general, the Anglo-Saxon invasions were at least as much a symptom of the inherent weaknesses of Romano-British society as they were a cause of its decline.

My route to this position was not direct. I began by accepting the conventional Germanist picture of the Anglo-Saxon invasions and hoped better to understand them by applying F. W. Maitland's technique of illuminating early and poorly documented events through comparison with later, better attested parallels. The results of a preliminary comparative study of the Anglo-Saxon invasions and the later Scandinavian conquests

[6] Reece, *My Roman Britain*, 128–37.

and settlements in Britain in the ninth and tenth centuries proved un-satisfying, however. Besides the inherently disquieting problem of com-paring an enigma with a mystery, I felt a progressive distrust in visions of massive folk movements with attendant agricultural and social revolu-tions and the displacement or worse of native peoples and cultures. My attempts to define the causes of the destruction of Roman culture in Britain lodged willy-nilly in the Roman period proper. A study beginning with the Gokstad Viking ship led to Emperor Claudius and his elephant.

My organization and methodology reflect this direction of movement from the early Middle Ages back into Late Antiquity. I have eschewed the advice given to Alice to begin at the beginning. The book is organized into six thematic chapters that fall into two parts. The first part examines and rejects the Germanist picture of the nature and effect of the Anglo-Saxon invasions. The second part presents the countertheory that Roman Britain was destroyed primarily by insular factors rather than by Germanic inva-sion. The first two chapters address a crucial problem in the study of the early medieval migrations. The continuity of Roman civilization in the areas occupied by Germanic tribes, or the lack thereof, is almost univer-sally attributed to the relative numbers of provincial (Romanized) to in-vasive (Germanic) populations. Where the provincial population was nu-merous and the invaders were an intrusive minority, Roman culture persisted. A gradation of Roman cultural survival from the Mediterranean coastal areas where *Romanitas* was triumphant to the Rhinelands where Germanic tribal culture prevailed marks, it is thought, this pattern of relative population densities. In this context Britain was long regarded as exceptional, a place where an unusually numerous Germanic settlement swamped what until recently was perceived to be a relatively sparse Brit-ish provincial population. A review of current estimates of Romano-British population and an examination of the archaeological and literary evidence for the scale the Anglo-Saxon migrations in fact dramatically contradicts the earlier interpretation. The Romano-British population of the fourth century A.D. emerges as surprisingly numerous, whereas the numbers of Anglo-Saxons are reduced to the modest levels typical of other Germanic tribal migrations of the Völkerwanderung. These Anglo-Saxon movements were by no means exceptional and hence fail to provide a sufficient explanation for the destruction of Roman civilization in Britain.

The problem remains, however, who or what was responsible for the ruin of Roman culture in Britain? The second half of this book begins in Chapter 4 with an examination of the early medieval British vision of the Roman past, as recorded in texts written between the fifth and ninth centuries. The vision of the Roman past that they reveal is largely nega-tive and hostile to Rome. Such an attitude within literate and Christian elements in Britain, the culture which should be most strongly associated with Roman values and traditions, raises the possibility that Britain was not so thoroughly or successfully Romanized as previously believed. The Britons themselves helped destroy the Roman legacy. Their motives are sought in Chapter 5, a study of political, social, and economic conditions within the later Roman diocese of Britain. Chapter 6 provides a study of the natural environment of fourth- and early fifth-century Britain, focusing particularly on climatic and coastal changes influencing late Roman economy and society. I conclude with an epilogue detailing the political events of A.D. 400–410, the final decade of the Roman occupation of Britain.

The raw materials for a study of later Roman Britain include archaeological evidence, the study of place-names, and a variety of inscriptions and literary sources. In a number of recent studies relating to the end of Roman Britain the archaeological evidence has been emphasized to the virtual exclusion of the literary evidence.[7] This is a conscious methodological choice to escape what some call a deductive trap of forcing the interpretation of material evidence to conform to preconceived historical interpretations based on classical texts. The texts themselves are few, and are plagued by problems of transcription and transmission, and by an inherently elitist bias. The New Archaeology also emphasizes methodologies currently more fashionable with scientific than with humanistic wings of study, and strives to be objectively empirical by using high levels of generalization. This approach has merit and has produced interesting results when applied to Roman Britain. Inevitably, however, the marginalization of texts in favor of constructs and theories based on areas of the Roman world with richer material and textual sources, or on analogies drawn from modern anthropological studies, results in the tendency to assimilate Britain into those preconceived patterns. This approach emphasizes external factors and sometimes suppositious forces at the expense of "positive" factors, such as the actions of the Britons themselves, and causal factors operating in a more narrow British context. As the ghost of J. B. Bury might say, such an approach cuts off Boudicca's nose. Thus the advantages of archaeologically based investigations over studies relying significantly on texts must be balanced against different but still potentially distorting problems of conception and interpretation.

Although the literary sources are often fragmentary, difficult, and suspect, texts are the backbone of this study. I have chosen the priests of Thebes over the rubbish heaps of Egypt. In the current minimalist cli-

---

[7] See the essays collected by Driscoll and Nieke, eds., *Power and Politics.* Cf. C. J. Arnold, *Roman Britain to Saxon England.*

mate, with confidence in written sources much eroded, this approach is unfashionable. Rather than constantly interrupting the narrative of my overall argument, I have defended a reliance on the texts in an appendix and numerous footnotes. The archaeological evidence is frequently suggestive and always tantalizing. While I have relied heavily in places on archaeological information, I have not attempted to duplicate or refine certain specialized studies that concentrate on coinage, pottery, and the question of urban or rural continuity. At least for the present, despite intense investigation, these lines of inquiry remain inconclusive. Place-name studies do not, in my opinion, provide trustworthy insight into the process of invasion or migration.[8]

The study of the end of Roman Britain has always fitted awkwardly into the traditional organization of British history. It is too often treated as a shabby epilogue to nearly four hundred years of Roman occupation or assumed to be a largely irrelevant prologue looming small in the medieval and ultimately national histories of England, Scotland, and Wales. Like the study of Late Antiquity in general, the study of the end of Roman Britain falls between the two stools of classical and medieval scholarship. Anyone attempting to straddle the gap risks double amputation at the hands of two distinct sets of experts. Yet it is from a variety of classical and medieval evidence that the early medievalist must cobble together a picture of what happened at the end of Roman Britain. The variety and difficulty of the evidence and the various technical skills required for its interpretation, and all that implies about an academic jack-of-all-trades, create both the fascination and frustration of this subject.

Little temptation exists for a student of the end of Roman Britain to succumb to the monocausal pitfall of earlier general theories of Rome's imperial decline. The subject of the collapse of Roman Britain is so complex and the evidence so problematic that conflicting perspectives valid in argument may coexist, suspended in tension. The evidence is too thin to create an interpretive context significantly independent of the imagination of the individual historian. In the sense of Isaiah Berlin's famous essay we must be foxes pursuing multiple hypotheses, not hedgehogs dominated by a single vision: "The fox knows many things but the hedgehog knows one big thing (Archilochus)."[9] In the narrower Romano-British context too little information survives in any one area satisfactorily to

---

[8] For a recent discussion and bibliography, see Copley, *Archaeology and Place-Names*. For an example of the growing skepticism about the value of place-names as a diagnostic tool to elucidate the pattern, extent, and chronology of the earliest Anglo-Saxon settlements, see Myres, *English Settlements*, 37–44. For a defense of place-name studies see Gelling, "Towards a Chronology."

[9] Berlin, *The Hedgehog and the Fox*, 1.

support a theory. A smorgasbord of factors including the nature of Roman colonialism, Romanization, the quality of Roman government and justice, social and economic organization, the actions of the Britons themselves, problems with internal and external security, and even the physical environment emerge as contributing to the destruction of Roman civilization in Britain. Long after these events and the eventual triumph of the Saxons in Britain, the Bretto-Norman author Geoffrey of Monmouth, in imagining the causes of the ultimate defeat of the Britons, diminished the significance of the Saxons. Foreign invasion, God's wrath, "the plague about which I have told you, the famine, and their own inveterate habit of civil discord caused this proud people to degenerate so much that they were no longer able to keep their foes at bay." In fact, just such a complex coven of troubles led to the end of Roman Britain.

Population and the
Anglo-Saxon Invasions:
The Archaeological Evidence

THE BARBARIAN INVASIONS are perhaps the most dramatic of the problems that ultimately destroyed the Roman empire in the West. The invasions, or the *Völkerwanderung*, conjure a popular cinematic image of massed crowds of savage warriors stretching from horizon to horizon, poised like a great curling wave ready to overwhelm the frail defenses of Roman civilization. Scholarly perceptions are more prosaic, and the numbers of German invaders shrink from millions to hundreds of thousands or even to tens of thousands. As Walter Goffart states of the German tribes and the invasions, "Those involved in it were a mere handful of peoples each numbering at the most in the low tens of thousands."[1] Estimates of German tribal or Roman provincial populations at the time of the invasions are much debated and of necessity highly speculative. Despite a lack of any reliable methodological basis for calculating the population of the various barbarian tribes, a general consensus places an upper limit of about 100,000 for the total population of the largest tribal confederations and far fewer (25,000) for smaller tribes.[2]

A conservative estimate of the total population of the Roman empire at the beginning of the third century is 50 to 60 million people, approximately half of whom lived in the European provinces.[3] Since the entire

---

[1] Goffart, *Barbarians and Romans*, 5. Contrast such a view with nineteenth-century perceptions, which could estimate a single tribe as a million strong. See, for example, Dahn, *Die Könige der Germanen*, 50; Pujol, *Historia de las instituciones sociales*, 308–15.

[2] See Appendix 3.

[3] See Appendix 1. The population of the empire probably grew substantially between the

population of German-speaking territories north of the Rhine and Danube in the third and fourth centuries is usually estimated at 3 to 3.5 million, and since only a fraction of this population was actually involved in migration, the relative populations (German:Roman) were grossly disparate.[4] German tribes or confederations, each numbering at the greatest some 100,000 souls with a war strength of approximately 20,000 men, conquered and settled Roman provinces in the West whose populations, even allowing for possibly severe depopulation during the third and fourth centuries, still numbered in the millions.[5] A rough estimate is that the invaders were less than five or six percent of the Roman population they conquered.[6] The barbarians were not, of course, intermixed with provincial populations like elements in a chemical compound. They settled in clusters and concentrations. Nor were the Germans unanimously hostile to Rome. The period is replete with examples of tribes fighting tribes and Germanic factions warring even within a single tribe at the behest of the Roman authorities. It would be a great mistake to conceive of the Germans as a cohesive or self-conscious unity. Germanic disunity even further exaggerated the demographic disparity between the invaders and the Roman provincial populations. Rarely in the course of western events have so many been conquered by so few. Viewed in this light, the fall of the empire in the West emerges in significant part as a sociological rather than a demographic problem, and in particular a problem of loyalty within the empire between the governors and the governed.

The numerical weakness of the Germans helps to explain their sub-

---

deaths of Augustus and Alexander Severus, possibly even doubling. For the European population see Appendix 2.

[4] The barbarian population in Germany and Scandinavia probably grew substantially between the first and third centuries A.D. Todd suggests that the total population grew from between 1 and 2 million at the beginning of the Roman Iron Age to a fourth-century total of not more than three million (*Northern Barbarians*, 4–5). Todd relies on the work of Mildenberger, who estimates the German population as 1 to 3 million but does not attempt to date this estimate to a particular century (*Sozial- und Kulturgeschichte der Germanen*, 25). Dixon follows Todd's estimate and puts the whole Germanic population before the migration at 2 or 3 million ("Continent in Ferment," 19). Russell's figures are very similar, 3.5 million population for Germany and Scandinavia c. 350 A.D. (*Late Ancient and Medieval Population*, 148; "Population in Europe," 36). Compare these figures with Schmidt, "Die Ursachen der Völkerwanderung," 347. Recent work in the Scandinavian area generally supports the level of these estimates. See, for example, Roesdahl, *Viking Age Denmark*, 18. McEvedy and Jones estimate the combined population of Scandinavia and Germany between A.D. 200 and 400 at something over 4 million (*Atlas of World Population History*, 50–51, 68–69).

[5] See Appendix 2.

[6] Starr, *History of the Ancient World*, 702: 5 percent; Pounds, *Economic History*, 43: 3 to 5 percent; Russell, "Population in Europe," 21: 1/16th; Wolfram, "Shaping of the Early Medieval Kingdom," 9: 5 percent; Vives, *Economic History of Spain*, 84: 5 percent; Katz, *Decline of Rome*, 105–6: 5 percent.

stantial assimilation and the continuity of much of the Roman order. It is one of the keys in interpreting the impact of the invasions and their aftermath. As J. M. Wallace-Hadrill noted of the Franks: "Even combined with all the Visigoths and other barbarians, their numbers could have been only a fraction of the total population of Gaul: and they had neither the desire nor the means to resist the process of romanization."[7] Such perceptions of the relative populations of the Roman provincials and the Germanic invaders have been decisively important in the historiographic debate between the Romanist and Germanist schools which stretches back into the nineteenth century.[8] It is implausible to maintain that so few invaders destroyed the Roman order while founding a new and largely Germanic one. Instead, historians suggest that something like a gradient of Roman influence and culture survived, stretching from the south and the Mediterranean littoral, where the Germans were largely absorbed, to the northern frontiers, where German culture to a great extent absorbed the Roman. Even in the provincial areas adjacent to the Germanic homelands, the provincial population was to a significant extent assimilated and Germanized rather than displaced and exterminated.[9] Medieval civilization was thus to a significant extent Roman and classical in its origins.

BRITAIN AND THE ANGLO-SAXONS

The Anglo-Saxon invasions of Britain historically have been regarded as a great exception to the general pattern of Germanic migrations. This is true both of comparative general studies of the *Völkerwanderung* and of many specialist studies concentrating on events in Britain.[10] The al-

---

[7] J. M. Wallace-Hadrill, *Long Haired Kings*, 1. The same idea is presented in J. M. Wallace-Hadrill, *Barbarian West*, 24–26. The actual numbers cited for various tribes, 30,000 to 100,000, seem too high. A more recent study estimates that the Franks represented c. 2 percent of the total population of their conquests. Geary, *Before France and Germany*, 114–15.

[8] Drew, *Barbarian Invasions*, 2. Drew, "Another Look," more recently emphasizes aspects of the Germanic role. For an even broader perspective see Bronson, "Role of Barbarians."

[9] Goffart, *Barbarians and Romans*, 32; Musset, *Germanic Invasions*, 116–52. This is a venerable idea and can be traced back at least to Pirenne, *Mohammed and Charlemagne,* 33–45.

[10] The most recent detailed examinations of Germanic settlement within the empire mark Britain as exceptional and exclude it from study. See Goffart, *Barbarians and Romans*, 32–34; Ferrill, *Fall of the Roman Empire*, 123. These are recent examples of a long-standing tendency to simplify the study of the invasions by regarding Britain as an anomaly that need not be considered with the continental migrations. Drew, *Barbarian Invasions*, 4, states, "To a certain extent it is not wise to include Britain in this study of the effects of the barbarian invasions since Britain is a very special case." Similar statements may be found in the classic studies of Musset, Wallace-Hadrill, Lot, Freeman and Bury. See Musset, *Germanic Invasions*, 100–106; Wallace-Hadrill, *Long Haired Kings*, 2; Lot, *End of the Ancient World*, 236, 406–7; Freeman, *Western Europe in the Fifth Century*, 36, 43. Bury refers to Britain as "the only

legedly unique nature of the Anglo-Saxon invasions is deduced from an undeniably different post-Roman aftermath in Britain, in which Roman institutions, the villa system, Romance language, and Christian religion failed to survive to anything like the same extent as in the continental provinces. In keeping with the principle that relative levels of population (invaders:indigenous) were decisively important in the cultural interrelation between provincials and invaders, both a great migration of Anglo-Saxons significantly more numerous than other Germanic migrations and a relatively underdeveloped Romano-British provincial population have been inferred. Further, so the argument goes, it was a movement involving an entire population including farming peasants and their families, not an essentially military movement as on the continent. Thus Lucien Musset writes of the Anglo-Saxon conquest: "The colonization of England stands out as a special case in the history of the great migrations. . . . It was effected not by a military elite, as with most of the barbarian kingdoms of the continent, but by whole populations."[11] In what was for long the standard history, F. M. Stenton described the Anglo-Saxon movement into Britain as a series of national migrations unique among contemporary Germanic settlements.[12] His basic assumption was that the Anglo-Saxons were very numerous, and unlike the other Germanic tribes, were populous enough to displace the native population and Roman culture in Britain.[13] Such conceptions of the Anglo-Saxon invasions are almost the last bastion of Gibbon's and Voltaire's hoary vision of a Roman world overwhelmed by a deluge of barbarians.[14] Recent studies of the transition between Roman Britain and Anglo-Saxon England evince a variety of conflicting opinion concerning the scale and nature of the invasions. A modified version of Stenton's thesis persists. Imagery of the deluge is still used and some modern accounts speak of waves, tides, and floods of invaders, of swampings and pourings. In contrast, some scholars shrink the num-

---

exception" to the pattern of conquest and synthesis between Romans and Germans in the West (*History of the Later Roman Empire*, 1:viii). His observation was echoed fifty years later by John Morris in his introduction to Gildas, *Ruin of Britain*, 1–2. In the standard history of Roman Britain, Peter Salway poses the still unanswered question "why the general picture A. H. M. Jones painted of the Germanic take-over in the west does not seem to fit Britain" (*Roman Britain*, 478). See A. H. M. Jones, *Later Roman Empire*, 1:248.

[11] Musset, *Germanic Invasions*, 109. Musset marked Britain as peculiar for a number of reasons, not only because of the numbers of the Anglo-Saxon invaders but also because of the actions of the Britons themselves (*Germanic Invasions*, 116).

[12] Stenton, *Anglo-Saxon England*, 277.

[13] Even the normally skeptical Goffart accepts the idea of an exceptionally large Germanic migration into Britain. So numerous were the immigrants that they dislodged and displaced the native Roman provincial population. Britain and the Balkans are the two exceptions to Goffart's general rule of small-scale Germanic migration (*Barbarians and Romans*, 32).

[14] The Rhenish and Danubian frontier districts are the other examples.

bers of the Anglo-Saxon invaders to a small, potent elite of only a few thousand immigrants.[15] Opposing perceptions of the scale and effects of the Anglo-Saxon migrations lie at the heart of the British historical equivalent of the Germanist-Romanist debate, in which the polar opposites might only half-jokingly be referred to as the tabula rasa school and the Celtomaniacs. A basic question, therefore, is how many Anglo-Saxons were there and how many Romano-Britons? But why should Roman Britain differ from the other western provinces? Why should the Anglo-Saxons differ from other groups of Germanic invaders?

As Gibbon remarked with typically sonorous understatement, "The number of subjects who acknowledged the laws of Rome, of citizens, of provincials, and of slaves, cannot now be fixed with such a degree of accuracy, as the importance of the object would deserve."[16] Despite the development of ingenious techniques of study, there are enormous difficulties involved in estimating even the trends of premodern populations.[17] These problems are particularly acute for periods such as the fifth century, which not only lack explicit contemporary statistics but have few written sources of any kind, and these of dubious quality. Archaeology is at best a palliative for the missing documentary evidence.[18] Nevertheless, given the significance of perceptions of relative populations in historical arguments concerning the *Völkerwanderung*, and given the ongoing debate over the scale and nature of the Anglo-Saxon migrations, it is well worth attempting an estimate and comparison of the numbers of Anglo-Saxons and British provincials. The range of potential error is great but this is one of the circumstances where a figure subject to 50 percent error is better than no figure at all.[19] The tolerable margin of error is very high in this case, for we seek not closely argued calculations but a simple comparison of orders of magnitude.

[15] For the floods image, see Whittock, *Origins of England*, 9, 70, 129; Randers-Pehrson, *Barbarians and Romans*, 279, 309; Ferrill, *Fall of the Roman Empire*, 123; Dixon, "Continent in Ferment," 7; Scullard, *Roman Britain*, 148; Sonia C. Hawkes, "The South-East after the Romans," 92. For a recent overview see Hills, "Roman Britain to Saxon England."

[16] Gibbon, *Decline and Fall*, 1:46.

[17] For an introduction to the study of premodern population see Willigan and Lynch, eds., *Sources and Methods of Historical Demography*; Hollingsworth, *Historical Demography*; Glass and Eversley, eds., *Population in History*; Swedlund and Armelagos, *Demographic Anthropology*; Zubrow, ed., *Demographic Anthropology*; Howells, "Estimating Population Numbers"; Acsádi and Nemeskéri, *History of Human Life Span*.

[18] For criticism of the methods used see D. H. Thomas, "The Awful Truth about Statistics in Archaeology"; Cicotti, "Indivizzie metodi negli studi de demografia antica"; Roberta L. Hall, "A Test of Palaeodemographic Models"; Petersen, "A Demographer's View of Prehistoric Demography"; Brothwell, "Stones, Pots, and People."

[19] See the comments in Brunt, *Italian Manpower*, 3–4; Glass and Eversley, *Population in History*, 6.

ROMANO-BRITISH POPULATION

Radical alterations in our perceptions of rural settlement patterns and of the density of population are perhaps the most revolutionary and significant developments in Roman British studies in the last thirty years. A generation ago it was conventional to suggest that Anglo-Saxon invaders perhaps numbering hundreds of thousands displaced or destroyed the provincial inhabitants of southern and eastern Britain who themselves numbered hundreds of thousands, a preponderant fraction of a total Romano-British population which at its height amounted to approximately a million people.[20] Britain was regarded as significantly less developed and populous than its western provincial neighbors.[21] The older conventional picture of the settlement pattern in Roman Britain was of a Romanized eastern and southern core surrounded by thinly populated, little-developed frontier districts in the north and west. Even in the south-eastern lowlands agriculture was supposedly confined to the lighter soils. Intensive exploitation of the heavier soils and extensive clearance of the woodlands seemingly began with the Anglo-Saxons.

Elements of this conception persist in some scholarly quarters, but an emerging consensus places the apex of Romano-British population not at hundreds of thousands or even several millions but at three or four million and conceivably more.[22] The greatly increased estimates of total population reflect dramatic upward revisions of the extent and density of rural

[20] Earlier estimates of Romano-British population proposed by Hall, Foord, Collingwood, Randall, Wheeler, Usher, Russell, Frere, and Henig and their methodologies are discussed in Michael E. Jones, "Climate, Nutrition, and Disease."

[21] The idea still persists. In contrast to the revised estimates numbering Romano-British population in the millions, Salmon presents a figure of .35 million, based on Russell's calculations. This contrasts dramatically with an estimate of population in Roman Gaul, cited in the same work, of 10 million. Salmon, *Population et dépopulation*, 33. Russell suggests a Romano-British population of .5 million, compared with 5.0 million for Gaul ("Population in Europe," 36). McEvedy and Jones estimate the peak of Romano-British population in the fourth century at .8 million, with a density of 4.5 to 9 inhabitants per square kilometer. In contrast, Gaul had double this density of population (*Atlas of World Population History*, 41, 21). A similar discrepancy in densities of population is described in Boserup, *Population and Technological Change*, 58–59. Hodges estimates the Romano-British population in A.D. 400 at only .3 million (*Dark Age Economics*, 164, fig. 40).

[22] Charles Thomas, *Celtic Britain*, 34: 3 to 4 million; Everitt, *Continuity and Colonization*, 352 n. 1: 4 to 6 million; Whittock, *Origins of England*, 128: over 3 million; Christopher Taylor, *Village and Farmstead*, 106: more than 4 million; James Campbell, "End of Roman Britain," 9: 3 or 4 million; K. R. Davis, *Britons and Saxons*, 18 n. 10–12, 130 n. 13: 2 to 4 million; Salway, *Roman Britain*, 544: 4 to 6 million; Anthony R. Birley, "The Assimilation of Britain," 1305: 4 to 6 million; Brandon, ed., *South Saxons*, 4: 4 million; Cunliffe, "Settlement and Population," 15: 4 to 6 million; Christopher Smith, "The Valleys of the Tame and the Middle Trent," 55: 5 or 6 million. This perception of a high Romano-British population has begun to enter our textbooks. See Clayton Roberts and David Roberts, *History of England*, 23: c. 4 million; Morgan, ed., *Oxford Illustrated History*, 58: more than double the Domesday population.

settlement in Roman Britain. These revisions in turn are the product of a combination of evidence—the results of aerial survey and photography, systematic field-walking applied in intensive regional studies, and excavation of specific farming sites. Regional patterns of extensive settlement and surprisingly intensive land usage are evident in virtually all of the distinct geographical zones comprising Roman Britain. These include a wide spectrum of soils and situations: gravels, limestones, loams, clays, and sandy soils.[23] Perhaps the most dramatic example of the changed perception of Roman settlement is the Nene valley area of Northamptonshire and Huntingdonshire. The 1931 Ordnance Survey map showed 36 Roman sites in the area (one every 25 square kilometers). In the 1956 edition of the map, 130 settlements were indicated (one every 7 square kilometers). Early in 1972, 434 definite settlements had been found (one every 2.3 square kilometers). This represents 300 newly discovered settlements in sixteen years.[24] Studies in Cumberland and Northumbria as well as of sites exposed through the extension of the M-5 motorway in Gloucestershire reveal a similar proliferation of newly discovered Roman sites.[25] With the exception of Cambridgeshire, fieldwork indicates surprisingly dense settlement in the Fens, Somerset, Wiltshire, Warwickshire, and Buckinghamshire. In certain evidently attractive areas, Roman settlement density exceeded 4 sites per square kilometer.[26]

Much of the new evidence for rural settlement is as yet ill-digested and chronologically imprecise. Few of the sites located by field-walking or aerial survey have been excavated. Since the Roman occupation lasted some three and one-half centuries, all of the great mass of settlements obviously cannot be contemporary. Excavation must follow survey before analysis penetrates below the level of crude generalization. On the other hand, a greater number of sites will doubtless be discovered in the future. There are no known great discontinuities in the overall pattern of rural settlement before the fourth century and there is limited evidence for the prolonged occupation of the whole range of soil types in the later Roman period. This suggests that many of the undated settlements were contemporary. Even if the number of inhabited sites calculated for a given period

[23] For a good survey of this topic see Christopher Taylor, *Village and Farmstead*, 83–106.
[24] Christopher Taylor, "Roman Settlements in the Nene Valley," 113–19. The number of newly discovered sites in the area continues to increase. A. E. Brown, ed., "Archaeology in Northamptonshire 1982."
[25] N. J. Higham, "Continuity Studies"; Jobey, "Notes on Some Population Problems"; Jobey, "Homesteads and Settlements"; Burgess, "Prehistoric Settlement of Northumbria"; Macinnes, "Settlement and Economy"; G. D. B. Jones and J. Walker, "Either Side of the Solway"; N. J. Higham and G. D. B. Jones, "Frontiers, Forts, and Farmers."
[26] Christopher Taylor, "Roman Settlement in the Nene Valley," 116.

is inflated by the inclusion of abandoned settlements or other duplication, a ten-fold increase in the number of Roman sites, including areas so inhospitable that only severe population pressure would probably have forced their cultivation, justifies a great increase in previous estimates of population.

Other evidence strengthens the conclusions drawn from the pattern of rural settlement. A structural demographic analysis of factors such as epidemic disease, climate, and public order which largely determined the trends of premodern populations, suggests that conditions were very favorable for population growth throughout much of the Roman era in Britain.[27] Botanical evidence supports the idea of a densely inhabited and fully exploited countryside.[28] In areas of the north and west extensive clearance of woodland occurred in the later Roman period.[29] Ironically, the changed perception of the level of population in Roman Britain fits very well with the subjective and impressionistic descriptions of British population in the primary evidence. These sources had often been dismissed as exaggerated rhetoric or the blind parroting of poorly informed Greek geographers. For example, Caesar stated that the British population was "innumerable," with a pattern of settlement similar to that of Gaul. Britain was regarded as very populous by Tacitus and Diodorus Siculus.[30] In fact, recent upward revisions in estimates of historical settlement patterns and densities of population in Britain are not confined to the Roman era. Recent perceptions of settlement in the pre-Roman Iron Age are entirely compatible with the Romano-British evidence and place the latter in a broad and consistent context.[31] Studies of Romano-British population are at last free from the blinders imposed by earlier attempts to tie the demography of the Roman period in some lineal fashion to the smaller levels of population associated with the Domesday survey and the early medieval era.

[27] Michael E. Jones, "Climate, Nutrition, and Disease," 232–39.

[28] For introductions to palaeobotanical studies and the application of pollen diagrams to settlement history see Judith Turner, "Evidence for Land Use"; Bartley, "Palaeobotanical Evidence"; Sawyer, *From Roman Britain to Norman England*, 148. Cf. Brian K. Roberts, *Rural Settlement in Britain*, 29–31.

[29] A number of regional studies have been published in *New Phytologist*, *Journal of Ecology*, and *Transactions of the Institute of British Geographers*. See, for example, Judith Turner, "Environment of Northeast England"; Bartley et al., "Vegetational History"; Tinsley, "Cultural Influences on Pennine Vegetation." For the north and west see also N. J. Higham, "Continuity Studies," 5ff.; Faull, "Roman and Anglian Settlement Patterns."

[30] Caesar *Gal.* 5.12; Tacitus *Ann.* 14.29–39; Diodorus Siculus 5.21.3–6.

[31] Salway, *Roman Britain*, 554; Peter J. Reynolds, *Iron Age Farm*, 77; P. J. Fowler, *Farming of Prehistoric Britain*, 32–36; Christopher Taylor, *Village and Farmstead*, 63–82; Knight, *Late Bronze Age and Iron Age Settlement*.

Because the evidence obtained from aerial survey and field-walking is chronologically imprecise, it is difficult to place the trend of Romano-British population into a convincing chronological framework. If the later first through late second century represented the heyday of Britannia's overall economic development, then population may have peaked in the same period. On the basis of simple analogy with the perceived general trends in population of the empire as a whole, we might expect that Romano-British population peaked in the mid-second century A.D. after a period of substantial growth and then declined during the third and fourth centuries. Alternatively, Britain might better be treated as a frontier province in which trends of population lagged behind those of the core area. Certainly Britain was added relatively late to the empire and her patterns of economic and probably demographic development were somewhat eccentric. A number of indicators suggest that, for the villa owners, the early fourth rather than the late second century may have marked the "golden age." This may reflect the moment of greatest prosperity for the rural population as a whole, although conditions for the Romano-British peasantry need not have paralleled those of the rural elite. Britain escaped the worst effects of the general crisis of the third century, and given the generally favorable external circumstances of the third and early fourth centuries, it is possible that the population peaked in this era and perhaps began to decline in the second half of the fourth century.

There are a number of essential problems associated with revised estimates that place the peak of Romano-British population at four million people or more. The range of potential error is very great. Given the inherent limitations of any study of early population, the new consensus represents a convergence of hypotheses rather than a demonstrated fact. As C. J. Arnold observes, there is a danger that a logical estimate may take on undue respectability simply through repeated citation.[32] The study of cemetery evidence for the provincial population is in its infancy and will doubtless continue to be hampered by difficulties of recognition and dating on the basis of distinctive material or physical evidence.[33] The relationship between the pattern of urban and rural development is still uncertain. The results of excavations are needed to fine-tune the evidence of aerial and field survey. More and more detailed regional studies are needed to flesh the bare bones of our current hypotheses concerning total population and demographic trends over time. Nevertheless, Roman Britain can

---

[32] C. J. Arnold, *Roman Britain to Saxon England*, 123.
[33] R. F. J. Jones, "Quantitative Approach to Roman Burial"; R. A. Chambers, "A Further Quantitative Approach."

no longer be treated as an exceptional case among the western provinces, an example of a region with a proportionally less developed pattern of settlement and a comparatively small population.[34] Even allowing for a hypothetically catastrophic demographic decline with a loss of a quarter of the population during the third and fourth centuries (probably an unreasonable and exaggerated assumption), literally millions of provincials must have inhabited Roman Britain at the beginning of the fifth century on the eve of the Anglo-Saxon invasions.

ANGLO-SAXON MIGRANT POPULATION

The question of Anglo-Saxon population during the era of invasions is fraught with difficulties. It is perhaps even more enigmatic due to the comparative paucity of sources and further complicated by the prolonged period of the transmarine migration and the relatively slow pace of political and military conquests in Britain. With methods like those used in analogous studies, however, it should be possible to produce an estimate of Anglo-Saxon population suitable for comparison with those of other German tribes. The surviving literary evidence, law codes, inscriptions, settlement archaeology, and cemetery evidence furnish the raw material for this study.

Physical Anthropology

The most direct approach to the problem of Anglo-Saxon population, as J. N. L. Myres long ago pointed out, is through physical anthropology. Theoretically it ought to be possible to discriminate between invasive and indigenous populations among burials in the pagan period cemeteries by using bone evidence, blood-typing, and DNA analysis. Within a given cemetery it is rarely possible to establish family relationships and descent using epigenetic traits, that is, skeletal characteristics such as dental anomalies that are genetically transmitted. Unfortunately, despite recent interesting work on blood groups and immunity characteristics which may one day have important archaeological application, Myres's statement is still correct that "neither the Romano-Britons nor the Anglo-Saxons can be regarded, in view of their previous history, as a sufficiently homogeneous group to enable such distinctions [skull form, eye and hair

[34] Kevin Greene, *Archaeology of the Roman Economy*, 98ff., has a good discussion of regional studies of settlement elsewhere in the empire. Leday's study of northern Gaul (*La campagne à l'époque romaine*) is particularly interesting in the context of rural settlement in Britain.

color, and so forth] to be used with confidence in their differentiation."[35] There may be an ethnic difference in average height between Germanic immigrants and Roman provincial populations in Britain and elsewhere. Several studies have suggested that Anglo-Saxon immigrant men were on average up to one and one-half inches taller than their Romano-British counterparts. As just noted, however, both the Germanic invaders of Britain and the Romano-British populations associated with towns and military sites were of heterogeneous composition. We do not know much about the rural population of Roman Britain, but presumably it was little affected genetically by exotic and cosmopolitan Roman elements. These considerations compromise and complicate the basis of any comparison between presumed invaders and suspected natives. Although there are several examples of Roman cemetery sites later reused by Anglo-Saxons, crucially missing from the available evidence is an appreciable corpus of studies of cemeteries continuously in use from clearly Roman contexts right through the early Anglo-Saxon period. Wasperton in Warwickshire may be a rare exception. Without such a context there is no reliable way to distinguish between newly arrived invaders and the surviving indigenous population. L. H. D. Buxton concluded in his study of Romano-British physical affinities that the Romano-Britons "are extremely closely related, if identity of measurement be a criterion of relationship, to the following peoples: the prehistoric peoples of Sweden, the Reihengraber people, the Merovingian and Belgian Franks, and the Anglo-Saxons, the differences being in all these cases extremely small."[36] The measured differences between the Anglo-Saxons and the Romano-Britons seem, in fact, to be well within the observed variation among individuals within one racial group. In other words, from the standpoint of physical anthropology, the Romano-Britons are generally indistinguishable from the Germanic invaders. This physical similarity parallels the confusion in early literary sources between Germans, Belgae, and Celts, who are ultimately separated not on physical or cultural bases but through linguistic differences. This being the case, the evidence of physical anthropology

---

[35] Collingwood and Myres, *Roman Britain and the English Settlements*, 426. On the subject of blood groups see Potts, "History and Blood Groups." A combination of studies of physical anthropology, grave orientation and limited classes of grave goods has yielded some speculative but interesting results concerning the survival of the Romano-British population and their appearance in "Saxon" cemeteries. See C. J. Arnold, "End of Roman Britain," 457; C. J. Arnold, *Roman Britain to Saxon England*, 121–41.

[36] Buxton, "Racial Affinities," 38–40. For a discussion of epigenetic traits and ethnic differences in stature see Härke, "Warrior Graves," 40–42. Other Roman sites where cemeteries may have passed uninterruptedly into Anglo-Saxon use include Kelvedon, Great Chesterford, Ancaster, Cambridge, Frilford, and Great Casterton. Burnham and Wacher, *Small Towns*.

remains inconclusive in determining overall relative numbers of immigrants and natives.[37]

Cemetery Evidence

The most prolific source of information for the Anglo-Saxons in Britain during the early fifth through the early eighth century is provided by the cremation and inhumation burials from more than fifteen hundred excavated cemeteries. As James Campbell aptly remarks, the early Anglo-Saxon archaeologist is a Resurrection Man, a haunter of graves. At first sight this corpus provides an attractive line of investigation for estimating average total population.[38] Unfortunately, the techniques involved require certain basic prerequisites for viable results, and these are rarely available for Anglo-Saxon cemeteries.[39] For example, each cemetery used must contain fifty graves as an absolute minimum.[40] Otherwise, chance distribution skews the results and deprives them of validity. Secondly, the entire cemetery must be excavated to ensure that the results are representative. Thirdly, a chronological framework must be available in order to adjust the numbers in the cemetery over time to produce an average population. Finally, the cemetery must be in a known relation to the pattern of overall settlement so that an average density of population may be calculated. Very few Anglo-Saxon cemeteries fulfill these requirements. The vast majority of excavated cemeteries are smaller than fifty graves, and thus useless for demographic calculations. Few of the larger cemeteries have been completely excavated (the cost and manpower involved in complete excavation is enormous for large cemeteries such as Spong Hill, ten years under excavation). Many of the cemeteries were dug before techniques of palaeodemography were developed, and excavations provided grave goods, not population figures. Even where large cemeteries were fully and scientifically excavated, as at Spong Hill, preliminary reports indicate that results may not be usable for demographic projections. At Spong Hill the ratio of female to male graves is so high that some external factor, either selective migration of men from the area or sexually selective burial practices, invalidates the body count for purposes of reconstructing population. Few settlement sites associated with cemeteries

---

[37] Hachmann, *Germanic Peoples*, 11–56; Goffart, *Barbarians and Romans*, 18–35; C. F. C. Hawkes and G. C. Dunning, "Belgae of Gaul and Britain."

[38] James Campbell, "End of Roman Britain," 27–29. See the population studies referenced above. See also Alcock, *Arthur's Britain*, 310–11.

[39] Willigan and Lynch, eds., *Sources and Methods of Historical Demography*, 39–56. See also the criticisms of these methods, referenced above.

[40] Hirst, "Some Aspects," 251. In the same volume, see also the histogram of cemetery sizes in the Upper Thames region (Rahtz et al., *Anglo-Saxon Cemeteries*, 27).

have been excavated and this also limits the demographic usefulness of the cemetery evidence.[41]

Speaking in general, the total number of excavated Anglo-Saxon graves in Britain is too few to represent the invading population, however small it may have been. The accident of discovery and perhaps the anthropological puzzle of burial practice and community may be at fault here. In Bernicia, for example, a population estimate based on a total body of cemetery evidence numbering thirty-eight graves would be ludicrously small.[42] A similar problem occurs in British archaeology for the later Viking settlement. The total number of graves definitely identified as Viking throughout the whole of Britain is currently about fifty.[43]

Chronology is perhaps the most intractable problem for cemetery studies, indeed for Anglo-Saxon archaeology in general. Dating rests on the uncertain and precarious chronology derived from typology—an arthistorical evolution based on changes of form and decoration of certain metalwork and pottery types. This process has many limitations and numerous critics.[44] Before the seventh century, Anglo-Saxon archaeology lacks any fixed points to date securely and anchor the typological sequences (such as the discovery in France of Childeric's tomb, identified by an inscribed ring and dated by a passage of Gregory of Tours). Furthermore, typological dating assumes a formal developmental process for the types of artifacts involved, an assumption made questionable in many cases by peculiarities of the Anglo-Saxon cemeteries producing the relevant artifacts. The cemeteries tend to be small and varied in their contents.[45] Even with the additional help of continental dating schemes it is rarely possible to date a particular artifact or collection to a period within fifty years, or even within a hundred years.[46] In demographic terms, therefore, available dating techniques cannot define a generation or even several generations. Without a more precise chronological framework, using the cemetery evidence to produce demographic estimates is nearly impossible. Dendrochronology offers some help in sites with timber preservation, but radiocarbon dating has too great a margin of error to be generally useful.[47] The chronological difficulties are particularly acute for the early

[41] Hills, "Anglo-Saxon Cremation Cemeteries"; Hills, Spong Hill: Part III; Hills, Penn, and Rickett, Anglo-Saxon Cemetery at Spong Hill. See Meany, Gazetteer.
[42] Miket, "Restatement of Evidence." See also Alcock, "Quantity or Quality."
[43] Campbell, "Scandinavian Viking-Age Burials"; D. M. Wilson, "Scandinavians in England," 396–97; D. Brown, Anglo-Saxon England, 76.
[44] Hills, "Anglo-Saxon Cremation Cemeteries"; T. Dickinson, "Present State of Anglo-Saxon Cemetery Studies," 12–16.
[45] Dickinson, "Present State of Anglo-Saxon Cemetery Studies," 19.
[46] Ibid.
[47] D. M. Wilson, "Introduction," 8–13.

Saxon period, the fifth through seventh centuries, precisely the period of interest for the migrations. Bruce Eagles's work with the cremation cemeteries of Yorkshire provides a good example of the chronological problems: of 550 cremation pots only 57 could be dated within a century or less.[48]

The problems outlined above suffice to demonstrate the limitations of archaeology as an independent line of inquiry into Anglo-Saxon population. A more fundamental question in archaeological theory, the relation of tribal identity or ethnicity to material remains, is also relevant to the discussion of cemetery evidence. Since the work of Gordon Childe, many archaeologists of British prehistory and protohistory have assumed as a basic tenet that differing associations of distinctive material remains (pottery, metalwork, grave goods, and so forth) defined ethnically or tribally distinct cultures. For example, if a grave containing certain pottery and jewelry associated with the fifth century is excavated, the person buried is assumed to be an Anglo-Saxon immigrant. On the other hand, if an inhumation without grave goods is found and the presumed date is the fifth century, it is taken to be the grave of a Romano-British provincial.

In general theoretical terms, there is a growing skepticism in some scholarly circles concerning attempts to match or identify archaeologically defined material cultures with particular migrating tribes or confederations. Instead of distinct and identifiable cultural units, tribes and confederations during the migrations are better understood as political units involving changing mixes of peoples and material cultures. Such perceptions blur the presumptive archaeological distinctions among invaders. It is fashionable to speak of a generalized *Nordseeküstengruppe* rather than distinctive Angle, Saxon, Frankish, or Frisian material cultures. The possibility of acculturation also greatly complicates attempts to distinguish between invading and indigenous populations on the basis of archaeology. This general caution has specific application for the study of cemetery evidence and important implications for attempts to estimate thereby the numbers of an invading population.[49] For example, N. Åberg argued long ago that buckle types deposited as grave goods and associated with invasive German settlement—the so-called Aquitanian buckles—were in fact neither Frankish nor Gothic but Roman.[50] A similar debate continues in a British context over the much discussed decorated buckles and belt-fittings that were originally used to locate early Saxon burials.[51]

[48] Eagles, "Anglo-Saxons in Lindsey," 286.
[49] See Goffart, *Barbarians and Romans*, 6–39; Dixon, *Barbarian Europe*, 11. Nordseekustengruppe: Myres, *English Settlements*, 55, 63–73. Nevertheless, Myres persists in defining tribal areas on the basis of material culture.
[50] Åberg, *Orient and Occident*, 3:40–64.
[51] Discussed in Hills, "Archaeology of Anglo-Saxon England," 298.

Similarly the Reihengraber, or row graves, once thought characteristic of
Frankish settlement in Gaul have recently been reinterpreted to represent
not tribal expansion but political influence. Frankish royal custom was
imitated by the Roman army (already heavily Germanized) and later by
other elements of the Roman population. As Edward James writes, "The
row-grave cemetery . . . is . . . to be associated with the spread of Frankish
lordship over Northern Gaul and not with the spread of the Franks themselves as a colonizing people."[52] The important principle of interpretation
is that burial custom can be a fashion, subject to change or imitation.
Roman provincials who had changed from cremation to inhumation earlier within the Roman period could have imitated German burial custom
just as they adopted barbarian hair style, trousers, and wives.

The debate regarding continental cemeteries has a British counterpart.
Martin Welch has argued that pagan-style burials in fifth- and sixth-
century cemeteries in Sussex contain a mixture of Britons and Saxons,
with both races using similar grave goods. If Welch proves to be correct,
then the whole method of distinguishing between Britons and Saxons on
the basis of distinctive material goods interred with burials must be modified or discarded.[53] Once the principle that burial custom is a changeable,
adoptable fashion is admitted, the use of cemetery evidence to trace patterns of intrusive or invasive settlement is greatly complicated. Tania
Dickinson now believes, for example, that in the Upper Thames region the
increase in numbers and geographical spread of "pagan" cemeteries, which
she originally interpreted as an increase in the Anglo-Saxon population,
may be an accident produced by flawed dating and/or a fluctuation in
burial custom over time. The practice of burial with grave goods may have
first declined and then revived in popularity.[54] A similar pattern of varying
fashion in burial has been suggested for the continent in the same period.[55]

In general, if burial custom is taken to be a fashion, and as such is seen
to be changeable and subject to imitation by people other than those who
originally introduced the custom, then many archaeological assumptions,
once strongly held, are replaced by uncertainties. Dickinson asks, "Can I
be sure that the geographical spread [of cemetery custom and grave goods]

---

52 Edward James, "Merovingian Cemetery Studies," 39. Lorren, "Early Medieval Cemeteries," recently interpreted the spread of row-grave cemeteries as a reflection of changing
cultural fashion and economic relationships rather than the displacement of Gallic provincials by expanding Franks. Young, "Barbarian Funerary Tradition," interprets the "Germanic"
graves in Gaul as an affirmation of new identity, a cultural rather than an ethnic marker.
53 Welch, "Saxon Cemeteries," 282; Welch, "Late Romans and Saxons in Sussex."
54 Tania Dickinson, "Present State of Anglo-Saxon Cemetery Studies," 23.
55 Ucko, "Ethnography and Archaeological Interpretation"; Edward James, Merovingian Archaeology, 97–160; Edward James, "Cemeteries and Frankish Settlement"; F. Stein, "Franken
und Romanen in Lotharingen"; Kidd, "Some Questions of Method."

reflects expanding Anglo-Saxon colonization, or do these so-called Anglo-Saxon cemeteries in fact represent or include a section of population that was British by origin and who by the sixth century wished or were obliged to conform to the Germanic cultural norm?"[56]

The above example of the problems of tribal identification by archaeology came from the Upper Thames and Sussex, areas that are generally accepted as having been early and densely settled by Anglo-Saxons. The problem of cemetery evidence and Anglo-Saxon population emerges most clearly, however, in England north of the Humber, particularly in the kingdom of Bernicia. Despite impressive archaeological activity, the number of identifiably Anglo-Saxon burials in Bernicia has remained tiny. The usual deduction from this fact is that the Anglo-Saxons were a small part of the Bernician population.[57] Roger Miket, however, has recently argued that the archaeological data is not a reliable indication of Anglo-Saxon population size in Bernicia.[58] Miket suggests that the British and Anglo-Saxon populations were "hybridized" and that burial customs were an amalgam of British and Anglian. In consequence, the body count of recognizably Anglo-Saxon graves may underrepresent the Anglo-Saxon population, who may have adopted British burial practices. If Miket is correct, this would be the archaeological inverse of British adoption of Saxon burial rites. The absence of any firmly defined late Roman or post-Roman British burial customs makes the argument very speculative. The question is further complicated by the mixture of religions, including Christianity, present in late and post-Roman Britain. Religious conviction must have influenced the potential for acculturation and the choice of burial rite.

In marked contrast to the archaeologically "visible" rites of furnished cremation and inhumation practiced by the Germanic tribes, the overwhelming majority of the indigenous British rural population disposed of their dead in a manner rarely recoverable by archaeology. They are largely invisible in the Iron Age, remain so throughout the Roman era, and continue to defy archaeological discovery in post-Roman contexts. Presumably, corpses were disposed of singly or in scattered groups in a fashion that time and modern agricultural plowing have mostly erased. The total number of graves discovered from the Roman period is less than 20,000, almost all from urban cemeteries. If extrapolations were made from this basis alone, this would represent an average total population for Roman Britain of only about 2,000 people, obviously a gross underestimate. Regional differences in burial, such as cremation in the southeast and unfur-

---

56 Tania Dickinson, "Present State of Anglo-Saxon Cemetery Studies," 27.
57 Alcock, "Quantity or Quality"; Faull, "British Survival."
58 Miket, "Restatement of Evidence," 298.

nished and often crouched burial elsewhere, evidently persisted after the Iron Age and continued to develop within the Roman period. New influences from abroad interacted with native rites, and influences traveled in both directions between cosmopolitan towns and conservative countrysides. Crouched burial, decapitation, and the inclusion of hobnailed footwear are various aspects of Romano-British regional burial customs. The urban dead of Roman Britain from such sites as Trentholm Drive (York), Lankhills (Hampshire), Poundbury (Dorset), and Ancaster (Lincolnshire) do illustrate one important principle. Within the Roman era, between roughly 150 and 250 A.D., burial practice changed from cremation to inhumation. Thereafter, regional differences tended to give way to a more standard rite, extended inhumation burial. Later still, by the fifth century, Christian influence can be traced in some British burials. These changes within a common political framework seem to result from indirect influences of fashion and religion rather than directly from migration and the arrival of new peoples. The change-over was evidently peaceful, and cremation and inhumation practices overlapped within the three generations of transition. Both the principle of changing fashion in burial customs, and the time frame of the change, hold significance for interpreting the later evidence from Anglo-Saxon cemeteries.[59]

The somewhat confusing double pattern of British use of Saxon custom and vice versa illustrates well an extremely important possibility. If burial custom and material goods are not certain indications of invasive or indigenous population (and I believe they are not), then archaeology loses much of its usefulness as a means of illustrating either relative population (British:Saxon) in a given area or the pattern of settlement. In fact, Childe's original assumption cast much of the archaeological investigations of the Anglo-Saxon settlement and conquest into a logical circle, and greatly prejudiced treatment of the question of British survival and post-Roman continuity. Acculturation (between Britons and Anglo-Saxons) can be defined as an interchange and amalgamation, whether of material goods or social customs such as burial. In contrast, to presume that tribal identity carried with it a distinct ethnic character, and then to define that ethnic distinction according to material remains, greatly prejudices the possibility of discovering amalgamation or interaction. The vulnerability of such principles in the context of early England is well demonstrated by an archaeological irony from two crucial sites, South Cadbury (Somerset) and Chalton (Hampshire). South Cadbury, the Dark Age British site par excel-

---

[59] For an overview see Reece, *My Roman Britain*, 77–88; Reece, *Burial in the Roman World;* Philpott, *Burial Practices;* McWhirr et al., *Romano-British Cemeteries;* C. S. Green, *Excavations at Poundbury.*

lence, produced only two decorated metal objects, a buckle and a saucer brooch, evidently both of Anglo-Saxon manufacture. Chalton, a "typical" example of an Anglo-Saxon village, has produced but one decorated (and thus distinctive) object, an enameled disc from a hanging bowl, a distinctively "British" object in a characteristic British style.[60] These two sites hardly offer resounding support for theories of distinctive material cultures.

I have taken some trouble to outline the difficulties posed in using the cemetery evidence as a primary or exclusive approach to the question of Anglo-Saxon population because a number of earlier estimates relied almost totally on the cemetery material. So far I have discussed the inadequate techniques of early excavations, the unsolved problem of chronology, the inadmissibly small size of many cemeteries, and the questionable principle of using material culture as a diagnostic tool. Any of these problems greatly compromises attempts to estimate population on the basis of cemetery evidence. Setting all these objections aside, however, there remains one supremely important consideration. In comparison with Germanic tribal cemeteries of the continent, the Anglo-Saxon cemeteries are both fewer in number and smaller in size. This may be an essential clue to the scale of the migration. Despite excavation of several large cemeteries such as Spong Hill which have greatly increased the total number of discovered burials in England, the total figure of all Anglo-Saxon cremation burials in Britain can be matched by a mere handful of cemeteries in the continental homelands, for example, Westerwanna, Issendorf, and Liebernau. The implications of the comparatively small scale of the Anglo-Saxon cemeteries in terms of overall population are consistent with the small sizes of early Anglo-Saxon settlements. The pattern of contemporary association between settlements and cemeteries is only beginning to emerge, but the scale and organization through the whole range of known settlements, including farms, hamlets, villages, and estate centers, suggest very small populations. As Philip Dixon remarks: "That the migrants settled down in small groups is further suggested by the cemeteries, few of which contain more than two hundred burials belonging to any one century: even allowing forty years to a generation, they must, in striking contrast to the great urnfields of Germany, have been serving local populations to be numbered in tens rather than hundreds."[61]

---

[60] D. Brown, *Anglo-Saxon England*, 46; Longley, "Hanging Bowls."
[61] Dixon, *Barbarian Europe*, 54. C. J. Arnold estimates that most of these communities numbered between twenty and forty individuals. C. J. Arnold, *Archaeology of the Early Anglo-Saxon Kingdoms*, 164–66; C. J. Arnold, *Roman Britain to Saxon England*, 124. For a review of settlements in relation to cemeteries see Welch, "Rural Settlement Patterns." Cf. Hodges, *Dark Age Economics*, 130–35.

Strictly and literally interpreted, the roughly 30,000 excavated inhumation and cremation graves from the Anglo-Saxon pagan era represent an average total population for the early fifth through early eighth century of only about 3,000 people. The equation used here to convert the overall cemetery evidence into an estimated average total population is adopted from one used for individual cemeteries:

$$\text{population size} = \frac{(\text{number of graves}) \cdot (\text{average life expectancy})}{(\text{period of occupation})}$$

For the Anglo-Saxon material this gives:

$$3,000 = \frac{30,000 \cdot 30 \text{ years}}{300 \text{ years}}$$

Some 4,000 of the burials are cremations, a fraction of which contain the remains of more than one individual. The average life expectancy for the period is uncertain, but probably ranged between 30 and 40 years. Even if the figures are adjusted to 35,000 burials (to compensate for cremation) and the higher life expectancy of 40 years is accepted, the projected average total population is tiny. What percentage of the actual historical total of burials is represented by the modern finds is anyone's guess. It might range between 1 percent or more to conceivably as little as 0.2 percent. Using the cemetery evidence, Leslie Alcock suggests that 50,000 to 100,000 might be a reasonable figure for the total Anglo-Saxon population of the sixth century. His estimate has gained some acceptance.[62]

Even allowing for the continued discovery of more pagan burials in the future, Alcock's projection of 50,000 to 100,000 for the specifically Anglo-Saxon population of the sixth century seems too high. It does not allow

[62] For numbers of burials see Hills, "Archaeology of Anglo-Saxon England," 318–19; Alcock, *Arthur's Britain*, 310–11. C. J. Arnold discusses the significance of the cemetery evidence for the question of population ("End of Roman Britain," 456–57). The equation is taken from Randsborg, *Viking Age*, 80. See Donat and Ullrich, "Einwohnerzahlen und Siedlungsgrösse." Estimates for the average life-span for the fifth century and after range between 33 and 36 for males, and from 27 and 33.1 for females. See Brothwell, "Palaeodemography." Alcock's figure is accepted by Laing and Laing, *Anglo-Saxon England*, 62. Whittock revises the estimate upwards to between 65,000 and 130,000 on the basis of the c. 1500 burial urns discovered at Lovedon Hill and Spong Hill between 1971 and 1973. In doing so he evidently failed to note that the possibility of newly discovered burials was included as a factor in Alcock's original estimate. Whittock also wrongly compresses the original chronology of Alcock's calculation from the sixth century to represent a population already established in the mid-fifth century (*Origins of England*, 126–29). The range of .2 to 1 percent is suggested by James Campbell, "Lost Centuries," 27–38. Using the original equation, this range of possibility produces an average population of 300,000 to 1,500,000. A transmarine migration on this scale is beyond belief.

sufficiently for the extended chronology of the pagan era (early fifth through early eighth centuries) and the unequal distribution of the cemetery evidence over this period. The pagan era extended for a considerable time beyond the migrations (fifth and early sixth centuries) and the graves of the period of the migrations are proportionally much less numerous than those of the later pagan era. The comparatively narrow geographical distribution of the early burials must also be added to the unequal chronological distribution and somehow factored into the estimate for total Anglo-Saxon population during the fifth and early sixth centuries. Even if Alcock's estimate for the sixth-century population is correct, the actual migrating population must have been fewer than 50,000 to 100,000, for some significant percentage of the cemetery evidence must represent natural increase over time among the original migrant population rather than new immigration. Some percentage of the discovered burials quite possibly represents native Britons and their descendants who adopted Anglo-Saxon burial customs.[63] My own estimate for the population of the Anglo-Saxon migration (fixed between roughly A.D. 410 and 550) is approximately 10,000 to 20,000 total. Earlier estimates based on archaeological evidence have been higher, generally about 100,000 total population.[64] Recent discussions present estimates for the migrating Anglo-Saxon population ranging between 10,000 and 100,000. The difference seems dramatic, but in a significant sense this is a squabble within the same order of magnitude. Given the inexact nature of any estimate, this is probably as much agreement as can be expected. There is an emerging consensus that the Anglo-Saxons represented a small minority of the total population in Britain at the time of the migrations, probably 5 percent or considerably less.[65] The upward revisions in our estimates of late

[63] James Campbell, "Lost Centuries," 27–38; Evison, "Distribution Maps." The rate of deposit in Anglo-Saxon cemeteries began with relatively few burials in the first half of the fifth century, sharply increased in the later fifth century, and peaked in the late sixth or seventh century. Hills, "Roman Britain to Anglo-Saxon England," 49.

[64] Kirsten, Raum und Bevölkerung, 293. Kirsten gives no specific arguments to support his estimate of 100,000. McEvedy and Jones, Atlas of World Population History, 67, reach the same figure of a migrating population of 100,000. They do not explain their estimate but evidently rely on the work of J. C. Russell. The estimate made by Alcock for the sixth-century population has been discussed (Arthur's Britain, 310–11). Russell once estimated that 200,000 Anglo-Saxons came to Britain between A.D. 440 and 470. This figure was based on very dubious logic. Russell estimated the military strength of the Britons at 100,000, from an overall fifth-century population in Roman Britain of only 200,000. He assumed that man-for-man the Britons were superior, so that the Anglo-Saxons must have outnumbered them. Russell, Late Ancient and Medieval Population, 97.

[65] Christopher Taylor cites the estimate of 10,000 Saxons arriving in Britain made by Charles Thomas and calls them "merely a hiccup in the history of settlement" (Village and Farmstead, 111). Thomas has suggested that no more than 1,000 or 2,000 Saxons need have been involved in the revolt described in Gildas. Charles Thomas, Christianity in Roman Britain,

Romano-British population emphasize the disparity in numbers. In any case, no matter how the cemetery evidence of the Anglo-Saxons is interpreted, it is impossible to justify thereby the notion of an Anglo-Saxon migrant population peculiarly large or greater in scale than the Germanic migrations on the continent.

Weapon Graves

Although the pagan Anglo-Saxon cemeteries in Britain are significantly smaller than those in the continental homelands, they contain a much higher proportion of weapon burials. This difference may provide a significant clue to the nature of the Anglo-Saxon migrations. These burials included single weapons such as a spear, shield, seax, ax or sword, or multiple weapons, or combinations of weapons in sets. Only exceptional graves were provided with helmets or chain mail. The origin of the weapon-burial rite is not well understood, but it may be associated with the breakdown of older kindred-based tribal societies in the fourth century A.D. and the emergence of warrior elites, uprooted and combined into new political communities by the migrations. In this context, weapon burials may have served an identity-forming function. They may have been the material and symbolic affirmation of newly formed social and "tribal" identities, in reality defined not by genuine, long-standing, hereditary or ethnic ties, but by the leadership (charisma) of warrior kings or military leaders and the shared dangers and political destinies connected with migration.[66]

In the Anglo-Saxon homelands of southern Scandinavia and northern Germany, the weapon graves are thinly spread within the cemeteries, with no evident consistent or significant difference between cremation and inhumation rites. Weapon graves represent roughly 4 percent or less of total burials. John Hines speculates that this archaeological pattern of thinly spread weapon burials corresponded with a thinly spread military elite, "an elite within which even the non-sword bearers could be

251. In contrast, E. A. Thompson estimates the Anglo-Saxons arriving in Britain in the fifth century as "many tens of thousands" (Saint Germanus of Auxerre, 112). Compare the remarks in the following accounts: Whittock, Origins of England, 128; Laing and Laing, Anglo-Saxon England, 62; Alcock, Arthur's Britain, 311; Dixon, Barbarian Europe, 56; C. J. Arnold, Roman Britain to Saxon England, 122–41; Hodges, Anglo-Saxon Achievement, 22–32, 186ff. A good example of changing attitudes is provided by the estimates accepted by Laing and Laing. In 1979 they cited the population of Roman Britain as c. 1,000,000 and the invading Anglo-Saxons as c. 50,000 to 100,000. In 1990, the population of Roman Britain had grown to 4,000,000 and the Anglo-Saxons had shrunk to between 10,000 and 25,000. Laing and Laing, Anglo-Saxon England, 62; Laing and Laing, Celtic Britain and Ireland, 69.
66 Hedeager, "Kingdoms, Ethnicity, and Material Culture," 280–83; Wolfram, History of the Goths, 1–18; Edward James, "Origins of Barbarian Kingdoms."

counted." This military elite may have held a practical military monopoly, since there is no evidence for a supporting host of massed peasants.[67]

In Britain, Anglo-Saxon burials in cremation deposits rarely include weapons. The incidence is perhaps 1.2 percent or less. This seems to mark a difference in practice from that of the continental homelands, one that cannot be explained simply by the archaeological difficulty of recognizing fragments of weapons associated with cremations. Because weapons were not deposited by peoples using cremation in England, we have no funerary measure of how warlike they were in comparison with their inhuming cousins. Nothing in their subsequent political and military history in England suggests that the groups practicing cremation were inferior in military resources or ferocity. In terms of inhumation burials, Anglo-Saxon cemeteries in England contain a startlingly higher proportion of weapon graves than those in the continental homelands. In a study of 54 burial sites including detailed examination of 47 inhumation or mixed cemeteries with some 3800 inhumations, Heinrich Härke found that 18 percent of all inhumations were accompanied by weapons. This compares with the rough figure of 4 percent for continental cemeteries. There are regional variations, but the overall figure of 18 percent represents 47 percent of all identifiably adult male burials.[68] That almost half of inhumed adult Anglo-Saxon men were buried with weapons is strongly suggestive. If the thinly spread weapon graves of the continent correspond to a thinly spread military elite among the general Germanic population, then as a natural corollary, the greatly higher percentages of weapon burials in England ought to represent a significantly more militarized version of Germanic society among the inhumation-practicing Anglo-Saxon immigrants. Among the Germans, possession of weapons was a mark of high status. We might expect a "status gradient" of the armed to the unarmed adult males on the order 1:10 or perhaps 1:5. A ratio of 1:2 requires explanation.

Speculating further, the circumstances of the invasion and settlement of Britain would have exercised strong pressures for a high degree of militarization among immigrating Angles, Saxons, and Jutes. As we shall see, the literary evidence records a pattern of initial mercenary recruitment followed by revolt and then invasion and colonization against active but ultimately unsuccessful British resistance. Such circumstances would account for a divergence in the level of militarization between the newly established Anglo-Saxon enclaves in Britain and the tribal homelands,

[67] Hines, "Military Context," 44.
[68] Härke, "Warrior Graves," 25–28; Härke, "Changing Symbols"; Härke, "Early Saxon Weapon Burials."

between the immigrating population, composed largely of warbands and their dependents, and those remaining behind. Besides being proportionally more numerous than weapon graves on the continent, weapon burials in Britain on average have fewer weapons per grave and simpler groupings of weapons such as a single spear and shield. As Hines suggests, this might be an archaeological reflection of the broadening and simplification of the military elite necessitated by the special circumstances of transmarine invasion and settlement in Britain.[69] It is possible that the poorer classes of Anglo-Saxon immigrants are underrepresented in Härke's sample of inhumation and mixed cemeteries. If the poor or ordinary folk were selectively buried elsewhere in as yet undiscovered locations, then the apparent highly militarized nature of the groups practicing inhumation would have to be reconsidered. Given the cemetery evidence of the continental homelands for burial of non-elites and given the level of archaeological investigation in England, this possibility seems unlikely, however.[70]

Interpreting the significance of Anglo-Saxon weapon graves in Britain is of course not simply a matter of treating a single weapon burial as the record of a single, once practicing warrior. There are regional variations affecting the frequency of weapon burials, and there are changes in the use of the rite over time within the same area. Many of the weapon sets are nonfunctional or incomplete and hence presumably symbolic. The cemeteries are not battle cemeteries. Indeed, many of the weapons deposited seem never to have been used. There is no obvious positive correlation between the frequency of the use of weapon-burial rites over time and what is historically known of varyingly intense periods of warfare. A number of weapon graves (8 percent) are associated with adolescents or children of fourteen years or younger, who are too young to have fought. Some weapon burials contain the remains of men who would seem to have been always physically unfit for war. Thus, as Härke has shown, neither the ability to fight nor actual military experience necessarily determined who was given a weapon burial. The weapon burial rite should thus be seen as an ideological, symbolic gesture by families within a weapons-owning social strata or class. In terms of religion, weapon burials may mark a preference for worship of war gods rather than fertility gods, but in any case weapon graves should be seen as a conscious expression of a warrior ethos and a claim to warrior status.[71]

---

[69] Hines, "Military Context," 44.

[70] For a discussion of attempts to rank the social groups within Anglo-Saxon cemeteries see Hodges, *Anglo-Saxon Achievement*, 38–42. Evison suggests that slaves were buried separately away from the Buckland Anglo-Saxon cemetery (*Dover*, 146–50).

[71] Härke, "Warrior Graves," 26–37. He suggests, however, that most of the weapons deposited may have belonged to the individual in whose grave they were found (35). Over time

Within the Anglo-Saxon inhumation cemeteries in Britain, weapon burials are on average more richly furnished than other inhumations. This may indicate greater disposable wealth. The weapon graves are also better provided with drinking vessels, perhaps a reflection of the heroic ethic of feasting and leisure associated with Germanic warrior society. Wealth and feasting would be in keeping with a military elite. Most intriguingly, men buried with weapons are an average of one to two inches taller than men buried without weapons in the same cemetery. Stature is a product of both genetic influences and environmental factors such as diet, illness, and stress in youth. Historically there are well-known examples of differences in stature between social classes. The correlation between greater average height and weapon burial in Anglo-Saxon cemeteries may be another in-dication of a distinct warrior elite and military class within a hierarchical society. Alternatively, this difference in height among inhumations may mark an ethnic difference between Anglo-Saxon invaders and native Romano-British men and their descendants. Some sample studies suggest that male Anglo-Saxon immigrants were an average of one and one-half inches taller than native British men. There is a risk of circularity in this argument if ethnicity is initially established on the basis of burial rites. Elaborating on the idea of an ethnic difference as an explanation for difference in average height within the same Anglo-Saxon cemeteries, a number of scholars have suggested that the shorter males without weapons may well represent a hybrid population containing significant numbers of surviving native Britons.[72]

Reflecting on the fact that roughly one-half of the men inhumed in the Anglo-Saxon cemeteries of his study sample were provided with weapons, Härke suggests that all men thus buried could not meaningfully be called "nobles" or "aristocrats."[73] Nevertheless, they can scarcely be considered ordinary agricultural peasants. The Anglo-Saxon weapon-burial rite pro-vides important evidence for the nature of their migration to Britain.

---

the distinction between a weapons-owning class and a weapons-using class may have become significant. For the period of the *adventus*, however, the difference between achieved and ascribed status was not yet likely to have developed.

[72] Härke, "Changing Symbols," 153–56; Härke, "Warrior Graves," 38–41. The alternative explanation for differences in height as reflecting pre-migration distinctions among different classes of Anglo-Saxons seems to be disproved by the fact that average height in males buried with weapons in Anglo-Saxon cemeteries actually decreases by five-eighths of an inch during the period from the fifth through the eighth centuries. Eventually the correlation between greater height and weapon burials vanishes altogether. This shrinking trend is better ex-plained by the gradual assimilation of Anglo-Saxons and native Britons than by some putative, unexpected, and unrecorded social revolution leading to the mixing of previously segregated strata within the Anglo-Saxon hierarchy. Fundamental changes in diet or nutrition do not seem a likely explanation for the changes in average height.

[73] Härke, "Warrior Graves," 43.

Although a number of what Catherine Hills calls ordinary folk may have participated, the movement was evidently highly militarized and thus qualitatively different from the social order in the continental homelands. This aspect of the *adventus* takes on enormous significance when set in the context of a Romano-British provincial population in southern and eastern Britain long accustomed to the protection of a standing Roman army and actively discouraged until the very last moment from bearing arms or even acting in large groups. Here is a vital clue to the conquest of the many by the few.

ARCHAEOLOGY AND THE *ADVENTUS*

Britain, like the rest of the late Roman world, was subject to a degree of "barbarization" through the agency of a Roman army that included significant barbarian elements. Inscriptions and literary evidence record the presence in Britain of Vandals, Burgundians, Alamanni, Marcomanni, Frisians, and Sarmatians, all introduced by the Roman authorities.[74] These barbarian soldiers sometimes left traces in the archaeological record. Frisians of the *numerus Hnaudifridi* are associated with fragments of a distinctive pottery. Within Roman cemeteries, inhumation graves furnished with weapons, barbarian styled brooches, and belts of office (the *cingulum*), are probably the burials of barbarian officers, since Roman inhumation custom did not conventionally include burial with such objects. These barbarians were an integral part of the Roman army and would have been significantly Romanized by the circumstances of their service.

The later Roman army in Britain was weakened by the authorized withdrawal of its manpower to reinforce threatened provinces elsewhere in the empire. The illegal and militarily wasteful adventures of a series of usurpers from Britain, ending in 407 with Constantine III, further depleted the strength of the remaining garrison. After the first decade of the fifth century, the Germanic and other barbarian military elements disappear with the rest of the regular Roman army from the history and seemingly also from the archaeology of Britain.[75] None of the later British or Anglo-

[74] Vandals and Burgundians: Zosimus 1.68; Alamanni: Ammianus 29.4.7; Marcomanni: Cassius Dio *Roman History* 72.16. For a discussion of the Frisians see Alcock, *Arthur's Britain*, 294, 278, 94, 177 (numerus Hnaudifridi). For the Sarmatians see Richmond, "Sarmatae."

[75] A possible exception may be the Frisians mentioned by Procopius (*De bellis* 8.20.7). The archaeology of York may yet connect some element of the late Roman army with the history of the successor kingdoms. The continued use of the *principia* is suggestive in this respect. In theory, local recruiting would eventually adulterate the Germanic character of any unit originally recruited on the continent and long stationed in Britain. Units of the field army, possibly

Saxon traditions preserved a memory of Germanic settlements persisting from the Roman era into the period of the Anglo-Saxon invasions. Such a survival is incompatible with the concept of an *adventus Saxonum*. In this sense Germanic barbarian history in Britain begins with Hengest and Horsa.

Myres and other scholars suggest, however, that beginning in the fourth century or earlier, Roman authorities sought to defend sections of the southern and eastern coasts of Britain with significant numbers of Germanic soldiers recruited from the homelands of the Angles and Saxons to serve as *laeti* or *foederati*. The area they defended became known as the Saxon Shore (*Litus Saxonicum*). *Laeti* were often barbarian peoples used to resettle lands depopulated by war. *Foederati* (federates) were groups of free barbarians settled within the empire who retained their own leaders and laws while fighting in exchange for Roman subsidies. Myres believes these free Germans remained in Britain with their families after the departure of the regular Roman army. Thereafter they overlapped with later Anglo-Saxon invaders arriving in the fifth century, interacting with them and augmenting their numbers. There is thus a demographic significance to Myres's thesis.[76]

In fact, there is no written evidence to confirm that either *laeti* or *foederati* were ever present in Britain. The only reference to the Saxon Shore comes from the *Notitia Dignitatum*, a late Roman source of uncertain origin, perhaps drawn up about 408 A.D. It lists a count for the Saxon Shore (*comes litoris Saxonici per Britanniam*) among the Roman military commands in Britain. The forts and units of this command may be considerably older than its specific designation as the Saxon Shore, a title which may originate as late as the end of the fourth or even early in the fifth century. This is the only "shore" frontier named anywhere in the Roman world. Perhaps the closest analogue is the *Ripa Gothica*, the Roman de-

---

heavily Germanic and brought to Britain during the late fourth-century emergencies, would either have returned to the continent following the crisis, or would later have been the units most likely to accompany the British usurpers to the continent. Similarly, more recently arrived *numeri* of Germanic origin would presumably have been more willing to leave Britain with the usurpers than units long stationed there with strong local ties. This perhaps helps to explain why there is not more archaeological evidence of their presence. See Welsby, *Roman Military Defence*, 125–32. There is limited archaeological evidence from the fifth or sixth centuries associated with some forts of Hadrian's Wall. Dark suggests, on this basis, that after the Roman army withdrew from northern Britain, the native Britons may have reconstituted elements of the former Roman command of the *Dux Britanniarum*. Alternatively, the archaeological material may be from residual British settlement left behind after the Roman military withdrawal. Dark, "Sub-Roman Re-Defence." Cf. Stephen Johnson, *Hadrian's Wall*, 113–16.
[76] For a recent discussion see Sonia C. Hawkes, "South-East after the Romans," 84–95. The final version of Myres's argument is *English Settlements*, 83–114. Compare his *Anglo-Saxon Pottery*, 62–119.

fences on the Danube constructed to resist the Goths. The basic issue is whether to interpret the Saxon Shore as an area defended against the attacks of Saxon pirates or as an area settled and defended by Saxon and other Germanic peoples. Linguistically either meaning is possible.[77] Lacking any textual support, Myres's scenario depends on archaeological interpretation.

Proponents of the idea of a shore settled by Saxons see certain material evidence in the archaeological record that they believe marks the presence of Saxon and other Germanic settlers in the fourth and early fifth centuries. These archaeological tracers include metal buckles and belt-fittings, barbarian styled brooches, and a particular type of pottery dubbed "Romano-Saxon." The pottery is so named because it was originally believed to be a Roman wheel-thrown ceramic designed to satisfy German (Saxon) tastes for pottery decorated in the style of the handmade wares of their homelands. Myres also suggests that a relatively small corpus of Anglo-Saxon cremation urns from eastern England (Caistor-by-Norwich) significantly resemble cemetery urns dating to the late third or fourth century found in the northern Germanic homelands. Finally, these various "Germanic" materials, including scattered Grubenhäuser (sunken-floored buildings), were thought to be distributed in significant relation to late Roman urban areas and road systems.[78]

These various archaeological arguments for significant Germanic settlement in fourth-century Britain have not withstood the scrutiny of recent revisionist studies. For example, the buckles and belt-fittings once thought to be peculiarly associated with Germanic soldiers were actually much more widely used in the Roman world. Although burials furnished with weapons and official belts are likely to be those of barbarian soldiers, the belts have also been found in female burials and were associated in everyday use both with the regular Roman military forces and with civilian bureaucrats. The discovery and excavation of kilns in Hertfordshire producing "Romano-Saxon" pottery place this material in a firmly provincial Roman context. The pottery was indeed produced in the

[77] Comes litoris Saxonici per Britanniam: Not. Dig. Occ. 1.36; 5.32. See Bartholomew and Goodburn, eds., Aspects. For a recent discussion of the Saxon Shore see Maxfield, ed., Saxon Shore. Donald A. White, Litus Saxonicum (settled by Saxons); D. E. Johnston, Saxon Shore, and J. S. Johnson, Roman Forts (defended against Saxons); J. G. F. Hind, "Litus Saxonicum," 317–24. Hind's article helps resolve the linguistic problem of interpreting "Saxon Shore" as an area defended against Saxons.

[78] For belts see Sonia C. Hawkes and G. C. Dunning, "Soldiers and Settlers"; Sonia C. Hawkes, "Some Recent Finds." For the pottery see Myres, Anglo-Saxon Pottery; Myres, Corpus of Anglo-Saxon Pottery; Myres and Green, Anglo-Saxon Cemeteries. Myres argues that a phase of controled settlement (360–410) preceded the end of Roman rule in Britain. His ideas are accepted by Evison in her survey of the archaeological evidence ("Distribution Maps," 126–40). In 1986 Myres restated his thesis (English Settlements, 74–103).

third and fourth centuries, and its style was indeed an imitation, but of more expensive Roman metal and glass vessels, not handmade cremation urns from northern Germany. These urns have been redated to the fifth century and this chronological change reverses the poles of imitation: the later Germanic material copies the Roman style and not vice versa. Except for scattered fragments found at Mucking (Essex), which may have originated in Roman plow soil accidentally incorporated into the pits of *Grubenhäuser*, no reasonably intact "Romano-Saxon" pots have been discovered associated with Anglo-Saxon structures. The idea that this pottery is a ceramic hybrid produced to Saxon tastes, or that its distribution is connected with the Saxon Shore, should be dismissed.[79]

The lack of a precise chronology overshadows the debate on the possibility of significant Anglo-Saxon settlement in fourth-century Britain. Archaeological dates for the earliest Anglo-Saxon cremations and inhumations derive from a series of overlapping associations. Pottery and metalwork in England are linked chronologically on typological grounds with closely similar objects in Germanic continental cemeteries. This Germanic material in its turn is ultimately linked to Roman coins and inscriptions through intermediate associations with imported Roman objects. Coins and inscriptions are dated within relatively narrow ranges by historically recorded careers of individual Roman emperors. Each link in this chain of dating by association tends to weaken its overall chronological precision. Moreover, archaeological dating systems developed from the cemetery material of southern Scandinavia or northern Germany must allow for extended periods of production and considerable longevity in use of particular pottery types or styles of metalwork. Associated Roman imports used in dating native Germanic materials were of high local value and may have been kept for long periods before being deposited as treasured heirlooms. Accordingly, the Germanic chronological systems take the form of overlapping phases. Within these phases individual objects are assigned approximate dates measured in units of a half century or a generation. Given these chronological limitations, what are the archaeological dates for the earliest Anglo-Saxon cremations and inhumations? Does the answer support or undercut the possibility of a significant Germanic settlement and population within fourth-century Britain?

Current archaeological dating schemes for northern Germanic pottery types and metalwork suggest that the earliest equivalent material from Anglo-Saxon cemeteries in Britain must date within the first half of the

---

[79] For a brief review of criticism of Myres's arguments see Sonia C. Hawkes, "The South-East after the Romans," 84. For buckles see C. J. Simpson, "Belt-Buckles and Strap-Ends." For the pottery see Gillam, "Romano-Saxon Pottery"; W. I. Roberts, *Romano-Saxon Pottery*.

fifth century.[80] A fifth-century rather than a fourth-century date is also indicated by archaeological distribution patterns within Britain. Myres interprets the close proximity of early Germanic cremation cemeteries to Romano-British sites such as Cambridge or Caistor-by-Norwich as evidence of the presence of fourth-century Germanic mercenaries employed for defense of towns by Roman or Romano-British authorities. Distinctly fourth-century Germanic metalwork is missing, however, from the fourth-century archaeological levels of the towns. Additionally, late Roman manufactured goods, such as wheel-thrown pottery, are not found in the Germanic cremation cemeteries in England. Such material segregation can scarcely be reconciled with the idea of fourth-century Germanic urban garrisons paid by Roman authorities. Since Germanic cemeteries on the continent in the fourth and fifth centuries did include Roman manufactures, presumably the Anglo-Saxon cemeteries were created after Roman manufactures ceased to be available in Britain. Precisely when Romano-British production and distribution collapsed is uncertain, but a date sometime between the ending of significant importation of Roman coinage in approximately 402 and 420 seems a reasonable estimate.[81] The implications of these distribution patterns complete the collapse on every level of the archaeological arguments for a significant Germanic settlement and a substantial population of Angles and Saxons in fourth-century Britain. Anglo-Saxon demography and the *adventus Saxonum* begin with the fifth century.

Although recent studies firmly place the earliest Anglo-Saxon pottery and metalwork in Britain within the first half of the fifth century, using archaeological arguments alone it is difficult to achieve greater chronological precision. Linking the archaeological pattern to historical evidence and specific events is equally problematic, for this requires synchronization of archaeological phases of fifty years' duration with the fast-

[80] For the continental material see Böhme, *Germanische Grabfunde*; Böhme, "Das Land zwischen Elbe- und Wesermündung." For a review of Böhme's *Germanishe Grabfunde* see Mildenberger. For the application of the Germanic chronologies to Britain see Böhme, "Das Ende der Römerherrschaft." Writing of the cremation cemeteries, Welch remarks: "Yet not one single Anglo-Saxon pottery urn from England can be shown to be earlier than the fifth century from the brooches or other finds they contained" (*Discovering Anglo-Saxon England*, 98). Sonia C. Hawkes comments of the metalwork: "There is not a scrap of official Late Roman military gear, whether fourth- or fifth-century in date, from any one of the great cremation cemeteries north of the Thames. . . . Except for the occasional broken and outworn heirloom, there is no fourth-century Germanic metalwork in any of our Anglo-Saxon cemeteries" ("The South-East after the Romans," 84–85).

[81] N. J. Higham, *Rome, Britain, and the Anglo-Saxons*, 173; Sonia C. Hawkes, "The South-East after the Romans," 84–85. Welch estimates that the unavailability of Roman pottery might date to the 420s or 430s (*Discovering Anglo-Saxon England*, 102).

moving history of the fifth century, when events of a decade or even a single year ushered in significant change. The historical evidence must refine the archaeological chronologies, not the reverse. Nevertheless, on purely archaeological grounds H. W. Böhme has dated the earliest Anglo-Saxon cremation cemeteries to roughly 420. These are distributed in an eastern pattern centered in East Anglia with associated brooch types that are characteristic of northwest Germany and southern Scandinavia, the traditional homelands of the Angles and Saxons. In a different and southerly geographical pattern, small groups of inhumation burials furnished with weapons, metalwork in the quoit brooch style, and Roman belt sets are scattered along both sides of the Thames. The metalwork and hybrid Roman-German burial rite are similar to those of Germanic soldiers from the Rhineland. Böhme detected in the metalwork the ethnic influences not only of Angles and Saxons, but also Franks, Alemans, and East Germans.[82] He dated these inhumation burials in southern England to the first half of the fifth century, possibly 420 or earlier. Important sites include Dorchester-on-Thames, Milton Regis (Kent), and Mucking (Essex). In the second cemetery from Mucking, the earliest inhumations (founder's burials) may date to the 430s or 440s.[83] The significance of Böhme's study of the metalwork of the fourth and fifth centuries in Britain lies not so much in the particular range of dates within the fifth century he assigns to Germanic (Anglo-Saxon) metalwork, but in his confidence that clear differences distinguish this Germanic material from metalwork in a fourth-century Romano-British context.

To conclude, the archaeological evidence suggests that the Anglo-Saxon migration to Britain began sometime in the first third of the fifth century. Although women, families, and ordinary people were included, the movement was heavily military in character and probably dominated by warrior elites. The total Anglo-Saxon immigrant population was probably considerably fewer than 100,000, numbering perhaps several tens of thousands. There is no archaeological evidence to distinguish the scale of the Anglo-Saxon migration as substantially greater than contemporary Germanic movements on the continent. If anything, the Anglo-Saxon movement was probably significantly smaller. At the beginning of this chapter, I suggested that the critical factor determining the Romano-German medieval synthesis was the relative numbers of invading and indigenous populations. If, as is here argued, the Anglo-Saxon migration

---

[82] Böhme, "Das Ende der Römerherrschaft," 522.
[83] Sonia C. Hawkes, "The South-East after the Romans," 87 (with references). Welch dates the Dorchester material to the 430s or 440s and believes the men buried with weapons and belt sets arrived at least two decades after 407 (*Discovering Anglo-Saxon England*, 102).

corresponded to the other Germanic movements of the period, and if Romano-British population corresponded to the population of the Roman continental provinces, then the distinctive pattern of events in post-Roman Britain must have resulted from something other than the Anglo-Saxons themselves.

CHAPTER TWO

The Scale of the *Adventus:*
The Literary Evidence

THE QUESTION OF THE scale and significance of the Anglo-Saxon immigration forms the marrow in the historical bone of contention regarding the nature of the transition between Roman Britain and Anglo-Saxon England. Given the limitations of the archaeological and anthropological evidence, the literary sources, however inadequate, are vital to any analysis of the numbers of invading Anglo-Saxons. The literary evidence is miscellaneous, consisting of laws, king lists, pedigrees, historical narratives, annals, a few early surveys such as the Tribal Hidage, and an offshoot of the literature, place-names. In my opinion, place-names, as a reflection of language, are a measure of political or cultural influence rather than an indication of population.[1] Changes in language do not necessarily stem from wholesale changes in population, as the history of the spread of English speech in the modern world illustrates. The Spanish conquests of Central and South America changed the language and place-names of an enormous area with a tiny force of priests and soldiers. This principle can be illustrated with examples more directly tied to the early medieval migrations. The small Irish colony of Dalriada, through military conquest, largely obliterated the Pictish language and place-names, although the surviving Pictish population very probably far exceeded the Dalriadic. Similarly, although they were evidently a minority of the population, the Anglo-Saxon invaders transformed language and place-names so that Bernicia was largely indistinguishable in this respect from the

---

[1] Hines, "Philology, Archaeology, and the *Adventus Saxonum.*" See now N. J. Higham, *Rome, Britain, and the Saxons,* 189–208.

other Anglo-Saxon kingdoms. Analogously, small Arab armies imposed their language in a vast area of North Africa. Of course the Romance languages of western Europe evolved from Latin, originally introduced to millions of Gauls and Spaniards by mere tens of thousands of Roman soldiers and merchants.

LAW CODES AND THE TRIBAL HIDAGE

It is very difficult to penetrate beneath the horizon of evidence provided by the seventh- and eighth-century sources, such as the earliest Anglo-Saxon legal codes and the Tribal Hidage, to the earlier world of the invasions and migrations. Already in the seventh century kingship was a well-established institution and a number of formidable kingdoms existed. The process of state formation is poorly understood, but probably the seventh-century kingdoms had grown during the sixth and seventh centuries by conquering and assimilating preexisting smaller and weaker political units. If so, these constituent units of the larger seventh-century kingdoms may provide clues concerning the political mosaic of the sixth century. By matching the earlier political units (termed *provinciae* and *regiones*) against the pattern of distribution of pagan artifacts, we may gain a rough notion of the scale and organization of the original Anglo-Saxon immigration which created the earliest territorial groupings. The key text is the Tribal Hidage, a document variously dated between the mid-seventh and later eighth century. It lists thirty-five peoples, each assessed for tribute in terms of numbers of hides (units of taxation). The hide was a unit without a precise modern value, but originally it may have represented the amount of land needed to maintain a single free family (possibly 120 acres). Many of the peoples listed are known from other sources and represent seventh-century political units. Many of these (perhaps all) had at one time been politically independent and had been governed by their own ruling families. Quite possibly, most of these provinces were in existence in the sixth century. If so, through inference and retrospection, we may find that these numerous small provinces suggest a relatively small original Anglo-Saxon immigrant population, settling in a number of autonomous units. Such an inference is compatible with the archaeological evidence for the small size of early Anglo-Saxon settlements and cemeteries, and fits with the generally slow pace of the Anglo-Saxon military and political conquest of southern Britain.[2]

[2] See W. Davies and H. Vierck, "Contexts of Tribal Hidage." For a discussion of the scale of early Anglo-Saxon settlement see Christopher Taylor, *Village and Farmstead*, 117–24; C. J. Arnold, *Roman Britain to Saxon England*, 124–25; Hodges, *Dark Age Economics*, 133–40. For the formation of kingdoms, see Basset, "In Search of the Origins"; Yorke, *Kings and King-*

English history is well provided with law codes, and the Anglo-Saxon laws furnish certain basic information that is useful for demographic purposes, but they offer little detail from which actual estimates of population may be derived. It is dangerous to generalize from the early laws associated with specific kings and kingdoms since conditions in early Kent and Wessex, for example, might have been significantly different. The earliest English laws from Kent and Wessex describe a hierarchical society.[3] The laws order compensations for crimes according to class, including provision for the officers of the Christian church. Unfortunately, there is no way to discover the relative numbers within each of the classes as defined in the laws. Each of the historical codes is associated with a single king (perhaps a political precondition of legal codification), and the laws reflect the political dominance of the aristocracy.

Certain incidental information in the laws is interesting for demographic questions. The existence of slaves and partially free classes is attested.[4] Several legal terms possibly imply the continued survival of a British population under Anglo-Saxon control. *Wealh* and possibly *laet* may represent a British element in the population.[5] Few of the statutes illuminate family size or structure in any fashion useful for demographic study. One class, the Kentish *ceorl*, has "loaf-eaters," slaves and other dependents.[6] The seventh-century West Saxon law of Ine (13.1) defines an army (*here*) as a force larger than thirty-five men. This suggests the possibility that armies in the early period may have been small, and it could even be an indirect clue to the scale of the Anglo-Saxon migration. Military population can sometimes be used as a rough index of overall population.[7] An "army" equivalent to a single ship's crew is suggestive.

---

doms, 9–15; Kirby, *Earliest English Kings*, 9–12. For the text of the Tribal Hidage see Dumville, "Tribal Hidage."

[3] Liebermann, *Die Gesetze der Angelsachsen*; Thorpe, *Ancient Laws and Institutes*; Attenborough, *Laws of the Earliest Kings*; Finberg, "English Society"; H. M. Chadwick, *Anglo-Saxon Institutions*, 87–113.

[4] One statute (Athelstan IV, 4 and 7) mentions the punishment of an offending slave by 80 other slaves. This perhaps suggests slaves were common, at least during Athelstan's time, and that they might be found in large groups, perhaps on estates. A passage in Bede suggests this might have been the case earlier, for a royal estate at Selsey in Sussex of 87 hides included 250 slaves. Sussex was once assessed at 7,000 hides, so by extrapolation a large slave population might be assumed. If 250 slaves for 87 hides is used as an average proportion and applied to the entire Tribal Hidage, this produces a figure of 500,000 slaves. There is no warrant for assuming the figure to be an average, but it does raise an interesting possibility. H. M. Chadwick, *Anglo-Saxon Institutions*, 373; Bede, *A History of the English Church and People* (hereafter cited as *H.e.*). A convenient Latin text with facing translation may be found in Bede, *Ecclesiastical History*, 4.13.

[5] Faull, "Semantic Development."

[6] Ethelbert 25; Finberg, "English Society."

[7] "We call up to seven men 'thieves'; from seven to thirty-five a 'band'; above that it is an 'army.' Ine 13.1, Whitelock, ed., *English Historical Documents* 1:366. Hollingsworth, *Historical Demography*, 43, 227–74.

NARRATIVE SOURCES

Relevant continental sources of the fifth and sixth century include Prosper's *Chronicle*, Constantius's *Vita Germani*, the anonymous Gallic Chronicles of 452 and 511, and the histories of Zosimus and Procopius.[8] These are valuable in creating a chronological framework for the Anglo-Saxon invasions, but for the most part provide little incidental detail suggesting the scale of those invasions. The *adventus Saxonum*, defined in keeping with British and Anglo-Saxon traditions of an original, identifiable settlement leading to permanent independent kingdoms, must be dated on the basis of the continental evidence to between 410 and 441/42 A.D.[9] The material providing the most suggestive line of enquiry into the numbers of arriving Anglo-Saxons is derived from the narrative accounts of Gildas, Bede, the *Historia Brittonum* ("Nennius"), and the *Anglo-Saxon Chronicle*.[10]

Except for Gildas, these narrative accounts are, strictly speaking, secondary sources separated by centuries from the events of the fifth century. Connecting them to the invasions requires plausible but largely unprovable inferences about oral traditions and lost sources. These are phrases that make even a medievalist's blood run cold. In fact, how to use the later narratives, or even whether to use them at all, has proved a divisive question for generations of historians.[11] A spectrum of opinions and approaches exists. At one extreme is the minimalist position that excludes all evidence except for first-class (strictly contemporary) primary sources, with the practical result that British history in the first half of the fifth century is virtually a prehistoric subject beyond the horizon of modern historical investigation.[12] *Testis unus, testis nullus*: unsupported testimony is no better than the complete absence of testimony. At the other extreme stand historians who believe Bede, the *Historia Brittonum*, and the *Anglo-Saxon Chronicle* not only preserve genuine traditions of fifth-

[8] For recent discussions of these sources in relation to the end of Roman Britain see Wood, "End of Roman Britain"; Wood, "Fall of the Western Empire"; Michael E. Jones and John Casey, "Gallic Chronicle Restored"; E. A. Thompson, *Saint Germanus of Auxerre*; Michael E. Jones, "Historicity of the Alleluja Victory"; Michael E. Jones, "Saint Germanus."

[9] Michael E. Jones and John Casey, "Gallic Chronicle Restored."

[10] For a general introduction see Whitelock, ed., *English Historical Documents*; Gransden, *Historical Writing*. Sims-Williams gives a more detailed treatment in two recent articles ("Gildas and the Anglo-Saxons," and "Settlement of England").

[11] Donald A. White, "Changing Views of the *Adventus Saxonum*"; Dumville, "Sub-Roman Britain"; Sims-Williams, "Settlement of England," 1–5.

[12] For example, Lot, "Bretons et Anglais"; Dumville, "Sub-Roman Britain"; Dumville, "Historical Value," 7–9. Probably the most famous statement of this position is by Kemble: "I confess that the more I examine this question, the more completely I am convinced that the received accounts of our migrations, our subsequent fortunes, and ultimate settlement, are devoid of historical truth in every detail" (*Saxons in England*, 1:16).

century events, but preserve them in little-altered form.[13] This latter position risks the overly credulous incorporation into modern historical reconstructions of anachronisms, alterations, and inventions deliberately created by synchronizing medieval authors and editors, and probably underestimates the problems associated with oral traditions and the accumulated errors of textual transmission.

But the evidence in Bede's account, the *Anglo-Saxon Chronicle*, and the *Historia Brittonum* cannot safely be simply ignored. To do so risks the creation of distortions of a different kind, for omissions of genuine tradition, even in dubious or adulterated form, can be as damaging as the inclusion of bogus material. As H. M. Chadwick remarks: "If one admits only evidence which is strictly first class . . . and rejects all late or indirect evidence and that of records preserved by oral tradition, one cannot but get an entirely erroneous impression of the British—or any other—Heroic Age."[14] Moreover, a hypercritical attitude toward later texts can impede the process of discovery and argument that reveals genuine early content.[15] Either of the extreme positions risks circularity of argument, and both have played crucial roles in the ongoing historical dialectic. My own position, like that of many others, is to accept the unavoidable risks associated with the use of material in Bede, the *Historia Brittonum*, and the *Anglo-Saxon Chronicle*, but to reduce these by using the later sources only in conjunction with more nearly contemporary evidence (principally Gildas) and with a skeptical eye wary of potential invention and contamination by synchronizing hands. From this material I have here abstracted the information relevant to population. Each of the sources will be dealt with in turn.

Gildas

The single most important source is Gildas's *De excidio Britanniae*.[16] Unfortunately for the historian, specific dates, places, names, and numbers were secondary in Gildas's writings to his primary exhortatory purpose. He was a preacher rather than an historian. Gildas found his inspiration and writing model in Jeremiah and the Old Testament. When Gildas

---

[13] See, for example, Morris, *Age of Arthur*, and to a lesser extent Alcock, *Arthur's Britain*.

[14] H. M. Chadwick and N. K. Chadwick, *Growth of Literature*, 1:142, n. 3.

[15] See, for example, the attempt to show that the fifth-century British entries in the Gallic Chronicle of 452 were derived from a later, Carolingian interpolation. M. Miller, "Last British Entry"; Bartholomew, "Fifth-Century Facts."

[16] Throughout this chapter I will use the text and translation of Winterbottom in Gildas, *Ruin of Britain*. The work is cited hereafter as *D.e.* Giraldus quoted the Latin title as *De excidio Britonum* (*Descriptio Cambriae* 2.2). Theodore Mommsen's version of the title is often used, *De excidio et conquestu Britanniae*.

composed the *De excidio* is not known. The work has usually been dated to the first half of the sixth century, roughly 540 A.D. As much as ten years may have separated Gildas's initial writing from the completion and publication of the work (*D.e.* 1.2). This possibility adds another element of uncertainty in estimating its date of composition. The traditional chronology rests on references within the *De excidio* to the siege of Mount Badon and to certain contemporary British rulers (tyrants) against whom Gildas directed his admonitions. These references can be dated approximately by using later British annals and genealogies, although the chronological reliability of this later material is suspect and the associated dates are insecure and sometimes contradictory.[17] The pivotal dating passage within the *De excidio* relating to the siege of Mount Badon is compressed in meaning to the point of obscurity and may also be corrupt in the surviving texts. Gildas relates (*D.e.* 25.3) that the Britons rallied under the leadership of Ambrosius Aurelianus and defeated the Saxons in battle:

> From then on victory went now to our countrymen, now to their enemies: so that in this people the Lord could make trial (as he tends to) of his latter-day Israel to see whether it loves him or not. This lasted right up till the year of the siege of Badon Hill, pretty well the last defeat of the villains [Saxons] and certainly not the least. That was the year of my birth; as I know, one month of the forty-fourth year since then has already passed. (Ex eo tempore nunc cives, nunc hostes vincebant, ut in ista gente experiretur dominus solito more praesentem Israelem, utrum diligat eum an non: usque ad annum obsessionis Badonici montis, novissimaeque ferme de furciferis non minimae stragis, quique quadragesimus quartus (ut novi) orditur annus mense iam uno emenso, qui et meae nativitatis est.)
>
> *D.e.* 26.1

---

[17] See Dumville, "Gildas and Maelgwn." Dumville first undercut the reliability of these dates, then restored them to a limited degree by checking the pedigrees and annals against an internal relative chronology built up from the sequence and probable duration of the events narrated by Gildas. This narrative is anchored by a reference to Magnus Maximus and, more controversially, to Agitius (Aetius). The *Annales Cambriae* date Badon to the equivalent of the year 516 A.D. The same source dates the death of Maglocunus (Maelgwn) to the equivalent of 547 A.D. This creates a contradiction in the context of Gildas, for if Maglocunus was alive to receive his admonition, Gildas cannot have written forty-four years after Badon (516 + 44 = 559/60). On the other hand, if Gildas originally addressed Maglocunus but waited ten years to publish his work, the discrepancy is reduced to a more acceptable level (c. 549 for the original drafting of *De excidio* and c. 547 for the death of Maglocunus). Dumville, "Chronology," estimated c. 500 A.D. for the siege of Badon and Gildas's birth, and c. 544 as the date for the composition of *De excidio*.

Winterbottom's translation catches the generally accepted meaning that Gildas was born in the year of the siege of Mount Badon and wrote forty-three years and two months after that event. Alternative antecedents have been suggested, however, to anchor Gildas's forty-four-year interval. These include (instead of the siege of Mount Badon) the victory of Ambrosius, the Saxon *adventus,* and some unknown era used by contemporary British authors.[18]

Ian Wood suggests that Gildas's forty-four-year interval should be counted from the victory of Ambrosius (*ex eo tempore*) and events preceding Badon. If so, the chronology of composition for the *De excidio* would accordingly be revised to an earlier date. Wood estimates this as sometime between about 485 and the 520s. Writing in the eighth century, Bede interprets Gildas to mean that the siege of Badon followed forty-four years after the *adventus:*[19] "Under his [Ambrosius's] leadership the Britons regained their strength, challenged their victors to battle, and, with God's help, won the day. From that time on [*ex eo tempore*], first the Britons won and then the enemy were victorious until the year of the siege of Mount Badon, when the Britons slaughtered no small number of their foes about forty-four years after their arrival in Britain" (*H.e.* 1.16). This may simply be an inference on Bede's part, or a misreading, or even a coincidence. He is, however, paraphrasing very closely and working from a text of the *De excidio* three centuries closer to Gildas than the earliest version now available. The association of Gildas's forty-four year interval with the arrival of the Anglo-Saxons might have some historical foundation. If so, we must find an earlier date for the *De excidio.*[20]

---

[18] Collingwood and Myres, *Roman Britain and the English Settlements,* 460–61; G. H. Wheeler, "Gildas, Chapter 26."

[19] Wood, "End of Roman Britain." Wood pairs Gildas's birth with Ambrosius's victory; the siege of Badon and the composition of *De excidio* follow forty-three years later. Charles-Edwards sees syntactical problems with Wood's translation (Review of *Gildas*). *H.e.* (trans. Colgrave and Mynors) 1.16.

[20] J. M. Wallace-Hadrill, *Historical Commentary,* 25–26, 212–15. Cf. M. Miller, "Bede's Use of Gildas." Sims-Williams follows Plummer's earlier suggestion that the forty-four years cited in Bede and linked to the *adventus* is simply a coincidence unrelated to Gildas's calculation of forty-three years and one month ("Settlement of England," 20). I think Bede's specific dates for the *adventus* are inventions based on a misunderstanding of Gildas. If the association between a forty-four-year interval and the *adventus* were correct, however, we could calculate a risky and speculative chronology using an insular date for the *adventus* independent of Bede (and Gildas), drawn from the *Historia Brittonum.* Calculations of the *adventus* in this last source center on the equivalent of the year 428 A.D. An elapse of forty-four years from this date places the siege of Badon about 471/72 (428 + 44). Gildas's princes of the post-Badonic generation act irresponsibly because they did not personally witness the miraculous British recovery at Badon and have forgotten the painful, associated political lessons (*De excidio* 26.2-4). Allowing a full thirty years for the maturation of this new generation of leadership gives a date of c. 500 for Gildas's time of writing (c. 471/72 + 30). Compare this with the table of dates in Sims-

Recent literary and linguistic studies of Gildas do not seem to support the traditional date of approximately 540 for the writing of the *De excidio*. Various aspects of the text appear to be inconsistent with our understanding of conditions and culture in mid-sixth-century Britain. The vocabulary, grammar, and diction of Gildas's Latin closely resemble the language of continental authors of the fifth and early sixth centuries and suggest that his work should be placed in the same chronological context. Gildas bears the intellectual thumbprint of a traditional classical education, perhaps received from a private *rhetor* continuing the tradition of defunct publicly supported schools that had prepared students for careers in the Roman bureaucracy. The rhetorical structure and style of the *De excidio* suggest that Gildas received training from a Late Roman *grammaticus*. Such an education is unlikely to have been available in Britain after the end of the fifth century, or indeed to have served any practical purpose after that date. These considerations also apply to Gildas's audience.[21] Literary and linguistic considerations thus suggest that Gildas was probably educated in the later fifth century and composed the *De excidio* at the beginning of the sixth century.[22] This controversial revised chronology has the significant effect of pushing Gildas a half-century closer to the events of the Anglo-Saxon invasions.[23]

These rough chronological limits help to define the potential period of Gildas's own memory for which, of course, he is a primary source. Independent of any specific chronology, however, Gildas provides a crucial clue which establishes his work, in an important sense, as a contemporary authority for the invasions. He states that the (degenerate) grandchildren of Ambrosius Aurelianus were living at the time he wrote. Since Am-

---

Williams, "Settlement of England," 15, and with Dumville, "Chronology," 83. The fullest discussion of the chronology of *De excidio* is O'Sullivan, *Authenticity and Date*. Cf. M. Miller, "Relative and Absolute Publication Dates." Miller gives 534–49 as the probable years of composition (p. 174); O'Sullivan suggests c. 515–20 (p. 178).

[21] See the studies collected in Lapidge and Dumville, eds., *Gildas: New Approaches:* Wright, "Gildas's Prose Style"; Orlandi, "*Clausulae* in Gildas"; Sutherland, "Imagery of Gildas"; Sims-Williams, "Gildas and Vernacular Poetry." See the review by Edward James, "Interpreting Gildas." I have relied particularly on Lapidge, "Gildas's Education." Even if Gildas had been educated in Gaul rather than Britain, as Kerlouégan suggests (*Les destinées de la culture latine*, 5), an educational time frame of the later fifth or very early sixth century seems indicated. On the basis of a relative chronology deduced from changing monastic influence in Gildas's works, Michael Herren suggests a date of composition for the *De excidio* at the very end of the fifth century or the beginning of the sixth ("Gildas and Early British Monasticism," 77–78).

[22] See now the massive study by Kerlouégan, *Les destinées de la culture latine*, 5: "Il rédigea, dans les premières années du VIᵉ siècle."

[23] A new consensus may be emerging in the most recent works that accepts the early sixth century as the date of composition for *De excidio*. Welch, *Discovering Anglo-Saxon England*, 9; N. J. Higham, *Rome, Britain, and the Anglo-Saxons*, 73–75; Kirby, *Earliest English Kings*, 14. Yorke, however, maintains a mid-sixth century date (*Kings and Kingdoms*, 2).

brosius was active during the Saxon *adventus* and revolt, Gildas had access to "living memory" in the form of men whose parents or grandparents witnessed the invasions.[24] For events that occurred before Ambrosius, however, Gildas must be treated as a secondary authority.[25]

Two passages in the *De excidio* are directly relevant to the numbers of the Saxons. Gildas writes of the first arrivals: "Then a pack of cubs burst forth from the lair of the barbarian lioness, coming in three *keels*, as they call warships in their language" (*D.e.* 23.3). These were followed by reinforcements: "The mother lioness learnt that her first contingent had prospered, and she sent a second and larger troop of satellite dogs. It arrived by ship, and joined up with the false units [the previously mentioned three keels]. Hence the sprig of iniquity, the root of bitterness, the virulent plant that our merits so well deserved, sprouted in our soil with savage shoots and tendrils" (*D.e.* 23.4). Gildas mentions no further reinforcements. It seems the Saxon force that ravaged eastern Britain consisted of three keels plus a larger additional force.

The use by Gildas of an Anglo-Saxon term, "keels" (Late Latin *cyula*, from Old English *ciol*), is sometimes cited to suggest that an Anglo-Saxon account underlies his description. A sixth-century Anglo-Saxon source would have to have been in oral form, of course, in the pagan, preliterate period before the conversion. The number three associated with a Germanic saga or origin story would be a suspicious convention, akin to the three ships of the Goths mentioned in Jordanes.[26] I find the notion that Gildas had an Anglo-Saxon informant rather far-fetched, for the *De excidio* creates the impression that Gildas was isolated from the Anglo-Saxon area of Britain.[27] He was probably simply spicing his account with

[24] *D.e.* 25. See Gransden, *Historical Writing*, 5. For a discussion of "living memory" see Morris, "Dark Age Dates," 151–52. Morris emphasizes that living memory acted as an audience-based control: "Living experience may be misinterpreted but it may not be invented."

[25] Sims-Williams, "Settlement of England," 6; Sims-Williams "Gildas and the Anglo-Saxons," 8, 24.

[26] Jordanes *Getica* 94–95. The suspicion that the number three is spurious has been voiced by numerous authors. Kemble, *Saxons in England* 1:16; James Campbell, "Lost Centuries," 26; Sims-Williams, "Gildas and the Anglo-Saxons," 22–29. Three of the founding expeditions in the *Anglo-Saxon Chronicle* are given as parties of three ships. *ASC*(E)s.a. 449, 477, 495, 501. The number three may thus be taken as simply a convention or a device—a formula "closer to myth than to history." Abels, *Lordship and Military Obligation*, 35. On the other hand, prominent historians see no difficulty in accepting the arrival in three ships as literally correct. Wallace-Hadrill, *Historical Commentary*, 21; Winterbottom in Gildas, *Ruin of Britain*, p. 150; E. A. Thompson, "Gildas and the History of Britain," 216. Myres went even farther and saw in the figure of three ships the evidence of a contemporary official document: "The most natural explanation of his reference to the Saxons coming in 'three keels' is that this was the number of ship loads specified in the first formal invitation which led to the *foedus* or treaty settlement" (*English Settlements*, 14).

[27] *D.e.* 10.2. Gildas seems to treat the Saxon territory of the "partition with the barbarians" in

an exotic term known to his audience. E. A. Thompson suggests that Gildas's readers probably knew the typical complement of a Saxon warship. At some point the term "keel" ceased to have a specifically Anglo-Saxon association. The *Historia Brittonum*, for example, used this term as slang to describe warships of all peoples. Thus the Scotti first reached Ireland in keels (*ciulis*) and the Romans invaded Britain in keels (*H.B.* 13, 37.20). Naval parlance is a dangerous basis for inference. Recall that the late Roman fleet patrolled the coast of Britain in craft nicknamed "Picts" (*Picati*)! Relevant to the possible significance of Gildas's use of "keel" is his correct use elsewhere in the *De excidio* of the non-Latin term "coracles" (*de curucis*) to describe the ships of the Picts and Scots. Recall that warships in the parlance of his latinate audience were *longis navibus*.[28] No one has suggested that the use of the term coracles implies the underlying presence of an Irish or Pictish source. I think keels and coracles alike are nothing more significant than an indication of technically correct information held on the part of Gildas or his sources. Neither term suggests the hidden presence of a foreign tradition any more than do the words Volvo or Volkswagen in modern English usage. It is misleading to treat the account (*D.e.* cc. 22–23) as a Germanic origin story or to dismiss the details included therein as a heroic formula or mythic convention.[29]

---

his day as a no-go area closed to the Britons. Such isolation would obviously impede any face-to-face transmission of a Saxon oral tradition to Gildas. Even assuming the possibility that Gildas used an early written account of the invasion somehow based on Saxon rather than British tradition, the source would necessarily have been transmitted in Latin, not Anglo-Saxon. When Bede later paraphrased Gildas's account he omitted his own native "keels" and recorded only *longis navibus* (*H.e.* 1.15). This is an appropriate cautionary example against an inference based on vocabulary. In fact, Bede used *longis navibus* to describe warships of all sorts including Anglo-Saxon, Pictish, and Roman (*H.e.* 1.1, 1.2). Any linking of the term "keels" with an early Saxon tradition is very problematic. E. A. Thompson, "Gildas and the History of Britain," 216; Vegetius *Epitoma rei militaris* 4.37. Howe suggests that Gildas used a barbarian word (*cyulis*) deliberately to express his horror at the event (*Migration and Mythmaking*, 58).

28 *D.e.* 19, 23.3.

29 The number three also has potential mystical religious meaning, and hence the potential for distortion. Gildas gives a three-hundred-year prophecy (*D.e.* 23.3) and his three appeals to Rome have sometimes been considered as a Celtic triad. On the whole, however, for all his faults, Gildas appears in the context of his times to be more rational than superstitious. He mentions only a single miracle. See Gransden, *Historical Writing*, 3. Gildas was not a modern sceptic, of course, and like Procopius he explained events by referring to a combination of divine action and human character. I detect no mystical or secret meaning in his numbers. The three consulships of Agitius is a good example. His three ships are unlikely to have theological overtones. It is interesting to compare the use of numbers by Bede, where some scholars see symbolic value in his use of seven and five. See Levison, "Bede as Historian," 122–23. Contrast J. M. Wallace-Hadrill, *Historical Commentary*, 10. I think it is possible to separate the sheep from the goats in this matter. Contrast the prosaic details of federates, *annonae*, and three ships plus a later, larger reinforcement in Gildas's account with the different, fabulous quality of the origin stories in the *Historia Brittonum*, Bede, and the *Getica*, quoted above. The *Historia Brittonum*'s preoccupation with the number three in the

As we shall see, Gildas's story is too precise and developed. He uses the vocabulary of late classical history and rhetoric, not Germanic saga. The disputed significance of Gildas's use of keel (*cyula*), however, does raise the general problem of his sources.

His own statement regarding his sources is typically obscure: "I shall do this as well as I can [tell the tale of Britain in the Roman era], using not so much literary remains from this country (which, such as they were, are not now available, having been burnt by enemies or removed by our countrymen when they went into exile) as foreign tradition [*transmarina relatione*]: and *that* has frequent gaps to blur it" (*D.e.* 4.4). This passage raises several questions. Are we to accept at face value the general conclusion that Gildas had no insular written sources, or is this an early version of a medieval modesty topos in which the author routinely denies his own competence or the competence of his materials, or decries the neglect of his subject by his predecessors?[30] It is also worth stressing that Gildas seems to be referring specifically to the Roman era (*temporibus imperatorum Romanorum*).[31] This would help to explain his ignorance of the fourth and early fifth centuries but would have no necessary bearing on his potential sources for the later Saxon *adventus* and the period of independent Britain. In any case, what did Gildas mean by *transmarina relatione*? Several possibilities, not mutually exclusive, include oral or written accounts from British settlements overseas (Gaul or Ireland), continental written sources, and perhaps even *relationes* similar to those of Symmachus.[32] Typically of his era, Gildas does not often explicitly acknowledge a source or quotation. He also paraphrases, which makes the identification of his sources more difficult. Besides the Bible and the *Aeneid*, Gildas used the *Church History* of Rufinus and several works of Jerome. He also probably used Orosius and evidently he quotes from a letter to Agitius. He may also have used inscriptional material, something like a *Notitia Brittaniarum*, and a Life of Saint Alban.[33] Beyond these we can

---

story of the Roman conquest of Julius Caesar is obvious. Caesar arrives in 60 ships (three score); after an interval of three years he returns in three hundred ships and conquers Britain in a third decisive battle. See *H.B.* 19–20; Marsh, *Dark Age Britain*, 73. Similarly, in the origin story of the Irish, thirty ships led by three brothers settled in Ireland. Each ship had thirty men and thirty women. See *H.B.* 13. Bede seems aware of the difference in quality between an origin story and the account in Gildas of the Saxon *adventus*. Contrast *H.e.* 1.1 with *H.e.* 1.15. J. M. Wallace-Hadrill, *Historical Commentary*, 8–9, notes Bede's appropriately cautious language and discusses the possibility that Bede was deliberately having fun with the origin stories by writing a "witty parody." Cf. Mayr-Harting, *Coming of Christianity*, 50.

[30] Compare the "Nennian" preface to the *Historia Brittonum*, translated by Morris, in Nennius, *British History and Welsh Annals*, p. 9.

[31] *D.e.* 4.4.

[32] Michael E. Jones, "Appeal to Aetius," 149 n. 24.

[33] Gildas *De excidio*, ed. Mommsen, p. 7. Stevens, "Gildas Sapiens," 356. Gildas's quotations from other sources are indexed by Winterbottom in Gildas, *Ruin of Britain*, 156–59. Neil

only speculate concerning a plausible mixture of living memory, oral tradition, folklore, personal observation, and now-lost written sources. The selectivity created by Gildas's moral purpose as an author makes it dangerous to conclude that his silence on a given subject necessarily results from simple ignorance.

Returning to the specific problem of the Saxon arrival in three ships with a later reinforcement, several features in his account indicate that Gildas used in this section a contemporary or near-contemporary written Latin source rather than a Germanic tradition. Gildas correctly employs the terms *foedus, annonae, hospites,* and *epimenia* in a technically accurate description of a federate (Saxon) settlement.[34] These terms were current in the fifth century and highly relevant to barbarian settlements within the empire during that time but have only a questionable relevance for sixth-century Britain, long separated from Roman control. To make this point another way, when Bede later paraphrased Gildas's account, he changed these technical terms because they no longer had contemporary meaning.[35] As James Campbell concludes: "His [Gildas's] account of how the beginnings of German power in Britain derived from the mutiny of mercenary forces is plausible, and uses vocabulary suggesting that he may have been drawing on a fifth-century source."[36] A second clue supports this conclusion based on vocabulary. The sudden shift in Gildas's narrative from a generalized to a very particular picture may well reflect the influence of a written source. This is accompanied by a marked change in rhetorical tone which perhaps also reveals the influence of a written account.[37]

The impression Gildas creates with his description of a force of three ships and "a second larger group" is scarcely that of a numberless invading multitude. The modest numbers do not accord with the otherwise florid

---

Wright adds Sulpicius Severus, an anonymous Pelagian tract, and possibly Euagrius's translation of Athanasius to texts used by Gildas ("Gildas's Prose Style," 107–14).

[34] *D.e.* 23.5: The barbarians who had been admitted to the island asked to be given supplies (*annonae*), falsely representing themselves as soldiers ready to undergo extreme dangers for their excellent hosts (*hospites*). The supplies were granted, and for a long time 'shut the dog's mouth.' Then they again complained that their monthly allowance (*epimenia*) was insufficient . . . and swore to break their agreement (*foedus*) and plunder the whole island unless more lavish payment were heaped on them.

[35] E. A. Thompson, "Gildas and the History of Britain," 217. Bede used *annonae* (food) but added *stipendia* (pay) and *alimenta* (supplies). He also used *foedus* (treaty) but in a crude, general sense (*H.e.* 1.15–16).

[36] James Campbell, "Lost Centuries," 23. Even so, Campbell thinks three ships might be a formula. Sims-Williams suggests caution concerning the allegedly technical nature of Gildas's vocabulary ("Gildas and the Anglo-Saxons," 22, n. 97).

[37] M. Miller, "Bede's Use of Gildas," suggests that differences in rhetoric indicate the use of a written source in the preceding section of *De excidio,* but I am unable to see this.

and exaggerated language of Gildas's narrative. Contrast the scale of the Saxon force with the 600,000 Israelites Gildas mentions in the preface to his work.[38] Other less explicit passages in the *De excidio* are consistent with this notion of relatively small numbers. Gildas states, for example, that the Britons' enemies were not stronger than the British themselves but that the Britons lacked a martial spirit and proper equipment.[39] The Saxons were invited into Britain originally to deal with the Picts and Scots. Implicit in this action was the judgment by the Britons that the Saxons were a lesser threat. Yet even the Picts and Scots are characterized as "wandering thieves," not an invasion far surpassing the British strength.[40] Gildas calls the Saxons more savage than the Scots and Picts,[41] and compares them to the Assyrians of the Old Testament.[42] They were a tremendously destructive force, but significantly, they are at no point portrayed as numerous.

Stripped of hyperbole, Gildas's story is a coherent and believable account of a classic mercenary revolt. (1) Faced by the threat of Scots and Picts the British invited a force of Saxons to combat the old enemy. This was a standard Roman tactic. (2) The Saxon force was joined by a second, larger contingent. (3) The Britons could not (or would not) supply enough rations, as promised in the initial agreement, to this increased Saxon army. (4) The Saxon mercenaries revolted and ravaged their former hosts. (5) The rebellion was ultimately controlled by the British. As he explicitly states, Gildas wrote in a time of relative calm and recovery following the struggle with the Saxons. The problems and dangers he laments and warns against include wickedness, immorality, injustice, and civil war. These domestic sins are untempered by fears of external attack and may again provoke God's wrath against the Britons. The Saxons remain in the background. Gildas refers incidentally to a partition with the barbarians.[43] Clearly, however, for Gildas and his contemporaries the Saxons pose no imminent threat. "External wars may have stopped, but not civil ones. For the remembrance of so desperate a blow to the island and of such unlooked for recovery stuck in the minds of those who witnessed both wonders [the Saxon revolt and final British recovery]. That was why kings, public and private persons, priests and churchmen, kept to their own stations. But they died; and an age succeeded them that is ignorant of that storm and has experience only of the calm of the present. All the controls

[38] *D.e.* 1.3.
[39] *D.e.* 18–19.
[40] *D.e.* 18.
[41] *D.e.* 2.
[42] *D.e.* 24.2.
[43] *D.e.* 10.2

of truth and justice have been shaken and overthrown. . . . " (D.e. 26.2–3).
A logical inference is that when Gildas wrote, the Anglo-Saxon population
in Britain was not so numerous as to present an obvious risk to continued
British security.

There is an odd juxtaposition between the prosaic details of Gildas's
description of the Saxon mercenary revolt and the extravagant language of
the jeremiad with which he narrates the effects of the revolt. The mention
of small numbers, keels, a partition, and a revolt over rations are, in my
opinion, strong evidence that Gildas used a factual source, for these details
are paralleled by analagous events elsewhere in the empire rather than
images cribbed from the Old Testament. They emerge despite, not because
of, Gildas's stated purpose and chosen literary style. It may be possible to
uncover the information of Gildas's source by removing the images and
matter obviously borrowed from the Old Testament and used in the De
excidio. A few examples paralleling Gildas and Jeremiah will illustrate this
point. Gildas explicitly states that Jeremiah and the Old Testament are his
model, "a mirror reflecting our own life."[44] His work, like Jeremiah's, is a
warning addressed to the princes and the priests. Gildas compares the
Saxons and Britain with the Chaldeans and Judea. In both cases God punished his people by invasion and purged them with fire and destruction to
return them to his will. The parallel between Gildas and Jeremiah, however, involves more than purpose and narrative structure. In significant
sections of the De excidio Gildas seems to use images derived from
Jeremiah, although these are not in the form of direct quotation. Thus in
Jeremiah "the whole country is in flight; they creep into caves, they hide in
thickets, they scramble up crags. Every town is forsaken, no one dwells
there" (Jer. 4:29 NEB). In Gildas the refugee Britons base themselves "on
the mountains, caves, heaths and thorny thickets" (D.e. 20.2). Later he
writes, "But the cities of our land are not populated even now as they once
were; right to the present they are deserted" (D.e. 26.2).[45] In Jeremiah the

---

[44] Gildas D.e. 1.4–7: I read how, because of the sins of men, the voice of the holy prophets rose
in complaint, especially Jeremiah's, as he bewailed the ruin of his city in four alphabetic songs.
And I could see that in our time too, just as Jeremiah had lamented, 'the city' (that is, the
church) 'sat solitary, bereaved; formerly it had been full of peoples, mistress of races, ruler of
provinces: now it had become tributary'. I saw that 'gold' (that is, the lustre of the word of God)
'had been dimmed and the best colour changed'. I saw that 'the sons of Sion' (that is, of the
holy mother church), 'once glorious and clad in fine gold, had embraced dung'. . . . I gazed on
these things and many others in the Old Testament as though on a mirror reflecting our own
life; then I turned to the New Testament also, and read there more clearly what had previously, perhaps, been dark to me: the shadow passed away.
[45] In these examples pairing Gildas and Jeremiah the images are very similar and represent
more than simply the use of Biblical language by Gildas. The specific Latin vocabulary in
these phrases from the De excidio, however, does not closely coincide with the Vulgate.

invaders are called "peoples of the North"; so too in Gildas the Picts and Scots are peoples of the North (Jer. 1:15; *D.e.* 23.2). In Jeremiah the invaders are introduced thus: "For I bring disaster out of the North. . . . A lion has come out of his lair, the destroyer of nations. . . . (Jer. 4:6–7). Gildas introduces the Saxons in the following manner: "Then a pack of cubs burst forth from the lair of the barbarian lioness. . . ." (*D.e.* 23.3).

Significantly, however, while Jeremiah's invaders were "hordes" (Jer. 4:16), "whirlwind" (Jer. 4:13), "clouds" (Jer. 4:13), and "thunder of the sea" (Jer. 6:23), Gildas breaks with the language of the Old Testament and states that the Saxon invaders comprised three ships' companies and a second, larger group. The only explanation I can offer for this break in the character and style of Gildas's narrative is that he either used a written source at this point or that his own information and the general knowledge of his audience precluded the use of exaggerated numbers and the imagery of the Old Testament. In either case the small number of invaders described by Gildas must be treated seriously by the historian.

Procopius

Procopius of Caesarea, a Greek historian of the mid-sixth century, is perhaps the most exotic source for the question of Anglo-Saxon population. A recent study by Averil Cameron has lifted a corner of Procopius's classicizing rationalist veil to reveal a mind strongly influenced by miracle, supersition, and the irrational.[46] The passage with potential relevance to the question of population is part of a geographical, ethnological "digression," one of a number in his work, with all the related problems typical of that particular element in ancient historiography.[47] The disconcerting mixture of fantasy and plausible detail is so intertwined within the

---

Elsewhere (*D.e.* 36) Gildas quotes Jeremiah (18.8) from a text differing significantly from the Vulgate. Overall, Gildas mixes numerous Old Testament quotations taken from the Vulgate, which is based directly on the Hebrew, with quotations from earlier versions of the Old Latin Bible derived from the Greek Septuagint. Some of his biblical material may be taken secondhand from other authors or even from otherwise unattested Bible texts. Gildas probably also quotes or paraphrases from memory. For Gildas's Bible see Burkitt, "Bible of Gildas"; Grosjean, "Bible de 'Gildas.'" For his biblical imagery see Sutherland, "Imagery of Gildas." For the lion image in biblical and Celtic literature see Sims-Williams, "Gildas and Vernacular Poetry," 185–88; Sutherland, "Imagery of Gildas," 159.

46 Averil Cameron, *Procopius.* See the review by Cherf.

47 Procopius *History of the Wars* 8.20 (*History of the Wars* 8 = *De bello gothico* 4). The "digressions" and "origins" in Procopius are discussed in Averil Cameron, *Procopius,* 207–22. "Far from being made up of discrete lumps of information, waiting to be dug out by modern scholars, Procopius' digressions and origins passages are complex, subtle and varied. The text is many stages removed from the simple transmission of information. It has been shaped by literary aims, personal opinion and wider changes in Byzantine policy" (213).

digression that no single statement can be used to disprove or validate another.[48] Procopius states of Brittia's (Britain's ?) population: "Three very populous nations inhabit the Island of Brittia, and one king is set over each of them. And the names of these nations are Angles, Frisians, and Britons who have the same name as the island. So great *apparently* [E. A. Thompson's italics] is the multitude of these peoples that every year in large groups they migrate from there [Brittia] with their women and children and go to the Franks. And they [the Franks] are settling them in what seems to be the more desolate part of their land, and as a result of this they say they are gaining possession of the island"[49] (*History of the Wars* 8.20.6–10). Procopius even explains his source—an embassy from the Franks to the court of Justinian had included some Angles to substantiate claims of Frankish overlordship of Brittia.[50] This seems plausible, and Stenton has argued that this reverse migration from Britain to the continent resulted from the British victory at Badon and the consequent restriction of land available for Anglo-Saxon (and "Frisian") settlement in Britain. This would indirectly confirm the account in Gildas.[51] Roughly one hundred years after the *adventus* began, such possible pressure of population might have resulted from natural increase, or just possibly, Procopius might be interpreted to support the idea of a numerous original Anglo-Saxon migration. Procopius himself, however, betrays doubts about this specific passage, and subsequent details in the chapter undermine its credibility as a clue to sixth-century population in Britain.[52]

---

[48] Averil Cameron, *Procopius*, 211.

[49] For the translation and a discussion with references see E. A. Thompson, "Procopius on Brittia"; Averil Cameron, *Procopius*, 213; O'Sullivan, *Authenticity and Date*, 172; Ward, "Procopius, *Bellum Gothicum*," 465. See E. A. Thompson's comments on variations within translations of this passage.

[50] The embassy is usually dated c. 553. Thompson, "Procopius on Brittia," 501. Alternatively, information may have reached Constantinople before 549 during the reign of the Frankish King Theodebert (533–48). Roger Collins, "Theodebert I," 10–12. There would have been obvious problems of communication and translation. The story may have reached Procopius second- or third-hand.

[51] Stenton, *Anglo-Saxon England*, 4–8. It is worth noting the oversimplification of three races and three kings as compared to the more complex mix of numerous kingdoms in sixth-century Britain. For a recent discussion of the Frisians see Bremmer, "Nature of the Evidence."

[52] It is disconcerting to reflect that Procopius evidently has no idea that the Angles and Frisians were recent invaders, not natives. See E. A. Thompson, "Procopius on Brittia," 506. Procopius presents overpopulation as the motive for the migration not as fact reported by his source but speculation ("it appears . . ."). My guess is that his inference is based on the imitation of classical authors such as Caesar, Strabo, and Tacitus, who described Britain as very populous. The fact of migration he learned from the Frankish embassy. Procopius put the two images together. The geographical descriptions in 8.20.4 and 6.15.4 may be compared to a similar digression in Jordanes *Getica* 2.12. The influence of earlier classical sources is readily apparent. See Alonso-Núñez, "Jordanes on Britain."

Procopius's evident uncertainty over this passage seems echoed by his geographical confusion concerning Britain. "The island of Brittia lies in this [the northern] ocean, not far from the shore, rather about two hundred stades away, approximately opposite the mouths of the Rhine; and it is between Britannia and the island of Thule. Whereas Britannia lies towards the west [of Brittia, presumably] opposite the extremities of the land of the Spaniards, separated from the mainland [of the Spaniards] by about four thousand stades, no less, Brittia on the other hand faces the rear of Gaul, the parts of it facing the ocean—clearly, to the north of Spain and Britannia" (*History of the Wars* 8.20.4–5, trans. E. A. Thompson). With both a Brittia and a Britannia we seem to have one Britain too many. If Britannia is Britain, where is Brittia? If Brittia is Britain then what can Procopius refer to as Britannia? A number of possible solutions have been offered to this geographical problem of identity, but each in turn creates a web of intractable secondary difficulties for interpreting Procopius's meaning. In the end, as E. A. Thompson concludes, "It would seem that on any interpretation we must ascribe a mistake to Procopius." Probably Brittia and Britannia are one and the same, but somehow confused in Procopius's mind or in the accounts of his sources. The division simply reflects Procopius's ignorance concerning sixth-century Britain. An alternative possibility is that Procopius refers to Britain as Brittia, while Britannia really means Armorica or Brittany. Brittia is specifically called an island while Britannia is not. In Brittia "men of olden times built a long wall, cutting off a large portion of it. . . . " (*History of the Wars* 8.20.42). This reference to a wall is naturally taken to mean Hadrian's Wall in Britain, although Procopius does not seem to know it was constructed by the Romans, a curious ignorance for a man so interested in buildings and fortification. Against this, Procopius consistently refers to Britain as Britannia in earlier chapters. No other author refers to Britain as Brittia, and no author before Procopius had yet called Armorica Brittany. A third interpretation equates Brittia with Jutland or Denmark. Ernst Stein and H. B. Dewing, the Loeb editor of Procopius, both support this idea. The suggestion makes some sense of Procopius's geography and places alliance, warfare, feud, and marriage among the Varni, Franks, Anglii, and Frissones in a credible context. The Brittones, however, seem obviously misplaced.

If Brittia really refers to Brittany or Denmark rather than Britain, then Procopius's statement on population and migration loses its British and Anglo-Saxon relevance. Of course if Brittia is Jutland or Denmark, and Procopius's testimony is believed, then the continental homelands of many of the Anglo-Saxon invaders are overpopulated, not depopulated, in the mid-sixth century at the end of the migration to Britain. E. A. Thompson concludes that Procopius's statement concerning overpopulation and the consequent migration by the Angles, Frissones, and Brittones to the lands of the Franks was conjecture: "Not a word of it is derived directly or indirectly from a British or English source."[53]

Next in Procopius's discussion occurs what has been called the earliest genuine historical romance in English history, the story of the "Bride of Radigis," the jilted maid of Britain.[54] In fact, as we have seen, the identification of Brittia as Britain is uncertain. In any case, this is a northern story probably originating among the continental Varni. In this tale a sister of the king of the Angles is betrothed to Radigis, a King of the Varni, who then jilted her in favor of a Frankish marriage alliance. Incidental details include a talking bird, the marriage to a step-mother, and an expedition of revenge led by the princess herself.[55] "She accordingly collected four hundred ships immediately and put on board them an army of not fewer than one hundred thousand fighting men, and she in person led forth this expedition against the Varni" (History of the Wars 8.20.26, trans. Dewing). Numeration was not a strong point for Procopius. Typical of classical authors, he greatly exaggerated barbarian numbers, even in situations relatively familiar to him personally. The cliché "not fewer than one hundred thousand" seems obvious and is certainly an exaggeration of epic proportions.[56]

Following this tale within the same chapter is a discussion with fantastic geographical details centering on a long wall dividing Brittia into two parts. "Many people dwell" in the temperate east, "but on the west side everything is the reverse of this, so that it is actually impossible for a man to survive there even a half-hour" (History of the Wars 8.20.45, trans.

[53] E. A. Thompson, "Procopius on Brittia," 506.
[54] Burn, "Procopius and the Island of Ghosts," 261.
[55] James Campbell, "Lost Centuries," 38, notes that this odd tale has Germanic elements (the prophetic bird).
[56] On numbers see Averil Cameron, Procopius, 148–49. On the cliché of a barbarian army of 100,000 invading Italy when Procopius was there, Cameron remarks: "When Procopius says blandly that the Franks are the most treacherous race of all he is no more reporting an objective fact than when he says that the invading army numbered 100,000" (210–11 and n. 20). For barbarian numbers in the Italian campaigns see E. A. Thompson, Romans and Barbarians, 80, 88, 278 n. 15, 280 n. 61, 282 n. 28. Speaking very roughly, Procopius's estimates of barbarians are about five-fold too high. This might be applied as a corrective to the passage above, but the fact that this figure is part of an obvious romance, itself embedded in a digression concerning the most remote of western peoples, makes the figure useless. Lopez, nevertheless, took the figure of 400 ships seriously ("Le problème des relations anglo-byzantines," 141). Simple division suggests that the numbers are bogus. No Germanic ship of the sixth century could transport 250 men (100,000 ÷ 400). Nor is the episode self-consistent. Hermegisclus advises his son Radigis to marry a Frank because potential aid gained from Brittia would take too long to reach the Varni. The Franks, in contrast, are only just the other side of the Rhine. Yet in this same episode 400 ships and 100,000 men come from Britain, and Procopius suggests the trip between Brittia and the continent is a row of one day and one night.

Dewing). Procopius concludes this chapter on Britain with a ghost story that details the ferrying over to Brittia of the souls of the dead. At this point even Procopius disavows his informants. Curiously, the story is possibly a garbled version of an ancient British myth rather than an Anglo-Saxon tale.[57]

There are obviously formidable problems with this chapter in terms of sources, language and transmission, Procopius's own style and aims, and the possible influence of Byzantine and Frankish policy and propaganda. These erect almost opaque filters between the modern reader and Procopius's sources, whatever they were.[58] Even so, it may well be that the fantastic elements in his account have some genuine historical basis potentially useful in characterizing political and diplomatic relations among the various peoples of the North Sea region.[59] Certainly his accounts provide an invaluable insight into Byzantine ideas concerning Britain. In terms of the problem of migrating populations, however, Procopius's value is slight. This particular element of his digression is better treated as a wonder-tale than as an historical clue.

Bede

Bede's famous *Historia ecclesiastica gentis Anglorum* was finished in about 731 A.D.[60] As the title suggests, the work is concerned with ecclesiastical rather than secular history and concentrates on events subsequent to the Anglo-Saxon invasion and settlement. In dealing with the Anglo-Saxon invasion, Bede incorporated Gildas, with the addition and alteration of a few important circumstantial details. Bede named Vortigern, the proud tyrant who invited the Saxons to Britain, localized the action in Kent, and also named the leaders of the invasion, Hengest and Horsa. Bede also dated the Anglo-Saxon arrival within the period 446–57.

---

[57] Would the Angles have known ancient British myths with Greek overtones? See Burn, "Procopius and the Island of Ghosts," 258–61. Burn hopes that an explanation of this story will somehow clear the way for acceptance of the rest of the chapter.

[58] Other sources of contact between Britain and Byzantium include the western seaways linking the Celtic west in Britain with the Mediterranean. Charles Thomas, *Celtic Britain*, 57–60. For a very speculative attempt to link the court of Maelgwn of Gwynedd with Byzantium see Ward, "Procopius, *Bellum Gothicum*."

[59] For the idea that a genuine historical core resides in this account see Wood, *Merovingian North Sea*, 3–12; James Campbell, "Lost Centuries," 38; O'Sullivan, *Authenticity and Date*, 172; Burn, "Procopius and the Island of Ghosts," 258–61; Averil Cameron, *Procopius*, 213: "There is just enough plausible detail, among the hearsay and the personal comment, to qualify as serious evidence, with sufficient distortion to make its interpretation highly problematic." In contrast, E. A. Thompson concludes: "Not a word of it is derived directly or indirectly from a British or English source" ("Procopius on Brittia," 506).

[60] Throughout this chapter I will use the translation of Sherley-Price in Bede, *History of the English Church*.

These additions and alterations raise the crucial question of Bede's sources and their tradition and transmission.[61] Some of the alterations and additions to Gildas made by Bede, such as the statement that war with the Huns prevented the Romans from aiding the Britons, and the probable alteration of Agitius to Aetius, can be traced back to Bede's classical sources such as Marcellinus Comes. These give insight into Bede's methods, synchronisms, and inferences.

The changes in Bede's treatment of the Anglo-Saxon invasion of Kent between his writing of the *Chronica maiora* in 725 and the *Historia ecclesiastica* in 731 are very informative and suggest the possible discovery of new material by Bede in the interval. Bede states in *Chronica maiora* that the Britons appealed unsuccessfully to Aetius in his third counsulship, and then asked for help from the Angles. Besides adding the Angles to Gildas's Saxons, Bede named the British leader (Vertigernus) and dated the *adventus* to the reign of Martianus and Valentinianus. The form *Vertigernus* suggests that Bede had an early Celtic source, either a fuller version of Gildas than we now have, or an early gloss on that work, or possibly an independent lost written source. Later, in *Historia ecclesiastica*, Bede repeats essentially the same story but changes the name of the British leader to "Vurtigernus" and also adds Hengest and Horsa, with their genealogy going back to Woden. Bede mentions Horsa's death and his monument in Kent.[62]

Some of Bede's material must have come from Kentish traditions preserved at Canterbury. In the preface to the *Historia ecclesiastica*, Bede acknowledged his debt to Kentish information conveyed by Albinus and Nothhelm. Thus Bede had this Kentish material secondhand, probably as an Anglo-Latin text. A Northumbrian monk would not have been familiar with Kentish oral tradition. Even if these traditions reached Bede in written form, however, they must ultimately have been derived from oral traditions, for the Anglo-Saxons were illiterate at the time of the inva-

---

[61] There are in fact several *adventus* dates in Bede. In *H.e.* 1.15 the *adventus* occurs within the period 449–55. In 1.23 and 5.23 another date (c. 446) is given. In 2.14 the same event is dated 446 or 447. Obviously these dates are calculated approximations. See M. Miller, "Bede's Use of Gildas," 241–61. Cf. Wallace-Hadrill, *Historical Commentary*, 20–21, 212–15. For Bede's chronological calculations, which are dubious for the *adventus*, see Sims-Williams, "Settlement of England," 8–21.

[62] *Chronica maiora* under the entries 483, 489; *H.e.* 1.14–15, 2.5, 5.24. H. M. Chadwick has a good discussion of this material (*Origin of the English Nation*, 35–38). For glosses of Gildas see Lindsay, *The Corpus*. On the historicity of Hengest see Turville-Petre, "Hengest and Horsa." Turville-Petre rejects Hengest and Horsa as historical persons. Against his arguments see Whittock, *Origins of England*, 41–51. On Bede's sources in general see Sawyer, *From Roman Britain to Norman England*, 2–20; J. M. Wallace-Hadrill, *Historical Commentary*, 16–23, 211–15; Myres, *English Settlements*, 4–10; Kirby, "Bede's Native Sources"; Sims-Williams, "Settlement," 5–26; Miller, "Bede's Use of Gildas."

sions. The earliest horizon for a written account of Kentish tradition would have been the arrival in Kent perhaps as early as 560 of the literate Frankish princess Bertha with her Christian retinue. A more probable time of record would be about 600–650. Even assuming a precocious Kentish written tradition, the early stages of the conquest lay beyond Anglo-Saxon living memory at the time of earliest record. The very earliest traditions of the conquest might have been transmitted before this in the form of king lists, genealogies, and alliterative poetry. Many changes, deliberate and accidental, would have occurred before the Kentish dynastic propaganda was ultimately recorded. Bede treated these traditions with caution ("It is said . . . ").[63]

Estimates of the reliability of Bede's traditional sources vary greatly. The question is a microcosm of the historiographic debate about the historical horizon of the early fifth century. For example, Stenton sees no reason to doubt their accuracy. In contrast, speaking of the Kentish royal genealogical material, P. H. Sawyer concludes, "It has no value as a statement about the realities of the English conquest." A popular theory is that Bede conflated several different "comings of the English." If Bede knew of other traditions relating to areas other than Kent, he did not see fit to include them in his history. Kent had a special place in his scheme, of course, for Augustine began the conversion of the English in that kingdom and Canterbury was the center of Roman Christianity.

In a passage over which much scholarly ink has been shed, Bede states: "These new-comers were from the three most formidable races of Germany, the Saxons, Angles, and Jutes. From the Jutes are descended the people of Kent and the Isle of Wight. . . . From the Saxons—, that is, the country now known as the land of the Old Saxons—came the East, South, and West Saxons. And from the Angles—that is, the country known as Angulus, which lies between the provinces of the Jutes and Saxons and is said to remain unpopulated to this day—are descended the East and Middle Angles, the Mercians, all the Northumbrian stock . . . and the other English peoples" (*H.e.* 1.15). It is the last part of this statement that is relevant to the question of numbers, for a migration leaving the land empty to the time of writing (450 and 731) certainly implies a wholesale shift of population. A most vexing question is the origin and reliability of this passage. It has been variously assessed by scholars as pure speculation on Bede's part, a later insertion based on some other source, or genuine early tradition.[64] It is certainly an oversimplifica-

---

[63] For the date of the marriage between Æthelberht and Bertha see J. M. Wallace-Hadrill, *Historical Commentary,* 34. Cf. Wood, *Merovingian North Sea,* 15–16; Kirby, *Earliest English Kings,* 31–32.

[64] Stenton, *Anglo-Saxon England,* 9; Sawyer, *From Roman Britain to Saxon England,* 13. For

tion.[65] The archaeological record and continental history both suggest that the peoples were culturally and politically more mixed in their origins than Bede believed. Bede's description is also anachronistic and shaped by the political and ecclesiastical interests of his own day.[66] Nicholas Howe suggests that Bede's creation (or simplification) of this ethnogeographic schema was a piece of effective "mythmaking." Gildas had provided an archtype or model for the history of Britain defined by a series of migrations across the sea into God's chosen island. Bede elaborated this idea into a paradigm by linking four of the languages of Britain (British, Pictish, Irish, and Latin) with four migration or origin myths. The arrival of the Anglo-Saxons completed the pattern by providing a people suitable to God's purpose. This is the essence of Bede's mythic interpretation of the past. Bede provided the chronological and geographical frameworks missing in Gildas's vague account of the *adventus* and thereby transformed a parable into a myth that could be fixed in popular memory. Bede thus performed the role of an Anglo-Saxon Vergil. Having fixed this myth in place and time, Bede could integrate the pagan *adventus* into his Christian scheme of history and create for his countrymen a usable past.[67]

Bede's statement that the Saxons came from Old Saxony, the Angles from Angulus, and the Jutes from (inferred) Jutland is plausible but suspiciously neat. Bede also wrote that the Britons came originally from Armorica (Brittany).[68] This is false and the suspicion is at once raised that the notion of Britons from Brittany, Angles from Angulus, Saxons from Saxony, and so forth, is a typical early medieval gloss, an unsubstantiated guess or inference. The statement that the land of the Angles is said to be deserted "from that day to this" sounds like the flourish of a tale or saga. Archaeology shows that Angulus was not completely deserted at the time

---

the passage as authorial speculation, see Sims-Williams, "Settlement of England," 21; H. M. Chadwick, *Origin of the English Nation*, 86; Alcock, *Arthur's Britain*, 108. For the passage as drawn from genuine tradition, with some support from archaeology, see Whitelock, *English Historical Documents*, 1:5; J. M. Wallace-Hadrill, *Historical Commentary*, 22; Myres, *English Settlements*, 46–49. The passage fits rather awkwardly into Bede's narrative and has the look of a later insertion. James Campbell thinks differences in the vocabulary of this passage compared with Bede's usual terminology mark it as deriving from a letter, rather than from Bede himself ("Bede's 'Reges,'" p. 13 n. 9). If so, Bede is spared the odium or credit, and we are left to speculate over secondhand speculation.

[65] *H.e.* 5.9. Cf. Procopius *History of the Wars* 8.4.20. Franks, Frisians, and Suevi should probably also be included. Alcock, *Arthur's Britain*, 278–301. For a recent review of the archaeology see James Campbell, "Lost Centuries," 30–37. For linguistics see H. M. Chadwick, *Origin of the English Nation*, 64–69.

[66] Stenton, *Anglo-Saxon England*, 9. According to Gransden, *Historical Writing*, 23, Bede was "reading history backwards."

[67] Howe, *Migration and Mythmaking*, 49–71.

[68] *H.e.* 1.1.

of the migrations or thereafter. A change in the settlement pattern occurred, and doubtless some deserted sites represent a movement to Britain. But the overall pattern of settlement throughout northern Europe changed at this time, and there is no way to estimate from a handful of excavated sites the magnitude of the movement into Britain, even if it were possible systematically to link the abandoned continental sites directly to sites in Britain (this has so far proved impossible). Medieval settlement was not fixed or immutable. Later changes that had nothing to do with migration overseas or invasion also resulted in deserted sites.[69] In any case, Bede himself seems less than certain concerning the realities of an empty Angle homeland. He prefaces the relevant statement with a cautionary "it is said" (*perhibetur*), a phrase that elsewhere in his work seems to indicate a fact not certainly known to him or a fabulous or legendary element.[70]

The other information in Bede relevant to the numbers of invaders which is not directly taken from Gildas seems to be mostly embellishment or the substitution for original phrases in Gildas unflattering to Bede's ancestral countrymen. As in the *De excidio*, the Saxons came in

[69] On the homelands of the Angli see Stenton, *Anglo-Saxon England*, 12–13; Chadwick, *Origin of the English Nation*, 103. These authors discuss the relevant passages in Tacitus, Ptolemy, *Widsith*, and Alfred's Orosius. The idea of deserted homelands is also found in the *Historia Brittonum*, but associated with islands. This is also the sense in Ohthere's report to Alfred. See *H.B.* 37–38; Ohthere 1.1.19. If the islands are related to *terpen*, mounds artificially raised above flood levels, then their abandonment need not involve the movement of many people. Land hunger as an engine driving the Anglo-Saxons to Britain does not seem consistent with completely deserted homelands, nor would land shortage in the tribal homelands really explain the secondary Anglo-Saxon expansion within England. See Witney, *Kingdom of Kent*, 74–75. Dixon has a good discussion of sites such as Ezinge, Wijster, Feddersen Wierde, and Gristede (*Barbarian Europe*, 44–63). No doubt the fifth-century discontinuity along the North Sea coast was sometimes directly related to migration to Britain. There are other horizons of discontinuity in the archaeological record of this area, however, that have nothing to do with Britain. In many regions the settlement area twelve miles inland is virtually unexplored, and until the complex of coastal and inland settlement and its dynamic is better understood, sweeping statements about a massive migration to Britain are crude generalizations. On the complexity of settlement patterns around the North Sea see TeBrake, *Medieval Frontier*, 100–132. It is salutary to consider that a migration of 10,000 Anglo-Saxons would have emptied the equivalent of 200 Wijsters. This puts our very limited settlement evidence into a more realistic context. On the uneven nature of the relevant settlement archaeology see van Es, "Introduction," 5–9.

[70] Bede uses the phrase when giving an unverifiable oral tradition rather than something known to him—for example, the outrageous origin story concerning the Picts (*H.e.* 1.1). The fact that *perhibetur*, and *perhibentur* occur in consecutive sentences in this section of Bede's account suggests to me that he was skeptical of either his information or his own speculation. Plummer is more hopeful: "And though it is going too far to say that this phrase implies critical doubts (in the modern sense) on the part of Bede, yet it does undoubtedly imply that he gives that part of the story as a tradition and nothing more." Plummer in Bede, *Venerabilis Baedae Opera Historica*, 2:28.

three ships. This group was augmented by a second force, as stated by
Gildas. Bede added that the larger second force was "a great body of warriors." In this combined force "such hordes of these alien peoples vied
together to crowd into this island that the natives who had invited them
began to live in terror."[71] A direct comparison between the relevant passages of Gildas and Bede, however, illustrates that the differences are too
slight to allow Bede a source for the numbers of the invaders in this
incident independent of Gildas.[72] Since his perception of the scale of the
invasion is largely derived from De excidio, Bede is of very limited value
in estimating the size of the Anglo-Saxon migration.

"Nennius" and the Historia Brittonum

The Historia Brittonum, of disputed authorship but traditionally ascribed to a certain "Nennius," provides the most detailed account of the
Anglo-Saxon conquest. The Historia as it has survived to the present was
compiled in about 829 A.D. but incorporated earlier materials.[73] Its highly
composite nature, along with disputed authorship, a complicated textual
history, and a typical early medieval mix of fantasy and plausible detail,
make the Historia Brittonum a notoriously difficult historical source. A
number of originally independent component elements have been recognized, of various dates and unequal historical value. These components
are in many cases themselves composites. Because of this, generalization
concerning the Historia is almost impossible. Each section or chapter
forms its own smaller world of controversy over authorship, origin, date,
and historicity. Some of the earlier written materials incorporated in the
Historia were at least as old as the seventh century, and perhaps contem-

---

[71] H.e. 1.15.

[72] Compare D.e. 23 with H.e. 1.15. These passages refer to the arrival of the first Anglo-Saxon
contingent and it is obvious that Bede used Gildas almost verbatim, only changing the insult-
ing "pack of cubs" to "Angles and Saxons." Gildas referred to the second contingent as "a
larger troop of satellite dogs," a phrase Bede also altered, using instead "men at arms" and in a
later passage "great companies of stranger folk." Bede added to Gildas the long passage concerning the tribal homelands which I have suggested is a typical speculative medieval gloss.
Bede's account concludes with what is obviously a borrowing from Gildas. Compare D.e. 26.1
with H.e. 1.16. Notice that the emendations by Bede delete the identification of the Britons
with Israel (now reserved for the Anglo-Saxons) and replace the obscure dating reference to
Gildas's birthday with a statement pertinent to an Anglo-Saxon audience.

[73] All translated passages are taken from Nennius: British History and the Welsh Annals,
translated by John Morris. All citations are to H.B. The attribution to Nennius occurs in only a
minority of the later manuscripts. For a discussion of date and authorship see Dumville,
"'Nennius' and the Historia Brittonum." The work survives in some forty manuscripts, and
varies greatly among the recensions. These are being edited by Dumville. See Dumville,
Vatican Recension.

porary or near contemporary with the late to mid-sixth century.[74] Beyond this historical horizon, historiographically speaking, be monsters. The scholarly community has been divided for generations over the value of the *Historia*'s depiction of fifth-century events. The sections describing the Anglo-Saxon invasion of Kent have been alternatively dismissed as ninth-century invention or upheld as reflecting early, local, and genuine traditions.

In the *Historia*, the English came to Britain as exiles, arriving in three keels. They were welcomed by the British chief Vortigern and given the island of Thanet in return for military assistance against Vortigern's enemies.[75] Trouble arose when the British could no longer feed the barbarians according to the original agreement. The numbers of the barbarians had increased, although the *Historia* does not state how.[76] This part of the narrative is contradictory, for although the British could not feed the barbarians already in Britain, Hengest managed to convince Vortigern to accept another contingent from Germany, sixteen keels of picked warriors.[77] Arriving with this force was Hengest's daughter. Vortigern fell in love with her (through drunkenness and Satan's power), married her, and gave Kent to Hengest as a bride price. The local British ruler in Kent, Gwyrangon, was betrayed to the barbarians.[78] Hengest's influence over Vortigern increased, and Hengest's son, Octha, together with the latter's kinsman, Ebissa, arrived from Germany with forty keels. They occupied "many districts" in the north, checking the Irish (*Scotti*) and Picts. This section of the *Historia* concludes: "So Hengest gradually brought over more and more keels, until they left the islands † whence † they came uninhabited; and as his people grew in strength and numbers, they came to the aforesaid city of the Kentishmen" (*H.B.* 38). Whether this passage refers to the arrival of sixteen and then forty keels or whether yet another reinforcement is meant cannot be determined from the text. The notion of an empty homeland is similar to a statement in Bede.[79] The passage is corrupt, however, and refers to islands rather than the mainland. In any case the population involved was not enough to wrest control of Kent from the Britons.

The next segment of the story details the conflict between Hengest and

---

[74] For the fantastic extreme see Paton, "Vortigern's Tower." For a discussion of the content of *H.B.* see Appendix 4 below. For the idea of a mid-sixth century historical horizon see Sawyer, *From Roman Britain to Norman England*, 18; Dumville, "Sub-Roman Britain," 189–90.

[75] *H.B.* 31. I have used the texts of the Chartres and Harleian manuscripts printed in Faral, *La légende arthurienne*, 3:4–62.

[76] *H.B.* 36.

[77] See H. M. Chadwick, *Origin of the English Nation*, 40–42.

[78] *H.B.* 37.

[79] *H.B.* 38; *H.e.* 1.15.

Vortigern's son, Vortimer. Vortimer thrice besieged the English in the island of Thanet "attacking, threatening, and terrifying them" (*H.B.* 43). Vortimer died, however, and the barbarians "returned in force" aided again by Vortigern. This time no leader came forth to organize British resistance. Hengest and the Saxons treacherously murdered the unarmed Britons during peace talks.[80]

The final section in the *Historia's* narrative outlines the campaigns of Arthur. Octha, Hengest's son, moved south from northern Britain to become king of the Kentishmen.[81] "At that time the English increased their numbers and grew in Britain." Arthur defeated the invaders in twelve battles, but failed to cut the invasion off at its source in Germany. "When they were defeated in all their campaigns, the English sought help from Germany, and continually and considerably increased their numbers, and they brought over their kings from Germany to rule over them in Britain, until the time when Ida reigned [c. 547 A.D.], who was the son of Eobba. He was the first king in Bernicia, that is, in Berneich" (*H.B.* 56). The above passage ends the narrative account of the Anglo-Saxon conquest. The next element of the *Historia*, the so-called Northern History, is a genealogical record with historical comment on the northern Anglo-Saxon dynasties. No further mention of migration from the continent to Britain is to be found in the *Historia*.

In comparison with other sources, the account of the Anglo-Saxon invasion in the *Historia* is both more circumstantial and more complex. In itself, despite the intermixing with obviously fabulous elements, the story is internally consistent and plausible. The numbers involved are greater than in the other primary sources. As in Gildas and Bede, the *Historia* begins with three keels followed by a further reinforcement. The *Historia* numbers this second group at sixteen keels. This combined force (nineteen keels) was evidently the army of conquest of Kent. Another larger group of forty keels led by Octha and Ebissa devastated the Orkneys and checked the Scots and Picts. This force occupied "very many districts," a phrase in keeping with the occupation of Kent by nineteen keels. The ambiguous statement following the account of Octha's force has already been discussed: "So Hengest gradually brought over more and more keels, until they left the islands † whence † they came uninhabited. . . ." I am uncertain whether this refers to the already detailed arrival of sixteen and forty keels or alludes to yet another reinforcement.

---

[80] *H.B.* 45–46. An interesting and similar tradition is preserved in Widukind, where Saxons first arrive in their country on the left bank of the Elbe, and slaughter the Thuringian *principes* during peace negotiations. The passage is discussed in Tischler, "Continental Background," 2.
[81] *H.B.* 56.

The next event mentioned is a summons by Hengest of "keels with a vast number of fighting men."[82] All of these Anglo-Saxon forces were defeated by Vortimer, however, and "they fled to their keels and were drowned as they clambered aboard them like women."[83] Vortimer's death enabled Hengest and his hosts to return but it is impossible to tell whether this represented a new migration or a return of the original surviving Anglo-Saxon force. I think the latter case more probable. The other mentions of migration in the *Historia* are vague. Twice used is a stock phrase—"at that time the English increased their numbers and grew in Britain."[84] Judged by the context of the relevant passages, this phrase in two instances is an implied contrast to new migration, and seems to signify that the forces in question had prospered through natural increase and had more firmly established their position. A similar phrase with a like meaning can be found in Jordanes's *Getica*, where no new migration can possibly be implied.[85]

All the records thus far discussed deal in numbers of "keels" rather than numbers of men in the invading forces. Fortunately, it is possible to develop a multiplier to convert a keel into a population figure. Elsewhere in the *Historia*, Nennius mentioned that a "keel" carrying a migrating group of Scotti contained thirty men and thirty women (sixty total). "Sixty" for a "keel" may well be a convention, but it is likely to be roughly correct. Matched against the archaeological record for ships of this period (examples include Nydham oak, Sutton Hoo, the recently discovered shipframes from Kongsgårde, and the Kvalsund vessel) sixty seems a high but acceptable number.[86] A passage from Hydatius detailing a fifth-century

---

[82] *H.B.* 43.

[83] *H.B.* 44.

[84] The phrase occurs three times in slightly different forms (*H.B.* 36, 56). (1) "At that time the English increased their numbers and grew in Britain" (*H.B.* 56). (In illo tempore Saxones invalescebant in multitudine et crescebant in Brittannia.) (2) "When they were defeated in all their campaigns, the English sought help from Germany, and continually and considerably increased their numbers . . . " (*H.B.* 56). (Et ipsi, dum in omnibus bellis prosternebantur, auxilium a Germania petebant, et augebantur multipliciter sine intermissione. . . .) (3) "But the barbarians multiplied their numbers, and the British could not feed them . . . " (*H.B.* 36). (At illi barbari cum multiplicati essent numero, non potuerunt Brittones cibare illos. . . .) Only in the second case does increase through additional migration seem to be implied.

[85] Jordanes *Getica* 51; "Here, then, they remained for some time and were much strengthened." The phrase is an ironically humorous use of strengthen in the sense of increase. "They" are a band of Amazons who could have been strengthened neither by new migration nor natural increase!

[86] *H.B.* 13. See Johnstone, *Sea-Craft of Prehistory*, 115–17; Archibald R. Lewis, *Northern Seas*, 107–9. The conventional way to estimate the size of a Scandinavian ship's crew is to double the number of oars. McGrail, *Ancient Boats*, 199–200. Two complete sets of oarsmen would allow one crew to rest. Besides arguments based on hull size, weight, and displacement, archaeological evidence from boat finds suggests the idea of a double crew, because complements of weapons outnumber oars. Gokstad ship, for example, had sixteen pairs of oars but

raid on Spain by German Heruls also supports the *Historia*'s figure of sixty men per ship.[87] Using 60 as a multiplier it is possible to convert the figures in Nennius into numbers of men:

Hengest	19 keels (16 keels + 3 keels)	× 60 = 1140 men
Octha	40 keels	× 60 = 2400 men
		Total = 3540 men

By modern standards this seems a tiny number for an invading army, but the armies of the early medieval period were small.[88] In Hans Delbrück's words: "So small were the armies which gave the great turn to the world's history, which put an end to the culture of the ancients, and destroyed what hundreds of years of peace had built round the Mediterranean Sea."[89] If, as the *Historia* states, Hengest's forces were made up of picked warriors, then an army of a few thousands would certainly have been sufficient to conquer portions of Britain. This would have been a formidable force in Theodosian Britain of 367, or in Clovis's Gaul, or Alfred's England.

Estimating the total invading force of the Anglo-Saxons is more difficult. Including forces proportional to Hengest's and Octha's and allowing for the initial conquests in Wessex, Sussex, Essex, and East Anglia as well as the archaeologically attested forces in the Upper Thames and

---

sixty-four shields slung inboard. A calculation based on this idea would give Nydam oak ship a crew of sixty (Nydam: 70 feet long, beam c. 10 feet, 30 oars). E. A. Thompson believes that a British audience would have known very well the complement of a Saxon warship, and that the knowledge would have acted as a control over the accounts of Gildas and Nennius ("Gildas and the History of Britain," 216). Vegetius describes the Roman scouting galleys in Britain as having roughly forty oars. They were meant to locate and sometimes intercept enemy ships. There is no rule of thumb for estimating a Roman ship's crew from the number of oars, but a crew of forty to eighty would be an appropriate size for the task described. Vegetius *Epitoma rei militaris* 4.37. See Alcock, *Arthur's Britain*, 335; Abels, *Lordship and Military Obligation*, 35, 219 n. 130. Interestingly, sixty appears to be a typical warship's company in the later entries of the *Anglo-Saxon Chronicle*. An entry for 897 explains that King Alfred had ships specially built to defeat the Danish ships that were almost twice as long as the Danish ones, and were equipped with sixty oars, some with more. Assuming a typical Dane would have thirty oars, this would imply a crew of sixty. Sixty is an acceptable estimate for the crew of the Gokstad ship. Since the *Chronicle* often describes the invaders as numbering so many ships' crews, some standardization of a typical ship's company might be assumed.
[87] The raid involved almost 400 men in 7 ships (400 ÷ 7 = 57). Hydatius *Chronicle* 171.
[88] These figures are discussed with references in Delbrück, *Numbers in History*, 70ff. Some comparative figures help to put the numbers in a meaningful perspective. The field army of Roman Britain was probably c. 6,000 strong. The Roman expeditions sent to Britain in the emergencies of A.D. 359–60 and 367–69 probably numbered only c. 2,000 to 3,000 men. It is doubtful that any medieval king of England could have maintained a standing army of 5,000 men. See James Campbell, "End of Roman Britain," 14. Clovis probably began his military conquests in Gaul with a nucleus of 400 to 500 warriors. Bachrach, *Merovingian Military Organization*, 4.
[89] Delbrück, *Numbers in History*, 61.

Midlands, a total of 5,000 to 7,000 men would seem reasonable. Allowing the usually accepted ratio of 1:5 for warriors to general population in a migrating tribe, 25,000 to 35,000 for the overall Anglo-Saxon population is a reasonable guess. This figure is consistent with the numbers estimated for the Germanic tribal populations on the continent in the same period (see Appendix 3). As we shall see, however, the logistical imperatives of a transmarine migration might have greatly reduced the number of dependents accompanying the invaders. Consequently, the overall population might have been much smaller, perhaps as few as 10,000 to 20,000.

The rest of the narrative in the *Historia Brittonum* is consistent with relatively small numbers of invaders. The Anglo-Saxons were three times shut up on the island of Thanet by Vortimer. This implies a relatively small Anglo-Saxon army. Such an incident is also in keeping with later examples of powerful kings being besieged on a small island.[90] In the *Historia* the British were able to deal with even the largest Anglo-Saxon forces. Arthur and Vortimer crushed their enemies. Gildas mentioned that numbers were not the British problem but a lack of martial spirit and equipment. Nennius explicitly states that the numbers of the Anglo-Saxons were not the reason for their victories. "But the barbarians returned in force, for Vortigern was their friend, because of his wife, and none was resolute to drive them out; for they occupied Britain not because of their strength, but because it was the will of God" (*H.B.* 45). An opposition of overwhelming numbers is certainly a frequently advanced excuse for the defeated. But significantly, not a single source, British or Anglo-Saxon, ever suggests that the Anglo-Saxon victories were due to great numbers. The British problem prominent in the literary record is disunity—father against son (Vortigern and Vortimer); British king against British king (Vortigern and Gwyrangon). Civil war was the target of Gildas's preaching. The British defeat in Kent resulted from a crisis of leadership: Vortimer died and "none was resolute to drive the English out."[91] The annals of early British history are replete with British disunity and fatal civil wars.

Descriptions of military forces among the various sections of the *Historia* are compatible. Hengest's three keels are a small force. Julius Caesar's second invasion force of three hundred keels is a great army.[92] Consistent also is the perception that the founding groups of migrating peoples were small. In the *Historia* the Scotti settled Ireland from Spain, arriv-

[90] The *Historia Brittonum* records that Theodoric, a powerful king of the northern English, was besieged three days and nights on the island of Lindisfarne (*H.B.* 63). The *Annales Cambriae* record for the year 629 that Cadwallon was besieged on the island of Glannauc.
[91] *H.B.* 45.
[92] *H.B.* 37, 20.

ing in a group only one thousand strong. Ultimately, colonization was successfully initiated by a single keel followed by gradual secondary settlement.[93] The notion that groups migrating by sea were small was evidently a shared historical perception in the early Middle Ages. Bede recorded that the Picts came to Britain "in a few longships" and without women.[94] Similar traditions appear in the *Anglo-Saxon Chronicle* concerning the Picts, the Anglo-Saxons themselves, and later the Vikings. The account of the *Historia* and the numbers therein are thus inherently credible, internally consistent, and in keeping with the other primary sources.

As noted earlier, the suggestion is sometimes made that the initial arrival of the Saxons in Britain in three ships is a piece of Germanic migration-legend unfounded in reality. For example, Jordanes records of the migration of the Goths: "You surely remember that in the beginning I said the Goths went forth from the bosom of the island of Scandza with Berig their King, sailing in only three ships toward the hither shore of Ocean, namely to Gothiscandza. One of these three ships proved to be slower than the others, as is often the case, and thus is said to have given the tribe their name, for in their language gethanta means slow"[95] (Jordanes *Getica* 94–95). In fact, significant differences separate the basic account of the Anglo-Saxon *adventus* in Gildas and the related story in Bede and the *Historia Brittonum* from legends such as the one narrated by Jordanes. Missing from the British material are telltale phrases such as "in the beginning" or eponyms for tribe or place. Bede's later embellishments may resemble Jordanes's account, including the "it is said" qualifications, but the core story of the *adventus* in Britain is more circumstantial than the equivalent story in Jordanes. It does not begin and end with three ships, nor are three ships used exclusively or artificially throughout the various accounts. All the sources are in agreement with the idea of development and the subsequent arrival of reinforcements, which are not in any formula of three. As we have seen, the language used in Gildas, the basic source, does not suggest the conventions of Germanic storytelling. Three ships, of course, is a handy size for such a force, capable of military success yet not too large to feed. In the event of disaster and the loss of one ship the remaining two could rescue survivors. Two analogues warn against the easy dismissal of "three ships" as a worthless convention along the lines of Jordanes. Tacitus records the story of a renegade cohort of Germans who mutinied in Britain, embarked in three ships, and attempted to return to Germany. Curiously, Bede described the force of

---

[93] *H.B.* 13.
[94] *H.e.* 1.1.
[95] Translation by Mierow in Jordanes *Getica* 78.

three ships of the Anglo-Saxon *adventus* as a cohort. The *Anglo-Saxon Chronicle* provides an instructive example. "In this year [787] . . . there came for the first time three ships of Northmen and then the reeve rode to them . . . and they slew him. Those were the first ships of the Danishmen which came to the land of the English." This *adventus*-type story with its three ships might easily be dismissed as a legend. The circumstantial details among the various versions of the *Chronicle* are so full, however, that the number three is almost certainly an accurate, contemporary figure.[96] In the case of Gildas, when we must decide whether we have an example of three ships of an actual expedition (like that of Columbus) or three of a legend (as in the Christmas carol), reality seems a stronger case.

The *Anglo-Saxon Chronicle*

The final source relevant to the question of the numbers of the invading Anglo-Saxons is the *Anglo-Saxon Chronicle*. In the form that we have, the *Chronicle* was compiled in Old English during the final decade of the ninth century and continued thereafter in a number of versions.[97] It drew on earlier materials, possibly including West Saxon records from the mid-seventh and eighth century.[98] The Anglo-Saxon struggle against the maritime attacks and settlements of the Vikings provided the immediate background for the *Chronicle*. This gives a potentially interesting perspective for a work whose early entries record the original Anglo-Saxon invasion and conquest of Kent, Sussex, and Wessex. The entries relating to the fifth-century invasions, however, must ultimately rest on oral traditions of folk memory, probably in the form of heroic saga poetry. Related difficulties in this context, having to do with dynastic propaganda, chronology, duplication, and bogus eponyms, have often been discussed, and there is marked disagreement over the historical value of this material.[99]

---

[96] Tacitus *Agricola* 28; *H.e.* 1.15. Other versions, possibly echoing the archetype, give the home of the invaders (Hörthaland, Norway), the name and home of the reeve (Beaduheard of Dorchester), and the landing place of the invaders (Portland).

[97] For a discussion of these versions see the introduction by Whitelock in *Anglo-Saxon Chronicle*. ed. Whitelock et al., xi–xxiv. The translations quoted in this chapter are taken from this edition.

[98] The compiler utilized an epitome of universal history, Bede's *Historia ecclesiastica*, some northern annals, genealogies, regnal lists, and episcopal lists, as well as the hypothetical earlier West Saxon annals. See *Anglo-Saxon Chronicle*, ed. Whitelock et al., xxii. For the genealogies see Sisam, "Anglo-Saxon Genealogies."

[99] The debate over the nature and value of material earlier than the mid-seventh century incorporated into the *Chronicle* may be followed in three articles. G. H. Wheeler, "Genealogy of the Early West Saxon Kings"; Stenton, "Foundations of English History"; Kirby, "Problems of Early West Saxon History." A good recent critical discussion of the *Chronicle* is Sims-Williams, "Settlement of England," 26–41. He concludes: "No convincing arguments have been produced to show that these early annals were composed as early as the sixth, the

The entries dealing with the fifth century are difficult to test conclusively with archaeological evidence. As E. T. Leeds demonstrated years
ago, the *Chronicle's* account of the conquest of Wessex is neither comprehensive nor complete in terms of its archaeological geography, since it
omits the presence of invasive groups of Saxons in the Thames valley.[100]
As for its chronology, the specific years assigned to the individual entries
represent a later calculation and are not accurate. The account of the
invasions is, at least in part, independent of the versions of Gildas, Bede,
and the *Historia Brittonum*. On the whole, the *Chronicle* is consistent
with Gildas but contradicts certain details in Bede.[101]

The origins of the kingdoms of Kent, Sussex and Wessex are given in an
intermixed series of entries and in an almost formulaic fashion. First, a
landing under a leader or leaders with a small invading force is described;
then follows a subsequent series of conflicts with the Britons ending with
the successful establishment of a kingdom.[102] The account of the invasion of Kent, with Hengest, Horsa, Vortigern and three ships (s.a. 449),
draws heavily on Bede's *Historia ecclesiastica*. This is followed by the
stories of the foundation of Sussex (one entry) and Wessex (three entries).

(477) In this year Ælle and his three sons, Cymen, Wlencing, and Cissa,
came into Britain with three ships at the place which is called
Cymenesora, and there killed many Britons. . . .

(495) In this year two chieftains, Cerdic and his son Cynric, came with
five ships to Britain at the place which is called *Cerdicesora*, and they
fought against the Britons on the same day.[103]

(501) In this year Port and his two sons Bieda and Maegla came to Britain
with two ships at the place which is called Portsmouth; and there they
killed a British man of very high rank.

(514) In this year the West Saxons came into Britain with three ships at
the place which is called *Cerdicesora*; and Stuf and Wihtgar fought
against the Britons. . . .

---

seventh or even the eighth century" (26). See also Dumville, "Genealogical Regnal List."
[100] Leeds, *Archaeology of the Anglo-Saxon Settlements.*
[101] Stenton, *Anglo-Saxon England,* 23; Alcock, *Arthur's Britain,* 41–44. H. M. Chadwick's
discussion is still valuable (*Origin of the English Nation,* 20–53). See also Bately, "Bede and
the Chronicle."
[102] James Campbell, "Lost Centuries," 26–27.
[103] The prefaces in the "A" and "G" versions of the *Chronicle* differ slightly from the account
of this annal.

The *Chronicle* mentions no later landings or subsequent reinforcements to these warbands. Antonia Gransden compares the *Chronicle* with a Russian nesting doll: it incorporated earlier annals which in turn incorporated still earlier ones.[104]

Her analogy can be extended to include an unfortunate aspect, for each doll bears too close a resemblance to the next, and we seem to be dealing in these early entries with imitation and duplication. Compare the entries for 495 and 514.[105] Unlike the account in Gildas, the repetitious entries for invading ships in the *Chronicle* (three ships of Hengest and Horsa; three ships of Ælle; five ships of Cerdic and Cynric; two ships of Port; three ships of Stuf and Wihtgar), drawn from preliterate traditions including bogus eponyms and duplications, might be considered a poetic convention. Curiously, the *Chronicle*'s tendency when numbering the contemporary ninth-century Viking fleets was probably to exaggerate, and the question is if the conventional numbering of the fifth-century invaders is plausible.[106] Alcock concludes: "It might be thought that 'three' was a conventional poetic number but for the fact that Cerdic and Cynric in 495 are said to have had five ships, and Port, Bieda and Maegla in 501 two only. But even if we are dealing with conventionalized, even partly fictional accounts, we can at least be sure that we have here the right order of magnitude."[107]

The importance of the *Chronicle* is as a touchstone with which to match traditions of the Anglo-Saxon conquest of Kent with events in Wessex. Taken together, Gildas, Bede, Nennius, and the *Chronicle* provide a surprisingly consistent picture of scattered landings by armies of a few hundred men overcoming local resistance and setting up small territorial units which ultimately unite under dynasties to form kingdoms. In his treatment of the sources for the Anglo-Saxon conquest Stenton concludes: "But it may at least be claimed that when four independent authorities agree in suggesting a coherent story, it is unlikely to be very far from the truth."[108] Stenton is not speaking here about the specific question of numbers of invaders, but his remark is equally pertinent to that issue. The literary sources—Gildas, Bede, the *Historia Brittonum*, and the *Anglo-Saxon Chronicle*—provide a coherent account surprisingly free of contradiction. They unanimously portray an Anglo-Saxon conquest of Britain by relatively small forces of military elites.

---

[104] Gransden, *Historical Writing*, 36.
[105] Stenton, *Anglo-Saxon England*, 22.
[106] Sawyer, *Age of the Vikings*, 120ff.; Abels, *Lordship and Military Obligation*, 35.
[107] Alcock, *Arthur's Britain*, 335.
[108] Stenton, *Anglo-Saxon England*, 31; H. M. Chadwick, *Origin of the English Nation*, 47.

CHAPTER THREE

The Anglo-Saxon Invasions

ONE OF THE FEW incontrovertible facts concerning the Anglo-Saxon migrations is that the invaders, however many there were, all reached Britain by
ship. Factors such as food supply, transportation, and communications
impose limitations on population levels of migrating peoples. In the case
of a marine migration these restrictions are particularly acute. The quality
and quantity of available shipping impose an absolute limitation. Thus
the logistics of a marine migration provide a useful check on the vexed
question of the scale and nature of the Anglo-Saxon immigration pursued
in the previous chapters. Does the archaeological and literary evidence
concerning the ships and seamanship of the Angles, Saxons, Jutes, and
other Germanic immigrants better support the thesis of a relatively small
and militarized migration, or the notion of a more massive movement of
entire agrarian communities involving the complete cross section of continental Germanic society, perhaps even entire tribes? This essential
question of early English social history has an inescapably nautical flavor.

As E. G. Bowen writes, "Peoples and cultures reaching 'the Atlantic
ends of Europe' by sea at any time did so on a small scale."[1] This is
particularly true of migrations moving across the North Sea or along the
North Sea littoral, a formidable task. Even when invasion or migration
crossed the narrow sea at the English Channel, the crossing still imposed a
severe restriction. As Sheppard Frere remarks: "In more primitive times
the existence of the Channel meant that, though settlement from overseas
was possible, it rarely took the form of a full folk-migration, owing to the

[1] Bowen, *Britain and the Seaways*, 9.

difficulties of transport; invaders came and conquered, but their numbers were usually small enough to be gradually absorbed."[2] In spite of such general acknowledgments of the restrictive influence of the sea upon migration into Britain, the Anglo-Saxons in their transmarine migration, as in so many other things, have been treated as the great historical exception. Hills concludes that "the quantity of fifth century Germanic material now known from eastern England is considerable. This includes not only moveable objects but also house types and burial rites which have their origins in northern Europe, outside the Roman Empire. This can be explained only in terms of substantial immigration of people who came in sufficient force to retain their religion and way of life—not to become absorbed into existing society but to absorb the remains of that society into their own. . . ." [3] Famous scholars of an earlier generation are even more emphatic. Stenton describes the Anglo-Saxon immigrations as national movements, unique among contemporary migrations.[4] H. M. Chadwick writes: "But the migration of the Angli is really exceptional in more than one respect. It is apparently the only case of a very large migration across the open sea. . . ."[5] If in fact the Anglo-Saxon migration was an exceptionally large-scale folk movement, if the North Sea was to them a thoroughfare rather than a barrier, then they must have commanded an exceptional maritime prowess, evident in both the quality and quantity of their shipping. Was this the case?

THE LOGISTICS OF INVASIONS

The relevant evidence consists of the pertinent literary passages, depictions of ships on coins, metalwork, inscribed stones, and most importantly, the excavated remains of the ships themselves or constructional details and impressions preserved in sand or soil. The ship remains are often distorted by conditions of their deposit and all too often incomplete and fragmentary. Despite these problems, however, the remains represent a benchmark, a record of what actually once voyaged. The descriptions of ships in late classical literature are notoriously inaccurate, a problem compounded by the frequently florid, contrived, and convention-laden

[2] Frere, *Britannia*, 1.
[3] Hills, "Archaeology of Anglo-Saxon England," 312–13. More recently, Hills has written: "The most convincing explanation is that there was indeed a migration of Germanic peoples across the North Sea during the fifth century" ("Roman Britain to Anglo-Saxon England," 52). This seems a more modest estimate of the scale of the migration.
[4] Stenton, *Anglo-Saxon England*, 277.
[5] H. M. Chadwick, *Origin of the English Nation*, 181.

writing style of the later Roman period.[6] Representations on coin or stone may be inaccurate, stylized, symbolic, or simply obscure.[7] Taken together, however, a picture of ships and shipping at the time of the Anglo-Saxon invasion (A.D. 400–600) may be constructed from this composite evidence.

The Anglo-Saxon migration involved a mix of Germanic peoples from Scandinavia and Germany, possibly from as far afield as southwestern Norway and northern France. The shipbuilding techniques of these various peoples for the period between the late Roman era and the seventh century are reflected in a corpus of boat finds from England and the continental homelands. In Scandinavia and northern Germany these include boats from Halsnøy, Nydam, Gredstedbro, and Kvalsund. Recently discovered fragments from Hjemsted and Kongsgårde in Jutland supplement this evidence. Boat finds from England include ships from Sutton Hoo, Snape, and Ashby Dell, and fragments from the Norfolk cemetery of Caister-on-Sea. In addition to these possible sea boats of plank construction, there are a number of smaller logboats, dugouts probably built for inshore work. Examples include the Slusegård boats from Bornholm in the Baltic and a recent find from the Snape cemetery in Suffolk.[8] The detailed evolutionary relationship among these various ships is the subject of much dispute. In general, a progressive elaboration in the constructional features and seaworthiness of the Scandinavian ship can be traced from Late Antiquity to a culmination in the superb Viking vessels of the ninth and tenth centuries, when the form of ship virtually ceased to evolve until the modern period. It is also likely, however, that throughout the Dark Ages relatively primitive forms continued in use with contemporary but more advanced vessels.[9]

Although there is a degree of variety in details and materials among these various ships, doubtless reflecting local building traditions and perhaps a different pattern between the Baltic and North Sea areas, certain common characteristics define pre-Viking Scandinavian shipbuilding. The vessels are clinker-built, that is, constructed of overlapping strakes

---

[6] Basch, "Reliability of Ancient Writers," 366. On learning and letters see Laistner, *Thought and Letters*; Glover, *Life and Letters*; N. K. Chadwick, *Poetry and Letters*.

[7] On the great difficulties of establishing dimension, numbers of rowers, rigging, and so on, from ancient ship depictions, see Basch, "One Aspect," 231.

[8] Boat finds from Britain, Scandinavia, and Germany are relevant to this discussion. Germany and Scandinavia represent the ancestral homelands, while Britain is the final destination of the invaders. For reviews of this evidence see Charles Green, *Sutton Hoo*, 48–65; Angela C. Evans, "Clinker-Built Boats"; Crumlin-Pedersen, "Boats and Ships."

[9] Greenhill, *Archaeology of the Boat*. This is the most conservative treatment of the subject. Brøgger and Shetelig, *Viking Ships*, is still a standard work on the evolution of Scandinavian ships.

reinforced by an internal system of braces. The vessels of the Anglo-Saxon invasions evidently lacked any provision for mast or sail and featured a flat-bottomed keel plank rather than a true T-shaped deeper keel. Incidentally, it may seem paradoxical to speak of Anglo-Saxon warships called *keels*, when the vessels lacked a developed keel. The original meaning of Old English *ceol* referred to the ship itself, not the lowest, central longitudinal member of the ship's hull (Old English *botm, bytme*). The word keel took on the latter meaning much later, probably under Scandinavian influence (Middle English *kele*, derived from Old Norse *kjolr*). The dual meaning persisted into the modern period, and keel could be either the lowest longitudinal timber, or a flat-bottomed vessel such as a lighter.[10] The vessels of the ship finds were in fact large, double-ended, undecked rowing boats almost certainly developed for war and piracy rather than trade or bulk cargo. Surprisingly, no trading vessels or "round ships" have been discovered in the context of the Anglo-Saxon invasions and settlement. The first positive archaeological evidence for mast and sail in Scandinavia is associated with the Oseberg and Äskekärr ships of about 800 A.D. This coincides roughly with the beginning of the Viking expansion in the late eighth century.[11]

The chronology of the various vessels is much disputed, but the finds seem to cluster around the beginning and end of the Anglo-Saxon invasions (about A.D. 400–600), with the majority of finds dating from the end of the period or even sometime after the invasions had ceased. The "missing middle" creates problems in interpreting the evidence. Three finds from Nydam in the area of south Jutland (the homeland of the Angles according to Bede) are the only representatives of shipping available in the tribal homelands at the onset of the invasions. The Ashby Dell boat might also be added to this group, although it may be too early, representing the Roman (early fourth century) rather than the Saxon era in Britain. The poor account which survives of the excavation suggests that the Ashby Dell vessel would have been scarcely seaworthy.[12]

The surviving Nydam oak vessel (see Figure 1) seems to date from the late fourth century. It was a long, narrow, plank-built boat, and the first

[10] For a glossary of technical terms used in this section see Bass, *History of Seafaring*, 306.
[11] Greenhill, *Archaeology of the Boat*, 165; Marcus, "Evolution of the Knörr"; Brøgger and Shetelig, *Viking Ships*, 178–87. Trading ships: Äskekärr, A.D. 830 ± 75; Graveney, tenth century; Bagart and Ralswiek, tenth century followed by a number of later finds beginning with Skuldelev. See the table in Fenwick, *Graveney Boat*, 254.
[12] Nydam ship: Åkerlund, *Nydamskeppen*; Shetelig and Johannessen, "Das Nydamschiff"; Engelhardt, *Nydam Mosefund*; Marcus, "Nydam Craft." Ashby Dell: The only surviving description of the find by Luck, written at the time of the excavation, is discussed in Charles Green, *Sutton Hoo*, 60–65. The vessel is probably a premigrations coastal craft of little relevance.

Figure 1. The Nydam ship. Reproduced by permission of the Archäologisches Landesmuseum, Schleswig.

intact example from northern Europe of a boat with oarlocks. The Nydam ship was thus propelled by oars that were pulled, not paddled like a canoe. The vessel has recently been reconstructed with a broader hull form and consequently increased seaworthiness. Even with this change, however, the Nydam vessel seems ill suited for the steep, active waves of the North Sea. Describing Nydam's sea potential, Charles Green recalls the lines from Sidonius Apollinaris about Saxons and shipwreck: "Moreover, shipwreck, far from terrifying them, is their training. With the perils of the sea they are not merely acquainted—they are familiarly acquainted."[13] Green wryly concludes that the risk of shipwreck in a vessel like Nydam was genuine.[14] The lack of a true keel would have made the Nydam oak vessel vulnerable to pressure on her hull. The ship would have been "crank" in choppy seas and liable to flooding when heavily laden. While its oars were certainly an improvement over paddles, the thwart arrangement was cu-

---

[13] Sidonius Apollinaris *Ep.* 8.6.14.
[14] Charles Green, *Sutton Hoo*, 49.

rious, and the oars seem too short to have been highly effective.[15] Parts of a second oak ship, deliberately destroyed at the time of its deposition, were recovered during Conrad Engelhardt's 1863 excavation, but these fragments have not survived. The third Nydam vessel, built of fir, is usually dated to about A.D. 400. It differs from the oak vessel not only in its softer material but in having more and narrower strakes, a more developed keel, and possibly a more elaborate stem. The Nydam fir vessel has not survived and discussion of its constructional details must rely on Engelhardt's report of 1865.[16]

The Gredstedbro vessel was discovered in the same general area as the Nydam finds. Only fragments survived, but from these it was possible to reconstruct certain important features. Radiocarbon dating placed the find to roughly A.D. 600–650.[17] The vessel had a broad keel plank similar to the Nydam oak vessel, although it had eight narrow strakes rather than the five of the Nydam. The planks were secured to the frame by wooden trenails (pegs) rather than the cleats of the Nydam oak vessel. Gredstedbro's construction was probably simpler and more economical than that of the Nydam vessel.

The Sutton Hoo vessel (see Figure 2), built about A.D. 600 or perhaps slightly earlier, had a keel and scarf (a joint uniting two pieces of timber to form a continuous piece), a construction similar to that of the Gredstedbro find. Sutton Hoo was broader in its form than the larger Nydam oak vessel and probably more seaworthy. For views of the two vessels, see Figure 3. Despite excavation and careful reexcavation, no trace of mast, sail, or sailing fittings has been found. The matter is inconclusive because a burial chamber had replaced the area amidships where a mast might have been.[18] A second smaller boat found at Sutton Hoo and the poorly recorded Snape boat find do not greatly add to our knowledge. Evidently the Snape boat did not share the broad and shallow hull form of the Sutton Hoo and Nydam finds, and was possibly built for inshore or estuary use rather than the open sea. Recently a second boat was found at Snape, a logboat possibly from the mid-sixth or early seventh century.[19]

Taken as a group (see Table 1), the boat finds for the period of the Anglo-Saxon invasion seem well suited to serve as troop transports to convey and land concentrated forces of pirates or invaders. The ships of the archae-

[15] Nouhuys, "Some Doubtful Points."
[16] Engelhardt, Nydam Mosefund.
[17] Crumlin-Pedersen, "Gredstedbroskibet"; Greenhill, Archaeology of the Boat, 182–88.
[18] Angela C. Evans and Rupert Bruce-Mitford, "The Ship"; Biddle et al., "Sutton Hoo Published," especially 259–62. The literature on Sutton Hoo is extensive. The two works cited give good bibliographies; see also Bessinger, "Sutton Hoo: Chronological Bibliography."
[19] Bruce-Mitford, "Snape Boat Grave"; Werner, "Zur Zeitstellung des Bootgrabes von Snape"; Filmer-Sankey, "New Boat Burial."

Figure 2. The Sutton Hoo ship (full view looking forward). Reproduced by permission of the Trustees of the British Museum.

ological record seem completely inadequate, however, for transporting large numbers of people including entire agrarian communities complete with dependents, equipment, and livestock. Lacking, so it would appear, mast and sail and true cargo vessels, the Anglo-Saxons would have had to rely on oared warships, the limited capacity of which would have made them an expensive means of transport. Compared to later Viking vessels, ships such as Sutton Hoo and Nydam would have been faster under oars, but their speed was achieved at the expense of stability and carrying capacity. Moreover, propulsion based on oar power alone creates a great difficulty for migration because the "cargo" would have to have been its own motive power. This is not a problem for a warband, but severely limits the transportation of the young and old. Since space was needed for the rowers and their necessary provisions, even large vessels such as Sutton Hoo would have had little room to spare, carrying at most twenty to thirty dependents and very little nonhuman cargo. Women could have rowed at intervals, just as Odin's wife rowed in earth's ship in the *Edda*. In this context, however, a line from the *Historia Brittonum* seems grimly

The Nydam ship showing the low rake of the end posts, and the narrow, shallow midships section.

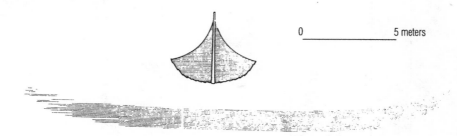

The hull shape and midships section of the Sutton Hoo ship, showing end posts similar to those of the Nydam ship.

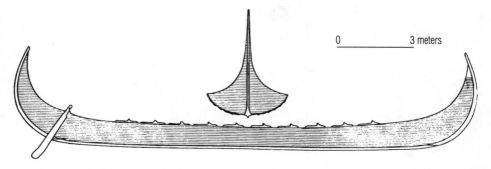

The larger of the two Kvalsund ships showing the tight curve of the end posts and the deepening keel section.

Figure 3. The Nydam, Sutton Hoo, and Kvalsund boats from the fourth through seventh centuries A.D. After Angela C. Evans, "The Clinker-Built Boats of the North Sea, 300–1000 A.D." In *The North Sea,* edited by Arne Bang-Andersen, Basil Greenhill, and Egil Harald Grude, 63–78. Oslo, 1985; reproduced by permission of the author.

Table 1. Scandinavian ship finds—Pre A.D. 700

Ship	Location	Estimated date	Possible origin	Approximate length	Excavated	Details
Halsnøy	S Norway	c. 200 A.D. votive?	?	?	1896	fragments only; found in bog
Nydam Oak	Schleswig	c. 350–400 A.D. votive	S Scandinavia N Germany	75 ft.	1864	complete hull; 30 oars
Nydam Fir	Schleswig	c. 400 A.D. votive	S Norway?	61 ft.	1864	survives from 19th-century plan; 22 oars
Larger Sutton Hoo	Suffolk	c. 600 A.D. funerary	East Anglia	89 ft.	1939 reexcavated 1965/67	nearly intact impression in sand and rivets; c. 40 oars
Sutton Hoo Mound 2	Suffolk	7th century funerary	East Anglia	22+ ft.	1939	poorly preserved as impression in sand
Snape	Suffolk	c. 600–650 A.D. funerary	East Anglia	50 ft.	1862	poorly recorded [a second boat burial discovered in 1987]
Gredstedbro	SW Jutland	600–650 A.D.? wreck?	Jutland	65 ft. ?	1945	fragments
Kvalsund	W Norway	disputed: 7th or early 8th century votive	Norway	60 ft.	1920	complete hull; 20 oars; accompanied by small boat
Ashby Dell	Suffolk	date uncertain, pre-Viking; funerary?	?	54 ft. ?	1830	local newspaper record only; 14 oars, no iron

Source: Michael E. Jones, "The Literary Evidence for Mast and Sail during the Anglo-Saxon Invasions," Studies in Medieval and Renaissance History n.s. 13 (1992), 36, Table 1. Reproduced with permission from AMS Press, Inc.

relevant. "They fled to their keels and were drowned as they clambered aboard them like women."[20] It is difficult to imagine the existence of an organized ferry service whereby thirty or so oarsmen rowed passengers to Britain, returning on a round trip to ferry more passengers. Accepting the most favorable reconstructions of each of the vessels, and also accepting the most generous estimates of their seaworthiness, I find it unlikely that these undecked rowing boats could have safely or regularly made the open-sea crossing between Jutland-Schleswig and Britain. Detlev Ellmers recently concluded that in the middle of the sixth century, nobody among the Franks, Frisians, Angles, Saxons, and Jutes was able to cross the North Sea directly from Scandinavia to the British Isles. Experiments with replicas of the Nydam and Kvalsund ships have revealed rather alarming features and suggested their limitations as vessels for crossing hundreds of miles of open water and weathering North Sea gales. This caution also applies to the more recent reconstruction of the Nydam ship. As Charles Green clearly saw, the alternative route for migration was a long and expensive coasting voyage down the North Sea coast and across to England via the relatively narrow passages of the Channel or just north of the Channel. The configuration of the Netherlands' coast was probably quite different then and it may have been possible to row within sheltered waters from the west coast of Jutland to the entrance of the Channel.[21] Allowing a very respectable average speed of three knots, a rowing trip from the continental homelands along the coasts to England would have required two to six months.[22] During this time stops would have been necessary to rest the crew, reprovision, dodge bad weather, and so forth, so that the trip must have been, on any consideration, an expensive venture. If the transporting ships were returned to the continent, return costs would also have to be taken into account. If the trip were one-way, then the cost of the vessel would be added to all the other expenses. Labor and materials necessary to construct a Nydam-type vessel would have been

[20] *H.B.* 44. For a fuller discussion of propulsion and cargo capacity see Michael E. Jones, "Literary Evidence for Mast and Sail," 57–58, 66 n. 78, 67 n. 80.
[21] The seaworthiness of these early vessels is much debated. Virtually everyone accepts, however, the limitations of the Nydam-style ship for oceanic voyages. Arenhold, "Nydam Ship at Kiel," 182–85; Marcus, "Nydam Craft," 66; Charles Green, *Sutton Hoo,* 49–52. For discussion of the migration routes see Charles Green, *Sutton Hoo,* 103–13; Crumlin-Pedersen, "Boats and Ships," 113: "Navigation was still based on landing or mooring offshore every night, except for the crossing of straits. Thus, all movements from Jutland to Britain were bound to be along the coastal regions of lower Saxony and the Netherlands." See also Ellmers, "Frisian Monopoly," 91. Binns has a good discussion of this question (*Viking Voyagers,* 5–12). For a dissenting view see Carver, "Pre-Viking Traffic." Carver's discussion of speeds and distances is useful, but he forgets to include the critical factor of safety in his calculations.
[22] Charles Green, *Sutton Hoo,* 103–13.

very costly.[23] Skilled labor would have been necessary and techniques for taking strakes from timber were wasteful. Some idea of the relative cost of such a ship is indicated by comparison with later, more settled and probably wealthier circumstances in Anglo-Saxon England, when a large warship represented the notional taxable wealth of several hundred families. Yet to make a cheaper vessel would have further reduced an already questionable seaworthiness. Taking all this into account, would moving village-sized or larger groups of agricultural laborers have been worthwhile or even feasible?

The implications of the archaeological evidence for the logistical possibilities of a maritime migration seem clear. How representative are the ship finds? Apart from the fact that there are so few examples of pre-Viking ships, these few come from archaeological contexts of ritual offerings or burials. Presumably no status-seeking family or Dark Age deities would have found a cargo vessel a suitable memorial for burial, hence the fact that all the ship finds seem to be warships. As Ole Crumlin-Pedersen points out, different archaeological contexts tend to produce different types of vessels. Ship finds from coastlines, harbors, and structures incorporating ship fragments are needed to balance the evidence from ritual deposits and burials. Fragments of the Gredstedbro ship discovered by dredging in 1945 and recent discoveries of ship fragments from Hjemsted and Kongsgårde, respectively from a seventh-century well and an old beach wall, are significant in this respect. The information conveyed by these fragments is limited, but consistent with the overall pattern of shipbuilding represented by the ship burials. Nor is it absolutely certain that ship burials involve only special and therefore perhaps unrepresentative vessels. The use of logboats in Scandinavian burials such as Slusegård and the recently discovered logboat grave from Snape in East Anglia complicate this question. Signs of wear including repairs indicate that some of the boats used for burials had been long in service and were perhaps selected because they had reached the end of their usefulness. The large ship from Sutton Hoo is a possible example. Charles Green suggested that the clinker-built Walthamstow boat from Essex, found inverted over a Viking grave, was probably a river barge used in the burial of a Viking chief when none of the Vikings' own ships could be spared for the purpose. Walthamstow dates after the period of the Anglo-Saxon settlement, but the example raises an important principle.[24] Strictly speaking, the ships of the archaeological record are Anglian or Jutish, since they were found in the

---

23 Greenhill, *Archaeology of the Boat*, 180.
24 Crumlin-Pedersen, "Boats and Ships," 98; Charles Green, *Sutton Hoo*, 63–64; Angela C. Evans and Rupert Bruce-Mitford, "The Ship," 394–95. Binns speculates that the Gredstedbro ship might have been a workboat rather than a warship (*Viking Voyagers*, 10).

traditional homelands of those tribes or in East Anglia. Given the ethnic and material mixture in these regions during the migrations, this is probably a false precision, but we have essentially no archaeological evidence for contemporary ships of the Saxons, Frisians, or Franks. On the other hand, the ships from Nydam probably represent either prizes taken on expeditions elsewhere, or ships of defeated invaders deposited as offerings by the victorious defending Angles. Differences in details of construction and materials suggest that the three ships from Nydam were not built in the same region. The Nydam fir ship was constructed of wood not naturally available in Schleswig and may have originated in Norway. The larger Nydam oak vessel may have come from northern Germany, perhaps even from a Saxon area, although this is speculation. Nothing from the evidence of later Anglo-Saxon shipbuilding suggests that Saxon ships differed significantly from those of the Angles or Jutes. On the basis of the literary evidence, Stéphane Lebecq suggests that until the end of the seventh century the Frisians, Franks, Varnes, and Chauks, like the Anglo-Saxons, used only oars to propel their ships.[25]

Another means of testing the representativeness of the boat finds is to match them against depictions of ships in the picture stones, coins, and small objects from the period of the Anglo-Saxon migrations and after. Depictions of ships from England for the period before roughly 700 are rare and reveal few details. An Anglian urn from the early seventh century found at Caistor-by-Norwich shows a wolf (possibly the Fenris wolf) chasing a ship. The freehand drawing is crude, but the ship has neither mast nor sail. A series of seventh-century Anglo-Saxon coins (sceattas) show ships with semicircular hulls, without mast or sail. The bronze model of a ship on a Kentish sword pommel of about 700 A.D. represents a double-ended rowing boat, but given its shape and purpose, it could hardly be decorated with a protruding mast.[26] This is thin evidence, but so far as it goes, it seems to confirm the tradition of shipbuilding preserved in the Anglo-Saxon ship burials.

The most extensive pictorial record of ships from the continental homelands is represented by approximately three hundred examples of picture stones from Gotland. These were probably erected as memorials between roughly 400 and 1100 A.D. The Gotland stones thus span the entire course of the Anglo-Saxon migrations. The various pictures and designs are engraved on loose stone slabs, mostly limestone. Individual stones are dated roughly within a particular century on the basis of stylis-

25 Åkerlund, Nydamskeppen, 121–22; Greenhill, Archaeology of the Boat, 182; Lebecq, Marchands et navigateurs, 1:177–81.
26 For an illustration of the pommel-boat see Fenwick, Graveney Boat, 199.

tic elements of the figural compositions and according to the shape of the stone. Sune Lindqvist pioneered the classification of the Gotland stones, dividing them into three major groups. An important motif of the first and earliest group included oared vessels, always of similar shape, associated with geometric designs. These crescent-shaped rowing vessels closely resemble ships such as Nydam and Sutton Hoo. No ships with sails appear on the stones of Lindqvist's first group. He dated these picture stones between approximately 400 and 600 A.D. Ships with sails first appear in Lindqvist's second group of stones, (about 500–700 A.D.). The sails depicted from roughly 600 seem to be of two different types, a diagonally plaited sail, and a rarer checkerboard design. Given an inescapably inexact chronology, the Gotland stones seem to confirm the archaeological pattern of the ship burials. The Anglo-Saxon migration falls within the first phase of Lindqvist's suggested scheme and is matched with the crescent-shaped oared vessels. The sailing ships depicted in Lindqvist's second group probably fall into the period after the ending of the migrations. Erik Nylén remarks of the first group of Gotland stones, "Strangely, the boats have no sails although the people of Scandinavia must by then have known about sails through their contacts with the Romans."[27] The picture stones of Gotland, together with the coinage of the Anglo-Saxon and Scandinavian areas, create a record extending from the fifth century until mast, sail, and merchant ships are well established in the pictorial corpus. The negative evidence of the absence of mast and sail before the seventh century in these materials is strengthened by depictions of ships with sails in the same material later on. Thus the depictions of ships in picture stones, coins, and small objects generally corroborate the archaeological evidence of the ship burials.

One final depiction of a Scandinavian ship must be discussed. In 1987 a small stone (twenty-two millimeters in diameter) was found on the east coast of Jutland at Karlby. One side was engraved with an elk, the other with a ship bearing an obvious mast and sail. This Karlby ship appears as the cover illustration of two recent works on early medieval maritime history and archaeology. Crumlin-Pedersen suggests that the engraving combined a "Sutton-Hoo-like hull" with a mast and sail and speculates that the Karlby stone might be pre-Viking, possibly seventh century in date. John Haywood describes the tiny ship carving as "clearly a Nydam-type ship carrying a single square sail," and concludes that this proves such ships could and did sail in the seventh century and might have done so much earlier during the Anglo-Saxon migrations. Such enthusiastic speculations far outrun the modest evidentiary limits of this small object.

---

[27] Nylén, *Stones, Ships, and Symbols*, 22. See Lindqvist, *Gotlands Bildsteine*.

The Karlby stone was a stray find with no archaeological context and hence no date. It might be as early as the seventh century, but equally possibly it may date from the ninth century or later. There is no way to tell. The inscribed ship is tiny (about twelve millimeters long) and this naturally limits the details of its shape and structure, which are the basis for its classification. The engraving of the ship is highly stylized and somewhat crude. Its trident-shaped steering oar is obviously not a naturalistic representation. Subjectively, the ship of the Karlby stone does not closely resemble the hull form of either the Nydam or the Sutton Hoo ship, nor does it closely resemble the crescent-shaped rowing vessels depicted on the Gotland stones, only with the addition of a mast and sail. To my eye, the Karlby engraving best resembles the banana-shaped ships depicted on the Dorestad coins of Charlemagne and Louis the Pious. It is as likely to represent a proto-hulc as any other type of ship.[28]

The corpus of pre-seventh century boat discoveries is coherent and largely homogenous. The vessels are too few in number and too scattered in place and time to allow inferences about their specific evolutionary relationships, but they do appear to reflect a gradual increase in sophistication and to improve over time. Ashby Dell, Nydam oak, Nydam fir, and Sutton Hoo show a slow, almost predictable advance in shipbuilding technique. Sutton Hoo and Gredstedbro, virtually contemporary vessels with good dating evidence, are remarkably similar in a great many features. The coherence of the evidence, therefore, lessens the danger of an undiscovered, unknown type. As Angela Evans points out, "Of all objects found during the period 300–1000 A.D. boats are the most conservative, with a fundamental shape that changes little over the centuries."[29] The similarity of the various finds accords well with the later, better-known conservatism of Scandinavian shipbuilding. An undiscovered, radically different tradition of sail-driven merchant vessels seems most unlikely.

The question of the quantity of shipping available for use during the Anglo-Saxon migrations is even more difficult than that of quality. The large-scale movements of population across water in the modern period were organized by national governments or large shipping interests like the twentieth-century steamship companies. No such organization is known for early Germany or Scandinavia, of course. Mixed and somewhat

---

[28] Crumlin-Pedersen, "Boats and Ships," 111; Haywood, *Dark Age Naval Power*, 21, 65. For a discussion of the seventh-century Merovingian strap-end from northern France, decorated with a crude depiction of a ship with mast and rigging, see Michael E. Jones, "Literary Evidence for Mast and Sail," 34, 59 n. 4. This ship is possibly a river craft rather than a seagoing vessel. It postdates the Anglo-Saxon invasions and may well be Romano-Celtic or Frisian rather than Scandinavian.

[29] Angela C. Evans, "Clinker-Built Boats," 64.

unstable tribal groupings seem to have been the largest political units in this period. The repeated maritime failures of the Goths after their entry into the Roman empire do not suggest a high order of seaworthiness or naval organization. The Vandals became notoriously successful pirates and raiders, but the only certain example of large-scale maritime transportation of a Germanic noncombatant population was accomplished by the Romans when they moved the Vandals and Alans from Spain to Africa in 429 A.D.[30] A significant law in the Theodosian Code (9.40.24) imposing a death penalty on anyone providing shipbuilding techniques to the barbarians is suggestive in this context. While it is possible that the Angles, Saxons, and Jutes located on the North Sea or Baltic coasts possessed a more lively maritime ability than some other tribes, the Goths and Vandals had migrated by sea (according to Jordanes) and had been active as pirates in the Black Sea earlier in the Roman era. Thus the comparative advantage of peoples living along the North Sea is somewhat presumptive.[31] The Franks, for example, on several occasions were obliged to capture the shipping they used for piratical forays against the empire. The East Anglian finds would seem to indicate that the Anglo-Saxons' shipbuilding technique was better suited to the Baltic than to the North Sea, right up to the end of the invasions.[32]

The onset of Saxon piracy, which appears suddenly in the Roman sources, may have been related to certain technological innovations. Detlev Ellmers has found several pottery shards from Trier, probably of the late fourth century, that he believes depict Saxon ships. Not only do these shards show vessels without mast or sail, they depict men paddling rather than rowing. It may be that the oar, oarlock, and true rowing techniques were only incorporated in Germanic and Scandinavian shipbuilding between the fourth and fifth centuries (the etymology of the oar technology in Germanic languages seems to be Latin). The Nydam vessel, which has oarlocks that allow rowing in one direction only and which is equipped with oars too short to be fully effective, may represent the transition between paddling and rowing.[33] While oar-powered galleys would have been effective for warfare, raiding, and piracy, thus creating a much

---

[30] Genzmer, *Germanische Seefahrt*; Archibald R. Lewis, *Northern Seas*, 3–110.
[31] Jordanes *Getica* 25. For the Vandals, see Victor Vitensis *Historia persecutionis vandalicae* 1.2; Procopius *B.V.* 1.5.18.
[32] The Angles may have been located in the Baltic coastal areas prior to their migration to Britain. A case has been made for believing that the Sutton Hoo ship was actually built in Sweden, so close are its affinities with Baltic tradition. N. E. Lee, "Sutton Hoo in Sweden?"
[33] If the techniques were borrowed from Roman examples, the very late acquisition after a long exposure together with a period of assimilation for the new technology would help explain why sailing techniques were not adopted until even later. See Crumlin-Pedersen, "Boats and Ships," 111–13.

more dangerous threat to Roman coasts, they would have been unsuitable for the wholesale movement of population.

Roman accounts of Saxon and Frankish piracy (Anglian pirates are not mentioned but Roman terminology was imprecise) stress mobility and surprise and seem to imply small numbers. This accords well with the British and Anglo-Saxon records already discussed. Saxon piratic operations evidently focused on the Channel and its approaches, an area where rowing vessels would be effective, rather than on the open sea.[34] The mobility of the Saxons and their ability to raid inland from the sea were a novel and difficult problem for Roman defense. Ammianus writes that "the Saxons are feared beyond all other enemies because of the suddenness of their incursions." And again, "Valentinian destroyed the Saxons, who had broken out with fearful violence, and always in parts where they were least expected."[35] Orosius writes in a similar vein: "The Saxons are a race situated upon the shores of Ocean, and in pathless morasses, and are terrible by reason of their valour and mobility."[36] So too, in a famous passage, Sidonius describes the Saxon warrior: "Unexpected he comes: if you are prepared he slips away. . . . For since a storm, should there be one, prevents observation and puts us off our guard, the hope of a surprise attack leads them gladly to imperil their lives amid waves and broken rocks."[37] Both Carausius and Valentinian I hit upon the same solution to Saxon raiders—to wait until they returned from their raids laden with spoil and then destroy them while recovering the booty. Although this tactic held an obvious incentive for the Roman crews (much of the recovered booty possibly stuck to their fingers), it may also be that tired Saxon rowers and vessels heavily laden with plunder were slower, less elusive targets for the Roman navy. If this surmise is correct, it would fit rowing vessels very well but would hardly seem applicable to sailing vessels. Thus, Roman tactics may support the archaeological evidence that Saxons rowed rather than sailed.

A final note is relevant to the question of the scale of the Anglo-Saxon seaborne migration. No signs survive in Anglo-Saxon literature of any tradition that tells of a truly large-scale folk migration across the North Sea. Instead, the sea was a place for exiles and wanderers in Anglo-Saxon poetry. Even long after the invasions, with revived trade and improved ships, great status accrued to a man who made three successful overseas voyages, the implication being that such ventures were rare and unusual.

---

34 Marcus, "Nydam Craft," 66; Eutropius *Breviarium ab urbe condita* 9.21.
35 Ammianus 28.2.12, 30.7.8, translated in R. W. Chambers, *England before the Conquest*, 61.
36 Orosius *Historia contra Paganos* 7.32.
37 Sidonius *Ep.* 8.6.14, translated in R. W. Chambers, *England before the Conquest*, 62–63.

Frisians dominated the trade of Anglo-Saxon England. When England was vexed by Danish piracy, the Anglo-Saxons were forced to import Frisian mercenaries or hire the pirates themselves for naval crews. This exiguous Anglo-Saxon maritime tradition and the lubberly deportment of the English in the early medieval period stand in contrast to the active maritime life of Scandinavia and Iceland. These facts seem impossible to reconcile with notions of a great seaborne Anglo-Saxon folk migration.[38]

Archaeological evidence from ship finds and notions (albeit vague) of the availability of shipping seem to indicate a migration characterized by small numbers, a multiplicity of landings, and a movement dominated by military elements. The inadequacy of vessels such as Nydam and Sutton Hoo for transporting a great populous migration is generally acknowledged. Historians who urge that the Anglo-Saxon migration was large and popular in the sense of involving the entire agrarian community are thus faced with a contradiction. To escape the logistical implications of the archaeological evidence a number of theories have been advanced. Perhaps substantial numbers of Germanic immigrants arrived in Roman shipping. Perhaps slaves pulled the oars of the immigration to Britain. Perhaps the Anglo-Saxons, Franks, or Frisians had sail-powered vessels as yet undiscovered by archaeology. If the archaeological record of ships is unrepresentative, perhaps this undiscovered, sail-powered type of vessel was the true vehicle of the migration.[39]

The thesis that significant numbers of Germanic settlers were permanently established in Britain by Roman authority before the end of the fifth century has already been discussed and rejected. As Gildas states, the Anglo-Saxons arrived in keels (cyules), not in Roman ships. While slave raiding and slave trading were certainly features of the early Middle Ages in Britain and northern Europe, there is not a shred of evidence to suggest that the Anglo-Saxon migration was slave-powered. Neither the Scandinavians nor the Romans seem to have powered their ships with slaves in the fourth through seventh centuries. Of course the use of slaves, of itself,

---

[38] *Gethynctho* 6: "And if a trader prospered, that he crossed thrice the open sea at his own expense, he was then afterwards entitled to the rights of a thegn." Translated by Whitelock, *English Historical Documents* 1:431–32. For the Frisians see Lebecq, "On the Use of the Word Frisian"; Ellmers, "Frisian Monopoly."

[39] For the idea of an Anglo-Saxon population transported in Roman ships along Roman sea lanes see Binns, *Viking Voyagers*, 5. For slaves see Carver, "Pre-Viking Traffic," 122. For the archaeologically unattested mast and sail see Alcock, *Arthur's Britain*, 301, 280–81; Haywood, *Dark Age Naval Power*, 70–73. Archibald R. Lewis, for example, suggests that Roman shipping or ship types were adopted by the Anglo-Saxons (*Northern Seas*, 105–8). Mast and sail have been linked to the Sutton Hoo vessel and Kvalsund craft in recent arguments. Angela C. Evans and Rupert Bruce-Mitford, "The Ship," 352; Marsden, "Mast and Sail," 140; Greenhill, *Archaeology of the Boat*, 186; Hodges, *Dark Age Economics*, 101.

does not improve the seaworthiness of the known ships of the migrations period. Every slave aboard would also reduce by one the potential for transporting free immigrants. M. O. H. Carver associates a particular social order with a migration powered by oars rather than sails: "The master-servant relationship was implicit between the rowed and the rowers, and in this respect complete reliance on sail marks a revolution in the sociology of travel."[40] The need for cooperation and initiative to complete safely the migration to Britain in an open, oar-powered ship suggests that "all in the same boat" might be a more useful social rule of thumb. In the second half of the fifth century, the Roman aristocrat Sidonius Apollinaris gave this description of a Saxon pirate crew: "[The Saxons] give the impression that every oarsman you see in their crew is a pirate captain—so universal is it for all of them simultaneously to issue orders and obey orders, to teach brigandage and to learn brigandage" (*Ep.* 8.6.13, trans. Anderson). As we shall see, Sidonius is an indifferent observer when it comes to barbarians and their ships. This particular passage, however, seems unconventional and may ring true.

If we may eliminate Romans and slaves as viable solutions to the logistical dilemma, what of the possibility of sail-driven ships in use among the immigrant Germans? Haywood has recently written, in support of the idea that the Anglo-Saxon migration was "a massive population movement," that "it is far easier to account for the completeness of the Anglo-Saxon migration if we assume that the settlers came in sailing ships with small professional crews who could make several return journeys in a season, building up the settlers' numbers rapidly."[41] In a similar bid to escape the logistical dilemma of the open rowing ships, the third edition of the British Museum's guide to Sutton Hoo pictures the ship under sail "to counter a climate of opinion which is unaccustomed to regarding the Sutton Hoo vessel as anything more than a big rowing boat."[42] The provision of sails for a vessel of the migrations would indeed ameliorate the logistical problems of transporting large numbers of people. A sail-driven boat could make a much shorter passage to England, perhaps even by a direct crossing in good weather rather than a longer, cautious coastal journey. Perhaps more important, a small crew could convey cargo or a larger body of dependents in space otherwise required for oarsmen. Lacking any archaeological evidence, the argument for the presence of mast and sail on the Sutton Hoo vessel in particular and among the ships of

---

[40] Carver, "Pre-Viking Traffic," 122.
[41] Haywood, *Dark Age Naval Power,* 73.
[42] Bruce-Mitford, *Sutton Hoo Handbook,* 76; Angela C. Evans and Rupert Bruce-Mitford, "The Ship," 424.

migrating Anglo-Saxons in general rests on a dual foundation.[43] A group of three texts has sometimes been interpreted so as to suggest the use of sails among the Anglo-Saxon invaders. The second part of the argument is a series of inferences relevant to the use of sails.

The first text is a line from the *De consulatu Stilichonis*, written by Claudian, a court poet who died in about A.D. 404: "Next spoke Britain clothed in the skin of some Caledonian beast, her cheeks tattooed, and an azure cloak, rivalling the swell of ocean, sweeping to her feet: 'Stilicho gave aid to me also when at the mercy of neighbouring tribes, what time the Scots roused all Hibernia against me and the sea foamed to the beat of hostile oars. Thanks to his care I had no need to fear the Scottish arms or tremble at the Pict, or keep watch along all my coasts for the Saxon who would come whatever wind might blow [*ne litore toto prospicerem dubiis venturum Saxona ventis*].'"[44] The first thing to notice about this passage is the poetical language abounding in literary conceits. Poets are notoriously inaccurate in descriptions of the sea, even Viking poets, and a court poet of Late Antiquity who most probably never saw a Saxon or their ships is an unreliable guide. As Peter Salway points out, Claudian's accounts cannot be accepted as accurate descriptions.[45] Claudian does not specifically mention sailing ships, mast, or sail. The only explicit reference is to oars ("the sea foamed to the beat of hostile oars"). Nevertheless, this passage is cited to support the idea that the Saxons used wind-powered vessels during their fifth-century raids and invasions. The necessary inference rests on the association of Saxons with wind, and the implied use of mast and sail. An alternative and simpler interpretation of Claudian's phrase, "whatever wind might blow," is that this must be a metaphor for the unpredictable and unexpected. A literary topos underlies the image. The stereotypic quality associated with Saxons in Roman literature was suddenness and surprise. An example drawn from Ammianus makes it clear that the literary association of Saxons with the wind suggested the sudden and unexpected, and did not imply use of mast and sail. "No one could guard against their unexpected coming, since they [the Maratocupreni, a brigand tribe from inland Syria] did not assail previously chosen places . . . breaking out wherever the wind took them [*quocumque ventus duxerat*]—the same reason that makes the Saxon feared before all

[43] Marcus, "Nydam Craft," 66; Marsden, "Mast and Sail," 104; Angela C. Evans and Rupert Bruce-Mitford, "The Ship," 352–435; Myres, Review of *Sutton Hoo*; McGrail, *The Ship*, 40; Haywood, *Dark Age Naval Power*, 70–73. For a survey of the literary evidence see Ellmers, *Frühmittelalterliche Handelsschiffahrt*.

[44] Claudian *De consulatu Stilichonis* II.247–55. For a full discussion of the translation see Michael E. Jones, "Literary Evidence for Mast and Sail," 38–42, 61 n. 15–16.

[45] Salway, *Roman Britain*, 419–24, 382 n. 1; Peter Foote, "Wrecks and Rhymes"; Basch, "Reliability of Ancient Writers," 366; Alan Cameron, *Claudian*.

other enemies for their sudden raids" (28.2.12, trans. J. C. Rolfe). In this example, the reference to desert Syria and the wind could scarcely have less to do with ships and the sea. Nevertheless the image that comes to Ammianus as a parallel is the Saxons, equally sudden and unpredictable, like the shifting winds. Even if Claudian's language is taken literally, no allusion to mast and sail need be implied. The strength and direction of the wind affect the movement of all vessels, not just sailing craft. Anyone who has rowed in the open sea appreciates how important to progress are sea conditions influenced by the wind. Tacitus recorded of the seas around Britain, "The sea was sluggish and heavy to the oars, and was not set in motion as much as other seas, even by the winds." As a later Anglo-Saxon gnomic verse pointed out, "weary shall he be who rows against the wind."[46] Finally, if Claudian's statement that the Saxons could arrive on any wind ("whatever wind might blow") is taken strictly and literally, this must suggest motive power independent of the winds, in fact oars rather than sails. Thus Claudian's testimony does nothing to strengthen the case for a hypothetical mast and sail among the Anglo-Saxons. If anything, he may be interpreted to strengthen the argument that the Saxons used oars alone.

The second text is a passage from a letter written by Sidonius Apollinaris (roughly 431–484), an aristocrat of distinguished Gallic family and a man of letters. Sidonius makes a tricky witness for matters maritime. On the one hand he sometimes shows good powers of observation and a love of detail. On the other hand his letters are the polished product of Roman epistolography and are derivative, highly conventional, and full of classical tropes and allusions. "In the letters," as C. E. Stevens has remarked, "the living man is smothered in the conceits of borrowed verbiage."[47] Sidonius's letters are not spontaneous first-person impressions but artificial and highly polished works designed for publication. They present a triple barrier between reality and Sidonius's descriptions of the Saxons and their ships—the borrowed conventions of classical rhetoric, personal ignorance, and cultural prejudice. There is no certain indication that Sidonius himself ever saw a Saxon ship. "When ready to unfurl their sails for the voyage home from the continent and to lift their gripping anchors from enemy waters," writes Sidonius, "they are accustomed on the eve of departure to kill one in ten of their prisoners by drowning or crucifixion. . . . [*praeterea, priusquam de continenti in patriam vela laxantes hostico mordaces anchoras vado vellant. . . .*]" (*Ep.* 8.6.15, trans. W.

---

[46] Tacitus *Agricola* 10, translation by Mattingly. The gnomic verse is quoted by Whittock, *Origins of England*, 134.

[47] Stevens, *Sidonius Apollinaris*, 174. For a full discussion of Sidonius, Saxons, and ships see Michael E. Jones, "Literary Evidence for Mast and Sail," 42–48, 62–64 n. 25–40.

B. Anderson). The reference to sails is part of a barbarian atrocity story. The language is highly poetic and hence deeply suspicious. The Latin has a pleasant alliteration equivalent to our "swelling sails" or "anchors aweigh"—*vela laxantes . . . anchoras vado vellant.* Elsewhere Sidonius seems to confuse the ships of the Saxons with the hide-covered coracle and curraghs of the Scots and Picts: "The Aremorican region too expected the Saxon pirate, who deems it but sport to furrow the British waters with hides, cleaving the blue sea in a stitched boat" (*Panegyric on Avitus* 369–71, trans. Anderson). No other Latin author links stitched or sewn hide boats with Germans or Scandinavians. Instead, seagoing hide boats are consistently treated as uniquely British or perhaps Irish (Hibernian). The language used by Sidonius is suspiciously similar to earlier descriptions of British hide boats in Pliny and Avienus. Sidonius may very well have borrowed from these and mistakenly applied the description of Celtic hide boats to Saxon ships, conflating the various types of ships used by the three groups of contemporary barbarian invaders of fifth-century Britain— the Scots, Picts, and Saxons. Just such a conflation occurs elsewhere in the same work of Sidonius, where he erroneously and anachronistically links the same triad of Scots, Picts, and Saxons as the foes of Julius Caesar's campaign in Britain.[48] After examining other passages in Sidonius concerning ships and the sea, O. M. Dalton concluded that "we learn nothing of naval matters" from Sidonius.[49] Another passage from Sidonius has actually been used to bolster the argument that the Saxon ships used only oars: "You had recently sounded the triumph of war in the fleet . . . and were roving the winding shores of Ocean to meet the curving (*pandi*) sloops (*myoparones*) of the Saxons, who give the impression that every oarsman you see in their crew is a pirate captain" (*Ep.* 8.6.13 trans. W. B. Anderson). Sidonius uses *myoparones*, an exotic term derived from the Greek, in reference to Saxon ships. "Curving sloops of the Saxons" and the description of the oarsmen seem appropriate when matched with vessels such as Nydam or Sutton Hoo, or picture stones such as Häggeby, Uppland.[50] Sidonius's evident confusion among the ships of the Irish, Pictish, and Saxon invaders of Britain and his poetic and artificial style make him an unreliable source, however. Certainly he cannot serve as authoritative textual support for an otherwise unattested technology.

---

[48] Pliny *Natural History* 4.102–4, 34.156; Avienus *Ora maritima* 94–134, both translated in Rivet and Smith, *Place-Names of Roman Britain,* 54–55, 79–80. Jonathan Wooding accepts that Sidonius probably borrowed from Avienus but suggests that the Saxons nevertheless may also have used hide ships. "Saxons Who Furrow the British Sea with Hides," 33–36. Julius Caesar, Scots, Picts and Saxons: Sidonius *Panegyric on Avitus* 88–92.

[49] Dalton, in Sidonius, *Letters,* cx n. 3, cxi.

[50] Charles Green, *Sutton Hoo,* 49; Crumlin-Pedersen, "Boats and Ships," 113.

The final relevant passage is taken from Gildas: "Then a pack of cubs burst forth from the lair of the barbarian lioness, coming in three *keels*, as they call warships in their language. The winds were favourable; favourable too the omens and auguries. . . . (Tum erumpens grex catulorum de cubili leaenae barbarae, tribus, ut lingua eius exprimitur, cyulis, nostra longis navibus, secundis velis omine auguriisque. . . .)" (*D.e.* 23.3). In terms of mast and sail, this seems to be an argument analogous to Claudian's shifting winds. The Latin is ambiguous, however, and the key phrase *secundis velis* may be translated to mean either favorable wind (through metonymy) or favorable sail, or perhaps more ambiguously, "smooth sailing." The association of *secundis velis* with prophecy and omen suggests this is not a description of actual sails. To complicate matters, *velis* is not found in all the manuscripts of the *De excidio*. *Secundus* seems inappropriate when paired with *velis* (sail), unless as a literary conceit. The more common phrase would be *secundis ventis*, meaning favorable wind or weather. An example from Cicero is instructive: "may you give to my talent favorable sails" (*des ingenio vela secunda meo*).[51] Elsewhere in the *De excidio* Gildas described the ships of the Britons, Scots, and Picts as having sails.[52] There is no equivalent unambiguous reference to Saxon sails. Although both drew on Gildas, neither Bede nor the author of the *Historia Brittonum* mentioned sails when describing the invading ships of the Saxons. Given the chosen purpose and style of Gildas's work (a jeremiad), we should be cautious in interpreting a highly literary passage such as the one in question.

The authors of these three texts—a prophet, a court poet, and a patron of letters—hardly constitute a gallery of naval experts. Even if their authority is admitted, however, the passages are ambiguous or vague. They may even be read to support the notion of oar-driven boats. We lack what would be most helpful in the literary record, a treatise on naval warfare in the vein of Vegetius, or even a deliberate historian such as Ammianus. The closest approximation to a narrative history is the work of Procopius, already discussed. His account of Justinian's wars includes several passages relevant to the controversy over Anglo-Saxons and sails. These are rarely quoted by those who advocate sail and mast. Speaking of an Anglian fleet from Brittia, Procopius writes: "And there are no supernumeraries in this fleet, for all the men rowed with their own hands. Nor do these islanders have sails, as it happens, but they always navigate by rowing

---

[51] For a discussion of the various translations and texts of this passage see Michael E. Jones, "Literary Evidence for Mast and Sail," 48–52, 64–65 n. 41–56. For Cicero and the use of *secundus* see Glare, *Oxford Latin Dictionary*, s.v.

[52] Gildas *D.e.* 25: exiles from Britain have sails; *D.e.* 16, 19: Picts and Scots have sails and coracles; *D.e.* 23.3: Saxons and the wind.

alone."[53] At last an unambiguous statement. It seems conclusive with respect to the invading Angles and their use of sails in the sixth century, but how reliable is Procopius? I have already rejected the numbers Procopius cites for the fleet in this passage, and it is always dangerous to pick and choose certain sentences while rejecting others. With respect to numeracy, however, Procopius seems consistent—his numbers are almost always gross exaggerations. This is a failing shared by many classical authorities who otherwise contain reliable information. For all of his faults, Procopius had one advantage as an authority for ships that sets him apart from the company of Claudian, Sidonius, and Gildas. Procopius had first-hand experience with warships and transports of the sixth century. His descriptions of the ships of the Byzantines and Vandals, though couched in somewhat archaic language, seem technically correct. He knew that Romans, Celtic peoples, and other Germanic groups such as the Vandals and Goths used sails. His claim that the Angles relied solely on oars thus deserves respect.[54] Procopius makes mention of one other peculiarity of the Angles, their ignorance of horses and habit of fighting on foot. This may be a general characteristic of barbarian armies in Procopius's eyes, but the practice certainly did typify the Anglo-Saxons who, in contrast to the cavalry-using Goths, Vandals, and Franks, fought primarily on foot until the Norman Conquest.[55] This accurate anecdote perhaps strengthens Procopius's credibility concerning Anglo-Saxon maritime practice.

Viewed as a whole, the literary sources hardly refute the evidence of archaeology that Anglo-Saxon vessels of the migrations period were powered solely by oars. The only explicit text, Procopius, strongly sup-

[53] Procopius *D.B.G.* 8.20.31, translated by H. B. Dewing.

[54] Some historians speculate that Procopius's information came from a Frankish embassy to Constantinople that included Angles. "If, as is probable, Procopius derived his strange tales from the Angles who were sent on embassy, in his time, to Constantinople, they have, in spite of their absurdity, some positive value." R. W. Chambers, *England before the Conquest*, 68. To escape the full implications of Procopius's statement, some historians have suggested that his description applied only to warships, not (hypothetical) sail-powered transports. This is not only speculative but inaccurate. Procopius specifically described a fleet transporting an army. His statement is not limited to a particular type of ship. It is a blanket statement: "Nor do these islanders have sails." Archibald R. Lewis and Timothy Runyan suggest that reliance on oar power perhaps was more characteristic of the Angles from the Baltic than the Saxons of the North Sea. They cite Sidonius for evidence of Saxon sails (*European Naval and Maritime History*, 12–13). This suggestion rests on a false premise, because Celtic and classical authors, including Procopius, drew no clear distinction between Saxons, Angles, or even Franks. To the Britons all the Germanic invaders were Saxons. See Myres, *English Settlements*, 104–6.

[55] The virtual absence of riding gear in the early weapon graves of Anglo-Saxon England, in contrast to grave goods of the continental cemeteries, supports Procopius's statement. The Northumbrians may later have added a cavalry force under British influence. See Alcock, *Economy, Society, and Warfare*, 265. R. H. C. Davis, "Did the Anglo-Saxons Have Warhorses?" has a different opinion.

ports this contention. Neither linguistic evidence nor later Anglo-Saxon literature contradicts the idea that the Anglo-Saxons lacked mast and sail in the period 400–600 A.D. The linguistic evidence is imprecise and difficult to interpret, but the terminology for rowing, mast, and sail in the various Germanic languages suggests that sailing terms entered their vocabularies after the fifth-century migrations had ended and the historical divergence of Old English and Old Norse. For example, words for mast in Old English (maest) and Old Norse (vida) evidently had different origins. The first explicit mention of a sail in Anglo-Saxon literature comes from Bede. The boat described is probably a coracle and its crew of three could carry it: this is obviously not a seagoing clinker-built ship. Probably the earliest certain Anglo-Saxon reference to a seagoing vessel with a sail is the poem *Andreas*, written about 800 A.D.[56]

The second part of the case for mast and sail during the Anglo-Saxon migrations consists of a series of inferences. The first suggests that the Anglo-Saxons must have been familiar with mast and sail from both Celtic and Roman practices in the same waters, or even through duty in Roman service. Thus they were likely to have adopted mast and sail into their own craft.[57] This argument is a merely presumptive one, and while possible, its conclusion is not necessarily probable. The whole push of Scandinavian shipbuilding over a two-thousand-year period is its conservative or "noninnovative" character. Techniques of construction in clinker boatbuilding and the mode of transmission of this skill made it difficult to innovate and experiment with new forms.[58] The Anglo-Saxons might have adopted the Liburnians or Picti of the British fleet mentioned by Vegetius, but no evidence suggests that they did so, anymore than they incorporated armored horsemen or catapults into their land fighting methods.

A second inference suggests that the Sutton Hoo hull was strong and broad enough to have supported a mast, and therefore did so.[59] It is certainly a stronger hull than Nydam's, although still a clinker-built longship, but with two hundred years having elapsed between these two examples, some evolution of hull form in Scandinavian shipbuilding might be expected. There is no need to resort to mast and sail to explain such a

[56] For Bede's mention of sail, see *H.e.* 5.1. For a discussion of the linguistic and literary material see Michael E. Jones, "Literary Evidence for Mast and Sail," 54–58; Kolb, "Schiff und Seefahrt"; Roger Smith, "Ships and Dating."
[57] Myres, Review of *Sutton Hoo*, 573; Marsden, "Mast and Sail," 140; Angela C. Evans and Rupert Bruce-Mitford, "The Ship," 422.
[58] Angela C. Evans and Rupert Bruce-Mitford, "The Ship," 434; Greenhill, *Archaeology of the Boat*, 178.
[59] Angela C. Evans and Rupert Bruce-Mitford, "The Ship," 422–24, quoting Akerlund, Marsden, and Christensen.

modification.[60] As Alan Binns points out, the argument over hull structure (recall Sutton Hoo lacked a true keel) confuses two very different problems. The theoretical possibility of carrying a mast and sail without destroying the hull is not the same as sailing effectively. If Sutton Hoo had possessed mast and sail, the ship would have had a tremendous leeward drift.[61] In fact, the unsuitability of Sutton Hoo's hull and keel design is an argument against her use as a sailing vessel. It is worth emphasizing that Sutton Hoo was not only excavated but reexcavated with meticulous care. Both cloth and metal survived in the burial but neither sail nor metal rigging parts were found. Three other boat finds, Ladby, Kvalsund, and Graveney, are sometimes cited as examples of ships which sailed but for which no archaeological evidence of mast or sail survived—the implication being that this state of affairs would admit a putative mast and sail for Sutton Hoo or other ships of the migrations despite the lack of positive archaeological evidence for such. Unfortunately for this argument, Ladby did in fact produce metal evidence interpreted as mast fittings.[62] In the case of the other two vessels, it is by no means clear or even likely that Kvalsund (see Figure 3) was a sailing rather than a purely rowing galley. Graveney is centuries later than Sutton Hoo, possibly five hundred years later, and is hardly a relevant example. Moreover, Graveney is an oddity. This ship may have been deliberately converted from sail for oared duties, and much controversy surrounds the interpretation of evidence for its mast and fittings.[63] These various inferences of why and how the Anglo-Saxons must hypothetically have availed themselves of the advantages apparent in the sailing ships of neighboring peoples are really circular arguments stemming from an initial assumption that the Anglo-Saxon migrations were on a grand scale. The circle, however, can also be drawn in the opposite direction. Before 600 A.D. the increasingly efficient northern European clinker-built rowing vessels served the purposes required of them in piracy, warfare, invasion, and migration on a limited scale. For example, the recipe for successful piracy in diverse periods and places required successful ambush, larger crews than those of the victims, and speed and maneuverability over relatively short distances. These were qualities possessed by the Nydam ship and refined in the ships of Sutton Hoo and Kvalsund. There was no need for special types of merchant vessels and no decisive cause for the adoption of sail.[64]

---

60 Ibid., 426; Crumlin-Pedersen, "Gredstedbroskibet."
61 Biddle et al., "Sutton Hoo Published," 259–62.
62 Crumlin-Pedersen, "Viking Ships," 9.
63 Fenwick, Graveney Boat.
64 Christensen, "Scandinavian Ships," 162; Greenhill, Archaeology of the Boat, 188.

One final point is often raised to argue that the earlier Anglo-Saxon vessels used mast and sail. In the Theodosian period the Romans erected a series of signal stations along the Yorkshire coast. This is taken as indicating the presence of Anglo-Saxon raiders who came directly across the North Sea rather than crossing near the Channel and coasting northwards up the British coast.[65] This in turn would suggest that the Anglo-Saxon vessels were sailed, since to row across the North Sea would have been extremely difficult and might have been fatally dangerous. There is a simpler solution. The British sources, including Gildas, clearly state that the Picts and Scots were raiding by sea.[66] Such raids would have outflanked the linear defense of Hadrian's Wall and necessitated some provision for warning along the exposed coast. No recourse to Anglo-Saxons is necessary to explain the Yorkshire fortifications. Hines suggests that settlers from southwest Norway may have made direct crossings of the North Sea to reach East Anglia and Humberside in the sixth century. Objects such as women's wrist clasps are found in Norway and England but are rare or absent along the coastlands of western Germany, the Netherlands, and Belgium. Leaving aside the controversy over whether such objects as wrist clasps reflect exchange, immigration, political emulation, or ideological alliance, there are difficulties in accepting Hines's thesis of direct crossings of the North Sea. As Hines acknowledges, the absence of evidence for contact between Norway and Scotland in the migration period, something we should expect if early medieval Scandinavians followed the direct crossing routes taken later by the technologically advanced ships of the Vikings, undermines his argument and is at least as significant as discontinuities in the trail of artifacts between southwest Norway and the coasts of western Germany and the Netherlands.[67] The distribution of the objects in East Anglia, the Wash, and Humberside cannot be used to prove direct crossings since these areas were a terminus for the circuitous coastal route linking England and the continent. In general the issue of direct sea crossing versus coastal routes is not subject to decisive archaeological confirmation. As M. O. H. Carver concludes:

---

[65] Myres, Review of *Sutton Hoo*, 573; Marcus, "Nydam Craft," 66.
[66] Gildas *D.e.* 16.
[67] Hines, *Scandinavian Character*, 277–78, map 6.1. See the criticism of Hines's thesis advanced by Welch, "Reflections." Interpretation of the clasps as evidence of migrating people rather than as signs of trade or exchange is made problematic by apparent differences in the use of these objects in Norway and England. In Anglo-Saxon cemeteries the position of the clasps in the graves does not always suggest they were attached to sleeves. In England the clasps are associated only with women. In Norway both sexes evidently used them. Hinton, *Archaeology, Economy, and Society*, 17.

Virtually all archaeological arguments for maritime contact derive from "trails" of similar objects, monuments, or behaviour, "trails" which are, unsurprisingly, only discovered on land. They can therefore be used to argue direct or coastal movement, *ad libidum*. . . . If Norwegian migrants did move along the eastern coastlines of the North Sea (rather than crossing it) but left no material traces until they arrived in Norfolk or Humberside, this must be a symptom of their political relations with the peoples who occupied or claimed to control the space through which they passed. Discontinuity in the trail, the "vanishing footprints" problem, is clearly a common problem for the migration period.[68]

The eastern coastlines of the North Sea were no tribe's exclusive maritime zone. Whether we speak of a "Merovingian" North Sea or an *Oceanus Fresconicus*, or look to a "Saxon" Shore, this maritime space was characterized by exchange, immigration, political emulation, and ideological alliance, all occurring together with piracy, raiding, and warfare. There is no reason to assume that Nordic peoples were barred from the coastal seaways. The limitations of ships such as Nydam, Sutton Hoo, and Kvalsund suggest that regular direct crossings of the North Sea were beyond the maritime capabilities of Scandinavian and Anglo-Saxon seamen.[69]

To conclude, this survey of the literary and archaeological evidence pertaining to ships and shipping in the period of the Anglo-Saxon migrations lends no support for the theory of an undiscovered type of Anglo-Saxon sailing vessel. Of course arguments from silence sometimes turn out to be lies of omission. Within the unexcavated burials of Britain and Scandinavia a seadragon's trove in the form of evidence for the use of mast and sail during the migrations may yet wait. On present evidence, however, the clinker-built rowing ships of the archaeological record form a logistical funnel through which all theories of the nature and scale of the Anglo-Saxon invasion and settlement must pass. A truly popular migration on a great scale seems logistically impossible. Instead, we should

---

[68] Carver, "Pre-Viking Traffic," 124. Binns suggests that Angles living on the east coast of Jutland began their journey to Britain by coasting northwards through Limfjord, but sometimes around Skagen. "One might see some suggestion of this route in some of the finds from Lindholm-Høje, overlooking the Limfjord, and in the cremation pottery and wrist-clasps common to a region of SW Norway and the Anglian parts of Eastern England but not recorded elsewhere." Binns, *Viking Voyagers*, 6. Thereafter the route led southwards down the coasts, perhaps crossing to England in the latitude of Great Yarmouth, a distance of about one hundred miles. Routes farther south connected the Hook of Holland and the Thames estuary, and the Dover Strait and Southampton Water.

[69] Welch, "Reflections," 255; Carver, "Pre-Viking Traffic," 119.

expect to see what the early medieval literature in fact describes, a pattern of scattered, relatively small and heavily militarized emigrant groups.

WARFARE

How suitable is the thesis of a relatively small and militarized Anglo-Saxon migration in the context of what is known concerning warfare and society in early Anglo-Saxon England? The historical debate over the nature and scale of the Anglo-Saxon migration is paralleled by a debate over the question who fought in Anglo-Saxon armies and why. The military counterpart of a large-scale "national" migration involving the entire spectrum of Germanic society is the concept of "the nation in arms," embodied in the military service of all free men, not just a warrior elite. From the idea of a migration centered on the *ceorl* (free peasant husbandman) extends the idea of a *ceorl*-centered army. Linked to these assumptions are related questions concerning the motivations behind the Anglo-Saxon migration. Was it essentially a movement of land-hungry peasants or of tribute-seeking warbands? To historians such as Stenton, service in the King's *fyrds* (royal military expeditions of an Anglo-Saxon kingdom) was the duty of peasants as well as nobles. This concept grew from romantic Victorian visions of prefeudal early Germanic societies in which all freemen defended their country in wartime. A free peasant society (or commonwealth) was defended by a free peasant militia. Such a conception of early Anglo-Saxon society has been sharply criticized by H. M. Chadwick and other historians who conclude that fighting was overwhelmingly, perhaps even exclusively, the preserve of the aristocracy, organized for warfare through the bonds of personal commendation. They affirmed a tripartite and exclusive social order of nobles who fought, peasants who farmed, and clerics who prayed. Such scholarly disagreement was and is possible because the limited extant sources will often support contradictory interpretations. The thesis of a "nation in arms" relies heavily on a particular interpretation and literal acceptance of Anglo-Saxon law books (specifically the single text of Ine, c. 51) and seems contradicted by anecdotal material from literary sources including Bede's *Historia ecclesiastica*, the *Anglo-Saxon Chronicle*, and certain of the Anglo-Saxon poems. Connecting either competing theory, or some synthesis of the two extreme views, to the fifth-century migrations requires a speculative retrospection from the seventh-century historical horizon for these Anglo-Saxon sources. In general, the Romantic vision of free peasant armies is currently in historiographic retreat both in Germany and Britain. Richard Abels has recently argued persuasively that the early Anglo-Saxon *fyrd* was composed of the king's personal followers—his immediate household—serving in expectation of reward, reinforced by his veteran landed retainers and their followings. Abels's position allows for military service by *ceorls*, but only in the context of personal lordship rather than national obligation.[70]

Perhaps the essential issue that ties warfare to the Anglo-Saxon migration is not so much the theoretical status of military service but the actual size and composition of early Anglo-Saxon armies. A truly large-scale popular migration might produce the military tradition and demographic basis of a numerous army. A smaller-scale migration, as a military corollary, ought to produce a pattern of small armies, in fact warbands on the scale of ships' companies. Throughout early Anglo-Saxon history the fundamental military unit was the warband and this was also evidently the agent of invasion of the fifth and sixth centuries. The warband revealed in early Anglo-Saxon works is recognizably akin to the *comitatus* described in Tacitus.[71] The primary bond of loyalty is between man and lord rather than any tribal allegiance. The warbands were evidently often of mixed composition.[72] A great leader would attract followers from a wide spectrum. Danes and Britons might be found in the retinue of an Anglo-Saxon chieftain even as Anglo-Saxon warriors served overseas in foreign retinues. The size of armies in this period was remarkably small by modern standards. The laws of Ine in the seventh century, for example, rate as a *here* (army) any band numbering more than 35 men. Thus in Anglo-Saxon terms a single ship's company might be considered an army. Such a small number, obviously a minimum, is given credibility by specific incidents. Private warbands of princes sometimes defeated Anglo-Saxon royal armies. This suggests that royal armies need not have been large. In this context the careers of Caedwalla and Guthlac are instructive.[73] In the example of Cynewulf's death in 786, a force of 85 men sufficed to kill a king. A political coup, of course, might involve fewer men than a representative army on campaign, but a few additional examples show that armies numbered only in the hundreds even at full strength. The total war strength of the kingdom of Dalriada, which resisted Pict, Briton, Angle, and Viking to absorb eventually the whole of Scotland, probably did not

[70] Abels, *Lordship and Military Obligation*, 1–42.
[71] Tacitus *Germania* 13–14; Woolf, "Idea of Men Dying"; Alcock, *Arthur's Britain*, 335–38; Abels, *Lordship and Military Obligation*, 11–37.
[72] Fisher, *Anglo-Saxon Age*, 130–32.
[73] Bede *H.e.* 4.12, 4.15; Felix *Vita S. Guthlaci* 16–18.

exceed 1,500 men.[74] That this represented a powerful military state is evident not only from Dalriada's eventual success but from particular events such as a battle with the *Miathi* described by Adomnan, where (to his astonishment) the host of Dalriada lost 303 men yet was victorious and even continued the campaign. In Dark Age warfare 300 is a recurring figure. The British expedition to Catraeth immortalized in the *Gododdin* poem numbered 300 men, and while this figure may be a poetic convention, it seems of the right magnitude. This army was gathered from several different British kingdoms, and even if the force is multiplied by a factor of two or three to account for nonnoble retainers or infantry, the force probably numbered less than 1,000. Penda's Mercian forces numbered 30 "legions." The idea that armies numbered only a few hundred warriors is consistent with archaeological evidence from the eve of the Anglo-Saxon migrations. A number of votive deposits of weapons in Jutland provide a clue to the size of armies there in the late third through the fourth century. Assuming that the ritual deposits such as those from Nydam and Ejsbol correspond to the size of the defeated army the worshipers wished to represent, these hierarchically organized armies ranged in size from as many as 300 to armed bands numbering in the tens rather than the hundreds.[75] In this context, Anglo-Saxon invasion forces numbering two, three, or five ships seem credible. The different patterns of the rapid collapse of Gaul and Spain in the face of the fifth-century barbarian invasions and the much slower pace of the piecemeal Anglo-Saxon conquest in Britain suggest that the Anglo-Saxon invaders may have been few in number. The century-long gestation between the fifth-century invasions and the emergence of established Anglo-Saxon kingdoms likewise seems to contradict the thesis of a large-scale "national" or even coordinated "tribal" migration, and better suits the thesis of smaller and scattered movements. This is also the implication of the unusual multiplicity of small kingdoms in early England, which as Stenton admitted was "a congestion of dynasties in southern England to which there is no parallel in Western Europe."[76]

---

[74] Calculated from the *Senchus Fer nAlban*.
[75] Hines, "Military Context," 38–39; Pearson, "Economic and Ideological Change," 86–87; Alcock, *Arthur's Britain*, 314–50; Alcock, *Economy, Society, and Warfare*, 223–311. For another discussion of numbers see Abels, *Lordship and Military Obligation*, 33–36. Adomnan *Life of Columba* 1.7–8. Aneirin *Gododdin* B.20, translated by K. H. Jackson. For a discussion of the poem see Davies, *Wales in Early Middle Ages*, 209–12. For numbers and *Gododdin* see Alcock, *Arthur's Britain*, 336–37. Penda's thirty legions: Bede *H.e.* 3.24.
[76] Stenton, *Anglo-Saxon England*, 38; Whittock, *Origins of England*, 122; Dixon, *Barbarian Europe*, 53.

SETTLEMENT AND SOCIETY

One of the central arguments in the traditional defense of a large-scale popular Anglo-Saxon migration was the apparently fundamental difference between the late Romano-British and early Anglo-Saxon settlement patterns and social orders. In his classic work Stenton writes that: "an invasion of Britain by a small number of chiefs, each accompanied by his personal followers, might perhaps have conquered the midlands and the south, but would not have produced the social order that is afterwards found there."[77] Stenton focuses on the agrarian order of what he considers to be free peasants (ceorls), a class he believes constituted the basis of Anglo-Saxon society. Even though the upper classes of Anglo-Saxon and British societies appeared to be very similarly organized around the military and aristocratic principles of the "Heroic Age" common to all of northern Europe in the early medieval period, the new social and agrarian order outlined by Stenton differs so greatly from the presumed Romano-British economy and society that he believes it warrants the assumption of "a series of national migrations"—"unique in any case among contemporary movements."[78] Stenton contrasts his typical ceorl, a free peasant landholder cultivating a hide of land, using a heavy plough in an open-field system of agriculture, and residing in a nucleated village, with what he considers to be the preexisting British pattern—upland settlement on light soils in scattered farms rather than village communities, placing heavy reliance on a pastoral rather than an arable economy. We have discussed the Victorian roots of the notion of a free peasant commonwealth. The actual evidence for the economic and social status of the ceorl is inconclusive. There is no etymological connection between the term ceorl and free status. Nor can the relative populations of the various classes of Anglo-Saxon society be established from the law codes. In fact, if the ratios of invasive to indigenous population argued earlier are even remotely correct, the majority of the inhabitants of the early Anglo-Saxon kingdoms were of Romano-British descent. Given the uncertainty of the evidence, it is fair to say that the centrality of the ceorl in the traditional vision of early Anglo-Saxon society rests on assumption rather than demonstration.[79] It is, however, recent landscape studies that have most undercut Stenton's paradigm.

Perhaps nothing in Anglo-Saxon studies has changed so drastically in recent years as the notion of the human landscape of the early Dark Ages.

---

[77] Stenton, *Anglo-Saxon England*, 277. See Loyn's comments on Stenton in "Anglo-Saxon England."
[78] Stenton, *Anglo-Saxon England*, 277.
[79] Abels, *Lordship and Military Obligation*, 37–42.

The techniques of aerial photography, together with field-walking and intense local settlement studies, have revealed just how inadequate the picture of the Anglo-Saxon and earlier landscapes, reconstructed from place-names, charter evidence, and the Domesday survey, had been.[80] Increasingly, it seems that the agrarian resources of early Anglo-Saxon England, Roman Britain, and even the later Iron Age were fully exploited. This changed perception of settlement geography has destroyed the dichotomy often encountered in the literature, which pictured Romano-British settlement as largely upland and Anglo-Saxon settlement as a new agricultural regime pioneering the forested heavy clay soils of lowland Britain. H. R. Loyn once wrote that "the story of Anglo-Saxon settlement, when looked at in depth, yields more of the saga of man against forest than of Saxon against Celt. It was a colonizing movement in the true sense of the word."[81] Pollen analysis, however, does not support the idea that the Anglo-Saxon migration was large enough to trigger an alteration in the exploitation of the countryside. If anything, the early Anglo-Saxon era is marked by reforestation rather than forest clearance.[82] Instead of a vista of Anglo-Saxon pioneers and a virgin landscape, Romano-British and Anglo-Saxon settlement areas in southern Britain broadly coincide. The farming technology of the Anglo-Saxons was probably very similar to that of the Britons. This would have eased the takeover and perpetuation of existing field systems. As D. J. V. Fisher sees it, "Corn growing on a large scale, the use of the heavy plough, and peasant settlement in nucleated villages were all characteristic of the last phase of Romano-British agriculture, which in these respects resembles that of the Anglo-Saxons."[83] Studies of animal bone assemblages suggest a continuum from the Roman era through the early Anglo-Saxon period (although there seems to have been a significant change in the Middle Saxon era).[84] Without the long accepted contrast between the general settlement patterns of Celt and Saxon, a warrant for a large-scale extraordinary settlement by the invading Anglo-Saxons disappears.

If a general coincidence in what might be called the macrosettlement patterns has been established, evidence for direct continuity between Romano-British and Anglo-Saxon eras at specific sites has proved elusive.[85] The Roman villa at Latimer (Buckinghamshire) and the Barton

---

[80] Sawyer, *From Roman Britain to Norman England*, 132–67.

[81] Loyn, *Anglo-Saxon England*, 36.

[82] For a brief recent survey see N. J. Higham, *Rome, Britain, and the Anglo-Saxons*, 77–80.

[83] Fisher, *Anglo-Saxon Age*, 53; Welch, *Dicovering Anglo-Saxon England*, 42.

[84] Biddick, "Field Edge," 106.

[85] Finberg, *Roman and Saxon Withington*; W. J. Rodwell and K. A. Rodwell, *Rivenhall*. For a study of continuity outside the Saxon areas of settlement see W. Davies, "Roman Settlements."

Court farmstead (Oxfordshire) are possibilities. The Roman villa at Rivenhall and the Roman town site at Great Chesterton have been suggested as examples of sites indicating peaceful interaction between Anglo-Saxon immigrants and British natives. In a sense, our ignorance concerning late Romano-British administrative organizations and our knowledge of a mere handful of excavated early Anglo-Saxon settlement sites together make the correlation of Romano-British and Saxon settlements a comparison of unknowns. Even the few early Anglo-Saxon villages known by excavation may be unrepresentative, for they are abandoned settlements which failed to survive, perhaps no more indicative of "normal" conditions than the abandoned British settlements of the uplands.[86] Chalton (Hampshire), Catholme (Staffordshire), West Stow (Suffolk), Mucking (Essex), Bishopstone (Sussex), and New Wintles (Oxfordshire) seem to have been small and relatively short-lived settlements. They followed no definable plan and were located on soils that could hardly be described as "good." A similar ignorance prevails for the earliest Anglo-Saxon field systems. The once popular contrast between British fields and the open fields associated with nucleated villages of the Anglo-Saxons has been effectively challenged.[87] No such field system has ever been found in an early medieval context in the Anglo-Saxon continental homelands, a fact undermining the notion that such practices were either characteristically early or Germanic. The evolution of a common-field or open-field system, in fact, more logically results from changes in population density and landholding as an inherent part of an agricultural dynamic related to local conditions. In general, differing agrarian systems in the early Middle Ages seem to be an outgrowth of various physical geographical conditions rather than ethnic or tribal distinctions.[88] Attempts to map the boundaries of late Roman estates in Britain and compare these with early medieval boundaries have yielded suggestive but inconclusive results. It may well be that later parish boundaries generally coincide with economic units (estates) existing in the Roman era. The movement or "drift" of the relatively short-lived settlements might have occurred within these more stable boundaries. Summarizing the evidence for early Anglo-Saxon settlement, Christopher Taylor concludes: "The Saxon period is not marked by any break in settlement pattern and type but is a direct continuation of the long-established situation. . . . The important conclusion that follows is that the coming of the Saxons as such did not have a profound effect on the settlement pattern. The changes that did

[86] Rahtz, "Buildings and Rural Settlement"; Welch, "Rural Settlement Patterns," 15–16; Christopher Taylor, *Village and Farmstead*, 109–24.
[87] Thirsk, "Common Fields."
[88] Dodgshon, *Origin of British Field Systems*.

take place were not as a direct result of this racial influx while the similarity of settlement over wide areas of England in these centuries, both
within and beyond those zones traditionally said to be settled early by the
Saxons, could only have resulted from a non-cultural explanation of the
settlement pattern."[89]

The studies of J. E. A. Jolliffe, G. R. J. Jones, and G. W. S. Barrow have
illuminated one particular agrarian organization, the multiple estate—a
number of dependent farms or hamlets organized around an administrative center.[90] They are found throughout England, being particularly evident in Kent, Northumbria, Scotland, and Wales. Throughout these areas
not only are the organizations of the multiple estates similar (as revealed
by charter, place-name and geographical studies), but some of the services
and rents paid by these estates to the administrative center clearly resemble each other in both British and Anglo-Saxon contexts. In some cases the
same technical terms for rents and services (*metreth*, for example) are
used for British and Anglo-Saxon rents.[91] As James Campbell notes:

> What is recognizably the same system of local organization stretches in
> a continuous belt from Wales, across northern England and far into
> Scotland. All told it seems highly probable that the institutions of local
> authority in much of northern England came from the Celtic past. There
> is comparable evidence elsewhere, above all in the West Midlands,
> where, for example, the British term *cylch* was used in the Middle Ages
> as far east as Staffordshire to describe certain renders.
>
> The evidence for the northern institutions of the kind just described
> having a British origin is specific. That for a similar origin for those of
> Kent is not, but depends on general similarities to the other. It is impor-
> tant to bear in mind that little is known about how Anglo-Saxons ar-
> ranged such matters left to themselves: not impossibly it was in very
> similar ways. Nevertheless, not only is it highly probable that the organ-
> ization of the countryside of the north went back to a Romano-British
> past, it is at the very least possible that the same is true of Kent.[92]

The multiple estate is only one form of agrarian organization, but notwithstanding the limited evidence, the entire range of known Anglo-

[89] Christopher Taylor, *Village and Farmstead*, 120–21. See Bonney, "Early Boundaries"; Bonney, "Pagan Saxon Burials."
[90] Jolliffe, "Northumbrian Institutions"; Jolliffe, *Pre-Feudal England: The Jutes*; G. R. J.
Jones, "Multiple Estates" (this work contains a bibliography of Jones's other writings on the
subject); G. W. S. Barrow, "Northern English Society." Compare the conclusions of Jolliffe,
Jones, and Barrow to those of Everitt, *Continuity and Colonization*, 69–92.
[91] W. Rees, "Survival of Ancient Celtic Custom."
[92] James Campbell, "Lost Centuries," 41.

Saxon settlement, from individual farm to nucleated village, can be paralleled by earlier Celtic and Romano-British types. Differences exist, but there is no justification for deducing a massive migration, "unique in any case among contemporary movements," on the comparative basis of agrarian social and economic orders.

British and Anglo-Saxon societies in the early Middle Ages in fact shared many essential characteristics. Both were hierarchical societies with grades of free and unfree. These grades determined privilege and liability in law. In both societies a wergeld system (payment made to relatives of victims to prevent bloodfeud) determined penalty and compensation according to status. Status in turn was calculated from landed wealth and royal service (German *wergeld* = Welsh *galanas*). Kingship in Anglo-Saxon and Celtic societies shared many features. Both cultures were organized for warfare along similar lines—military aristocracies formed warbands supported by units of tribute or rent based upon a formula for the property of one family.[93] Lordship carried the same ideal in each society—protection and generosity were given in return for service. Although very different in form, the heroic poetry of the Welsh and the Anglo-Saxons shared a common ethos. The elegies that Taliesin and Aneirin wrote for their noble British patrons would have been entirely suitable for the Anglo-Saxon warriors who killed them.[94]

The similarities evident between British and Anglo-Saxon societies can be explained in several ways—mutual influence, convergent evolution, or an inheritance common to both from an Indo-European past. Certain similarities between Anglo-Saxon vernacular building traditions and Romano-British architecture seem to represent a hybrid insular style. For example, the farms of Anglo-Saxon Catholme (Staffordshire) resemble the plan of the Romano-British homestead at Dunston's Clump (Nottinghamshire). Since there are no known parallels to this hybrid style in the Germanic continental homelands, at least in the case of architecture, the similarity likely resulted from interaction and mutual influence.[95] The source of the similarity is less important to my argument than its undoubted existence, for the common features undermine the thesis of a cataclysmic displacement of British society by an Anglo-Saxon invasion of unparalleled scale and the erection of a novel replacement. The sim-

[93] Hodges speculates that similarities between Romano-British and Anglo-Saxon buildings suggest that household structures formed in Roman Britain survived into the Anglo-Saxon era. In turn, this may suggest that units of assessment levied on households (such as the hide) may also have originated in Roman Britain. Hodges, *Anglo-Saxon Achievement*, 36. But see Charles-Edwards, "Kinship."
[94] Sawyer, *From Roman Britain to Norman England*, 51–56.
[95] Dixon, "How Saxon Is the Saxon House?"; S. James et al., "An Early Medieval Building Tradition"; Losco-Bradley and Wheeler, "Anglo-Saxon Settlement."

ilarity of the cultures explains their close interaction during the early medieval period both in terms of conflict and alliance. More important, the similarity explains how many people and extensive territory were vanquished by small numbers of invading warbands. The process must have been to a great extent the displacement of like by like. Military victory both removed a rival and freed a tribute system for new masters. Brian Hope-Taylor's excavation at Yeavering may well be an archaeological example of this process. Thus even the Anglo-Saxon's beloved mead-hall may not have been entirely his own. Large timber halls such as Yeavering, Cowdery's Down, and Doon Hill have no precise parallel in the Germanic world. They may be the physical headquarters of rural territorial units inherited from late or sub-Roman Britain which perhaps provided the infrastructure of the Anglo-Saxon royal centers (*vills*) and their dependent settlements (*regiones*).[96] The respective military aristocracies were like hybrid flower blooms—differing in color, shape, or texture but products of the same root stock, leaf, and stem. Similarly, although disguised by differences in language, material goods, and some customs, the aristocratic warbands were ultimately supported by a continuing agriculture and peasantry. If the allegedly radical differences in social and agrarian order purportedly resulting from the Anglo-Saxon invasions are stripped away from the traditional paradigm, then no justification remains for maintaining the peculiarity or uniqueness of the Anglo-Saxon invasion and settlement from the course of events elsewhere in the Barbarian West. The argument returns naturally to the original question as stated in Chapter 1. If the Anglo-Saxon invasions were no different in scale or nature from other Germanic invasions of the period, why then does Britain alone among the ex-Roman provincial areas lose so much of Roman civilization? My belief is that the answer lies within the elements of Romano-British society itself, and the circumstances of the "Romanization" of the British provinces. This hypothesis is the subject of the next two chapters.

[96] Hope-Taylor, *Yeavering*; Foard, "Administrative Organization"; Millett and James, "Excavations at Cowdery's Down."

CHAPTER FOUR

Romano-British Attitudes: *Romanitas* and the Vision of the Roman Past

IN RETROSPECT, Roman Britain ended in a native revolt.[1] An occupation of more than three and a half centuries seems to have unraveled in the span of a single generation (380–410), perhaps even in a single decade. For reasons that are obscure, in 406 A.D., exactly a century after the elevation in Britain of Constantine the Great, three usurpers followed one another in Britain in quick succession. Little is known of Marcus, the first pretender in the mutinous triad. He may have been a soldier, but was quickly toppled and replaced by Gratian, a civilian magistrate and a native Briton. After only four months Gratian was in turn deposed by Constantine (Constantine III), who is described in hostile sources as a common soldier. Actions in Britain may have been linked to concerns about the safety of the Rhine frontier, an increasingly constricted and unreliable umbilical cord for Britannia's garrison and merchants. On the last day of 406, Germanic invaders broke through the Rhine frontier and began to ravage

---

[1] I use "native" in the sense of indigenous. See Dyson, "Native Revolts." Dyson's study is restricted to "nativistic" revolts in the early stages of Romanization, and these are not strictly comparable to the chronologically much later revolt in Britain described by Zosimus. There are, however, a number of interesting parallels and implications. Some common causal factors drawn from Dyson's model and applicable to Britain include the memory of former revolt (Magnus Maximus and Constantine, for example); governmental loss of prestige due to recent defeats; the absence of the army from the scene of the revolt; significant external pressure (Saxons); disturbed psychological state of the province; a Romanized rebel leadership; a sense of identity and cooperation among the rebels fostered by the Roman occupation; confusion engendered by civil war; and general discontent. Zosimus's wording, in fact, justifies the application of the more specific label of "nativist" to the British revolt, for he stated that the Britons "no longer submitted to Roman law, and reverted to their native customs." Zosimus 6.5. The translation is by Ridley in Zosimus, *New History*, 128.

Gaul. Constantine III stripped Britain of soldiers and crossed to the continent in an unsuccessful bid to become emperor. He failed in part because
one of his trusted generals, a Briton named Gerontius, betrayed him. The
consequences of failure were extreme. Barbarians invaded a now exposed
Britain, and the ensuing military and political crisis triggered yet another
rebellion. The Greek historian Zosimus, probably writing very early in the
sixth century and possibly drawing on the fifth-century history of Olympiodorus, gives a few enigmatic details.

> Gerontius . . . winning over the troops there (in Spain) caused the bar-
> barians in Gaul to rise against Constantine. Since Constantine did not
> hold out against these (the greater part of his strength being in Spain),
> the barbarians from beyond the Rhine overran everything at will and
> reduced the inhabitants of the British Island and some of the peoples in
> Gaul to the necessity of rebelling from the Roman Empire and of living
> by themselves, no longer obeying the Romans' laws. The Britons, there-
> fore, taking up arms and fighting on their own behalf, freed the cities
> from the barbarians who were pressing upon them; and the whole of
> Armorica and other provinces of Gaul, imitating the Britons, freed
> themselves in the same way, expelling the Roman officials and estab-
> lishing a sovereign constitution on their own authority.[2]

The passage illustrates the complex interaction of causal factors and the
fine line between external invasion, civil war, and internal revolt characterizing the immediate ending of Roman rule in Britain. The British native
revolt was triggered by a barbarian invasion, itself prompted by the
disastrous collapse of security linked to the failure of a British usurper
(Constantine III) and his rebel general (Gerontius).[3] Specifically which
group of Britons rebelled in roughly 410 A.D. and against which group of
Romans is unclear.[4] Zosimus's description seems to convey something
unusual and significant, perhaps a generalized rejection of all Roman authority. Some modern historians see an overtly anti-imperial sentiment in
the actions of the Britons, perhaps connected with a rejection of the entire
Roman social order. Whatever the immediate goals of the rebels, probably
all parties would have been surprised to learn that the revolt permanently
severed Britain from the rest of the empire. No subsequent reoccupation

[2] Zosimus 6.5. Translation by E. A. Thompson, "Britain, A.D. 406–410," 306. See Stevens,
"Marcus, Gratian, and Constantine."
[3] See the epilogue below for a detailed discussion.
[4] For the date of the rebellion see Michael E. Jones and John Casey, "Gallic Chronicle Restored," 379–92. Zosimus twice states that the rebellion occurred during the tyranny of
Constantine but never makes him the explicit object of the revolt: the Britons rebel "from the
Roman empire." Zosimus 6.5–6.

by any Roman authorities has ever been demonstrated. Indeed, in the mid-sixth century Procopius writes: "And the island of Britain revolted from the Romans, and the soldiers there chose as their king Constantinus [Constantine III], a man of no mean station . . . and Constantinus, defeated in battle, died with his sons. However, the Romans never succeeded in recovering Britain, but it remained from that time on under tyrants."[5]

The attitude toward Britain in Zosimus and Procopius is significant, for it must be seen in the general context of optimism and imperial recovery in the period between Anastasius and Justinian that culminated in an initially successful reconquest of parts of the western empire. Why should Britain have been considered exceptional and beyond imperial recovery? There seems to be a similar western tradition associating a final ending of Roman rule in Britain with the events of roughly 410. Bede connected the fall of Rome with the end of Roman rule in Britain and thought this important enough to include in his selective chronological summary at the end of the *Historia ecclesiastica*.[6] This might be simply a lucky guess or inference on his part, not evidence of a western tradition independent of Zosimus or Procopius, but there is evidence of such a western perception in earlier sources. The *Narratio de imperatoribus*, for example, states that *Brittaniae Romano nomini in perpetuum sublatae* (The Britains were removed from Roman authority forever) and associates this with the sack of Rome.[7] The Gallic Chronicle of 452 is less explicit, simply recording a Saxon invasion of Britain, but it associates that event with the fall of Rome in 410 and the loss of lands to the barbarians in Gaul and Spain.[8]

The fact of the British revolt and the significance given to events of roughly 410 by the late Roman and Byzantine sources raise important questions. How committed to *Romanitas* were the Britons after 410 A.D.? To what extent did the concept of *Romanitas* mold attitudes within independent Celtic Britain?[9] In a crucial sense, Roman Britain ended when the Britons themselves thought it did. As Wood recently suggested, "Ultimately the end of Roman Britain is the history of fifth- and sixth-century

---

[5] On possible anti-imperial sentiment, see E. A. Thompson, who calls the British rebellion "a revolt of separatists" ("Britain, A.D. 406–410," 310–16). For the quotation, see Procopius *History of the Wars* 3.2.31–38. Translation by Dewing.

[6] *H.e.* 5.24: "409. Rome was stormed by the Goths, after which the Roman rule in Britain ceased." *H.e.* 1.11: "Now Rome was taken by the Goths in the eleven hundred and sixty-fourth year after its foundation; after this the Romans ceased to rule in Britain. . . . " See Myres, *English Settlements*, 6. Bede was apparently ignorant of the work of Procopius and Zosimus. His statement therefore suggests an independent, confirming western tradition. See Wood, "End of Roman Britain," 1–2, 24–25.

[7] *Narratio de imperatoribus*, MGH AA 9:630.

[8] Gallic Chronicle of 452 s.a. Honorius xvi. For a discussion of the entry see Michael E. Jones and John Casey, "Gallic Chronicle Restored," 379–92.

[9] Dumville, "Sub-Roman Britain," 174.

opinion."[10] The whole question of loyalty and Romanization can be approached as an aspect of the *l'histoire des mentalités* and traced along a thin and delicate vein running through the British native sources.

In a famous passage Theodore Mommsen wrote that "it was not Britain that gave up Rome, but Rome that gave up Britain."[11] The loyalty of Britannia to Rome and the success of Romanization have long been accepted. The attitude and loyalty of the Britons to Roman culture, the circumstances surrounding the end of Roman Britain, and the character of the Anglo-Saxon invasions are inextricably linked in the traditional historical picture. *Romanitas* in Britain was strong, the Britons fiercely loyal, the Anglo-Saxons exceptionally numerous and inimical. Britain was from Rome's bosom untimely slashed by the seax, the Saxon knife.

One essential prop in this historical theory has been removed by the study of population. If a Romano-British population of millions faced an Anglo-Saxon population numbering in the tens of thousands, deep suspicion must greet the notion that the Britons fought to the death to preserve *Romanitas*. It would be surprising if they had. Everywhere else in the western provinces invasion led to accommodation and synthesis. In this respect the fall of the Roman empire is a sociological problem of allegiance and loyalty. What in fact were the British attitudes towards Rome and her civilization? What was the Roman legacy in the historical memory of post-Roman Britain? The most straightforward way to assess British attitudes and loyalty to Rome is by an examination of the literary evidence from late Roman and sub-Roman Britain.

The writings of Saint Patrick, Gildas's *De excidio*, and the *Historia Brittonum* comprise the essential literary corpus.[12] As we have seen, virtually every aspect of these sources has been the focus of scholarly debate. In this chapter, however, I am concerned less with the accuracy of the specific historical details in these works than with the general attitudes towards Rome that they evince. The three works share some important

---

[10] Wood, "End of Roman Britain," 1–2.

[11] Mommsen, *Provinces*, 1:194.

[12] For an introduction to these sources see Alcock, *Arthur's Britain*, 1–41. I have not included in this discussion the famous Pelagius or the "Sicilian Briton." Pelagius's thought very possibly reflects attitudes and intellectual currents of Rome and the Mediterranean rather than those of his native Britain. He was educated in Rome and spent his adult life in the Mediterranean region. Caspari's arguments for making the anonymous author of a series of Pelagian letters a Briton are not conclusive. The author in question seems to refer to "home" as *ad Urbem*, a phrase most naturally interpreted as a reference to the city of Rome. Adding this Pelagian material would risk the contamination of the discussion of native British attitudes with foreign ideas, and compromise the whole point of the chapter. The popularity of Pelagian ideas in Britain, however, does give them potential significance in illuminating British social and religious attitudes. This aspect of the problem is taken up in the next chapter. See Caspari, ed., *Briefe*; Morris, "Pelagian Literature"; Wood, "End of Roman Britain," 7.

attributes: all are Christian in outlook and all are written in Latin. The background for all three sources thus has a partially Roman tincture through Latin and Christianity. The individual authors also have a degree of Roman connection. Patrick, as details in his own writings make clear, came from an ostensibly Romanized background, the son a decurion and a deacon, and was strongly motivated by Roman Christianity. Gildas in some ways had a personal outlook and sympathy culturally more Roman than British, so much so that later medieval writers thought it necessary to invent an explanation for his presumed anti-British attitudes.[13] He too was strongly Christian. The authorship of the *Historia Brittonum* is disputed, but at least one manuscript tradition identifies "Nennius" as the disciple of Elvodug (Elfoddw), a British churchman partly responsible for reconciling the British "Celtic" church with the Roman Christian order.[14] Given this background to the sources, a historian interested in interpreting their content might expect and be prepared to adjust for a pro-Roman bias. It is all the more surprising, therefore, to encounter a negative picture of British loyalties to Rome.

SAINT PATRICK

Patrick describes himself in his *Confessio* and *Epistola* as the son of Calpornius—a deacon and sometime decurion, a slaveholder owning an estate (*villula*) near the *vicus* Bannavem Taberniae. Patrick's grandfather was Potitus, a presbyter.[15] This autobiographical introduction with its Latin names, Christian offices, *vicus*, and estate certainly suggests a thoroughly Romanized background. Patrick's dates are uncertain. Basically there are two alternative chronologies—his birth may be placed late in the fourth century with a career extending into the mid-fifth, or his life may

---

13 A. O. Anderson, "Gildas and Arthur," 154. Anderson quotes Giraldus Cambrensis: "And of Gildas, who inveighs so bitterly against his own nation, the Welsh say that he wrote . . . in offence because of the death of his brother."
14 Nennius, *British History and Welsh Annals,* preface. In 768 Elfoddw changed the date of Easter in the British church to bring its practice in line with Rome's. See Ifor Williams, "Notes on Nennius," 380–81.
15 *Conf.* 1: "Ego Patricius . . . patrem habui Calpornium diaconum, filium quondam Potiti presbyteri, qui fuit vico Bannavem Taberniae; villulam enim prope habuit, ubi ego capturam dedi." *Epistola* 10: "Ingenuus fui secundum carnem, decorione patre nascor." For an introduction to the texts of St. Patrick's writings see Hood in Saint Patrick, *Writings and Muirchu's Life,* 17–22. Quotations used in my text are from Hood's translation. See also Bieler for the best critical edition with notes. Saint Patrick, "Libri epistolarum." I have had access to the "C" text (London, British Museum, Cotton Nero E. 1), c. A.D. 1000. A facsimile edition of the oldest text (Armagh) of the Patrician documents, including Muirchu's Life, can be studied in Gwynn, *Book of Armagh.* I have used only those writings generally accepted as genuinely Patrick's: the *Confessio,* the *Epistola,* and the *Dicta.*

be confined within the fifth century with a career ending possibly as late as 493.[16] Patrick's own experiences, plus the memories of his parents' generation, cover a critical period spanning the Indian summer of later Roman Britain and the subsequent insecurity of the barbarian invasions. As a teenager, Patrick fell victim to an Irish raid and was twice in his lifetime made a captive. Personal experiences and the style and intent of his writings create a vivid impression of the period. In many ways he is the most revealing figure of the fifth-century British church, and as R. P. C. Hanson remarks, "One could almost go further than this and say that Patrick is the first British personality in history whom historians can know. . . ."[17]

Given his Romanized environment, Patrick's attitudes to Rome as evidenced by the *Confessio* and *Epistola* are disappointing to the historian interested in secular events and institutions. He never refers to Rome or the Romans outside an ecclesiastical context. The first mention of Romans comes in the *Epistola*: "With my own hand I have written and composed these words to be given, delivered, and sent to the soldiers of Coroticus—I do not say to my fellow-citizens [*civibus meis*] nor to fellow-citizens of the Holy Romans [*civibus sanctorum Romanorum*], but to fellow-citizens of the demons, because of their evil actions. Like the enemy they live in death, as allies of Irish and of Picts and apostates."[18] Patrick writes to condemn the abduction of some of his Irish converts by the soldiers of Coroticus, a British warlord. Most striking in this passage is the implied distinction between fellow citizens (meaning Britons) and fellow citizens of the Holy Romans (meaning, most probably, Christians). To equate "fellow citizens" in the first instance with "Romans," as many scholars have done, destroys the sense of the distinction between Patrick's two groups (fellow citizens/fellow citizens of the Holy Romans) and

---

[16] On Saint Patrick's dates see R. P. C. Hanson, *Saint Patrick*, 171–188; R. P. C. Hanson, "The Date of St. Patrick"; Morris, "Dates of the Celtic Saints," especially 369–72. For a critique of Hanson see P. A. Wilson, "St. Patrick." For recent discussions of the question of chronology see Charles Thomas, *Christianity in Roman Britain*, 314–27; E. A. Thompson, *Who Was Saint Patrick?* 166–75. The latest fashion in this matter is to take the later date, but there is no orthodoxy and no decisive argument. A number of chronological studies are presented in Dumville et al., *Saint Patrick*. Relying on linguistic clues, John Koch has suggested an even earlier period for Patrick's activity. See Widmer, "Dating Saint Patrick." Koch suggests c. 350 to 430 A.D. for Patrick's dates. In terms of the arguments advanced in this chapter, the earlier Patrick's dates, the more rapid appears the failure of *Romanitas* in the western regions of Britain associated with him.

[17] R. P. C. Hanson, *Saint Patrick*, 200. See also John Morris's comments in Saint Patrick, *Writings and Muirchu's Life*, 16.

[18] *Ep.* 2: "Manu mea scripsi atque condidi verba ista danda et tradenda militibus mittenda Corotici—non dico civibus meis neque civibus sanctorum Romanorum sed civibus daemoniorum, ob mala opera ipsorum. Ritu hostili in morte vivunt, socii Scottorum atque Pictorum apostatarumque."

makes the passage unnecessarily repetitive and unclear.[19] What would be
the point of distinguishing between fellow Romans and fellow Holy Romans in a Christian Roman empire? The implied sting in Patrick's rebuke
has been traditionally taken to mean that Coroticus must have regarded
himself as a Roman.[20] I disagree. The implied sting is that Coroticus
considered himself to be a good Briton. Patrick suggests that no self-
respecting Briton would consort with Picts and Scots, his people's traditional enemies. The second, parallel rebuke in Patrick's letter links the
idea of Holy Romans (Christians) with apostates, mortal enemies of the
church. Patrick speaks in another passage of "our nationality" in a context
where he seems to mean Britons.[21] If the Coroticus addressed by Patrick is
the contemporary ruler of Dumbarton of that name, then Patrick's letter is
a very early example of an important Brittonic tendency—the inclusion of
Britons north of the late Roman frontier and outside the bounds of the late
empire with their fellows within the Roman diocese to form a common
group.[22] In contrast, it is difficult on any reckoning to see how Coroticus
and his soldiers could meaningfully be described as Romans.[23] The reference to Roman citizens in this passage is clearly an allusion not to the
empire but to the fellowship of the Christian Church, for Patrick calls
them "Holy Romans" and contrasts them with the fellow citizens of the
demons. The context for non-British "Roman" citizens thus seems to be
religious rather than secular. This conclusion is reinforced by another
passage which refers to Gaul: "Here is the custom of the Roman
Christians in Gaul; they send suitable holy men to the Franks and other

---

[19] The following authors interpret Patrick's "fellow citizens" to mean Romans: Wood, "End
of Roman Britain," 22; R. P. C. Hanson, *Life and Writings,* 59–61; Smyth, *Warlords and Holy
Men,* 16–18; E. A. Thompson, *Who Was Saint Patrick?* 130–33.
[20] E. A. Thompson, *Who Was Saint Patrick?* 130, follows J. B. Bury and H. M. Chadwick.
[21] *Conf.* 42: "Et de genere nostro qui ibi nati sunt nescimus numerum eorum." Thompson
translates this as "of those who were born there [in Ireland] of our nationality we do not know
their number" (*Who Was Saint Patrick?* 110). R. P. C. Hanson translates, with a similar sense,
"and I cannot reckon the number from those of our race who have been born there [in Ireland]"
(*Life and Writings,* 110–11). To translate Patrick's meaning as "of Christians" or "of Romans"
seems forced. Hood, for example, gives "and we do not know the numbers of our family of
faith who have been reborn there" Saint Patrick, *Writings and Muirchu's Life,* 50. For a
discussion see E. A. Thompson, *Who Was Saint Patrick?* 110 n. 8.
[22] The identification is not certain. There is another Coroticus in Cardigan, and E. A.
Thompson recently suggested that Patrick's opponent was a British warlord resident in Ireland. If so, the implication of including within the category of "fellow citizens" British groups
outside the old bounds of the empire is still significant. E. A. Thompson, "St. Patrick and
Coroticus," 15–17; E. A. Thompson, *Who Was Saint Patrick?* 126–37; Tolstoy, "Who Was
Coroticus?" M. Miller points out the common view among Welsh, Irish, and Scottish sources
that Brittonic territory reached to the Forth-Clyde line ("Bede's Use of Gildas," 244 n. 1).
[23] J. B. Bury made a spirited attempt (*Life of Saint Patrick,* 191). But see Charles Thomas,
"Saint Patrick and Fifth Century Britain," 80. Cf. Smyth, *Warlords and Holy Men,* 16–18.

peoples . . . to ransom baptized captives."[24] To Patrick, the Gauls are not fellow political citizens of the Roman empire, but fellow Christians dwelling in Gaul, in contrast to the pagan Franks who live in the same region. The other reference to Gaul in the *Confessio* is similar. Gaul is not described as a province of the empire, as such, but the home of Christian brethren and holy men: "I would have been only too glad to do so, to see my homeland and my family; and not only that, but to go on to Gaul to visit the brethren and to see the face of my Lord's holy men. . . ."[25] "My brethren" is also used to address fellow Christians in Britain and Ireland.[26] Patrick thus defines himself as a Briton and also a Christian, but significantly, not as a citizen of the Roman empire. This seems a subtle confirmation of the implications already discussed in the passages from Zosimus and Procopius—the Britons had successfully rebelled and separated themselves from the Roman empire.

Patrick's fundamental world-view is a simple dichotomy—inside and outside, those within the Christian communion and the rest of the world. Of the peoples active in his sphere, he gives only a few details which seem to emphasize his spiritual as opposed to secular outlook. The Irish (*Scotti*) are barbarians, foreigners dwelling at the ends of the earth, until they convert to Christianity, whereupon they become, in Patrick's eyes, his children and Christian brethren.[27] Indeed, if the *Dicta* are contemporaneous with Patrick, the barbarian Irish become "Roman" at their conversion.[28] The people of Gaul, as has already been mentioned, are *Gallia fratres* or *Romani Galli Christiani*. The Franks and the Scots are pagans. The Picts seem particularly odious to Patrick.[29] He seems to use "Roman" in a wholly spiritual sense, as a synonym for Christian. There is no hint of the imperium in his writing. Patrick seems oblivious to the instrument of Roman government and the empire plays no providential role. His usage seems peculiar and anticipates later developments in several ways. Patrick's inclusion of a barbarian people outside the empire (the Irish) within the rubric of Christian-Roman labels would most probably

[24] *Ep.* 14. The "P" text (Paris B. N. lat. 17626) omits *Christianorum*. See Bieler's note in Saint Patrick, "Libri epistolarum" (1951), 203. See also 92, 211. Bieler points out that *Romanorum* alone can denote "Roman Christians."

[25] *Conf.* 43: "Unde autem etsi voluero amittere illas et ut pergens in Brittanniis—et libentissime paratus eram quasi ad patriam et parentes; non id solum sed etiam usque ad Gallias visitare fratres et ut viderem faciem sactorum Domini mei. . . ."

[26] *Conf.* 41, Cf. *Ep.* 16: where "fratres" is also used with Irish converts.

[27] For "the ends of the earth," see *Conf.* 1.

[28] *Dicta* 3: "Aeclessia Scotorum immo Romanorum; ut Christiani ita ut Romani sitis ut decantetur vobiscum oportet omni hora orationis vox illa laudabilis Curie lession, Christe lession." Cf. Saint Patrick, "Libri, epistolarum," 211. Bieler suggests that *Romani* may mean either citizens of the empire or citizens of the city of Rome.

[29] On the Picts see Grosjean, "Les Pictes apostats."

have shocked Augustine and represents an eccentric and precocious vision in the fifth century.[30] Patrick's simple equation of Roman with Christian, although it would scarcely require comment in the intellectual framework of the eighth century, or perhaps even the later sixth century, is striking in the fifth. Augustine, Orosius, Salvian, and Sidonius, Patrick's contemporaries, could scarcely define themselves or their church without reference to the empire. The Roman state was psychologically integral even to the vision of its critics, yet it finds no place in Patrick's thought world.[31]

The secular political world surfaces in Patrick's writings only when it intrudes in a gross way on his mission of conversion. The incident with Coroticus and his warband has already been mentioned. Coroticus refused to follow the instruction of the church (in the form of Patrick's messenger), and his sin is the same as Patrick's sin in his youth—refusal to obey the priests.[32] Coroticus will suffer accordingly, with punishment in the future life and exile (through excommunication) in the present one, just as Patrick was made captive and exiled for his sins. Coroticus and his soldiers will thus become part of the "outside." It is interesting to note that in Patrick's mind God's punishments are personal and directed at the individual sinner. There is no hint of punishment for entire kingdoms or peoples such as is found later in Gildas. This perception further emphasizes Patrick's lack of concern with the secular order. A few other examples of secular contacts are found in the Confessio, such as payment of protection money or bribes to "judges" in Ireland, and Patrick's often dangerous interaction with local kings or princes in the pursuit of his mission.[33]

Patrick mentions his British homeland (patria) with evident affection in several passages. He also seems to have retained a strong fondness for his family and kinsfolk. His primary loyalty, however, is to the Christian church, especially his new Irish converts whom he calls his children.[34] The only other examples of loyalty or allegiance in Patrick's autobiographical writings are personal and negative. He refuses in the rather bizarre ceremony of sucking the nipples of the ship's crew to commit to a secular loyalty oath even in order to escape from slavery.[35] The other

30 Peter Brown, Augustine, 26. But see now Charles-Edwards, "Palladius, Prosper, and Leo."
31 Ullmann, "Use of the Term." Bieler has an interesting discussion of Patrick's use of the synonyms gens, natio, plebs, and populus ("Libri epistolarum" [1951], 92, 203–11).
32 Ep. 6.
33 Conf. 35, 52, 53.
34 For homeland and family, see Conf. 17, 23, 27, 36, 43; Ep. 1, 10, 11. Patrick thrice uses the phrase "country and kinsfolk," which alliterates in both Latin and English (Ep. 1; Conf. 36, 43). See R. P. C. Hanson, Life and Writings, 59.
35 Conf. 18.

example is the keen disappointment Patrick feels at the betrayal of a confidence (a confession of boyhood sins) to his ecclesiastical enemies by a close friend.[36] Patrick's work contains no favorable examples of secular loyalty and even in a Christian context shows only slight signs of possible ties to the monastic communities of Gaul, and none to the Pope or to the City of Rome. Patrick's personal horizon does not seem to extend beyond Britain and Ireland and perhaps Gaul. Rome appears only as an abstraction connected with the Christian church of his immediate experience.

The only specifically Roman civil or military office Patrick mentions is decurion, a local office of councillor in the Roman municipal system. In the later empire this office was unpopular due to certain incumbent duties such as tax collection, for which decurions were personally responsible and liable. The office was hereditary. Patrick writes, "I was free-born according to the flesh; my father was a decurion. I sold my good birth (not that I am ashamed or regret it) in the interest of others. In short, I am a slave in Christ to a foreign people. . . ."[37] Even this passage shows Patrick's concentration on the spiritual and his rejection of the secular, for he is here contrasting his own actions with those of Coroticus. He balances the surrender of his privilege and birthright against the greed of Coroticus, who instead of sacrificing for his fellow (Irish) Christians sacrifices them to the pagan Scottish or Pictish slave dealers.

It has been suggested that Patrick's father became a deacon to avoid the duties incumbent on decurions, but still managed to retain his property (deacons were exempt from civic duties but were also supposed to divest themselves of personal property). If so, it might be possible to see in the father's supposed civic irresponsibility or fraud the seeds of the son's rejection of the secular. The father's actions might also be a rejection of the Roman order and values, a specifically British example of the civic failure characteristic of the Roman west. The conjunction of decurion and deacon in Patrick's father and the continued possession of a slave-farmed estate has been urged as evidence that the Christianity of Patrick's home was a sham to acquire civil immunities.[38] This in turn might explain Patrick's early lack of deep Christian piety or faith. The above argument rests on a series of questionable assumptions. Decurions probably were not a universally demoralized class unwilling to perform their civic duties.[39] More important, it is nowhere stated in Patrick's writings that his father was

---

[36] *Conf.* 32.
[37] *Ep.* 10. See above for the Latin text. E. A. Thompson, *Who Was Saint Patrick?* stresses Patrick's class and its associated values. See my review.
[38] R. P. C. Hanson, *Saint Patrick*, 176–78.
[39] Garnsey, "Aspects of the Decline." Garnsey's study, however, does not extend beyond the Severan period.

simultaneously deacon and decurion. This is modern conjecture only, and in fact the passages concerning deacon and decurion are segregated in Patrick's works. Patrick's grandfather was a presbyter, and we could as easily conclude that he relinquished his property and his obligations to his son before taking church office, and that Patrick's father did likewise. Alternatively, Roman law may not have run in Britain at this time; Gildas claims that Roman law and custom had ceased in Britain at the time of Maximus.[40] Finally, in the confused conditions of the late fourth or early fifth century "decurion" might imply no more than a form of address or an honorary title. In this period inference of the full substance of an institution or office from a mere title is notoriously chancy. Attribution of Patrick's early lack of genuine or deep Christian faith to crass motives in his father's religious conduct is in fact unnecessary. Historians too often fail to take into account the vagaries of religious faith within families. Augustine's case was not unique. The son need not be like the father, nor must faith stretch unbroken through the generations. Patrick nowhere intimates that his family's faith was otherwise than genuine. The significance of church office as a tradition in Patrick's family is perhaps more Gibbonesque—it may reflect the disturbed conditions of the times, in which a spiritual order might well supplant the secular in the hierarchy of men's thoughts, thereby undermining loyalty to political Rome.

Patrick's lack of early zeal for Christianity raises an important caution—the danger of attributing a variety of aspects of Roman culture to individuals or localities because a single or different element of Roman influence is present. Despite the external trappings of Patrick's evidently Romanized background, he wrote and probably spoke Latin with difficulty, as a foreign language.[41] It seems clear from passages in his writings that Patrick was at odds with what appear to be the most Romanized and cultured elements of the Britons with whom he has contact, the learned rhetoricians.[42] Patrick perceived these men to be against his mission, against the Irish, hostile to the poor, and especially disdainful of the uneducated. The tone of Patrick's remarks is very similar to that in certain writings of Martin and may reflect the tension between the new monastic and the long established aristocratic leadership within the church.[43] Patrick's attitude toward wealth certainly echoes attitudes

---

[40] Gildas D.e. 13.1.
[41] R. P. C. Hanson, Saint Patrick, 118–19; Mohrmann, Latin of Saint Patrick, 33. For another view, see O'Rahilly, Two Patricks, 33. In Conf. 9, Patrick seems to refer to Latin as a foreign language. E. A. Thompson, however, thinks Patrick was a native Latin speaker (Who Was Saint Patrick? 40–41).
[42] Grosjean, "Dominicati Rhetorici"; Conf. 11, 13.
[43] It is interesting to note that the Book of Armagh containing Patrick's writings includes also a Vita of Saint Martin.

found in continental writings and Pelagian works of the same period frequently attributed to Britons. These may, in fact, represent social, economic, and perhaps even class tensions in the society of the day. Certainly the early missions to the barbarians and the spread of Christianity from the cities into the countryside were simultaneous. They were associated with the ascetic monasticism of Saint Martin and his followers, in stark contrast to the position of the church under the leadership of wealthy and worldly bishops such as Sidonius Apollinarius. Finally, Patrick's writings show signs of a millennial outlook. He associates his ministry to the Irish (who live on the edge of the world) with the prophecy and latter days described in Scripture. He several times refers to the evidently imminent end of this world.[44] A sidelight to this outlook may also be present in the tone of his address to Coroticus, which perhaps reflects the antimilitary attitudes prevalent in some circles of the western Christian church at this time.[45]

The picture of Patrick's loyalties and his attitudes to Rome, revealed by an examination of his writings, hardly justifies the view that he was consciously and enthusiastically pro-Roman in his outlook.[46] Despite his family background, his Romanization seems thin on close scrutiny, even if allowance is made for his abduction during adolescence, for it lacked in his youth both well-developed Latin and Christianity, two of the most important hallmarks of Roman civilization. Ultimately his religious conversion is the product of the jolting experience of captivity and slavery, not the outgrowth of a boyhood spent on a decurion's estate with a Christian family. Patrick's loyalties are supremely placed at last in the church, with special affection reserved for his family and his native country. There is no hint of a secular allegiance to Rome or any other political order. Finally, in the insecurity and helplessness that grew out of Patrick's captivity and continued even during his ministry, and still more in the eschatological attitudes he expresses, we see the echoes of profound anxiety. R. P. C. Hanson points out the lack of any Christian historical vision in Patrick's writings and suggests that he shared with many fifth-century Christians a notion that "civilization, the very fabric of society, and the course of history itself were about to collapse."[47] Patrick reminds his audience that the contemporary, political world, including Coroticus and his warband,

---

[44] *Ep.* 5, 19.
[45] *Ep.* 9.
[46] Hanson feels Patrick obviously fostered and valued his Roman citizenship. I find no evidence of this. Hanson writes that "by the fourth century the Celtic peoples under Roman rule felt no sense of oppression or yearning to be free. On the contrary, they appear to have wanted romanization." R. P. C. Hanson, *Saint Patrick,* 185–86.
[47] Ibid., 201.

is "a miserable temporal kingdom which will in any case pass away in a moment." Wicked kings will count for nothing when Christ and the righteous "judge the nations." Patrick seems to represent not Romanized values and pro-Roman imperial traditions, but the negation of secular Rome that is symptomatic of its decline. He symbolizes the failure of the Roman political order and the fragility of its accomplishments in Britain. This Romano-Briton's attitudes are a world apart from *Roma Aeterna* and the glory of empire.[48]

It is almost impossible to generalize on the basis of attitudes expressed by Patrick. He is an isolated figure, the only surviving voice from mid-fifth century Britain.[49] His missionary activity was unconventional. Charles Thomas calls it "markedly un-Roman."[50] Is Patrick unique or does he mirror in some important ways the general qualities and attitudes of his "fellow citizens" the Britons and of the British church which sponsored him? We know he had enemies and critics within that church, but he must also have had significant support.[51] Although the corpus of his work is small, its retrospective, eschatological nature reveals much about Patrick's loyalties and self-definitions.[52] Overall, two salient features stand out from Patrick's writing. His silence regarding the secular Roman order may denote at least a noteworthy indifference. When paired with a second aspect—Patrick's definition of "fellow citizens" in political terms as Britons rather than Romans—this silence takes on a particular significance. In the introduction to this discussion I suggested that in a meaningful sense Roman Britain ended when the Britons ceased to consider themselves to be Romans. Patrick's work may indicate that in some British quarters, already in the fifth century and perhaps even very soon after the events of 410, *Romanitas* politically and secularly understood may have been quickly fading. This notion is in keeping with an apparently rapid retribalization of the political order in Britain, creating warlords and native kings. The suggested distinction between Britons and Romans, and its historical significance, rest on somewhat delicate inferences regarding Patrick's works. These find an interesting confirmation and development in the writing of Gildas.

---

48 *Ep.* 19. See Paschoud, *Roma aeterna*.
49 E. A. Thompson, *Who Was Saint Patrick?* 153–57.
50 Charles Thomas, *Celtic Britain*, 124. Charles-Edwards points out the interest of Prosper and Leo the Great in the spread of the church among barbarian people beyond the widest bounds of the empire. Prosper and Leo, however, keep one eye on Rome the city or Rome the empire and this comparative aspect is missing in Patrick's work. ("Palladius, Prosper, and Leo the Great: Mission and Primatial Authority").
51 *Ep.* 1.
52 I think it is significant that, despite Patrick's eschatological concerns, he nowhere explicitly mentions the sack of Rome or any of the cataclysmic misfortunes of the empire.

GILDAS

De excidio Britanniae, "The Ruin of Britain," was written sometime between roughly 490 and 540 A.D. by a British churchman living probably
somewhere in western Britain.[53] The bulk of the work is a critical ha-
rangue rebuking certain secular rulers and elements of the British church.
The main hortatory section is preceded by a short historical sketch (Chapters 1 through 26) which presents historical lessons and attempts to explain how the flawed state of Gildas's present world came to be. The
purpose of Gildas in writing the *De excidio* has been the subject of much
discussion. To my mind, the historical section is purely secondary and
dependent on the main purpose, a theological and moral message on the
lines of Jeremiah's denunciations and warnings in the Old Testament.[54]
Gildas, like Salvian, believes that sinful peoples and sinful rulers are punished in the present by God through the agency of earthly calamity. The
sins and consequent afflictions of the Israelites furnish Gildas with a
model. History merely illustrates the truths of theology.

There are few geographical clues within the *De excidio*. Gildas seems
to interpret events from a broadly western British viewpoint, but his horizon in the historical section is probably best judged as including all Britain: it is not restricted to any particular region. Gildas's concept of *patria*
involves more than the orthodox Roman idea of one's native province and
includes the entire Roman diocese and even beyond. In the *De excidio*,
patria, *Britannia*, and *insula* seem essentially interchangeable.[55] This

[53] The oldest extant manuscript of Gildas's *De excidio* is British Museum, Cotton Vitellius A.
vi, a tenth-century work. The first seven chapters were destroyed by fire in 1731, but the text
had been printed in 1528 and 1568 and the early chapters have been restored from these copies.
The critical edition is Gildas, *De excidio*, edited by Mommsen. For background to Gildas see
Gransden, *Historical Writing*, 1–12; Winterbottom in Gildas, *Ruin of Britain*, 1–12. Translation and textual citations in the notes will be from Winterbottom's edition unless otherwise
stated. Another version of Gildas with text, translation, and notes may be studied in *Gildas*,
ed. and trans. Hugh Williams.
[54] Against this view see M. Miller, "Starting to Write History." For a recent discussion see
Brooks, "Gildas' *De Excidio*." Brooks suggests that both the historical section and the homi-
lies in *De excidio* directed to contemporary British rulers served the same purpose. They
provided an agenda for social reform and a "revolutionary" blueprint for kingship. In this
context it is interesting to recall John Morris's suggestion concerning Pelagian literature and
events in Britain in 410 ("Pelagian Literature," 34). Both denunciation and suggested social or
moral reform are inseparable parts of the Old Testament prophetic model. To my mind,
Gildas's vision is rooted in this tradition. Jeremiah served as his particular model and is the
source of Gildas's vision of himself as dangerous social and political critic. He expected some
kind of backlash from his remarks concerning contemporary politics (*D.e.* 37.2). See Dumville, "Chronology," 80. In some ways Salvian seems a good parallel. Gildas's identification
with Jeremiah was filtered and probably reinforced by the work of Jerome (*Prolegomena in
Jeremiam*) and Rufinus. See Bolton, *History of Anglo-Latin Literature*, 33.
[55] Myres refers to Gildas's western perspective as a "Highland Zone Mentality" (*English*

geographical perspective is reminiscent of Patrick's, whose idea of "fellow citizens" was evidently conceived to include all Britons independently of reference to the old imperial frontier or the historical geography of the late empire. The use of *cives* by Gildas and Patrick, in fact, seems similar in a number of ways. It is tempting to view both Patrick and Gildas, with an eye to Roman and Byzantine perceptions of a permanent break between Britain and Rome in roughly 410, as expressing a nascent, precocious British sense of nationality.[56] Gildas, like Patrick, defies precise location. Details in later medieval lives of Gildas, and they are of questionable accuracy, make him a northerner, perhaps from Clyde. He may have acquired his education in South Wales and it is to the rulers of southwestern and western Britain that he addresses his admonitory work. Later traditions link Gildas with both Ireland and Brittany.[57]

Gildas "Sapiens" enjoyed great learned repute in the Middle Ages, but he subsequently came to be seen as an isolated, obscure, and peculiar Latin stylist. Recent revisionist literary and linguistic studies have upgraded his image and reputation among modern scholars, who have begun to locate Gildas, and perhaps his audience, firmly within a context of late classical education. His language, political vocabulary, imagery, rhetorical devices, and prose style seem identifiably late Roman and may be compared to the writing of Sidonius, Cassiodorus, or Caelius Sedulius.[58]

Settlements, 12). For the idea that Gildas saw Britain as a whole see Wright, "Gildas's Geographical Perspective." This is the same conclusion reached by Sims-Williams, "Gildas and the Anglo-Saxons," 5–15. In contrast, E. A. Thompson has argued that Gildas lived and wrote in the north with a historical horizon limited to that area ("Gildas and the History of Britain," 214–26). M. Miller suggests that Gildas presented a historical narrative first for northern events and then, in a discrete section, one for the south. M. Miller, "Bede's Use of Gildas"; M. Miller, "Stilicho's Pictish War." Dumville thinks it impossible to define the area of Britain that Gildas was writing about, but favors the northwest of England ("Chronology," 78–79).

[56] See Charles-Edwards, review of *Gildas*, 120. The similarity of the two men's views might be explained in several ways. If the later chronology for Patrick (death c. 492) and the earlier chronology for Gildas (writing c. 500) are accepted, then the two men were contemporaries. Moreover, both may have been from the frontier region of northern Britain in the area between Clyde and Carlisle. In that case the similar attitude would be unsurprising. Alternatively, if both men were only vaguely "western" and the earlier chronology for Patrick (death c. 461) and the later chronology for Gildas (writing c. 540) are accepted, then the similarity in their outlook must reflect a common British intellectual tradition transmitted over time.

[57] There are two later *Vitae* for Gildas, one from the eleventh century and one from the twelfth century. See *Vita sancti Gildae*, ed. Mommsen. Kenneth H. Jackson has argued that the spelling in *Arecluta regione oriundus*, a phrase in the earliest *Life*, suggests a sixth-century contemporary source for this information (*Language and History*, 42).

[58] Some of the earlier studies of Gildas's prose suggest similar conclusions. See Bolton, *History of Anglo-Latin Literature*, 27–37; Kerlouégan, "Le Latin du *De excidio*"; Winterbottom in Gildas, *Ruin of Britain*, 5–11. Linguistic and literary studies are collected in Lapidge and Dumville, eds., *Gildas: New Approaches*. These include Wright, "Gildas's Prose Style"; Orlandi, "*Clausulae* in Gildas"; Sutherland, "Imagery of Gildas." See the reviews by E. James,

These various traits imply a great deal concerning the nature of Gildas's education, which seems to resemble in important ways the secular and classical education of the fifth century, traditionally designed to prepare students for imperial careers and office.[59]

Gildas's attitudes to *Romanitas* and the empire are complex, seemingly even paradoxical. On the one hand rest his latinity and classical education together with his civilian and highly Christian perspective. On the other hand, despite these Roman cultural trappings, Gildas perceived himself and his countrymen to be Britons, distinct from the foreign Romans. This is paradoxical because the very process of late classical education supposedly created a uniformity of cultural environment, a linguistic and literary identity that united the upper classes in a sense of solidarity that precluded separatist regionalistic or nationalistic feeling. As Chester Starr observes, successful Romanization created "true identification with Rome and the Romans so that a provincial did not think consciously or unconsciously of 'we' and 'you.'"[60] But the distinction between Britons and Romans permeates Gildas's historical vision. It is compounded by a perception of antagonism that, for Gildas, characterized the entire Roman period in Britain from its inception and the revolt of Boudicca to its conclusion with the revolt of the Magnus Maximus. In fact, the distinction between Britons and Romans lies at the heart of the most original aspect of Gildas's work—his startling departure from the traditions of Latin Christian historiography. In the historical section of the *De excidio* Gildas breaks from contemporary conventional historical genres of universal chronicles, church histories, imperial biography, and secular compendia of imperial history to write the particular history of Britannia and the Britons. There is no known earlier western parallel for the history of a Roman province or a former Roman provincial people. In significant ways the *De excidio* anticipates later histories of the Goths, Franks, and Anglo-Saxons. E. A. Thompson rightly emphasizes the originality of Gildas's historical conception. "In the history of British historiography he was the greatest innovator of all. He invented it! . . . He was the first man in the entire West to write a provincial history." The decision to break with traditional historical models must have been a conscious rhetorical innovation, for Gildas was evidently familiar with Rufinus of Aquileia's Latin version of Eusebius's *Ecclesiastical History* and quite possibly also knew

"Interpreting Gildas," and Charles-Edwards. The fullest treatment is by Kerlouégan, *Les destinées de la culture latine.*
59 Lapidge, "Gildas's Education."
60 A. H. M. Jones, *Later Roman Empire,* 2:1021–24. Starr, *Roman Empire,* 96.

portions of Orosius's *History against the Pagans*. In the context of attitudes and loyalties, the remarkable innovation represented by the creation and dissemination of a history of their own for the Britons and Britannia is obviously tremendously significant.[61]

Gildas's attitude toward the Britons is also complex. To the idea of historical antagonism and the distinction between Romans and Britons he adds a harshly critical judgment of his fellows. As he explains in the preface to the *De excidio*, Gildas did not regard his own attitudes toward his countrymen as hostile. The powerful criticism and exhortation to reform were sympathetic and kindly intended to forestall God's terrible wrath from striking the current generation of Britons.[62] This attitude very possibly arises from his understanding of the Old Testament, particularly the book of Jeremiah. One of the chief parallels Gildas draws between Jeremiah and his own British past involves the idea that unjustified rebellion is punished by God with calamity.[63] The terrible effects of the Saxon revolt and the arrogant pride of the tyrant and his council mark the penultimate consequence of the repeated and unjustified rebellions of the Britons against Rome. In his adaptation of Jeremiah, Gildas substitutes the Britons and Romans for the Jews and Chaldeans. Because he wrote during a period of relative prosperity, his jeremiad could cite no contemporary disaster analogous to the Babylonian captivity of the Jews, but Gildas did his best to paint a picture of capture and exile for the Britons in the preceding period. He returns to an admonitory and prophetic posture in the later sections when addressing the contemporary secular and ecclesiastical leaders of Britain. Thus an Old Testament paradigm provided Gildas with a motive for his harshly critical attitude toward his fellow Britons and his comparatively indulgent treatment of the Roman occupation. Significantly, the incidental, circumstantial insight he provides into the darker side of the Roman occupation of Britain emerges despite, not because of, his rhetorical purpose and model. This makes his characterization of the nature of Roman rule all the more valuable and significant. It must reflect general British attitudes and traditions, not Gildas's personal rhetorical agenda.

These mixed attitudes regarding Rome and the Britons are clearly expressed in Chapters 5 through 7 and 13 through 18 of the *De excidio*. For example, Rome gives to the Britons the priceless gift of universal peace and a flame of civilization that all the seas surrounding Britain cannot

---

[61] E. A. Thompson, "Gildas and the History of Britain," 208. On Gildas's use of Rufinus and Orosius see Wright, "Did Gildas Read Orosius?"; Wright, "Gildas's Prose Style." E. A. Thompson rejects the idea that Gildas read Rufinus or Orosius ("Gildas and the History of Britain," 210). Cf. Mommsen, *MGH AA* 13:7.
[62] Winterbottom, "Preface to Gildas"; O'Sullivan, *De Excidio*, 23–32.
[63] See T. H. Robinson, *Prophecy and Prophets*, 120–142.

quench.[64] These gifts pave the way for the introduction of Christianity into Britain. In these passages Gildas allots a providential role to the empire's expansion into Britain. The Britons, however, are too proud, stupid, and untrustworthy to accept Rome's blessings, and the relationship between Britain and Rome centers on mutual inconstancy—the Britons are inconstant in their loyalty and allegiance, reverting periodically to treason and rebellion, and the Roman occupation is intermittent. In Gildas's narrative they arrive and decamp several times. The interaction between these two inconstancies promotes instability, which in turn engenders a harsh Roman subjugation of the Britons. Gildas succinctly describes Britain's history under Roman rule—"obstinacy, subjection, rebellion, her second subjection, and harsh servitude."[65] Gildas places the blame for conflict between the Romans and the Britons mostly on the shoulders of his countrymen. He introduces the Britons into his historical preface and sounds the note of his Old Testament theme in the following manner: "Ever since it was first inhabited, Britain has been ungratefully rebelling, stiff-necked and haughty, now against God, now against its own countrymen, sometimes even against kings from abroad and their subjects."[66]

Offered universal peace by the Romans, the Britons reply with feigned submission and later treachery. Rome provided a rule of law, but for the Britons the "obedience to the edicts of Rome was superficial: their resentment they kept repressed, deep in their hearts."[67] Finally, the Britons were too cowardly and inefficient to take advantage of Roman military aid and create security against barbarian invasion.[68] When victory over the invaders is finally achieved, the lion's share of the credit goes to Ambrosius Aurelianus, "a gentleman," almost the last of the Romans, a man whose family "had worn the purple."[69] Gildas thus perceives the Britons' con-

---

[64] *D.e.* 5: "Potioris famae viribus firmassent, non acies flammae quodammodo rigidi tenoris ad occidentem caeruleo oceani torrente potuit vel cohiberi vel extingui." See Hanning, *Vision of History,* 57ff.

[65] *D.e.* 2: "De subiectione, de rebellione, item de subiectione ac diro famulatu. . . . "

[66] *D.e.* 4: "Haec erecta cervice et mente, ex quo inhabitata est, nunc deo, interdum civibus, nonnumquam etiam transmarinis regibus et subiectis ingrata consurgit."

[67] *D.e.* 5.2: "Sed transfretans insulae parendi leges nullo obsistente advexit, imbellemque populum sed infidelem non tam ferro igne machinis . . . in superficie tantum vultus presso in altum cordis dolore sui oboedientiam proferentem edictis subiugavit." (Crossing the strait, and meeting no resistance, it brought the laws of obedience to the island. The people, unwarlike but untrustworthy, were not subdued, like other races, by the sword, fire, and engines of war, so much as by mere threats and legal penalties. Their obedience to the edicts of Rome was superficial: their resentment they kept repressed, deep in their hearts.)

[68] See *D.e.* 15, 17.

[69] *D.e.* 25.2–3: "Ne ad internicionem usque delerentur, duce Ambrosio Aureliano viro modesto, qui solus forte Romanae gentis tantae tempestatis collisione occisis in eadem parentibus purpura." (Their leader was Ambrosius Aurelianus, a gentleman who, perhaps alone among

duct as Roman provincials in an almost wholly negative light. It is difficult to know whether his position arose from inherited tradition, conviction, ignorance, or as a rhetorical device to pave the way more persuasively for a denunciation of his own contemporary political scene. Ignorance seems to have played an important part.

Few classical sources other than the Bible have been identified in his writings.[70] Lamenting his lack of historical information, Gildas explains that in attempting to write his historical sketch, "I shall do this as well as I can, using not so much literary remains from this country (which, such as they were, are not now available, having been burnt by enemies or removed by our countrymen when they went into exile) as foreign tradition: and that has frequent gaps to blur it."[71] Gildas uses a Latin tag to summarize what little he describes of Britain's pre-Christian past, calling the pagan era "long past years."[72] He mistakenly attributes a statement to Porphyry that suggests Britain's political misbehavior was notorious even in distant places: "Britain is a province fertile of tyrants."[73] Besides supporting tyrants, disobedience and cowardice, the Britons also fail to take full measure of the greatest gift of the Roman occupation, Christianity.[74] Finally, in the face of foreign invasion, the Britons fell into internal disorders while relaxing in laziness and torpor rather than taking necessary precautions against barbarian attack.[75] Variations of all these British shortcomings as outlined in the historical section are also found in the second part of Gildas's work, the denunciation of the contemporary rulers, and this parallel construction certainly gives the two parts of the De excidio a unity and rhetorical persuasiveness. Given the earnest tone of the work (to put it mildly) and accepting as genuine the motives Gildas offers for writing in his preface, rhetorical purpose, conviction, and inherited tradition seem to influence Gildas's view of Britain's Roman past.

In contrast to his harshly critical view of his fellow Britons, Gildas places the initial Roman conquest of Britain into a perspective favorable to Rome and acceptable to a Christian viewpoint. In the De excidio, the Roman conquest is virtually bloodless. The Romans impose peace through superior prestige (fama) throughout the world and then enforce

---

the Romans, had survived the shock of this notable storm: certainly his parents, who had worn purple, were slain in it.)

[70] For a discussion of sources and literary influences see Wright, "Gildas's Prose Style." Compare Mommsen, MGH AA 13:6–7. For a speculative treatment of Gildas's sources see Wade-Evans, "Some Insular Sources."

[71] D.e. 4.4.

[72] D.e. 4.3.

[73] D.e. 4.3–4.

[74] D.e. 9.1.

[75] D.e. 19.4, 18.1.

submission on the British, who, being completely unwarlike, do not resist.[76] Following an account of the "unjustified" British rebellion against Rome, Gildas introduces the major theme of Christianity. His description of the coming of Christianity to Britain is as long as the entire secular history outlined in Chapters 3 through 14 of the *De excidio*. Gildas deliberately chooses to exclude the pagan period from his historical sketch. Roman *pax* and order are seen to be conducive to the spread of the Gospel. He gives partial credit to the emperor Tiberius, thereby associating Roman rule with God's precious gift: "Meanwhile, to an island numb with chill ice [Britain] . . . Christ made a present of his rays (that is, his precepts). . . . This happened first, as we know, in the last years of the emperor Tiberius, at a time when Christ's religion was being propagated without hindrance: for, against the wishes of the senate, the emperor threatened the death penalty for informers against soldiers of God."[77] Britain also shared with the rest of the empire, through the unifying action of the church, the gift of the martyrs.[78]

When disaster strikes Britain in Chapter 13 of the *De excidio*, the true beginning of its troubles and the agency of its ruin is the British-sponsored tyrant Magnus Maximus.[79] Maximus was actually Spanish, not British, and it is revealing of Gildas's perspective and in keeping with his purpose that he makes Maximus the product of home-brewed British treason, thus portraying Britain as the cause of its own destruction. Maximus attempts to conquer the empire, and to do so removes Britain's soldiers, governors, and youth to the continent. Here he kills one legitimate Roman emperor and puts to flight another while conquering great territories. He ultimately fails, however, and Britain, now defenseless, must appeal to Rome for aid against the barbarians. Overlooking previous treason, the Romans twice rescue Britain from its foes, and having helped prepare defenses for the British citizens, they finally leave, never to return. This ends the Roman period in Gildas's narrative.

Gildas clearly attempts to show that the Britons were at fault for their misfortunes, while the Romans were justified and even generous in their actions.[80] The incidental information in his account of Roman deeds and the results of their policy are, however, of crucial interest as evidence of opinions about Rome current in fifth- and sixth-century Britain. Gildas prefaces his historical sketch of Roman Britain with these words: "I shall

[76] *D.e.* 5.
[77] *D.e.* 8.
[78] *D.e.* 10.
[79] Zosimus 4.35.3. See Jarrett, "Magnus Maximus"; John F. Matthews, "Macsen, Maximus, and Constantine."
[80] *D.e.* 17. Gildas describes the Romans as "illustrious helpers."

simply try to bring to light the ills she [Britain] suffered in the time of the
Roman emperors and inflicted on other men, even those far away."[81]
From the start of his narrative it is evident that the Roman period is
remembered not as a golden age, but as a time of conflict. In fact, the
closest thing to a prosperous age in Gildas's work is the time of post-
Roman British independence.[82]

In the *De excidio*, things Roman almost always have an incidental,
circumstantial description casting them in a slightly or often wholly sinister light. The Roman law, for example, is called a law of obedience. It acts
as an instrument of subjection, subduing the Britons through legal penalties. The law can persecute not only the Britons but the church, as in the
case of Diocletian's "wicked edicts." British obedience to the law is superficial, masking deep resentment and ultimate rejection at the time of
Maximus.[83] Gildas feels that the British rebellions against Rome were
unjustified, but his descriptions of the Roman response are chilling. The
Romans in charge after the rebellion of Boudicca, for example, are "whips
for the backs of the inhabitants and a yoke for their necks."[84] As punishment, the rebelling Britons are slaughtered except for a few kept as slaves
for Rome. The name of Roman servitude is ground into the very soil of
Britain and the people so tormented that "the island should be rated not as
Britannia but as Romania, and all its bronze, silver, and gold should be
stamped with the image of Caesar."[85] The Romans are here seen to be a
scourge or punishment, as bad as barbarian invaders, like the Saxons, and
plague.

Gildas thus presents as harsh a view of Romanization as can be found in
literature, nor does he use the postural prose of a Roman aristocrat with an
idyllic view of barbarian values. He is hardly an enthusiastic witness
either to the success of Romanization as a political process or to the pro-
Roman allegiance or loyalty of the bulk of his fellow countrymen. In fact,
the *De excidio* arguably calls into question the alleged success of Roma-

---

[81] *D.e.* 4.4.

[82] *D.e.* 21.2, 26.3.

[83] For Roman law see *D.e.* 5.2, 13. *D.e.* 5.2: "Who gave to the edicts merely a skin deep
obedience, with resentment sunk deep in their hearts." See also *D.e.* 12.

[84] *D.e.* 7. Gildas seems to be describing Boudicca's rebellion here. It is significant not only
that memory of this long-past event was still so vivid, but also that Gildas selected it as the
example to color his description. For an opposing view see A. Birley, *Life in Roman Britain*,
164–65.

[85] *D.e.* 7: "Solo nomen Romanae servitutis haerere facturos ac non tam militari manu quam
flagris callidam gentem maceraturos et, si res sic postulavisset, ensem, ut dicitur, vagina
vacuum lateri eius accommodaturos, ita ut non Britannia, sed Romania censeretur et quic-
quid habere potuisset aeris argenti vel auri imagine Caesaris notaretur." See also *D.e.* 22, 24.

nization in Britain.[86] Certainly by the time Gildas wrote (roughly 490–540 A.D.) Romans and Britons are antipathetic parties rather than an integrated whole. Gildas sees the Roman period as an age of unrest rather than a golden era of peace and prosperity to be reconstituted if at all possible. The primary relation between Britain and Rome is rebellion, not cooperation. Rome provided law, but not a law Britons could accept.[87] Rome enforced peace, but Roman rule engendered rebellion. Rome gave military security, but not dependable security, and as a consequence British loyalty was also undependable. The relationship between security and loyalty is explicitly stated in Chapter 15 of the De excidio: "As a result of their [Scots and Picts] dreadful and devastating onslaughts, Britain sent envoys with a letter to Rome, plaintively requesting a military force to protect them and vowing whole-hearted and uninterrupted loyalty to the Roman empire so long as their enemies were kept at a distance."

Gildas attempts to explain and excuse the periodic breakdown of Roman security.[88] Magnus Maximus, a tyrant supported by the Britons, is the root cause of Britain's defenselessness. Gildas also believes that the Britons are simply more cowardly than everyone else (and thus practically impossible to help). Finally, the Picts and Scots are really just bandits, unworthy of serious Roman military attention. The Britons ought not to need help in dealing with such a small threat.[89] Despite the attempted whitewash, the basic fact remains that, in Gildas's view, Britain was not secure under Roman rule. The reasons Gildas gives for the periodic withdrawal of the Romans reveal their essentially selfish interest in Britain. They first leave because they are not paid. Next they leave because Britain has been emptied of wine and oil.[90] Each of the two subsequent military interventions also end in Roman withdrawal, although they leave behind fortifications and an injunction to learn self-defense. Even here there is a hint that the British money and labor used to build the fortifications were coerced or conscripted. As the De excidio reveals, Gildas was no simple Roman loyalist. Nor must we assume that the traditions he preserved

---

[86] For example, Millet concludes, "Thus during the third quarter of the fourth century Britain was utterly Roman. Legally and culturally there was little to distinguish her inhabitants from those of any other province" (Romanization of Britain, 212). Compare Haverfield, Romanization; Salway, Frontier People. See Michael E. Jones, "Failure of Romanization."

[87] For Britain and Roman law, see D.e. 5.2, 12, 13.

[88] Security is linked to loyalty in D.e. 15: "Ob quarum infestationem ac dirissimam depressionem legatos Romam cum epistolis mittit, militarem manum ad se vindicandam lacrimosis postulationibus poscens et subiectionem sui Romano imperio continue tota animi virtute, si hostis longius arceretur, vovens." See R. P. C. Hanson, "Date of St. Patrick," 71.

[89] For Maximus, see D.e. 13, 14; for unwarlike Britons, see D.e. 5.2, 6.2; for Picts and Scots, see D.e. 18.1.

[90] For land or rents, see D.e. 6.1; for wine and oil, D.e. 7. For conscripted resources see D.e. 18.2.

hostile to Roman rule were simply the memory of the humble elements of Britannia's population.[91] His complicated and conflicted disposition toward imperial government may be paralleled among the attitudes of postcolonial elites of other periods. For Gildas and his learned, presumably aristocratic audience, the unpleasant aspects of Roman governance were well remembered. Clearly in the *De excidio* neither security nor prosperity was associated with Roman rule. It is hardly surprising that significant numbers of Britons evidently felt no allegiance or loyalty to Rome.

"NENNIUS" AND THE *HISTORIA BRITTONUM*

As we have seen, the *Historia Brittonum* is a work shrouded in scholarly controversy. Of all the literary sources relevant to the question of British attitudes toward Rome, the *Historia* is perhaps the most difficult of interpretation and application. The major points of dispute center around three interrelated issues—authorship, method, and purpose; historical reliability; and the highly composite nature of the work.[92] The compiler of the *Historia Brittonum* evidently sought to produce something like a British version of a world history by integrating, or at least grouping, a variety of component elements from different periods. His underlying assumption reflects a British (Welsh) perspective found throughout the early Middle Ages—the Island of Britain (*Ynys Prydain*) was a geographical, historical, and political unity rightfully belonging to the native Britons, who had been oppressed through a series of foreign conquests (*gormes*) that had for a time fragmented that union.[93] The attitudes expressed in the various sections of the *Historia* and the overall tone of the work are markedly and unambiguously hostile to Rome. The basic question is whether this hostility reflects a consistent, traditional antipathy within the relevant component sections of the *Historia*, or whether the anti-Roman attitude is the late creation of a synchronizing editor and

---

[91] For a discussion of patriotism and political sentiment in Gildas see O'Sullivan, *De Excidio*, 23–32. Compare Kerlouégan, *Les destinées de la culture latine*, 559–76. I do not accept E. A. Thompson's conclusion that "the tradition which Gildas preserves is the memory of the rank and file of the population . . . to whom Roman rule brought no paradise" ("Gildas and the History of Britain," 213).

[92] Dumville is preparing a text of the *Historia*, but until the complete publication of that work Mommsen's critical text remains the basic reference (Nennius, *Historia Brittonum*). A criticism of Mommsen can be found in Ifor Williams, "Mommsen and the Vatican Nennius." Other printed texts may be found in Faral, *La légende arthurienne*; Lot, *Nennius*. I have used the Harley 3859 manuscript of the British Museum. John Morris's translation of this text with some variants is presented in Nennius, *British History and Welsh Annals*. Translations quoted in my work are taken from that version.

[93] Gransden, *Historical Writing*, 10; Sims-Williams, "Some Functions," especially 101–7.

reflects the political concerns and attitudes of the ninth century. To a significant degree this is a rhetorical question, since the idea of a distinct British identity and a geographical and political unity seem clearly reflected in the work of Gildas, as does the theme of British antipathy toward Rome. In a more subtle form, similar ideas may be seen in Patrick's writing, and these attitudes, evident in the fifth and sixth century, can hardly be a ninth-century invention. Indeed, the notion of an antagonistic historical distinction between Britons and Romans had already passed into Anglo-Saxon traditions before the compilation of the *Historia Brittonum*.[94]

The attitudes of the Britons toward Rome were not simple or uniform, as Gildas's views show. The civil wars among the Britons during the fifth and sixth centuries were to a degree probably a reflection of divided loyalties and attitudes toward Roman rule and its sequel. Gildas recorded several appeals by Britons for Roman help, although he couched these in terms of British self-interest. The instruction of the emperor Honorius to the Britons in roughly 410, recorded in Zosimus, was presumably the reply to a petition by some group of prominent Britons. Some group of Britons appealed either to the Gallic bishops or the pope for aid against the Pelagian heresy sometime before 429. Gildas described Ambrosius, the heroic leader of British resistance against the Saxons, as "perhaps the last of the Romans." It is tempting to imagine that the views of British loyalists are reflected in pro-Roman aspects of Gildas's work and to read the anti-Roman sentiments in the *Historia Brittonum* as preserving the historical viewpoint of a British separatist faction. The respective treatments in Gildas and the *Historia* of Magnus Maximus, Vortigern, and Ambrosius are suggestive examples.[95]

The intellectual environment of ninth-century Wales and the specific political and cultural context of the court of Merfyn of Gwynedd, the most likely candidate for the locus of compilation of the *Historia*, do not provide very compelling arguments for the novel creation of anti-Roman attitudes. In a general European sense, the dominant ideology of the period centered on the papacy and the Carolingian revival of empire. Neither of these was likely to inspire anti-Roman perceptions in a work that in some

---

[94] For example, Bede, *H.e.* 1.11–13. The interrelation among the sources creates a danger of circular argument. Some of Bede's attitudes may be traced back to Gildas, of course. For the relation of *H.B.* to *H.e.* see Chapter 2 above. The *Anglo-Saxon Chronicle* is less obviously related to Gildas but the content of its relevant entries may also be ultimately based on Bede. There are, however, some suggestive entries not obviously dependent on him. For example; "In this year the Romans collected all the treasures which were in Britain, and hid some in the ground, so that no one could find them afterwards, and took some with them into Gaul." *Anglo-Saxon Chronicle*, entry for year 418, trans. Whitelock.

[95] Fletcher, *Arthurian Material*, 19; Wood, "Fall of the Western Empire," 261.

ways prepared the Britons for an intellectual reentry into Latin civilization. There is no hint within the *Historia* of the struggle of the British
"Celtic" church against the Roman tonsure or the Roman Easter, topics
that so interested Bede. In fact, one tradition links the authorship of the
Historia Brittonum to the disciple of a Romanizing bishop. Merfyn's
brother-in-law, Cyngen of Powys, evidently died while visiting Rome.
There seems to be no religious or moralizing ninth-century purpose behind the *Historia's* anti-Roman attitudes.[96]

Ninth-century realities and concerns could be expected to have re-
shaped the origin stories, genealogies, and attitudes from the earlier component sources of the *Historia*. Immediate political courtly requirements
might well have influenced a synchronizing author's manipulation of panegyric, genealogy, and prophetic poetry.[97] Welsh ninth- and tenth-century
genealogical collections sometimes assign Roman imperial or Christian
ancestry to ruling families by including figures such as Constantine the
Great, Magnus Maximus, or the Virgin Mary. Pedigrees based on figures of
the northern native aristocracy such as Cunedda sometimes include Romanized names like Aeternus, Paternus, or Tacitus. These various connections with the era of the Roman past in Britain, even in the case of the
usurper Magnus Maximus, are often interpreted as claims to a sanction
derived from Rome and added to native aristocratic traditions. In this
context, it is difficult to see how the invention of anti-Roman attitudes
about 830 by the compiler of the *Historia Brittonum* might have served
the specific dynastic needs of Gwynedd or some other royal court. The
royal genealogies are notoriously difficult to interpret correctly for they
are beset by problems of dating, fabrication, corruption, and transmission.
Roman-sounding names and figures such as Constantine may in fact indicate post-Roman Christian influence rather than a Roman political legacy
and the power of imperial association. Thoroughly Celtic names are interspersed with Latin ones in the same genealogies. Speaking in general,
however, the anti-Roman sentiments within the narrative of the *Historia*
seem independent of ninth-century dynastic and genealogical interests.[98]

---

[96] Liebermann, "Nennius," 25–44.

[97] Sims-Williams, "Some Functions," 101.

[98] Just how much earlier traditional material may have been incorporated into the existing
ninth- and tenth-century versions of collections of British royal pedigrees is problematic. See
M. Miller, "Historicity and the Pedigrees of the Northcountrymen." Nora Chadwick believes
that the pedigrees preserved a genuine historical tradition from the sixth century or even
earlier and that genealogies began to be preserved shortly after the Roman period ("Early
Culture and Learning in Wales," 35). Compare W. Davies, *Wales in the Early Middle Ages*, 94–
95. See Bartrum, *Genealogical Tracts*. Dunville is highly skeptical of the historical value of
the pedigrees for the period before c. 800, but accepts that there was an older secular antiquarian corpus of genealogical work ("Historical Value," 6–11).

Ninth-century concerns including renewed Saxon aggression may have reinvigorated British patriotic traditions, but it seems reasonable to conclude that anti-Roman attitudes within the *Historia* originated in an atmosphere earlier than the ninth century and are the product of component sources and traditions drawn from a long period of time stretching back to within a century of Gildas.

The contents of the *Historia Brittonum* vary considerably among surviving manuscripts and are a mixture of fact and fancy containing both historical and legendary material. The major elements include origin myths of the British, Irish, and Picts, including genealogies; a sketch of the Roman era; a selection dealing with the activities of Guorthigirn (Vortigern); a section concerning Saint Patrick; a segment relating the deeds of Arthur; Anglian genealogies with a Welsh historical commentary; and a chronological outline. Chapters 1 through 30 contain the material relevant to the Roman period.[99] The origin stories and the sketch of the Roman past in the first thirty chapters are obviously full of fantastic elements and historical inaccuracies. This portion of the *Historia* is derivative, based on an intermixture of material drawn from Gildas, Jerome, Orosius, and Prosper, inextricably mingled with popular traditions and antiquarian speculations of doubtful value. The attitudes presented are, however, significant for the history of ideas, and bear an unmistakable similarity to the vision of the past recorded in Gildas. T. M. Charles-Edwards makes the point this way:

> We can perceive, already existing in Gildas, the kernel of the later British and Welsh view of the past: the Britons were the earliest settlers of the island and gave their name to it; the subsequent settlements of Picts, Irish, and Saxons were due to successive invasions—violent seizures of land that belonged by hereditary right to the Britons. The British sense of nationality was thus far more intimately linked to their land . . . than was the sense of nationality of either the Irish or the English. . . . We cannot know how far the origin legends of the Picts and the Irish had developed in Gildas's day; what we do know is that, for Britain, the origin legends concerning the Britons and the Picts used by Bede only expressed in another language Gildas's view of the movement of peoples.[100]

---

[99] British Museum, Harley 3859, folios 174–98. The material relevant to the Roman period is in folios 177A-179B. The Chartres text is the most divergent and includes little of the Roman material other than the genealogies. It does, however, include the pro-British account of Julius Caesar's invasion of Britain. The Chartres text is printed in Lot, *Nennius*, 227–32. See Appendix 4.

[100] Charles-Edwards, review of *Gildas*, 120.

The material in the *Historia* specifically relevant to British attitudes toward Rome can be considered in three sections: the origin stories and genealogies, including two basic variants (Chapters 10 and 11 and Chapters 17 and 18); a list of Roman emperors who visited Britain together with some historical details (Chapters 19 through 27); and a sketch of Roman-British relations describing the end of Roman rule (Chapters 28 through 31).

Genealogies

The *Historia* states that four races inhabit Britain, the Irish, Picts, Saxons, and Britons. Rome first enters the *Historia Brittonum* in the person of Britto (Brutus), the eponymous founder of Britain and a Roman consul. Two distinct versions of Brutus's genealogy occur, with a fair amount of variation in the manuscripts and some contradictions. Chapter 10 gives the origins of the inhabitants of Britain through Brutus. Ostensibly drawn from Roman sources, this version derives the Britons from both the Trojans and the Romans. Brutus-Britto's ancestry is traced back to Aeneas and the sack of Troy. Son of Silvius and the grandson of Aeneas, Britto does not have a happy relationship with his parents, the founding family of Rome. Fulfilling a prophecy, he kills both of his parents—his mother dies in childbirth and he later kills his father with a stray arrow. Driven from Italy, Greece, and Gaul, he finally comes to Britain, "which is named Britannia from his name and filled it with his race, and dwelt there. From that day Britain has been inhabited until the present day."[101] A variant within the *Historia* portrays Brutus-Britto not as an exile but as a ruling Roman consul. A similar variety of tradition typifies the origin myths of other peoples in the *Historia Brittonum*.[102] The second major variant of Brutus's origins occurs in Chapters 17 and 18 of the *Historia*. Here he is traced to Hessitio, a son of Alanus of the race of Japheth, the son of Noah. (Historical peoples are always founded after the Flood.) Hessitio's sons are Francus, Romanus, Britto, and Albanus.[103]

These genealogies in the *Historia* serve one principal role—to create for the Britons a heritage and ancestry equal in nobility and venerability to Rome's.[104] Thus in the first version Britto is a grandson of Aeneas from

---

[101] *H.B.* 10.

[102] The multiple genealogies and origin tales, and the lack of agreement even within the same manuscript, suggest that the compiler of the *Historia Brittonum*, as he claimed, really did find these variants rather than invent them. The variety also suggests a "heaping" methodology.

[103] *H.B.* 17–18.

[104] Against this view see Hanning, *Vision of History*, 104. Hanning argues that the purpose of one variant within the *Historia* was to attach the Britons to the ancient world and make them heirs of Rome's greatness. I disagree. These genealogies create for the Britons a competitive

whose sons also descend Romulus and Remus, the founders of Rome. In the second major variant, Britto (Britain) and Romanus (Rome) are sons of the same father, Hessitio; as brothers they are equals. The other significant factor in this genealogical material is the element of conflict. Britto is forced to leave Italy because of violence (patricide). Alternatively he conquers Britain as a successful Roman consul, but this act is heinous because the Britons through common ancestry are really kinsmen with the Roman conquerors. Thus the "conquest" is really civil war and fratricide. Geoffrey of Monmouth later elevates this element into a major theme in his historical romance, *The History of the Kings of Britain*. In this work he often alludes to the tragic irony of unnecessary war between the Britons and Romans—kinsmen and equals, yet striving to obtain sovereignty each over the other.[105]

Roman Emperors in Britain

The *Historia* lists nine visiting emperors: Julius, Claudius, Severus, Caritius (Carausius), Constantine (son of Constantine the Great), Maximus, Maxim(ian)us, another Severus, and Constantius. The list is not historically accurate, but the emperors who were remembered and included provide an interesting insight into British historical traditions.[106] The *Historia* presents each of these emperors in turn, with some historical comment. The commentary provides a not very accurate history of the Romans in Britain. Following Gildas, the *Historia* prefaces the Roman invasion as follows: "When the Romans acquired the mastery of the whole world they sent legates to the British, to demand hostages and taxes from them, such as they received from all countries and islands. But the British were arrogant and turbulent, and spurned the Roman legates." Echoes of Gildas are several times evident in the *Historia*, but what is not incorporated from Gildas is a more revealing clue to the author's intentions. From the plethora of disapproving and critical comments directed at the Britons in Gildas's *De excidio*, the above is the only one included in the *Historia*, and the compiler clearly adopts both a more secular and a

---

and equal pedigree, not a derivative one.

[105] On Geoffrey of Monmouth see B. F. Roberts, "Geoffrey of Monmouth." For the theme of Rome versus Britain see Geoffrey of Monmouth, *History of the Kings*, pp. 9–45, especially 10; see also Gransden, *Historical Writing*, 205–7.

[106] The location of the imperial list varies among manuscripts. Wade-Evans thought "Nennius" was attempting to integrate the account of Roman Britain in Gildas's *De excidio* with a contradictory "old British list" of seven Roman emperors who had stood on British soil (*Nennius*, 19).

more strongly pro-British attitude than Gildas did.[107] The introduction of Christianity into Roman Britain gets fewer than thirty words in the *Historia*, whereas it filled fully one half of Gildas's historical sketch. Also in contrast to Gildas, the Roman conquest of Britain is presented as a severe conflict. Gildas, you will recall, made the Britons surrender without a fight.[108]

Julius Caesar, who is treated in the *Historia* as the first emperor, is twice defeated by the Britons before he can subdue them. Following the murder of Julius, the Britons pay taxes to Augustus (Octavian), but this is presented in the *Historia* as a singular event.[109] The theme of taxation figures prominently in the short account of Roman rule. The second emperor to visit Britain, Claudius, must like Julius Caesar fight a great and bloody battle before ruling Britain. Claudius also succeeds in conquering the Orkneys, but before his death, the Britons cease to pay taxes to Rome.[110] The demise of emperors who visit Britain is a litany repeated with evident relish in the *Historia*.

Severus, the third emperor to visit Britain, provides the "subject" provinces of Britain with a wall stretching from sea to sea as protection against barbarian invasion from the Picts and Scots. Soon after this Severus dies in Britain. One manuscript variant adds, "he was killed at York with his generals."[111] Not a great deal of gratitude shines through this account of Roman measures for the defense of Britain, and the ominous variant "he was killed with his generals" is developed in Chapter 24 of the *Historia* in a way to suggest that the author thought that Severus was killed by Britons, not by the invading barbarians. Carausius becomes ruler because of the death of Severus. He takes vengeance for his murdered predecessors: "He [Carausius] struck down all the little kings of the British, and took the purple over Britain."[112] The manuscript version containing the *Capitula* offers this summary: "How the emperor Carausius avenged Severus and was sated with the blood of the British and where he built a triumphal arch in memory of his victory." It is interesting to notice the presence of the "little kings" in this passage and the evident conflict between Britons and Romans even in the face of barbarian invasion.

Constantine, son of Constantine the Great, is the fifth imperial visitor to Britain—some manuscripts call him Constantius. He dies at Caer Seint

---

[107] For the vernacular in "Nennius" see M. Miller, "Starting to Write History," especially 459; Hanning, *Vision of History*, 95.
[108] On Gildas and Nennius see Lot, "Nennius et Gildas"; Dumville, "Sub-Roman Britain," 180 n. 31. Hanning, *Vision of History*, 108.
[109] *H.B.* 20.
[110] *H.B.* 21.
[111] *H.B.* 23.
[112] *H.B.* 24.

(probably Caernarfon), the only emperor in the list of whom something complimentary is said: "He sowed three seeds, of gold, of silver, and of bronze, on the pavement of that city [Caer Seint], that no man should ever live there poor; and its other name is Minmanton."[113] Curiously, Constantine the Great, although first proclaimed emperor while in Britain, is not included in the list. The sixth visiting emperor was Maximus, and the seventh Maximianus (a duplication of Maximus).[114] The *Historia* states that British tradition ends with this second Maximus but that Roman sources claimed nine rather than seven emperors visited Britain.[115] The eighth was another Severus, and the ninth was Constantius. Maximus (Maximianus) is clearly the pivotal figure in this treatment of the Roman rule in Britain. He appears in Chapter 27 in more detail than any other Roman ruler except Julius Caesar, and a further chapter is devoted to him to preface the end of Roman rule (Chapter 29). Finally, in Chapter 31 of the *Historia*, the death of Maximus along with the war between Britons and Romans are the two events specifically linked to "the end of the Roman empire in Britain." As mentioned above, Gildas made Maximus responsible for Britain's subsequent difficulties. The *Historia* affirms his role as a source of troubles. Maximus goes forth from Britain to Gaul with the British army and kills the emperor Gratian, but afterwards refuses to send the army of Britain home. The soldiers settle instead in Armorica, leaving Britain without defenders: "That is why Britain has been occupied by foreigners, and the citizens driven out, until God shall give them help."[116]

The *Historia Brittonum* implies that British traditions of Roman emperors end with Maximus and it is interesting in this context to note that Maximus is the only Roman emperor to occupy an important place in later British folklore. He is also present in the dynastic genealogies of several British kingdoms in the post-Roman period.[117] Maximus, however, is hardly a copybook model of a Roman emperor. He is a usurper and tyrant, the killer of a legitimate Roman emperor, and he uses the army in Britain to conquer Roman provinces on the continent. In this sense, Maximus seems almost an instrument of British revenge against the empire. He is much changed by British tradition, which equips him with a British wife and a son who becomes a British holy man. Maximus is, in short, thoroughly assimilated into a British, not a Roman, hero.

---

[113] *H.B.* 25.
[114] Maximus = Maximianus and Macsen. Maximus is called Maximianus in some Latin texts. He is Macsen in the later Welsh vernacular.
[115] *H.B.* 27.
[116] *H.B.* 27.
[117] See Dumville, "Sub-Roman Britain," 180–81. n. 32–33. See Matthews, "Macsen, Maximus, and Constantine."

The End of Roman Rule in Britain

The relations between Britain and Rome after the reign of Maximus are detailed in Chapters 28, 30, and 31 of the *Historia Brittonum*. The chief significance of these chapters is the way in which they portray the end of Roman political control over Britain. The author of the *Historia* clearly believed that the Britons expelled Rome, not that Rome abandoned Britain. "Hitherto the Romans had ruled the British for 409 years. But the British overthrew the rule of the Romans, and paid them no taxes, and did not accept their kings to rule over them, and the Romans did not dare to come to Britain to rule anymore, for the British had killed their generals."[118] Chapter 30 expands this tale. The British kill the Roman generals on three occasions, but each time the barbarian attacks on Britain force them to request military aid and the return of the Romans. To gain military aid, the British sent envoys who abased themselves before the Roman consuls, bribed them with great gifts, and "promised to swear to accept the yoke of Roman law, although it was harsh."[119] The Romans return with an army, place emperors over Britain again, and install generals to rule. They then return home. The cost of Roman aid is great, besides the yoke of Roman law: "The Romans came to bring help to the empire and defend it, and deprived Britain of her gold and silver and bronze, and all her precious raiment and honey, and went back in great triumph."[120] The author of the *Historia* is closely following Gildas throughout this section, but whereas Gildas presented his descriptions in a rather confused way, the *Historia* more clearly perceives a particular pattern active for "348 years."[121] I earlier described Roman-British relations as a mutual inconstancy. The author of the *Historia* perceives the same problem. The Roman army appears and disappears, and when it is absent the Britons rebel and kill the generals who govern them. In contrast to the testament in Gildas, the *Historia*'s rebellions are not unjustified treachery on the part of the deceitful Britons, but the actions of a people driven to rebellion by the "oppression of the empire."[122]

---

[118] *H.B.* 28. The chapters seem out of sequence because the story in Chapters 28 and 30 is interrupted by a second chapter on Maximus, Chapter 29.

[119] *H.B.* 30.

[120] *H.B.* 30. There is an interesting aside in this chapter. The Romans intervene not for the sake of Britain as such but for the "empire": "Romani autem ad imperium auxiliumque et ad vindicandum veniebant et, spoliata Brittannia auro argentoque. . . ." A similar emphasis may be found in Gildas's *De excidio*. Here the Romans intervene to save their prestige (the Roman name), not because of any love of Britain (*D.e.* 17).

[121] *H.B.* 30.

[122] *H.B.* 30: "propter gravitatem imperii."

The final relevant passage is perhaps the most significant. Chapter 31 begins the story of the *adventus Saxonum*. "It came to pass that after this war between the British and the Romans, when their generals were killed, and after the killing of the tyrant Maximus and the end of the Roman Empire in Britain, the British went in fear for 40 years. Vortigern ruled in Britain, and during his rule in Britain he was under pressure, from fear of the Picts and the Irish, and of a Roman invasion, and, not least, from dread of Ambrosius. Then came three keels, driven into exile from Germany." A number of scholars see in this passage a fragment of contemporary or near contemporary fifth-century record.[123] If it is indeed early and genuine, we have additional support, independent of Gildas, for the presence of strong anti-Roman feeling in fifth-century Britain, and an illumination of the issues at stake in the conflict between Ambrosius, "almost the last of the Romans," and Vortigern.

The vision of the Roman past presented in the *Historia Brittonum* is thus decidedly anti-Roman. The Roman rule begins in violent conflict, continues amid rebellion, and ends in forcible expulsion. There is no notion of a *pax Romana*. Roman security is inadequate. Despite Roman fortification and occasional interventionary forces, the threat of the Scots and Picts continues and even increases. Moreover, the inadequate protection of Rome is too dearly bought. Taxes, the "harsh yoke of Roman law," and the loss of Britain's precious metals, even its raiment and honey, are the cost. The equation between Roman government and the generals in Chapters 28 through 30 of the *Historia* is an interesting insight into the author's perception of the intolerable "weight of empire."[124]

My examination of the insular British literary sources reveals a substantially negative attitude toward the Roman past. There are, however, certain obvious criticisms of the methods and findings. The most important criticism is the thinness of the evidence and the possibility that it is not representative. There are only three basic sources, and since "Nennius" is dependent in part on Gildas, not even three entirely independent sources. Moreover, the material is scattered over a considerable period of time, the fifth through the ninth century. Against this criticism is the melancholy fact that only this literary evidence has survived. The very fact that it has survived, however, bespeaks an acceptance of the popularity and value of these works by men who troubled to copy and preserve them. The authors enjoyed a reputation for learning and sanctity, at least in the early medieval period. With typical enthusiasm, John Morris re-

[123] Myres, *English Settlements*, 15–18; Salway, *Roman Britain*, 472; Alcock, *Arthur's Britain*, 39; Liebermann, "Nennius," 40.
[124] *H.B.* 30.

marks of Gildas: "But Gildas did not write in vain. On the contrary, few books have had a more immediate and far-reaching impact than his. He uttered what tens of thousands felt."[125] British literary attitudes hostile to or critical of the Roman empire do not stand in an isolated intellectual context. Although historians often suggest that the empire was remarkably free from regional or ethnic prejudice, Britain seems to be a significant exception. British hostility can be matched with a possibly general anti-British prejudice and persistently negative image of Britons in late Roman writings. This is detectable among Gallic aristocrats such as Rutilius Namatianus and Ausonius of Bordeaux. Ausonius, for example, in a series of six epigrams lampooned one Silvius Bonus, the only British poet named in classical literature, on the basis of his British origin. As H. G. Evelyn White notes, evidently a "good man" and "a Briton" were regarded as a contradiction in terms so that a Briton named Bonus (Good) was ironically humorous.[126]

Epigram 110
No good man is a Briton. If he should begin to be plain Silvius, let the plain man cease to be good.

Epigram 111
This is Silvius Good, but the same Silvius is a Briton: a plainer thing—believe me— is a bad Briton.

The Gallic stereotyping of Britons sounds a hostile note that differs from friendly banter about banquet-loving Gauls. Given the powerful influence of Gallic aristocrats at the imperial court, negative preconceptions about Britons could be seen as politically sinister. Ausonius and his Gallic circle influenced or controlled the powerful office of Praetorian Prefect of Gaul, the government official who ultimately controlled the British diocese and was subject only to the emperor himself. Britain had a reputation for political and military instability. In Jerome's much quoted words, Britain was "a province fertile in tyrants." He wrote this in 415 A.D., and his attitude may reflect the recent impact of the succession of usurpers in Britain in 406-10.[127] In general Roman historians and panegyrists failed

125 Morris in Gildas, Ruin of Britain, p. 2.
126 Ausonius Epigrams 107-12. Rutilius Namatianus De reditu suo 495-506. These passages are discussed more fully in Chapter 5. For the idea of a general anti-British prejudice see A. Birley, Fasti of Roman Britain, 328; A. Birley, People of Roman Britain, 159. Compare Salway, Oxford Illustrated History, 283. For the idea that Romans in the western provinces had little or no racial prejudice or idea of nationality see Sherwin-White, Racial Prejudice; E. A. Thompson, Who Was Saint Patrick? 109-13.
127 Jerome Ep. 139.9. Zosimus implies that the soldiers in Britain were the "most stubborn and violent" in the empire (New History 4.35.2).

to distinguish among Britons residing lawfully within the diocese, rebels, and Britons living beyond the frontier. The language of the panegyrics is of course laden with convention and stereotype, but even after centuries of Roman rule Britain was portrayed as outlandish and barbaric. In 400 A.D. Claudian proclaimed: "Next spoke Britannia, dressed in the skin of some Caledonian beast, her cheeks tattooed, her sea-blue mantle sweeping over her footsteps like the surge of Ocean." Recent modes of literary analysis suggest that such descriptions serve to define "the other" and are a form of segregation and denigration.[128]

In the religious sphere there are hints that some British clerics were respected by cultured Gauls of the fourth century. However, Pelagius, the most prominent religious figure to emerge from Roman Britain, was eventually condemned as a heretic. He suffered from personal and vicious attacks directed in part at his British origin. Jerome and Orosius, a partisan of Augustine, variously depicted Pelagius and an unnamed Pelagian, almost certainly to be identified as Pelagius himself, as bull-necked and pointy-headed, a monstrous Goliath, and a huge alpine hound. Jerome insinuated that Pelagius was a Scot, thus identifying him as an out-and-out barbarian, by implication something even worse than a Briton.[129] Indications of anti-British feelings are not confined to literature. Several game boards from the period of the Tetrarchy associate the Britons with the Parthians, the archenemy of Rome. The boards are on floors of public places in Rome and Trier and proclaim, "The Parthians have been killed; The Britons vanquished; Play Romans!" This propaganda message would have been literally under foot for the citizens of these key imperial cities.[130]

Some of these examples of anti-British feelings can be excused as special cases applying to heretics or usurpers. There is, however, no counterpoint of inscriptional material or literary records of native Britons attaining high imperial office through conventional means or otherwise winning prominence, esteem, and fame in the later Roman empire. Com-

---

[128] Claudian *On the Consulship of Stilicho* 2.247–50. On the concept and use of "the other" see Edward Said, *Orientalism*.

[129] Jerome *Commentary on Jeremiah* Prologue 4, 3.1; Jerome *Dialogue against the Pelagians* 1, 3.16; Orosius *Book in Defense against the Pelagians* 2, 16, 31. Pelagius is discussed more fully in Chapter 5. On respected British clerics see N. K. Chadwick, "Intellectual Contacts," 200–203.

[130] The game boards consist of six groups of spaces or letters aligned in three rows on stone slabs. The name of the game and its rules are obscure. See McCormick, *Eternal Victory*, 33–34. The boards are an example of the extension of "victory ideology" into the Roman citizens' daily leisure hours.

PARTHI	OCCISI
BRITT[O]	VICTVS
LVDIT[E]	ROMANI

bined with the suggested evidence for mutual antipathy between Romans and Britons, this political and cultural lacuna is distinctly ominous. The suspicion grows that something went wrong with Romanization in Britain.[131]

Despite differences in focus and various dates of composition, the early British sources are in accord in evincing a negative view of Rome that is more persuasive in its cumulative effect than in its constituent parts. The Patrician documents, and to a lesser extent Gildas's work, are specialist ecclesiastical writings, not straightforward histories, and the inferential deduction of secular attitudes is a delicate task. Patrick seems to ignore secular Rome altogether, but secular Rome is not replaced by any coherent view of a Christian state, and his silence perhaps indicates a negative view of Roman government. Gildas is in many ways the decisive witness, for his observations are at least partly founded on a personal sympathy with *Romanitas*. Despite this, a negative view of the effects of Roman rule emerges in his writings. The view of the *Historia Brittonum* is removed from Roman Britain in time and influenced by Gildas and other early sources to a considerable extent. Gildas is not slavishly incorporated into the *Historia*, however, and "Nennius" has the best claim of all surviving works to represent the full development of traditional British attitudes toward *Romanitas* and the Roman past in that portion of the British population, literate and Latin-writing, who maintained their independence from barbarian invasion. The *Historia Brittonum* presents a wholly negative memory of the Roman era.

Over time, the British sources reflect an interesting progression or development in attitude. In the fifth century Patrick ignored secular Rome. Gildas in the sixth century justifies Rome but does not conceal the ugly side of Roman actions in Britain. By the early ninth century the *Historia Brittonum*, probably incorporating earlier perceptions, is unambiguously hostile to the Roman tradition. Moving one step farther from the events of the Roman occupation, later British traditions, particularly the twelfth-century *History of the Kings of Britain*, elevate the conflict between Britain and Rome to the central theme of British history, more important even than the struggles with the barbarians.[132]

Patrick, Gildas, and "Nennius" alike portray a political world that is already medieval—the warband and the church have squeezed out Roman political institutions. The traditional strengths of Roman civilization, *pax* and law, also fail to inspire affection in the British writings. Instead of *pax*

---

[131] Michael E. Jones, "Failure of Romanization."
[132] B. F. Roberts, "Geoffrey of Monmouth," 32. Geoffrey of Monmouth, *Historia regnum Britanniae*, bks. 4–5.

there is a well-developed sense of British-Roman conflict. The Roman law is remembered with loathing as an instrument of Roman oppression, a burden and a yoke. The Romans themselves are remembered as inconstant defenders but capable plunderers. The literary sources have their inherent limitations, but their evidence makes it difficult either to retain the earlier historiographic view of a strongly loyal and Romanized British province, or to avoid the conclusion that the failure of *Romanitas* to survive in Britain was to some significant extent due to the hostility of substantial portions of the British population—in short, it was a failure of loyalty.

Speaking of the revolts in Britain beginning with Magnus Maximus, Gibbon observes:

> It is not very important to inquire from what causes the revolt of Britain was produced. Accident is commonly the parent of disorder; the seed of rebellion happened to fall on a soil which was supposed to be more fruitful than any other in tyrants and usurpers; the legions of that sequestered island had been long famous for a spirit of presumption and arrogance; and the name of Maximus was proclaimed by the tumultuary but unanimous voice both of the soldiers and of the provincials.[133]

Unlike Gibbon, modern historians would give much to know a little about the underlying reasons why Britain's soil was so fruitful for the seeds of rebellion, its garrison peculiarly arrogant and presumptive, and its provincials so tumultuous.

[133] Gibbon, *Decline and Fall*, 3:143.

CHAPTER FIVE

The Roman Provinces of Britain

WITHIN THE CHANGING FASHIONS of historical explanation for the decline and fall of the Roman empire, one factor has become increasingly important. Misgovernment is seen as contributing to the political, economic, social, and religious influences that encouraged apathy among the Roman provincial populations and that even led them to support conquest by relatively small numbers of barbarian invaders. The broad outlines of the decline are well known: barbarian invasion, political instability bordering at times on anarchy, a harsh, often precarious material existence for the bulk of the population—all followed by a Draconian solution. To preserve the empire, Diocletian and his successors created a new system that included destructively high taxation, the proliferation of an increasingly inefficient bureaucracy and army, and the consequent necessity of economic compulsion. This, in turn, engendered corruption, evasion, and injustice. Ramsay MacMullen has argued that a crucial change in mores occurred among the governors and soldiers in the north and west of the empire, altering the relation between private and public power. Formerly the networks of private patronage had been linked more or less constructively with the official Roman government. A toleration of favors and favoritism intensified, however, and changed to the pursuit of private profit at public expense. The cumulative effects further undercut the efficiency of government and eventually compromised even its military security. Thus the will of a great empire dissolved in the uncontrolled impulses of private enterprise.[1] While these conditions afflicted the entire

[1] MacMullen, *Corruption and Decline*, 197). The argument thus returns to Gibbon's idea that

empire, the degree, timing, and effect varied from province to province. Some areas of the empire prospered while others declined. It is important, therefore, to establish in a specifically British context the organization and quality of late Roman government and the nature of the provincial response. In the following sections, I discuss (1) the organization of the Roman administration in Britain; (2) the quality of Roman government; and (3) the general conditions of Romano-British society in the fourth century, including religious belief as it pertained to political loyalties.[2]

ROMAN ADMINISTRATION

Probably by 313 A.D. Diocletian's new organization had subdivided the original Roman province of Britain into four separate provinces, to which a fifth may have been added later.[3] The emperor Severus or Caracalla, his son and successor, had earlier divided Britain into two provinces (Britannia Superior and Inferior), probably in order to reduce the garrison under any one governor, thereby diminishing the temptation for rebellion.[4] Diocletian must have shared such a concern in the aftermath of British rebellions under the pretenders Carausius and Allectus. Little is known of the location or configuration of his new provinces except their names: Britannia Prima, Britannia Secunda, Maxima Caesariensis, Flavia Caesariensis.[5] The fifth province, Valentia, was created after the "Pict"

moral and civic decline led to the fall of the empire. For the subject of patronage and Roman society see the essays collected in Andrew Wallace-Hadrill, ed., *Patronage in Roman Society.* For the system of patronage centering on the Christian church see Peter Brown, *Power and Persuasion.* In contrast to MacMullen, Averil Cameron suggests that the increase in patronage may not be an essential cause or symptom of decline (*Later Roman Empire,* 108, 217).

[2] The evidence is thin but various and includes inscriptions relating to the careers of Roman officials serving in Britain, narrative historians such as Tacitus, Ammianus, and Herodian, as well as gossipy letters and epigrams recording the prejudices and perceptions of the social and political elite. The Pelagian letters edited by Caspari reveal a semiapocalyptic Christian vision. The evident consistency of such diverse kinds of evidence gives me some confidence that the composite picture they create of conditions in later Roman Britain may be substantially correct.

[3] The four provinces of Britain are included in the Verona list of A.D. 312–14. An inscription dates the reunion of the provinces of Numidia before A.D. 314 (*Corpus Inscriptionum Latinarum,* VIII, 18905). Since the Verona list mentions two places called Numidia, it must have been composed before 314, which in turn dates the division of the British provinces. See A. H. M. Jones, "Date and Value." See also the discussion in Anthony R. Birley, *Fasti of Roman Britain,* 168–72.

[4] Herodian 3.8.2. Britain was divided sometime after the defeat of Albinus in A.D. 197.

[5] The Council of Arles in A.D. 314 included church delegations which were often led by a bishop from the capital of the province. If this was the case for Britain, then the capitals of the represented provinces can be deduced. The British delegation was as follows: (1) Eborius episcopus de civitate Eboracensi provincia Britannia; (2) Restitutus episcopus de civitate

war of A.D. 367–70.[6] Collectively the British provinces formed a diocese commanded by a *vicarius*. There were twelve dioceses in the empire. The Vicar of Britain did not have direct access to the emperor under Diocletian's system. Instead, the British provinces were in the charge of the Praetorian Prefect of Gaul whose command included Transalpine Gaul, Spain, and Britain. Two consequences of the reorganization were important. In a political world where patronage and personal influence were crucial, Britain's rulers lacked direct access to the imperial court. Previously the British governors had ruled directly under the emperor. Secondly, the proliferation in the number of provinces multiplied the bureaucracy and costs of government in Britain. Resulting tax increases cannot have been popular.[7]

Before the reforms of Diocletian, financial administration was separated from other military and civilian government and formed an independent command. Financial governance under the *Procurator Augusti* headquartered in London was probably more important in everyday life for the bulk of the population than the civil and military command of the governor. The procurator was responsible for imperial property, estates, mines and industries, and most important, for the collection of taxes, both of money and kind, levied as land tax, poll tax, corn tax, and excise. The large military garrison in Britain required a large revenue. Local administration embraced a variety of municipal organizations. Britain included four *Coloniae*—Colchester, Gloucester, Lincoln, and York—and at least one *municipium*, Verulamium.[8] Additionally, many *civitates* existed, urban centers with dependent surrounding territories. Early distinctions of prestige and constitutional privilege among these various kinds of municipal structures blurred with the grant of universal citizenship in the third century. Also important in local government were the *vici*, settlements that had grown up around military posts, and *pagi*, rural areas either lacking an "urban" center or subdivisions of a given *civitas* with more than one concentration of population.[9] The various forms of municipal organi-

---

Londiniensi provincia suprascripta; (3) Adelphius episcopus de civitate colonia Londiniensium [Lindinensium?]; and (4) Exinde Sacerdos presbyter, Arminius diaconus. Assuming that Lindinensium was miscopied (Lincoln was a colony but London was not), York, Lincoln, and London were provincial capitals. In the fourth case no bishop is mentioned and on the basis of known parallels at Arles, the priest and presbyter substituted for an absent bishop of the unfortunately unlocated capital city. Cirencester is a possibility. See Mann, "Administration of Roman Britain."

6 Recent opinion favors the idea that the fifth province was perhaps a renaming or a subdivision of a preexisting province (possibly York) or that Valentia was territory recovered from rebels acting within the diocese. See J. G. F. Hind, "The British Province of Valentia and Orcades."

7 Van Sickel, "Diocletian and Decline."

8 Richmond, "Four *Coloniae*."

9 There were a number of different classes of town. *Colonia* and *municipia* held charters of

zation were each governed through a local senate (*ordo*) of one hundred or so men of property called *decuriones*, many of whom had previously held magistracies. Four magistrates were elected each year, one pair to manage judicial affairs (*duoviri jure dicundo*) and one pair in charge of public buildings and finances (*duoviri aediles*). The local tribal aristocracies largely filled these posts. On a provincial level, representatives of each *civitas* met yearly in the provincial council whose main function was related to the official cult of emperor worship and a restatement of provincial loyalty. The council also provided in extraordinary circumstances a means of appeal to the emperor which bypassed official channels dominated by the governor of the province.

This outline of the main features of Roman administration in Britain is schematic and must be seen as somewhat artificial in contrast to actual practice. Diocletian's scheme blurred the old segregation between the governor (*legatus*) and finance officer (*procurator*). Governors (*praesides*) of the new smaller provinces held some financial responsibility. The division between military and civil authority which Diocletian hoped to create was evidently delayed until the reign of Constantine I. The *praeses* Aurelius Arpagius, for example, ostensibly a civilian governor, is recorded by an inscription from Birdoswald as responsible for military defense of the northern frontier. There may well have been a greater complexity and variety in the administration of the diocese than the standard definitions suggest.[10]

THE QUALITY OF LATE ROMAN GOVERNMENT

The quality of late Roman government in Britain is difficult to assess. Britain lacks the numerous inscriptions or literary sources used to evaluate Roman administration in Gaul and other provinces. When British affairs are recorded, as in Ammianus for example, the notice exists because of something extraordinary. The few literary sources for fourth- and

independence. *Coloniae* were originally settlements of Roman citizens (in Britain discharged veterans) who enjoyed full privileges of self-government. In the provinces, sufficiently "Italianized" communities were first extended Latin rights, with a municipal charter of Roman style, and later might be granted full Roman citizenship. A *civitas* was an alternative organization in areas such as Britain which lacked *municipia* or a strong urban tradition. Non-Roman, nonurban tribal centers (cantons) were organized as *civitates*. This was the least-privileged grade of self-governing municipal community possessed of local autonomy. Governors and procurators worked through these local units, relying on the tribal aristocracy for tax collection and other duties. For each *civitas*, a council, magistrates, and consititution would be fixed according to local custom. See the entries for *civitas* and *municipium* in Hammond and Scullard, eds., *Oxford Classical Dictionary*. Wacher has written in detail of British conditions in *Civitas Capitals* and *Towns of Roman Britain*.

[10] Frere, "Civitas—A Myth?"

fifth-century Britain are thus in some senses atypical and must be used with caution in attempting to generalize on "normal" conditions within the province.[11] It would be surprising beyond belief if Britain had escaped the general malaise of government in the later Roman empire, including problems of inflation, corrupt and venal justice, disproportionate concentration of wealth, and the host of other difficulties plaguing Roman imperial administration.[12] Here and there, however, glimpses of the career and quality of Roman officials governing in Britain allow more direct argument rather than analogy.[13]

Of the major officials, the governors, legates, procurators, and *juridici*, much is known from the early period of Roman rule. The governors are particularly well attested.[14] Unfortunately, nothing like as much evidence is available for the third or fourth centuries. Before its subdivision, the British province's garrison of three and sometimes four legions made it a command second only to Syria in prestige. The governors reflected the military nature of the command, being for the most part active and ambitious men. This would not have been the kind of governor necessarily preferred by the provincials, of course. A notable exception to the aggressive governors, Trebellius Maximus, evidently a mild and cautious man, was ousted by his military staff in the Roman equivalent of a colonels' coup.[15] From the standpoint of the inhabitants and taxpayers, the military tail may often have wagged the civil dog in Roman Britain.

From the mid-third century onwards, the epigraphic evidence is slight, a problem compounded by confused and unstable political conditions. Even allowing for the changed nature of the evidence, however, the later governors of Britain seem to have been largely undistinguished men who rarely achieved the supreme honorific of consul. This of itself need not imply inadequate government, but at the same time, comprehensive or long-enduring solutions to Britain's problems were never found. Of fifteen attested governors of Britannia Inferior, details of the careers of only two are known. Inscriptions from Caerwent, High Rochester, and the famous

[11] See, for example, the classic trilogy by Dill: *Roman Society in Gaul; Roman Society in the Last Century; and Roman Society from Nero.* The British sources are edited by Moore, *Romans in Britain.* Also useful are *Literary Sources for Roman Britain,* edited by Mann and Penman, and Greenstock, ed., *Some Inscriptions.* The inscriptions from Roman Britain may be read in two sources: Collingwood and Wright, eds., *Roman Inscriptions of Britain,* and *Corpus Inscriptionum Latinarum* (hereafter *CIL*).
[12] Walbank, *Awful Revolution;* Peter Brown, "Later Roman Empire."
[13] Anthony R. Birley has collected the relevant evidence from inscriptions and literary evidence in *Fasti of Roman Britain* and *People of Roman Britain.* These can be usefully supplemented with A. H. M. Jones et al., eds., *Prosopography.*
[14] Anthony R. Birley, *Fasti of Roman Britain,* 37–424.
[15] During the turbulent year A.D. 69, Trebellius Maximus was forced from power by the legate of XX Legion, Roscius Coelius. Interestingly, Trebellius may have been a Gaul.

Marbre de Thorigny track the career of Tiberius Claudius Paulinus. Although he governed in Britain for perhaps only a single year or less (between 219 and 221), the details of his relations with Sollemnis, his client and *assessor* (judicial adviser), provide a British example of the ties of personal patronage that ran as private and sometimes sinister undercurrents beneath Roman provincial administration.[16] The first inscription, from Caerwent (*Venta Silurum*), was erected shortly before A.D. 220 and is now housed in Caerwent Church: "To [Tiberius Claudius] Paulinus, legate of the Second Legion Augusta, proconsul of the province of Narbonensis, emperor's propraetorian legate of the province of Lugudunensis, by decree of the council, the *civitas* of the Silures."[17] This inscription records the corporate act of the community of Caerwent, set up by a motion of the *ordo* honoring Paulinus, onetime legate in Britain, later promoted to a command in Gaul. Taken at face value, the inscription might simply represent a gesture of esteem to commemorate good service, or an attempt to curry favor with a powerful and influential man. The Marbre de Thorigny, a Gallic inscription, honors a certain Sollemnis, a client of Claudius Paulinus, and was erected at the behest of the Council of the Three Gauls in A.D. 238.[18] The base of a statue erected in Sollemnis's native village is inscribed on the front with the details of his career and bears on one side a letter about Claudius Paulinus, (written in A.D. 223):

Copy of a letter of Aedinius Julianus, prefect of the Praetorian Guard, to Badius Comnianus, procurator and acting governor. Aedinius Julianus to Badius Comnianus, greeting. When I was serving as *quinquefascalis* [acting governor] in Gallia Lugdunensis, I observed a number of worthy men, among whom was that Sollemnis, native of Viducasses and priest, whom I began to esteem for his sobriety of life and honorable ways. In addition, when certain persons who thought they had suffered at the hands of my predecessor Claudius Paulinus (according to their deserts) attempted to instigate an attack on him in the Council of the Gauls, as if by a consensus of the provinces, that Sollemnis of mine resisted their motion. He demanded return to the previous business, on the grounds

---

[16] For general background to the question of Roman provincial administration see Brunt, "Provincial Maladministration"; Abbot and Johnson, *Municipal Administration*; G. H. Stevenson, *Roman Provincial Administration*; W. T. Arnold, *Roman Provincial Administration*.
[17] When I last viewed this inscription in the summer of 1981, it was serving as a pediment for the local flower arrangement contest. A text and translation of the inscription may be found in Greenstock, ed., *Some Inscriptions*, no. 133. See Salway, *Roman Britain*, 533–34.
[18] See Pflaum, *Le Marbre de Thorigny*; *CIL*, XIII, 3162. A partial translation may be found in N. Lewis and M. Reinhold, eds., *Sourcebook*, 445–46. I have quoted MacMullen's translation, *Corruption and Decline*, 106.

that his own state, when making him delegate with the others, had given him no instructions for this motion and had rather offered its praises; and at this argument, everyone abandoned the accusation. I began more and more to esteem and value the man. Confident of my respect for him, he came to the city [Rome] to see me and, on his setting forth again, asked me to recommend him. You have thus done well if you favored his requests.

This letter fits with a portion of the inscription describing Sollemnis as "a friend of Tiberius Claudius Paulinus, imperial propraetorian legate of the province of Lugdunensis, and his client, and afterwards *assessor* to him when he was imperial propraetorian legate in Britain, attached to the sixth legion, and Paulinus sent him his salary and other gifts, many more of them." A third portion of the inscription records a letter from Paulinus himself, the only known letter from a British governor. In this letter Paulinus apologizes for his delay in securing for Sollemnis a commission as tribune, but honors him with certain "small gifts" including cloaks, brooches, a British rug (*tossia*), and not least, 25,000 sesterces in gold. The inscriptions fit together to reveal the following story. Paulinus passed from Britain to be a governor in Gaul, then back to Britain as a governor. An attempt was made to appeal his alleged past misconduct in Gaul to the emperor, using the only means available to sidestep the official channels dominated by the governor. The appeal made in the provincial council (of the Three Gauls) was blocked by Sollemnis, who as priest of the cult of Rome and Augustus was also chief priest of Gaul and president of the provincial assembly. (The holder of this office was elected by the Gallic Assembly.) Sollemnis used his position to check the appeal to the emperor against Paulinus. For this service he was rewarded both by Paulinus and his successor, Aedinius Julianus. Paulinus, now governor in Britain, appointed Sollemnis as his *assessor*, the judicial adviser assigned to the governor. The *assessor*'s salary was paid from public funds, usually amounting to approximately one-tenth the salary of the officer he advised. The known cases place the figure at from one to ten pounds of gold per year. Evidently Sollemnis received his salary in advance. The rich presents (pay-off?) awarded to Sollemnis are touchingly British—besides the gold, they included British rugs and cloaks, probably the famed *birrus Britannicus*, and a sealskin. We do not know if the charges made in the Council of the Gauls were legitimate grievances or, as the inscription with its text of a letter suggests, the sour grapes of unobtained patronage. Inscriptions are generally erected by the winners. These inscriptions may well record an example of how a web of patronage subverted the function of a provincial assembly. If so, we have the chilling scenario of a corrupt governor moving on to rule in Britain and appointing a corrupt client to act as his judicial adviser. The effect on the quality of justice in the British province can be imagined. Had the charges against Claudius Paulinus been approved in the Council, however, they could have led to his prosecution in Rome and the end of his career. Claudius Paulinus's letter to Sollemnis concludes with the sentiment that "with the favor of the gods and the emperor's sacred majesty [Sollemnis] would obtain rewards more fitting to his loyalty." In fact Sollemnis evidently never obtained his commission as tribune. Claudius Paulinus was replaced in Britain for unknown reasons.[19]

M. Antonius Gordianus is the other governor of Britannia Inferior whose career is known. After governing in Britain he evidently achieved the consulship and in 237/38 became proconsul of Africa at the ripe age of seventy-nine. In a bizarre incident following the murder of a procurator, Gordianus was caught up in a local conspiracy in 238 and proclaimed emperor. He wore the purple for only twenty-two days before hanging himself. A seventy-nine-year-old emperor was remarkable, but a governor of Britain appointed in his late fifties is also curious. An elderly man may have been a "safe" appointment in a province with a powerful garrison. Dio claimed that Caracalla tried to eliminate political enemies by appointing them "to uncongenial provinces, the climate of which was deleterious to their health, exposing them to excessive heat or cold on the pretext of giving them great honor." The description of Gordianus in the *Historia Augusta* supports the thesis of an unthreatening governor. "There is nothing you can say that he ever did passionately, immoderately, or excessively. His love of sleep was enormous; he would doze off even at table, if he was dining with friends, and without any embarrassment."[20]

Of the major officials besides governors—the legionary legates, *juridici,* and procurators—but little is known. In the late Roman period the British legates were not "high-fliers."[21] The *juridici* of the early Roman period were prominent men, but nothing can be said of the quality of their successors in the third and fourth centuries. A rare mention of Britain in the legal records of the fourth century concerns the obligations of decurions, a passage sometimes interpreted as indicating a conflict between Celtic and Roman tenurial custom.[22] The first two procurators to

---

[19] It is possible that he died in office. See Anthony R. Birley, *People of Roman Britain,* 42–43; Anthony R. Birley, *Fasti of Roman Britain,* 188–90. For a somewhat different interpretation of the Marbre de Thorigny see MacMullen, *Corruption and Decline,* 105–6.
[20] Dio 77.11.6–7. The passage from *Historia Augusta* is quoted in Grant, *Roman Emperors,* 142. For a good discussion see Anthony R. Birley, *Fasti of Roman Britain,* 184.
[21] Anthony R. Birley, *People of Roman Britain,* 43–56.
[22] *Cod. Theod.* 11.7.2, "De exactionibus." See Stevens, "Possible Conflict."

serve in Britain provide a Hyde and Jekyll contrast and illustrate the worst and best of Roman provincial government. The craven Decianus Catus helped imperil Roman control in Britain.[23] According to both Dio and Tacitus his rapacity sparked Boudicca's revolt. His successor, Julius Classicianus, emerges through the veil of Tacitus's dislike as an able man, successful even in dismissing the victorious but over-vengeful governor and thereby aiding in the restoration of long-term Roman rule.[24] Classicianus was probably a native of northern Gaul; perhaps it was his birth that made him show fellow feeling for the British tribes in rebellion. His selection as procurator in the sensitive period following the rebellion reflects credit on Roman statecraft. Interestingly, however, except for an unnamed *vicarius* from Belgica referred to by Ausonius, Classicianus seems the only northern Gaul recorded as holding a major position of power throughout the long Roman tenure in Britain.[25] Of later procurators, few personalities emerge. In the civil war following the murder of Commodus, Britain had backed its own governor, Clodius Albinus. He was defeated by Severus in 197 at Lyons. After taking possession of Britain, Severus appointed a relative as provincial procurator, Sextus Varius Marcellus. As Salway suggests, this appointment doubtless guaranteed that collection of taxes in the recently conquered province was in reliable and merciless hands. Subsequently in Severus's reign, Marcus Oclatinius Adventus was made procurator. He was a barely literate soldier of humble origin whose sinister preparation for office included a career in the military police (*speculator*) and the head of the secret police (*princeps peregrinorum*). These skills added to control of Britannia's tax records must have made him an effective agent in confiscating the properties of Albinus's supporters. The bare outlines of one other procurator emerge from late third-century sources. The infamous Allectus, *rationalis summae rei* (chief finance officer) murdered and replaced his patron Carausius. In the aftermath of his own defeat the inhabitants of Britain were menaced by his mercenary army of ferocious Franks.[26] During the reorganization of administrative careers in the later third century the office of (equestrian) procurator lapsed. In the fourth century, finances including taxation were controlled by the *comes sacrorum largitionum* (count of the sacred largesses), the praetorian prefects, and their staffs. In Britain, the *ration-*

---

23 Dio 62.2; Tacitus *Ann.* 14.32, 14.38.3.
24 Tacitus *Ann.* 14.38.3.
25 See the entry for C. Julius Alpin(i)us Classicianus in Anthony R. Birley, *People of Roman Britain*, 172; Frere, *Britannia*, 186–87.
26 For Marcellus and Adventus see Salway's comments in his *Oxford Illustrated History of Roman Britain*, 166. The official sources for Allectus are, of course, hostile. For a full discussion see Shiel, ed., *Episode of Carausius and Allectus*.

alis (comptroller) headed the finances of the diocese assisted by the *praepositus thesaurorum* (treasurer) located in London.

Little evidence survives concerning the personnel and organization of Roman administration in Britain after the restoration to imperial control and the implementation of Diocletian's schemes. We have evidence for only about twenty men from the high officials and senior officers serving in Britain during the final century of Roman rule there. The bare name of the first *vicarius* of Britain, L. Papius Pacatianus, is recorded in the Theodosian Code.[27] He had earlier been *praeses* of Sardinia. Ammianus recorded a few additional details of later *vicarii* in Britain.[28] Following the defeat of the usurper Magnentius, Constantius II dispatched to Britain a certain Paulus, nicknamed "the Chain," to restore the province's loyalty. The nickname referred to the fate of all, guilty or innocent, who fell in the hands of Paulus. Martinus, the vicar of Britain, tried without success to curb Paulus's excesses. In the end Martinus was reduced to the expedient of attempted murder. Failing to kill Paulus, Martinus fell on his own sword. The episode is an unhappy variation of the earlier struggle between the procurator Classicianus and governor Paulinus. Ammianus's epitaph for Martinus, "thus died a most just governor," provides a chilling indictment of the court and policies of Constantius II and places the working of central authority and the aftermath of imperial intervention in an unfavorable light. Martinus's successor, the vicar Alypius, was complimented as an excellent governor by both Julian (then caesar) and Libanius, the famous orator. Julian singled out Alypius's rule as, "active administration tempered by mildness." Was this exceptional? Ammianus called Alypius "a mild and charming man." In late Roman politics, however, the mild inherited neither the earth nor peace and Alypius was eventually exiled on false charges.[29]

The remaining characters of late Roman government in Britain of whom details survive are mostly usurpers: Magnentius, Magnus Maximus, Marcus, Gratian, and Constantine. The usurpers will be discussed later but a few references to legitimate governors of the fourth century survive in the poetry and letters of the Gallic aristocracy. Ausonius's *Parentalia* preserves an attractive portrait of his kinsman Flavius Sanctus, a *praeses* in Britain: "You, Sir, who love jests and merriment, you who hate all moroseness, neither fearing any man nor causing any man to fear, who entrap no man by trickery nor vex him at the law, but mildly and wisely live an upright life, come with reverent lips and words of good

---

[27] Preserved in a rescript dated 20 November 319. *Cod. Theod.* 11.7.2.
[28] Ammianus 14.5.9.
[29] Libanius *Ep.* 327; Julian *Ep.* 402D-404B; Ammianus 23.1.2, 29.1.44.

omen to do honour to the peaceful shade and the remains of kindly Sanctus. His service he performed diligently without tumult; with him for governor the Rutupian land rejoiced."[30] This poem carries an implied contrast between Flavius Sanctus and those governors of Britain who had to deal with rebellion, and it hints perhaps that the cause of such trouble was misgovernment.

Finally, details of the last two British vicars, Chrysanthus and Victorinus, survive in a passage of Socrates's *Ecclesiastical History* and a poem by Rutilius Namatianus.[31] Chrysanthus's father was a teacher at the court of Valens, who later became a bishop in Constantinople (albeit of the heretical Novatian sect). Chrysanthus's career included governing an Italian province (as *consularis*) and promotion to the vicarate in Britain. He was later obliged to follow his father as a bishop in Constantinople. In this last office, Chrysanthus evidently showed a sterling character, refusing a bishop's salary while distributing his own wealth to the poor. Rutilius praises his friend Victorinus, providing the backhand compliment that, although trouble and unpopularity were the expected lot of governors in Britain, his rule had been peaceful:

> The ocean to his worth
> Can witness bear, Thule can witness bear
> And every field the savage Briton ploughs,
> Where his curbed power as Prefect's deputy
> Has lasting tribute of affection great.
> That spot retired to earth's extremest bound
> Yet, as it were in City's midst, he ruled.
> It is more glorious to have striven to please
> Those whom to have failed to please is less of shame.
>
> (*De reditu suo* 498–506)

Again, in the last line is an allusion to trouble with governing Britain being a norm rather than exception. As we have seen, an anti-British prejudice is detectable in other writings of the aristocracy of southern Gaul. Ausonius, whose *Parentalia* has already been quoted, lampooned the one poet known to us from Roman Britain, Silvius Bonus, in a sequence of epigrams.[32]

---

[30] Ausonius *Parentalia* 18 (translation by Evelyn White).
[31] Socrates *His. ecc.* 7.12.1. Rutilius Namatianus *De reditu suo* 491–508; see the translation by Keene in Rutilius Namatianus, *De reditu suo,* 498–506.
[32] Ausonius *Epigr.* 107–12. Evelyn White comments: "Apparently 'a good man' and 'a Briton' were regarded as a contradiction in terms, and a Briton surnamed Bonus as something extremely humorous. The expression 'good Indian' (= dead Indian) is somewhat similar" (*Aus-*

CVIII

"This is Silvius 'Good'." "Who is Silvius?" "He is a Briton." "Either this Silvius is no Briton, or he is Silvius 'Bad.'"

CIX

Silvius is called Good and called a Briton: Who would believe a good citizen had sunk so low?

CX

No good man is a Briton. If he should begin to be plain Silvius, let the plain man cease to be good.

CXI

This is Silvius Good, but the same Silvius is a Briton: a plainer thing— believe me—is a bad Briton.

CXII

Thou Silvius art Good, a Briton: yet 'tis said thou art no good man, nor can a Briton link himself with Good.

The collected biographical details of Roman administrators in Britain provide an interesting albeit fragmentary and anecdotal picture of the nature and quality of Roman rule. From the evidentiary base it is impossible to tell if Britannia's government was significantly worse than elsewhere in the empire. In an age of patronage such as the third and fourth centuries, literary prejudice can be assumed to exaggerate both the good of those praised and the iniquity of those condemned. Notwithstanding this bias, however, at least two conclusions seem warranted: (1) a general expectation existed that Britain would be a particularly troublesome place to govern; and (2) Roman administration in Britain manifested to a high degree the general imperial governmental problems of instability, violence, venality, and incompetence.

Although Britain unfortunately lacks any detailed equivalent account of Late Roman society such as Salvian provided for Gaul, Orosius for Spain, or Augustine for North Africa, two sources illuminate conditions of particular British concern. The first of these two works is an anonymous collection of Pelagian Christian letters which on the basis of biographical details C. P. Caspari believed were written by a Briton.[33] Morris further

---

onius, 2:214–15). The translations quoted are Evelyn White's, line-breaks added. See also Anthony R. Birley, *People of Roman Britain,* 56, 159.

[33] Caspari, *Briefe.* The relevant texts may be studied as follows: *De vita Christiana* in *PL* 40:1031–46; *De virginitate* in *CSEL* 1:225–50; *Ad Celantiam* in *CSEL* 56:329–56; *De lege* in *PL* 30:105–16.

refined Caspari's argument and somewhat dubiously dubbed the anonymous author the "Sicilian Briton."[34] The letters provide exceptional insight into late-fourth- and early-fifth-century Roman society, but their relevance to social history and class relations has been hotly debated.[35] Certainly the character of Roman justice and the quality of Roman administration provide the author with his most virulent materials. The attribution of these letters to a native Briton is very speculative, but the undoubted popularity of Pelagian ideas in Britain gives the attitudes expressed a strong Romano-British relevance. A long quotation illustrates the tone of much of the work:

> We see before us plenty of examples . . . of wicked men, the sum of their sins complete, who are at this present moment being judged, and denied this present life no less than the life to come. One can easily understand it if, through changing times, one has been waiting for the end of successive magistrates [iudices] who have lived criminally; for the greater their power, the bolder their sins . . . and since while they judged over others, they were unafraid of the judgement of any other man, they were prompt to sin. Thus it is fitting that those who had no man to fear when they gave vicious judgement would feel God as a judge and avenger . . . . Those who freely shed the blood of others are now forced to spill their own. . . . Others who unjustly killed vast numbers of people have individually been torn limb from limb. . . . Their judgements killed many husbands, widowed many women, orphaned many children. They made them beggars and left them bare. . . . [36]

Political turmoil evidently resulted in the death of one set of officials. Another passage chillingly describes a Roman magistrate in action. We see perhaps the ghost of a Paulus Catena or Oclatinius Adventus: "You sit upon the tribunal. . . . Under your eyes the bodies of men like you in nature are beaten with [whips of] lead, broken with clubs, torn by the claws or burnt in the flames."[37] Throughout the letters a curiously antiquated and antagonistic attitude towards involvement or participation in Roman government is evident. For the author, Constantine might never have been converted nor the apocalyptic fervor of the early church

[34] Morris, "Pelagian Literature," 26ff. For a criticism of this argument see Wood, "End of Roman Britain," 7.
[35] Myres, "Pelagius and the End." Compare the arguments of Myres and Morris with Liebeschuetz, "Social Aims," and Liebeschuetz, "Pelagian Evidence." Cf. Peter Brown, "Pelagius and His Supporters."
[36] Translated in Morris, "Pelagian Literature," 34.
[37] Ibid., 49.

dimmed. The negative view of Roman justice and law, however, is clearly consistent with the later British traditions discussed in Chapter 4.

The second source relevant to late Roman government in Britain presents a much less passionate view of the problems of the age. Reform, not segregation, is advocated by this author. The anonymous work entitled *De rebus bellicis* dates between approximately A.D. 366 and 378.[38] The author is not explicitly concerned with Britain, but his observations are particularly relevant to a western province with a fleet and a large garrison.[39] In contrast to the "Sicilian Briton's" view of affairs, the anonymous author of *De rebus bellicis* presents a sectarian and comprehensive outlook. He perceives that the successful defense of the frontiers, his primary concern, ultimately depends on necessary reforms of social and financial aspects of imperial administration. The relevant sections, addressed as appeals to the emperor's attention, discuss the following subjects: the reduction of public grants; the origin of governmental extravagance and greed; fraudulent practices of the mint and their correction; the corruption of provincial governors; methods of economy in military expenditure; a series of inventions useful to the military; the defense of the frontiers; removing the confusion of the laws and enforcing justice. This last topic ties directly to the complaints of the "Sicilian Briton." The author of *De rebus*, however, discreetly blames misjustice on the confusion of the laws rather than the character of the magistrates: "One remedy designed to cure our civilian woes awaits Your Serene Majesty: Throw light upon the confused and contradictory rulings of the laws by a pronouncement of Your August Dignity and put a stop to dishonest litigation. For what is so alien to decent conduct as to give vent to one's passion for strife in the very place where the decisions of Justice distinguish the merits of individuals?"[40]

The measures in *De rebus* aimed at tax relief combined a suggested reduction in public grants with proposed reforms of coinage and the operation of the mint. Also included was an explanation of how the problem had gotten out of hand. This section highlights the well-known problem of overtaxation in the late empire.[41] Problems of avarice and the quality of late Roman government are highlighted in the section of *De rebus* entitled "The Corruption of the Provincial Governors": "Now in addition to these injuries, wherewith the arts of avarice afflict the provinces, comes the

---

[38] *De rebus bellicis*, in E. A. Thompson, ed., *Roman Reformer*.
[39] Stevens, "Roman Author." Most recently see Hassal and Ireland, eds., *De Rebus Bellicis*. Stevens later withdrew his suggestion concerning a British context for the author.
[40] *De rebus bellicis* 21.
[41] A. H. M. Jones, *Roman Economy*, 161–85; Deleage, *La capitation du Bas-Empire*. I am not convinced by Hopkins, "Taxes and Trade."

appalling greed of the provincial Governors, which is ruinous to the tax-payers' interests. For these men, despising the respectable character of their office, think that they have been sent into the provinces as merchants, and are all the more burdensome in that injustice proceeds from the very persons from whom a remedy should have been expected."[42] This idea is closely paralleled in a passage of the "Sicilian Briton" (dressed in more biblical language) where Roman misjustice creates widows and orphans, while preying on "hapless toilers."[43] Interestingly, the author of *De rebus* blames the governors and the "exactors," the local tax agents who are associated with individual *civitates*, but has no criticism for the *rationalis* or finance minister.[44]

In the final two sections of *De rebus*, the reforming author levels criticisms particularly relevant to the governance of Roman Britain with its numerous garrison. Officials evidently juggled pay books, allowances, and muster lists for recruits and relief forces. In what seems to be a reference to the *annona militaris* and compulsory purchase, the author states, "To these men the enlistment of recruits, the purchase of horses and corn . . . are time-honored sources of profit and the eagerly awaited opportunity for robbery."[45] There is no evidence that *De rebus* ever found an audience, but the anonymous comments substantiate modern notions that frontier provinces and heavily garrisoned areas felt an unequal and heavy weight of taxation in comparison to lightly garrisoned "core" areas. Britannia clearly falls in the first category.

The various thin strands of evidence—prosopography, literary accounts, and analogy—provide significant glimpses into the quality of imperial government of late Roman Britain. A background of governmental abuses provides a fitting introduction to a discussion of conditions within the British provinces in the fourth century.

BRITANNIA IN THE FOURTH CENTURY

The crisis faced by the Roman empire during the third century has become a commonplace in modern historical accounts. Britain escaped the worst immediate effects of the crisis, but the events molded subsequent imperial policy which did directly impinge on Britain.[46] The basic problems

---

42 *De rebus bellicis* 4.
43 Translated in Morris, "Pelagian Literature," 34.
44 *De rebus bellicis* 4.
45 *De rebus bellicis* 4–5.
46 For general discussions of the third century and after see A. H. M. Jones, *Decline of the Ancient World*; Anthony King and Martin Henig, eds., *Roman West*. Cf. Averil Cameron, *Later Roman Empire*, 1–12, 209–10.

confronting imperial authority in the aftermath of the crisis were twofold: (1) a period of prolonged civil conflict and wars of succession wasted lives and treasure, devastating the economy and destablizing the frontiers; and (2) external enemies of increasing numbers, capability, and aggressiveness threatened virtually the entire frontier system. These enemies included the Sassanian Persian empire in the east, the Sarmatians and Goths along the Danube, and tribal confederations of Germans on the Rhine. The cumulative costs of civil and frontier wars, and an increased military and bureaucratic establishment necessary to cope with now endemic "emergency," gravely disrupted the Roman economy, impoverishing substantial numbers of the population.

At the height of the third century crisis, the emperor Decius (249–51) was killed by the Goths, and Valerian (253–60) was captured by the Persians. Several areas within the empire broke away in order to guarantee local security and prosperity. Britain was included in the "Gallic" empire of the rebel Postumus.[47] This period of momentary autonomy is a convenient point at which to pick up the various threads of conditions in the British provinces. Analysis will be divided into four sections; political order, military security, economic and social order, and finally, religion.

Political Order

Britain was a passive, perhaps even willing participant in the Gallic empire. In the period A.D. 260–273, under the pretenders Postumus, Victorinus, and Tetricus, no sign of British political unrest is recorded. Numerous inscriptions of loyalty to the pretender emperors, a prolific coinage, and archaeological evidence suggestive of economic well-being indicate that this period was prosperous.[48] Shielded by the forces in Gaul and isolated by the sea, Britain suffered less from civil or foreign violence than the other areas of the empire. Aurelian (270–75) reestablished imperial control over Britain, but frequent political trouble thereafter, in contrast to earlier quietude, indicates that elements within the British provinces may not have been happy with the reunion. An unsuccessful British coup was suppressed in A.D. 276–77 but in 286 the usurper Carausius successfully created an *insulae imperium*, and ten years elapsed before Constantius recovered Britain for the empire. In July 306 Constantius's son Constantine was illegally proclaimed emperor by the British garrison.

[47] Postumus was the emperor Gallienus's lieutenant on the Rhine. Postumus murdered the praetorian prefect and Gallienus's son at Cologne. He then declared himself emperor with the support of the armies in Britain, Gaul, Spain, and Germany. The entire Roman northwest for a period of thirteen years formed an independent state within the empire. See Salway, *Roman Britain*, 273–84; Drinkwater, *Gallic Empire*.

[48] Salway, *Roman Britian*, 276–85.

British politics remained turbulent for the remainder of the century. The usurper Magnentius (350–53) evidently commanded wide support in Britain and Magnus Maximus (383–88), perhaps the best-remembered Roman figure in later British history and legend, was proclaimed emperor in 383 by the British garrison.

The explanation for British military and political discontent must lie to a great extent with the adjustments made by the Roman government to cope with the problems of the third century and after. Rebellion in Britain naturally takes the form of military revolt, but given local recruitment, the army's long residence in Britain, and the consequent web of ties of patronage, kinship, and marriage, it would be a false distinction to separate the actions of the army in Britain, or the consequences of those actions, from the civilian population or civil government. Leaders of rebellions in Britain were not always military commanders. Gratian was called *municeps tyrannus*. Throughout the empire draconian measures of an authoritarian state forced the payment of greatly increased taxes. Diocletian increased the numbers of a Roman army already swollen by the actions of Septimius Severus.[49] By the end of the fourth century the cost of the military establishment had probably doubled. Mobile enemies and a frontier that was nowhere firmly secure dictated a shift in focus to cavalry forces acting as central reserves and also serving to protect the person of the emperor.[50] Troops disposed along the traditional linear frontiers declined in status and privilege relative to the new field armies led by counts. Britain possessed no field army under the new deployment schemes and these changes must have been resented by a British garrison which, by the fourth century, was probably in large part locally recruited. Another source of resentment was possibly caused by the governmental reorganization that placed Britain under the prefect of the Gauls. Increasingly isolated from the patronage and power of the imperial court, ambitious men serving in Britain may have reacted by promoting one of their own number as an imperial pretender. It is significant in this context that no examples of native British senators, governors, or legates are known from the era of the later empire. The presence of a western emperor at Trier in Gaul throughout much of the fourth century does not seem to have promoted the careers of Britons into the higher levels of imperial service.

[49] The army of Severus counted 33 legions of 6,000 infantry each, plus auxiliary forces. The army numbered about 300,000 men. The *Notitia dignitatum*, which includes army lists, indicates Diocletian doubled the number of legions. See A. H. M. Jones, *Decline of the Ancient World*, 32; MacMullen, "How Big Was the Army?"; Eric Birley, "Septimius Severus."
[50] Elements of the field army included at various times the praetorian guards, *protectores*, and *scholae*. In addition, the comitatus might include three or four legions and detachments drawn from frontier legions. An interesting discussion of changes in Roman strategic thought is Luttwak, *Grand Strategy*, 127–94.

Costs of supporting the military and bureaucracy were made greater by the shift from taxes paid in money to taxes collected in kind, with consequent increased waste and peculation. Financial disruption, debasement, and inflation connected with the third-century crisis led to the collapse of the silver coinage used for payment of taxes and the salaries of soldiers and officials. In the fourth century the army was paid in significant part by requisitions, payments in kind, and compulsory purchases made by the state. Problems with security, spoilage, and the costs of transportation resulted in the need to raise supplies as near as possible to the troops. This in turn increased local burdens of production (*annona militaris*) and also transportation (*munus, angareia*) since the taxpayers not only had to produce the goods but also transport them to the designated recipient. As Averil Cameron recently remarked: "If such a system worked at all, it was bound to be unreliable, clumsy and extremely burdensome on local populations, who never knew what was going to be demanded from them or when." Such developments must have increased the tax burden in Britain, with its large garrison. In the first century A.D., the Britons had evidently been particularly sensitive to the abuses associated with taxes paid in kind and the delivery of such goods. Reform of these practices was a major policy for Agricola.[51] The increased importance of taxes paid in kind in the fourth century was very likely accompanied by a return of old abuses and British discontent. This load was further increased when disastrous barbarian inroads into Gaul and Germany shifted the burden more directly onto Britain for partial support of these areas.[52] Britain had perhaps always been too small for her military boots. Strabo and Appian had correctly guessed in the first century that Britain would not repay the costs of conquest. Before the third-century crisis these costs were defrayed in part through importation from other provinces. A reduction in the size of the garrison in Britain may have offset some of this burden, but as we shall see, environmental changes may have significantly reduced overall agricultural production in Britain in this period.[53] Heavy taxes must have increased discontent and paved the way for local usurpers, particularly when, as often happened, the security needs of Britain were sacrificed to imperial concerns elsewhere.

Another imperial policy contributing to political instability in Britain was the practice of exiling untrustworthy elements to "the land beyond

---

[51] Averil Cameron, *Later Roman Empire*, 36. Cf. A. H. M. Jones, *Later Roman Empire*, 448–62. See also Tacitus *Agricola* 13, 19.

[52] Julian *Ep. ad Ath.* 280A, translation from *Literary Sources*, edited by Mann and Penman; Ammianus 18.2.

[53] Strabo 4.5.3; Appian *BC* pr. 5. See Fulford, "Demonstrating Dependence." For the environment see Chapter 6 below.

farthest Ocean." Several examples are known. In the fourth century, Palladius the Antiochene, a former master of offices and thus a powerful bureaucrat, was exiled to Britain by the emperor Julian.[54] Sometime shortly before 367, Valentinus, brother-in-law of a prefect of the Gauls, was exiled in Britain. Frontinus, aide to a powerful African official convicted of treason, was banished to Britain.[55] Magnus Maximus sent two heretics into British exile during his purge of the Priscillianists.[56] As this action was taken instead of execution, it is tempting to speculate that in the eyes of his court, Britain may have represented a fate worse than death. If the numerous barbarians moved to Britain in the wake of tribal defeats were sent more to remove them from sensitive, valuable areas than to protect Britain, the province takes on the aspect of a Roman Devil's Island, a dumping ground too far away from the heart of the empire to be a danger.[57] In one certain case this policy backfired. Valentinus organized a revolt among fellow exiles (evidently numerous) and rebellious troops that temporarily wrested control of a portion of Britain from imperial authority. Ammianus describes the plot: "A certain Valentinus, who was a native of Valeria in Pannonia, a proud man, whose sister was the mate of the pernicious Vicar Maximinus, had been exiled to Britain for a serious offense. Like some dangerous animal he could not stay quiet; he pushed ahead with his destructive, revolutionary plans, nourishing an especial loathing for Theodosius. . . . However, Valentinus was exploring many possibilities both secretly and openly, and as his immoderate ambition became increasingly swollen, he approached exiles and soldiers, and promised them, as opportunity allowed, alluring rewards for the rash adventures he proposed."[58] Ammianus thus portrays a figure who, like Milton's Lucifer, would rather rule in hell than serve in heaven. The Roman practice of exiling to Britain, besides fueling an already volatile political scene, is most significant as a revelation of attitudes towards Britain held in the highest circles of court and palace. This attitude in turn helps explain the resentment and disloyalty of sections of Romano-British society.

For the losers in the later empire, the costs of political instability,

---

[54] Ammianus 22.3.3.

[55] Ammianus 28.1.21.

[56] The Church curbed Magnus Maximus's purge of this group of heretics, who were the first to be judicially murdered by Christian Roman authority. St. Martin of Tours interceded to stop their execution.

[57] Anthony R. Birley suggests that Britain was "a kind of Siberia or dumping-ground for undesirables" (*Life in Roman Britain,* 155). Marcus Aurelius, Probus, Julian, and Magnus Maximus sent political suspects, heretics, or defeated barbarians to Britain. Salway would disagree (*Roman Britain,* 395 n. 2).

[58] Ammianus 28.3.3–5, translation from *Literary Sources,* ed. Mann and Penman, 45.

particularly of failed coups, were high. In Britain an unfortunate pattern can be discerned in which rebellion, failure, and consequent punitive sanctions closed a circle of self-generating political insecurity. A British example of post-rebellion repression by Roman authorities has already been discussed in the person of Paul "The Chain." Ammianus's description of the aftermath of Magnentius's rebellion is probably also relevant to the whole succession of rebels thrown up by Britain, including Clodius Albinus, Carausius, Allectus, Magnus Maximus, Marcus, Gratian, and Constantine: "This was how Paulus carried out his crimes, and he returned to the emperor's quarters steeped in blood, bringing crowds of men almost swathed in chains and in the deepest squalor and despair. Upon their arrival the racks were made ready and the executioner prepared his hooks and instruments of torture. Of these men many were proscribed, others exiled, and a number executed with the sword. No-one readily recalls any man who was acquitted in the reign of Constantius, once such charges had reached the level of a whisper."[59]

Rebellion and attempted usurpation placed British landholders, officials, and soldiers in an insidious dilemma. If they remained loyal to a distant emperor, their lands and lives were forfeit to the local pretender. If they backed a local candidate and he later lost (even ten years later), their lives and fortunes were imperiled by imperial revenge. Herodian succinctly described this problem in the case of Clodius Albinus: "Albinus crossed with an expeditionary force from Britain to the nearest part of Gaul and sent word to all the neighboring provinces, telling the governors to send money and provisions for the army. Some obeyed and sent them— to their cost, for they paid the penalty in due course. Those who ignored his instructions made their decision more by good luck than good judgement and were safe. Their decision proved right or wrong according to how the war happened to go."[60]

For Britain, the wars happened to go badly for every usurper except Constantine the Great. The costs in terms of political stability, military security, and economic prosperity must have been immense. After the defeat of Albinus in the savage battle at Lugdunum, his wife and sons were murdered and his body and those of the senators who had fought with him were mutilated. The Severan purge extended to numbers of local aristocrats in Gaul and Spain. They were executed and their estates confiscated. In Spain the olive trade was disrupted. In Gaul factories producing *terra sigillata* pottery were destroyed or ruined when their owners were killed.

---

[59] Ammianus 14.5.9. See Graham Webster, "Possible Effects." For some of Paul's other activities see John Matthews, *Roman Empire of Ammianus*, 82, 92, 217.
[60] Herodian 3.7.1, translation from *Literary Sources*, edited by Mann and Penman.

In Britain there is less evidence of reprisals. We have discussed the Severan procurators. There is tentative evidence for changes of ownership of some British villas at this time. Possibly civilian support for Albinus was weaker in Britain than in Gaul or Spain. Perhaps there were simply no British senators to execute. Alternatively, problems with the Caledonians and Maeatae in northern Britain may have overshadowed the political reprisals in Britain in the limited written evidence.[61] Only in the aftermath of Valentinus's rebellion was leniency certainly adopted by Roman officials, and circumstances rather than official desire dictated gentle handling: "Eager for action, determined with high purpose to punish the plot he had uncovered, [Theodosius] handed over Valentinus and a few others who formed his immediate circle . . . for capital punishment; but drawing on the military experience in which he was pre-eminent . . . and looking to the future, he forbade investigations into the conspiracy to be pursued; he wanted to prevent fear spreading and the troubles in the provinces which he had lulled to rest being brought to life again."[62] All too often troubles in Roman Britain were renascent.

Military Security

The pattern of Britain's security problems in the fourth century and after has its own distinctive features and timing, but also mirrors on a smaller scale a number of the interacting elements of the earlier general third-century crisis. Meddlesome intervention in politics by locally recruited armies brought conflict between Roman factions with attendant attrition of Roman manpower. The periodic absence of frontier garrisons off supporting a pretender's claim to the imperium encouraged increasingly formidable barbarians to ravage the provinces. The link between civil conflict and barbarian threat is well illustrated by events in Britain. Imperial victory over a British pretender almost always required an expedition to chasten the tribes of the northern frontier. The drain on British military resources was almost certainly a factor in the later inability of the inhabitants effectively to resist barbarian attack. For Gildas the loss of British troops in civil wars, particularly during Magnus Maximus's reign, was a primary cause of later British defeats at the hands of Pict, Scot, and Saxon. "Rather it [Britain] cast forth a sprig of its own bitter planting, and sent Maximus to Gaul with a great retinue of hangers-on. . . . Applying cunning rather than virtue, Maximus turned the neighboring lands and

---

[61] Frere, *Britannia*, 283–84; Anthony R. Birley, *Septimius Severus the African Emperor*, 125–26. Cf. Salway, *Oxford Illustrated History of Roman Britain*, 166.

[62] Ammianus 28.3.6. Salway believes Aurelian encouraged reconciliation. He spared Tetricus, the last Gallic emperor.

provinces against Rome. . . . After that Britain was despoiled of her whole army, her military resources. . . . Quite ignorant of the ways of war, she groaned aghast for many years, trodden under foot first by two exceedingly savage overseas nations. . . ."[63] At a time when Persians and Germans posed an increased danger to Roman security, the northern tribes in Britain evidently formed confederations of increased size and military effectiveness. The process is faintly traceable in Roman sources, where tribes such as the Venicones and Vacomagi vanish to reemerge in the fourth century as Maeatae, Caledonians, and Picts. The danger these large confederations posed is evident in Dio's account of the campaigns of Severus in north Britain.[64] The Maeatae and Caledonians coordinated their opposition, the Romans waged a costly war (although Dio probably exaggerated Roman casualties at 50,000), but failed to achieve a decisive battlefield victory. The quiet frontier secured by Severus's sons was in part purchased through bribes. Agricola's Mons Graupius would never be duplicated, and control of the northern British tribes involved repeated campaigning and periodic bribery. The Picts survived all the Roman measures and emerged as Britannia's most dangerous enemy in the post-Roman period.

Besides the northern tribes, Britain faced new enemies at the close of the third century. An onset by Irish tribes (the *Scotti,* together with the mysterious Attacotti) began with raiding and ended with eventual settlement all along the west coast of Britain.[65] To complicate the problems of defense, the Irish raiding coincided with Frankish and Saxon piracy in the Channel. Dramatic evidence of Roman security problems in Britain can still be seen in the massive fortifications of the "Saxon Shore." Roman military organization in Britain changed to meet these new dangers, albeit somewhat belatedly.[66] Defense of the south was organized in a new command under a *dux* and later a *comes,* the Count of the Saxon Shore. Forces in the north were also augmented by the new units listed in the *Notitia,* but the inadequacy of even these reorganized forces is revealed by the necessity for repeated intervention by the emperor or his lieutenant with portions of the western field army. British provincial resources and leadership were unequal to their tasks, the most obvious example being the disastrous performance of the British command in the barbarian conspiracy of A.D. 367.[67] Ammianus recorded that the Count of the maritime

[63] Gildas *D.e.* 13–14.
[64] Dio 76.13.1–4, 76.12.1–5. See also Herodian 3.14–15. Mann, "Northern Frontier."
[65] Charles Thomas, "Irish Colonists"; Richards, "Irish Settlements"; Charles Thomas, "Irish Settlements."
[66] *Notitia dignitatum* (west) 28; Bartholomew and Goodburn, eds., *Aspects.*
[67] Ammianus 27.8.1, 28.3.8.

region was killed, the *dux* Fullofaudes was surprised and cut off, and the *arcani* (*areani*) leagued with the barbarian invaders. Moreover, a portion of the garrison deserted to loot the province and one area of the diocese evidently seceded in rebellion under the leadership of a certain Valentinus, a political exile. Even allowing for the unusual combination and coordination of the barbarian raiders, we must judge the performance of the British command as poor, and the obvious problems of morale and basic loyalty within the Roman ranks suggest longstanding problems and bad governance rather than a momentary collapse during a crisis.[68] Stilicho perhaps finally provided Britain with its own field force commanded by a count, but shortly thereafter circumstances in Italy forced the withdrawal of a "legion" from Britain to defend Italy.[69] The strength of the Roman army in Britain during the fourth century is uncertain. At its height in the second century the garrison in Britain probably numbered between 45,000 and 53,000 and represented more than a tenth of Rome's entire military strength. This strength was drawn down during the third century to meet continental provincial needs. At the beginning of the fourth century the army in Britain may have numbered 20,000 to 25,000 men. Simon James, in a recent deliberately minimalist argument, suggests that by the late fourth century the Roman army in Britain might have shrunk to as few as 12,000 men, including the new field army. At the other extreme, estimated from the list of units preserved in the *Notitia dignitatum* and with different assumptions concerning the average strength of the units, the army in Britain in the late fourth century might have numbered as many as 33,500 men. Even accepting the higher figure, however, the strength of the army in Britain suffered a major decline from second-century levels.[70] The military problems of the Romans in Britain had thus come full circle from the reluctance of Augustus to invade or Agricola's failure fully to subdue Britain due to problems elsewhere in the empire, to Stilicho's unwilling reduction of the garrison in Britain below any margin of safety. The Britons were thereafter forced to find their own path to security, and the search led them to a separation from the empire.

Perhaps the key element in the Roman failure to provide Britain with an effective defense lay in the changed nature of the threat to Britain—a shift from assault by enemies across defended land frontiers to attacks by sea. The linear defenses shielding the Roman areas from the northern

[68] Theodosius appointed a new commander as Vicar of Britain, a certain Civilis, thereby completing a clean sweep of the British command.

[69] W. Douglas Simpson, "Stilicho in Britain"; Claudian *Consulatu Stilichonis* 2.247–55; Claudian *On the Gothic War* 404–18.

[70] Simon T. James, "Britain and the Late Roman Army." Cf. Breeze, "Demand and Supply," 268.

tribes (the Hadrianic and Antonine Walls) were initially conceived with their flanks anchored and sheltered by water.[71] Indeed coastal ports helped supply the garrisons. The Roman scheme was sensible unless the enemy took to boats to outflank or bypass the defended zone. The Picts, for reasons yet unknown, acquired a maritime capability late in the third century. At approximately the same time Scots and Saxons began raiding by sea and with these maritime threats Britain became the most exposed target in the Roman West, as virtually the whole island was vulnerable from the sea. The problem was compounded by the lubberly nature of Roman military thought. The episode of Carausius illustrates this problem. Carausius, a Menapian seaman, organized effective naval operations against the Franks and Saxons but used the newly created naval power to defy successfully his rivals in Roman politics. The more characteristic Roman attitude is seen in the actions of Asclepiodotus, Constantius's lieutenant who, after slipping past units of the British fleet, burned his shipping the better to concentrate on a traditional land engagement. Rome's inability to deal with sea-borne enemies was not confined to Britain. The resurgence of piracy in the Mediterranean, the ravages of the Heruls, Goths, and especially the Vandals highlight an inherent weakness, but Britain was particularly exposed and vulnerable to maritime attack. Barring an efficient fleet (and even this would not have provided immunity, as Constantius's victory over Allectus shows), a possible solution to the surprise and mobility of sea-going raiders would have been decentralized political and military control crudely analogous to the feudal system, the later Western European response to the ninth-century invasions. Late Roman tactics relied heavily on regional field armies composed of higher quality regiments, the *comitatenses*, to act as strike forces against barbarian invasions. These field armies supplemented largely immobile garrison units, the *limitanei*. The British field army was a late creation and small, numbering perhaps only about 3,000 men. Neither its size nor its mobility proved adequate. Viewed in this context, political rebellions in Britain climaxing in the early fifth century can be seen as an attempt to find security through local action and autonomy.

One final aspect of the effects of the military establishment remains to be considered—the social and economic costs of conscription.[72] The empire managed to avoid widespread conscription until the fourth century, probably from a combination of a desire not to antagonize the landholding class by increasing their labor problems and also a belief that better sol-

---

[71] Breeze, *Northern Frontiers.*
[72] A. H. M. Jones, *Later Roman Empire,* 1:198; Salway, *Roman Britain,* 439, 457, 487–88, 508–10.

diers were recruited through inducements for volunteers. The ultimate resort to conscription no doubt further alienated provincials, in Britain as elsewhere. The costs of taxation and the burden of conscription must have contributed to disloyalty. After all, the expensive military, even when augmented by half-barbarous German units in the field forces, failed to provide effective security while jeopardizing prosperity and safety by sponsoring pretenders. In Britain, certain elements of the garrison (the *areani* or *arcani*) passed beyond mere ineffectuality to outright collusion with the barbarian invaders and had to be disbanded. These *areani* are mysterious. They gathered intelligence and evidently ranged north of the frontier but may have been civilian inhabitants of the paramilitary zone between Hadrian's Wall and the *Vallum* to the south.[73]

The Lower Social Order

In contrast to the revolts, usurpations, and purges attesting to the troubled relations between the central imperial administration and the army and aristocracy in Britain, the corresponding record for the conditions of the lower social orders, the *coloni*, peasants and slaves, is a literary blank. We may safely assume, however, that the social order in Britain was not immune to the complex of woes afflicting the Roman West. Driven by a need to collect greater revenues in a period of prolonged crisis, the government relied on coercion to freeze men in their occupations and forcibly collect the necessary taxation. The rich proved better able to dodge the weight of these measures (not surprisingly, since they were often the collecting agency), and a disproportionate burden of taxation fell on the poor. "Taken as a whole the peasantry were an oppressed and hapless class. Enough has been said already of the many ways in which they were exploited by the tax collector, if they were freeholders, and by the landlord's agent if they were tenants. In times of shortage it was they who were the first to suffer."[74] The poor reacted by seeking, through patronage, the protection of a powerful private person against the demands of the state. In return for protection against the tax collector's demands and favorable treatment by the landholding aristocracy, the poorer elements surrendered their land and mobility. The rich gained a dependable rural work force.[75] This process of commendation and patronage created a circular pattern destructive to the authority and resources of the state. The network of private loyalties corrupted tax collection and justice in the courts,

---

[73] Ammianus 28.3.8. See J. F. C. Hind, "Who Betrayed Britain?" Cf. Frere, *Britannia*, 337, 340–41, 350 n. 28.
[74] A. H. M. Jones, *Later Roman Empire*, 2:810.
[75] Percival, "Seigneurial Aspects."

forcing more and more poor men to seek the protection of a patron. The government helplessly watched the creation of a governing order erected within the state but independent of it. The ineffectual but shrill efforts of a series of emperors to curb the problem are recorded in the surviving record of imperial legislation. Most of the entries originated in the eastern provinces. The problem was almost certainly greater in the West, however, due to the greater power and control exercised there by the aristocracy. The plight of the poor in fifth-century Gaul is eloquently described by Salvian: "But what else can these wretched people wish for, they who suffer the incessant and even continuous destruction of public tax levies. To them there is always imminent a heavy and relentless proscription. They desert their homes, lest they be tortured in their very homes. . . . The enemy is more lenient to them than the tax collectors. . . . This very tax levying, although hard and inhuman, would nevertheless be less heavy and harsh if all would bear it equally and in common. Taxation is made more shameful and burdensome because all do not bear the burden of all. They extort tribute from the poor man for the taxes of the rich, and the weaker carry the load for the stronger."[76] Patronage provided an alternative to flight. "Except for one reason only I might well wonder that all the poor and needy taxpayers do not flee in a body to the barbarians. They do not do it, because they cannot carry with them their few little possessions, households, and families. . . . Therefore, because they are incapable of doing what they really prefer, they do the one thing of which they are capable. They give themselves to the upper classes in return for care and protection. They make themselves the captives of the rich and as it were, pass over into their jurisdiction and dependence."[77] The landed aristocracy of the West, ensconced in their great estates, protected by private forces, and able to defy the government's agents, were arguably as fatal a problem for the empire as the barbarians. Indeed, they survived as a powerful force into the Middle Ages after the Roman imperium perished.[78]

A third possibility existed for the disaffected lower classes—resort to organized brigandage or even organization of a polity to replace the Roman government. Such peasant movements were called *Bagaudae*.[79] Active rebellion was rarer than might have been expected. The *Circumcellions* in Africa and the Bagaudic movements in Gaul and Spain are the only known examples.[80] Since the literate classes deliberately suppressed references to events of this sort, however, the literary record is almost certainly an

---

[76] Salvian *De gubernatione Dei* 5.7, translation from Salvian, *Writings of Salvian*, 138.
[77] Salvian *De gubernatione Dei* 5.8, translation from Salvian, *Writings of Salvian*, 141–42.
[78] John Matthews, *Western Aristocracies*.
[79] E. A. Thompson, "Peasant Revolts"; Landsberger, ed., *Rural Protest*.
[80] Baldwin, "Peasant Revolt"; Minor, " 'Bagaudae' or 'Bacaudae'?"

underrepresentation. Bagaudic outbreaks became more frequent in the late fourth and early fifth centuries and at different times afflicted much of Gaul and Spain. The threat to Roman government was evidently serious.[81] The *Bagaudae* organized their own armies and courts and necessitated the sustained operation of large Roman armies before their eventual suppression.[82] Of these *Bagaudae* Salvian writes, "I am now about to speak of the *Bagaudae* who were despoiled, oppressed and murdered by evil and cruel judges. . . . For, by what other ways did they become *Bagaudae*, except by our wickedness, except by the wicked ways of judges, except by the proscription and pillage of those who have turned assessments of public taxes into the benefit of their own gain and have made the tax levies their own booty?"[83]

Recent studies have suggested that the *Bagaudae* were not exclusively peasants but may also have included failed local magistrates and landowners or perhaps provincial elites asserting their influence in territories where imperial power was in abeyance. Thus Bagaudic movements were probably more complicated than simple class conflicts between the poor and the elite, the *humiliores* and *honestiores*. Some of the recent interpretations, not necessarily mutually exclusive, suggest that *Bagaudae* were: (1)indigenous rural populations under the patronage and leadership of local aristocrats; (2)refugees with their free and servile dependents relocated on lands outside the Roman or barbarian orbits; (3)poor rural classes carrying out secessionist movements; and (4)common outlaws or bandits. One circumstance unites these various interpretations. Bagaudic activity occurred in a vacuum, in regions free from Roman or barbarian control. The majority of recent studies suggests that once this developed, there was a strong reluctance to be reabsorbed into the Roman state and a strong inclination to act independently for local interests in disobedience to Roman rule.[84]

Some historians have identified the separatist rebellion in Britain in 410 A.D. recorded by Zosimus as a Bagaudic incident, specifically a revolt by the poor rural classes against the empire. "So the Britons took up arms and facing danger for their own safety they freed their cities from the barbarians who threatened them; and all Armorica and the other prov-

---

[81] Wightman, "Peasants and Potentates."

[82] They were capable of besieging and taking even large fortified towns, like Autun in 271 A.D.

[83] Salvian *De gubernatione Dei* 5.6, translation from Salvian, *Writings of Salvian.*

[84] For the Marxist interpretation of Bagaudic revolt as class conflict see Dockès, "Révoltes bagaudaes." Cf. E. A. Thompson, *Saint Germanus of Auxerre,* 34–36, 62–63. For the idea of *Bagaudae* as local aristocratic elites and their clients, see Van Dam, *Leadership and Community,* 41–48. For *Bagaudae* as refugees see Drinkwater, "Bacaudae." Van Dam dissents from the idea of Bagaudic separatism: "They 'revolted' to remain Romans" (*Leadership and Community,* 48).

inces of Gaul followed the British example and freed themselves in the same way, expelling their Roman governors and setting up their own administrations as best they could." The inference that this otherwise unspecified British revolt was Bagaudic is tenuous and requires a number of assumptions concerning the chronology and character of revolts in Gaul before and after 410.[85]

If a Bagaudic rebellion in Britain in 409/10 A.D. seems problematic on the evidence of Zosimus, certain other details of conditions within Britain strongly support the probability of a troubled social order. In fact, there are hints in Ammianus's description of the barbarian conspiracy of 367–69 that suggest poorer elements within the Romano-British provincial population actively joined with the barbarian invaders and army deserters to loot the province. Ammianus uses the suggestive terms "mob" and "natives." "Theodosius learned from the confessions of the captives and the reports of the deserters that the widely scattered enemy, a mob [plebem] of various natives [gentium] and frightfully savage, could be overcome only by secret craft and unforeseen attacks."[86] Admittedly gentium is ambiguous, but in the passage immediately preceding this one, Ammianus refers to the barbarian raiders as "the predatory bands of the enemy" (vagantes hostium vastatorias manus). These bands had taken booty and captives and exacted tribute, presumably from the wealthier elements of Romano-British society. Other references to the invaders include "barbarians" (barbarica conspiratione), "the enemy" (hostilibus insidiis), and specific tribal names including Picts, Dicalydones, Verturiones, Attacotti, and Scots.

The fourth century in Britain evidently witnessed some major changes in regional rural economies.[87] Large areas of the southeast, particularly Surrey and East Anglia, perhaps underwent large-scale transformations from a predominately arable economy into a mixed or even largely stock-raising economy.[88] This change, occurring in a relatively brief time, was

[85] Zosimus 6.5.3, translation from Literary Sources, 53. E. A. Thompson believes that this passage is evidence for Bagaudic rebellion in Britain. His argument is a series of linked assumptions tied to Zosimus's statement that the rebellion of 410 spread from Britain to Armorica and other parts of Gaul. Based on this British-Armorican link, Thompson infers that the revolts in both areas were of a common nature. Since later fifth-century rebellions in Armorica were sometimes Bagaudic (417, 435, 442), Thompson concludes that the revolt of 410 was of the same sort. Therefore, the revolt in Britain must also have been Bagaudic. The argument is highly conjectural. See E. A. Thompson, "Britain A.D. 406–410," 310–14.

[86] Ammianus 27.8.9: Diffusam variarum gentium plebem, et ferocientem immaniter, non nisi per dolos occultiores, et improvisos excursus, superari posse, captivorum confessionibus, et transfugarum indiciis, doctus.

[87] Charles Thomas, ed., Rural Settlement; Rivet, "Rural Economy."

[88] Applebaum, "Roman Britain," 226–49.

evidently paralleled by increased exploitation of lands in northwest Britain for cereal production which previously had been pastoral regions.[89] Agrarian transformations of this sort inevitably entail considerable dislocation of the rural peasantry and of traditional relations between classes. The late fourth and early fifth centuries were therefore most probably a time of increased social tensions in large areas of Britain, tensions which may well be reflected in the turbulent politics of the period. It may be too much of an imaginative leap to see in these changes a case of "sheep that eat men," analogous to the later medieval and Tudor clearances, but the circumstances in Roman Britain seem to have had much in common with later enclosures, including the construction of expensive houses by the rural landowners.[90]

Another element in the agrarian scene was the increase throughout the empire of absentee landowning. The emperor, the Church, and the senatorial class commonly owned lands in a great variety of locations. The list of lands given by the biographer of Melania the Younger, for example, included estates in Britain.[91] Absentee landholding probably exacerbated the problems of the rural poor, for such landowners could exert little protection or patronage for their tenants, who were thus more exposed to exploitation and illegal practices. The impact of the third-century crisis in Gaul may also have affected landholding practices in Britain. There is some archaeological basis for suspecting a shift of investment from troubled Gaul to relatively more secure Britain in this period. New villas seem to have been built there, and the villa economy of Gaul seems to have suffered a parallel decline.[92] The abuses that sparked peasant revolts in Gaul may thus have entered Britain, since the landholding class and the practices of estate management must have been similar to a degree in both areas.

Another important influence on the rural poor in Britain was the growth of imperial estates and monopolies fueled by confiscation and extortion of lands owned by men involved in unsuccessful rebellions. An early example of expropriation on a grand scale followed the forfeiture of Brigantian lands during the reign of Antoninus Pius, who "deprived the Brigantians in Britain of most of their territory because they too had taken up arms. . . ."[93] To meet the emergency needs of the state the imperial lands must have been ruthlessly exploited. The well-known example of the arbitrary increase of Britain's grain exports to the Rhine legions by six

89 Manning, "Economic Influences."
90 Salway, *Roman Britain*, 281, 628.
91 *Vita S. Melania Junioris* 11.
92 Salway, *Roman Britain*, 280–84, 600.
93 Pausanias 8.43.3. See Salway, *Roman Britain*, 199 n. 1.

hundred shiploads in Julian's reign provides a literary confirmation of archaeological evidence interpreted as an indication of increased taxation.[94] So-called corn-drying ovens proliferate at the end of the Roman period in Britain, a phenomenon possibly linked to increased taxation in kind. The ovens may, however, have been used for malting rather than drying cereal. "The impression is gained of a situation in which the niceties of life had declined and production was regarded as all-important."[95] The payment of taxes in kind, such as the grain shipped from Britain to the Rhineland, was often associated with official corruption. An arbitrarily low price might be set by officials, if increased demands were paid for by the authorities, or a dishonest measure might be used to record weights. These very problems were singled out in the De rebus bellicis.[96] In addition to deliberate abuses, the generally high inflation of the late Roman period placed the taxpayers (cereal growers) at a great disadvantage.[97] Taxes and levies had to be paid in kind, but official purchases were paid in an inflated currency at artificial rates.

The plight of the rural poor in Britain was almost certainly worsened by climatic changes which brought in their wake flooding and coastal inundation in eastern regions. Areas of the northwest where arable farming had only recently been introduced lay on the margin of cultivable land. The cooler, wetter weather may have caused widespread agricultural failure in these areas. The details of these climatic changes are discussed more fully in Chapter 6, but the large-scale changes in Britain's rural economy, probably reflecting a measure of official government pressure, in combination with deteriorating weather patterns, would have resulted in decreased harvests, desperate peasantry, and ever greater hardship from taxation. Official demands and agricultural expansion could result in natural disasters for British farmers, as the failure of the Roman settlement of the Fens clearly shows.[98] The necessity for increased taxes, a cold-blooded attitude on the part of Roman officials, and natural environmental changes must have been a fatal combination for many of the rural British population. Under these circumstances the attitude of the poor in rural Britain can hardly have been an asset to the Roman administration. It would be surprising if they failed to show deep antipathy toward Roman justice, taxation, and government. If not active in aiding barbarian invasion or political rebellion, the lower social orders in Britain would have

[94] Ammianus 18.2.3; Zosimus 3.5. Julian Ep. ad Ath. 279D–280A–C.
[95] Applebaum, "Roman Britain," 230.
[96] See also Tacitus Agricola 19. De rebus bellicis 4–5.
[97] A. H. M. Jones, "Inflation"; Ravetz, "Fourth Century Inflation."
[98] Phillips, ed., Fenland.

failed to support the government or the landowning elite with labor, blood, or treasure beyond what the government could compel by force.

Religious Belief and Political Loyalty

One final aspect of life in the British provinces is relevant to conditions there and to the willingness or ability of the Romano-Britons to defend the Roman order. Religion is sometimes an important resource in the preservation or expansion of a culture or state. The rise of Christian Europe and the growth of the Arab world under Islam are good examples. In the later Roman world the advantages brought to the emperor and the empire with the adoption of Christianity are a commonplace of historical commentary. Caesaropapism or imperial control of the church—with its wealth, powerful networks of patronage and communication, organization, the tremendous influence and support of energetic bishops—strengthened the late Roman state and aided the preservation of *Romanitas*. Recent revisions have stripped away the idea of a death struggle between pagans and Christians or even the reality of a general pagan revival in the fourth century. Tensions between pagans and Christians are revealed in the sources to be disputes between members of the same class rather than a conflict between classes. Older views of a sharp struggle between pagans and Christians in fourth-century Rome have been shown to rest on false assumptions. The bark of antipagan legislation was doubtless worse than its bite. Nevertheless, as Averil Cameron recently emphasized, disputes over Christian heresies played a central role in fourth-century history. Even if attempts to outlaw or persecute paganism were the exception rather than the rule, tensions between pagans and Christians involved significant social and cultural factors. In the Christianizing tradition, paganism is portrayed as declining and somehow religiously bankrupt. Christianity expanded to fill a spiritual void in an age of intense spirituality. Such a view tends to minimize the tension, dislocation, and consequences following from the Constantinian union of empire and Christian Church.[99]

MacMullen has recently surveyed the Christianizing of the Roman empire. He marks the combination of "flattery and battery" in that process, and the role of mobs, armed force, and antipagan legislation that allied with flattery, persuasion, and material reward. Religion may aid in the preservation and expansion of a state but it is a two-edged sword. Gibbon added bishops and Christianity to the barbarians in his list of causes of Rome's decline. At the very least we must be prepared to recog-

[99] For a recent review of pagan-Christian relations see Averil Cameron, *Later Roman Empire*, 66–84, 151–69.

nize the exasperation and alienation in the minds of non-Christian Romans.[100] The deleterious effects of Christianity on the Roman empire have been often discussed. These effects may be conveniently grouped into four headings: (1) The loss of manpower and resources alienated from the Roman state into the Christian church; (2) an increase in instability caused by the Christian apocalyptic expectation; (3) an increase in violence and disorder initiated by the Christian pursuit of a single orthodox belief, forcibly imposed by the power of the state on both heretics and pagans; (4) a subtle undermining of allegiance through the creation of an alternative focus of loyalty, best typified in works written by ostensibly patriotic Romans such as Augustine's *City of God.*

The first point affected Roman strength both directly and indirectly. Money and manpower supporting the growing monastic element in the Christian church were a direct loss. Celibacy and the influence of dualistic antimaterial philosophy mortgaged the future as well as the present. Christian prejudice against participation in either the army or civilian service weakened Roman manpower and morale. Tertullian wrote, "Nothing, then, is more foreign to us than the state."[101] This attitude persisted, especially in the West. At the Council of Elvira (306), the bishops ruled that no Christian serving in an official secular post could be allowed to enter a church. Constantine's pro-Christian sympathies failed to eradicate this attitude toward state service. In 313 at the Council of Arles, the church decreed that political officeholders must be excluded from holy communion.[102] A series of popes excluded those in government service from holy orders. Killing by Christians even in army service could be treated as murder and punished by excommunication. The lives of Saint Martin and Paulinus of Nola record Christian antipathy to military service even into the fifth century.[103] The psychological trauma and disruption created by Christian apocalyptic visions waned with the passage of time. The sack of Rome in 410, however, called the vision back into force. The belief that the world would soon end and that "eternal" Rome would perish bordered on treason in the eyes of Roman secular authorities.[104] The use of force by the state to compel obedience to Christian orthodoxy is best seen in the imperial edicts where Manichees, Donatists, Priscillianists, Pelagians, and others are attacked.[105] Pagan re-

100 MacMullen, *Christianizing the Empire.* For pagan vitality see Lane Fox, *Pagans and Christians.*
101 The passage from Tertullian may be read in translation in Grant, *Fall of the Roman Empire,* 186.
102 *Ecclesia Occidentalis,* ed. Schwartz, 396–415.
103 Hoare, trans., *Western Fathers,* 3–44; Coster, *Late Roman Studies,* 183–204.
104 McGinn, *Visions of the End,* 1–65; R. P. C. Hanson, "Reaction of the Church."
105 N. Q. King, "Theodosian Code."

sistance seems to have been mostly passive, but by the fourth century, with church and state so closely intertwined, any apparent assertion of pagan practice might be interpreted as anti-authority, antisocial actions.[106] Certainly the separation between pagan and Christian must have further divided an already unraveling society. Ambrose, for example, preached against "mixed" marriages between Christians and pagans. After Stilicho's death pagans were for a time excluded from the army because of their doubtful loyalty to a now Christian state. The greatest religious violence, however, grew from clashes between differing Christian sects rather than conflict between pagan and Christian.[107] After Constantine, the emperor presided in person as the champion of Christian orthodoxy.[108] Through persuasion, reward, and coercion, a succession of emperors pursued the mirage of Christian unity to buttress a failing state. The emperors reluctantly intervened in christological controversies and local religious conflicts such as the Donatist schism in Africa.[109] In 407/8 heresy was declared a public crime and non-Catholic Christians were excluded from court. Augustine and others pioneered the "just" use of force against heresy. In 384 the first heretics had been executed by the state. If, as Peter Brown has argued, the Christian homogeneity, created in part by state intervention, played a vital role in the survival of the Roman empire in the East, the western Catholic "orthodoxy" frequently placed church and secular authorities in opposition.[110] Religion divided town from countryside and retarded the assimilation of German Arian Christians into Roman society, thereby contributing to the creation of barbarian Europe rather than the preservation of Rome.[111]

It is difficult to apply the religious developments of the later empire to a narrow British context. Britain is one of the most poorly documented of the western provinces in matters of religion.[112] There is a strong temptation to study Romano-British Christianity through the rearview mirror, influenced by the potent hindsight that Britain alone among the western provinces failed to preserve a strong, episcopally dominated church. The most vexing difficulty is simply to determine the extent of Christianity in Britain by the fourth and fifth centuries. The most authoritative monograph does not resolve this question[113] and scholarly opinion remains

[106] Momigliano, "Introduction: Christianity and the Decline," 1–16.
[107] Peter Brown, *Religion and Society.*
[108] Setton, *Christian Attitude.*
[109] Barnes, "Beginnings of Donatism"; Peter Brown, "Religious Dissent."
[110] Peter Brown, "Later Roman Empire."
[111] Baker, ed., *Church in Town and Countryside.*
[112] Radford, "Christian Origins"; Frend, "Religion in Roman Britain."
[113] Charles Thomas, *Christianity in Roman Britain.* Cf. Watts, *Christians and Pagans,* 215–30.

divided between contrasting positions. A minimalist argument opts for a relatively small Christian community in Britain largely confined to communities in the towns.[114] The opposing school posits a significant Christian element in the population spread throughout all levels of British society. Using scattered textual references together with the archaeological evidence of hoards, mosaics, baptismal tanks, and other Christian-influenced material remains, it is possible to plot a rough chart of the progress of Christianity in Britain. The texts confirm the presence of Christians, with representatives of British churches attending councils on the continent, but they do not allow a reconstruction of their numbers in Britain or of their social background.[115] Neither does the archaeological evidence lend itself to exact interpretations. Artistic themes in Christian silver plate from hoards such as Water Newton, and pagan imagery coexisting with Christian themes on mosaics such as those from Frampton, perhaps unexpectedly show Christian links with pagan custom. The owners within the Romano-British elite must have had rather heterodox ideas. Absorption rather than destruction of pagan tradition seems indicated. As W. H. C. Frend remarked of the Mildenhall treasure, "At this period the combination of pagan and Christian elements in a single treasure suggests a Christian owner of great wealth who nonetheless accepted the reality of traditional religious motives, especially when expressed on objects of beauty.[116] In general, the progress of Christianity in Britain seems to develop somewhat anemically, but in parallel with the growth of Christianity in Gaul. The most significant fact emerges only after the Roman period—the failure of the Christian church to survive in recognizable form in the most Romanized sections of southeastern Britain and the related failure of the British church to convert the Anglo-Saxon invaders. Even in the western British areas long free of Anglo-Saxon control, the church survived in a form in which monastic organization dominated the diocesan structure.[117] The condition of Christianity in Roman Britain is thus a contentious subject, but in my opinion it can best be understood by assuming that Christianity throughout the fourth century remained very much a minority religion. *Romanitas* and Christianity were intimately interrelated in the late Roman era.[118] If Christianity was not as well established in Britain as in the other western provinces, then a strong

---

[114] Frend, "Ecclesia Britannica." For a recent survey see Henig, "Religion in Roman Britain." See also Frend, "Pagans, Christians."

[115] *Councils and Ecclesiastical Documents*, edited by Haddan and Stubbs, 1:4–21; Barley and Hanson, eds., *Christianity in Britain*; Frend, "Romano-British Christianity."

[116] Frend, "Pagans, Christians," 123. Cf. Henig, "Religion in Roman Britain," 227–30.

[117] Owen Chadwick, "Gildas and the Monastic Order."

[118] Palanque and de Labriolle, *Church in the Empire*.

presumption exists that Romanization was likewise underdeveloped in Britain. In this context the possibility of a so-called "Celtic Renaissance" in fourth-century Britain—the revival of native artwork at the expense of imperial styles—may take on political and cultural significance. Such an inference is complicated by continued use of late imperial styles. A possible parallel may be drawn with a resurgence of native styles in Syria and Egypt and the use of Coptic and Syriac languages. Here the religious context is Christian rather than pagan, but inter-Christian rivalries seriously disturbed relations between these regions and the imperial government. K. S. Painter has suggested that the evident failure of Latin to spread among a Celtic-speaking rural population in Britain may have isolated Christianity in urban and aristocratic circles.[119] Some scholars have seen in the revived native styles a "nativist" rejection of Roman culture.[120]

Archaeologists and historians have long discussed the idea of a pagan revival at the end of the Roman era.[121] Such a revival in fourth-century Britain, partially coincident with the Celtic revival, has been urged on the basis of certain shrines and sanctuaries (often located on hillfort sites) being refurbished and reused after long periods of disuse. The crucial site for this theory is Lydney Park, Gloucester.[122] If a pagan revival in opposition to a now-Christian government could be added to the evidence of a revived native Celtic art-style—a rejection of Roman styles and fashions—then the next step of deducing a strong anti-Roman current in fourth-century Britain would not be farfetched. Unfortunately, reexcavation at Lydney in the summer of 1981 failed to confirm the site's pivotal role as an example of fourth-century pagan revival. Instead of reuse following a long period of abandonment, the excavation suggested that occupation at Lydney had been continuous, perhaps ending in the late fourth century. Pagan sites at Woodeaton, Frilford, Pagan's Hill, and Nettleton all provide examples of what seem to be pagan temples enjoying strong popular support throughout the fourth century. Instead of a fourth-century revival, we should probably see the continued strength of Romano-Celtic paganism in Britain. Compared to what happened in other areas of the empire, this seems exceptional.[123]

The archaeological picture of religious life in Roman Britain is very mixed.[124] Native British cults, eastern mystery cults, and Christianity are

119 Painter, "Villas and Christianity."
120 MacMullen, *Enemies of the Roman Order*, 229.
121 Bloch, "Pagan Revival."
122 Stephen Johnson, *Later Roman Britain*, 34; R. E. M. Wheeler, *Report on the Excavations*.
123 Frend, "Pagans, Christians," 127.
124 M. J. Green, *Corpus of Religious Material*; Warwick Rodwell, ed., *Temples, Churches, and Religion*; M. J. T. Lewis, *Temples in Roman Britain*.

all confirmed in a fourth-century context. The destruction of the Mithraea at Carrawburgh and Rudchester on Hadrian's Wall and evidence of an attack on the Wallbrook Mithraeum in London provide surprisingly early evidence of pagan-Christian friction in Britain in the first decades of the fourth century. The earliest known attack on a Mithraeum in the city of Rome itself was in 377 A.D. Mithraism, an eastern mystery cult derived from Persian Zoroastrianism, was popular in the western province among army officers and merchants. It was one of Christianity's strongest rivals.[125] Christian influence is most spectacularly revealed in "house-churches" such as Lullingstone.[126] So far, however, no evidence for large churches or identifiably Christian communities in urban contexts (intramural churches) has been found. Intramural churches, as the seats of bishops, are associated with a powerfully established church. The church at Silchester, where a congregation of fifty would have been uncomfortably crowded, remains the largest Christian structure known from the Roman period. The identification of the building as a church is not universally accepted. The site seems to end in squatter occupation about 370 A.D. Several other putative Romano-British intramural churches are larger than Silchester, but a comparison of the congregational areas of probable Romano-British extramural and intramural churches with their European contemporaries suggests that Romano-British congregations were smaller than those of neighboring provinces. Icklingham provides a British example of a cemetery church, the third major late Roman type. The safest overall conclusion based on current evidence is that religion in fourth-century Britain was very diverse. As Martin Henig concludes in a recent survey of the evidence, "It is abundantly clear that even in the fourth century, Christianity did not oust more traditional forms of religion."[127] Lack of religious homogeneity and the failure of the Christian church to secure a position of religious dominance minimize the potential aid that the Romano-British church might have offered the government in the diocese during a period of great stress. As a corollary, the scope for alienation between the bulk of the pagan population and an intensely Christian court and government must have been significant.

If Christianity in Britain was more or less on track with continental developments until the mid-fourth century, what factors intervened thereafter to stunt the spread of Christianity in Britain? Although Ninian and Patrick represent missionary activity in the British church, in the

---

[125] Harris and Harris, *Oriental Cults.* For Mithraea see Merrifield, *London,* 211–12.
[126] Painter, "Villas and Christianity."
[127] Charles Thomas, "Churches in Late Roman Britain." The intramural sites of Richborough and St. Paul-in-the-Bail (Lincoln) are larger than Silchester. See Watts, *Christians and Pagans,* 143–45, 221–22. Henig, "Religion in Roman Britain," 230.

fourth century the Romano-British church in southern Britain evidently produced no equivalents to Martin of Tours, Paulinus of Nola, and Victricius of Rouen, or to their arousing of popular religious fervor and agressive evangelizing among the pagan country folk of Gaul. This may well be a vital missing ingredient. Britain seems never to have undergone "the very short and decisive third period" in MacMullen's recently proposed scheme of conversion.[128] Insular political history may provide a few clues. In the aftermath of Magnentius's failed usurpation, his supporters in Britain were savagely punished by the agents of Constantius II. Britain had been Magnentius's launchpad and Ammianus recorded the pattern of retribution there. Magnentius's pagan sympathies and probably those of many of his supporters injected a religious element into Constantius's retribution.[129] This emperor was agressively antipagan and enacted laws punishing pagan sacrifices with death. Perhaps the policy backfired in Britain and created a legacy that hindered subsequent Christian proselytizing. It is interesting to note that at the controversial Council of Arminium (359/60) Constantius's offer of state hospitality was refused by almost all the bishops there except for three from Britain. Constantius II was followed by the pagan emperor Julian (361–63). There followed a brief but confusing shift of gears in the realm of state religion and imperial patronage. Julian's attempt to restore paganism in the empire failed. The single greatest act of provocation against the Christians during his reign was his attempt to restore the Jewish Temple at Jerusalem, aimed at confounding a popular Christian prophecy and refuting Christ's own words (Matt. 24:2). Interestingly, he appointed to this task Alypius, "a former *vicarius* of Britain." For a time this man known as the former vicar of Britain must have taken center stage in the hatred and fear of Christians throughout the empire. He eventually came to a bad end, condemned and sentenced on a charge of poisoning. Such trials of sexual misconduct, poisoning, and magic may reflect the tense conditions of cultural and social relations between pagans and Christians.[130] Julian's successor was Valentinian I (364–75), who restored Christianity as the state religion, but in a relatively tolerant form. Julian and Valentinian collectively may have provided Romano-British paganism an opportunity to recover from Constantius's reprisals. Frend recently suggested that the impact of "the barbarian conspiracy" of A.D. 367 may have been the decisive influence that stymied the development of Christianity in late-fourth-century Britain. The barbarians struck at a particularly sensitive time.

---

[128] MacMullen, *Christianizing the Empire,* 119.
[129] Graham Webster, "Possible Effects," 247–54.
[130] Ammianus 23.1.2, 29.1.44. Cf. Averil Cameron, *Later Roman Empire,* 97, 163.

The evidence seems to converge. Down to c. 360 the Christian Church was making significant headway. It was in the mainstream of Christian doctrine, liturgy and art. After that date its slow progress contrasts with its ever more rapid advance on the Continent. . . . Something had knocked the heart out of rural Christianity in areas where previously it had been making most progress. The finger of suspicion points to the years 367–369 as decisive for its fate. The "barbarian conspiracy" wrought its havoc just at the time when paganism and Christianity were finely balanced. Associated too much with the defects of the imperial system and with the villa-owning aristocracy, Christianity failed to surmount the crisis. When in the 440s the Anglo-Saxon invasion began in earnest the Christian Church was unable to provide the same rallying point as it did with success on the Continent.[131]

If Christianity was a minority religion in fourth-century Roman Britain, its ranks were evidently not troubled by divisive heresy. Despite Gildas's charge to the contrary, the Christian church in Britain was apparently a staunch and consistent supporter of the Council of Nicea. Only in the early fifth century do we have evidence of a heresy disrupting Romano-British Christian circles. The heresiarch was a native son.

The best-known, or perhaps infamous, Briton of the fourth and fifth centuries was Pelagius, a theologian, moralist, and condemned heretic. Although authorship is disputed, a number of his works survive. He was active in Rome in the period roughly 380–400 A.D., gathering aristocratic support and building a reputation as an ascetic and reformer. About 402–5, Pelagius strenuously objected to Augustine's doctrine of grace, predestination, and free will. Augustine stressed the essential sinfulness of humanity, stemming from original sin, and the helplessness of the individual in the face of an overwhelming, predestined divine plan. Salvation came only to the elect through the agency of divine grace (*gratia*). In contrast, Pelagian leaders, including Rufinus the Syrian, Celestius, and Pelagius himself, rejected the doctrine of original sin and championed the idea of man as a free moral agent, created by God with the capacity to resist evil and choose good. Individuals thus carried significant responsibility for their actions. Grace was theoretically necessary for salvation, but appeared as an aid to human will in the form of divine teaching and revelation. These opposing views were refined and expounded in hot debate through a series of treatises and letters. About 409 Pelagius left Rome for Carthage and eventually Palestine. The doctrinal enemies of the Pelagians pursued them in a number of synods and church councils.

---

[131] Frend, "Pagans, Christians," 131.

Celestius was condemned at Carthage in 411. The African bishops spearheaded the anti-Pelagian drive, eventually convincing the imperial court and papacy of the dangers posed by Pelagian doctrines. In 418 the Emperor Honorius condemned the Pelagians and banished them from Rome. In the same year Pope Zosimus excommunicated both Pelagius and Celestius. The controversy continued, however, and the heresy spread from Italy into Africa, Palestine, Spain, and eventually into Gaul and Britain.[132]

Aspects of Pelagian doctrines have tempted some historians to link theological and moral principles with social and political conditions. Michael Grant, for example, associates Augustine's doctrine of providence, predestination, and grace, in which the individual is helpless within an overwhelming predeterminism, with fatalism, apathy, and inertia. In contrast, the Pelagian doctrines are closer to classical humanism and the idea of achievement through human endeavor. While acknowledging that Pelagius was primarily concerned with spiritual salvation, Grant suggests that these doctrines were also applicable to the earthly survival of a failing Roman state. "If people bestirred themselves more and tried harder, it could be deduced from Pelagius, they would be better men. And that also meant, though he did not put it in such a way, that they would be better able to come to the rescue of their country. . . . Pelagius believed that man makes his own history on his own account." By extension, such a doctrine and outlook might help to explain the Britons' exceptional revolt and separation from Rome and the equally uncharacteristic, prolonged resistance to barbarian conquest. J. N. L. Myres suggests that British Pelagianism, although expressed confusedly in theological language, may actually have been an essential element in a political revolt led by well-to-do British landowners in 410 A.D. The revolt unseated the Roman system of governance and administration and was "an attack on the social corruption inherent in a totalitarian regime." Along somewhat similar lines, John Morris argues that the Pelagians had been active in Britain since the late fourth century, forming a socially radical and egalitarian influence in Romano-British politics. These Pelagians recommended a social agenda for good government to the rebel regime emerging from the tumult of 406–11 A.D.[133]

---

[132] For a detailed treatment of the Pelagian heresy see B. R. Rees, *Pelagius*. Charles Thomas gives a useful brief overview in *Christianity in Roman Britain*, 53–60. The Augustinian passage that triggered Pelagius's reaction was *Confessions* 10.29. See Pelagius, *The Letters of Pelagius*, trans. B. R. Rees.

[133] Grant, *Fall of the Roman Empire*, 192. Myres, "Pelagius and the End," 26; Myres, "Introduction," 6. John R. Morris, "Pelagian Literature," 34; John R. Morris, "Literary Evidence," 61–73.

Problems of context and chronology undercut these interesting attempts to link Pelagian teachings with the social and political arena of later Roman Britain. There is no clear evidence that Pelagius or his contemporaries ever regarded themselves as political or social reformers or their movement as anything except an attempt at ascetic reform. Prominent scholars doubt that late Roman heresies possessed socially translatable aims, but see them as theological conflicts confined within ascetic, largely aristocratic circles.[134] Moreover, the surviving evidence fails to establish the presence of Pelagians in Britain prior to about 429 A.D. Strictly speaking, the Pelagian heresy seems to have begun in Rome. It was there that Pelagius first encountered Augustine's extreme doctrine of predestination and grace and began his conflict with Augustine and Jerome. It was in Rome that Pelagius first met Celestius and Rufinus of Syria, the other prominent spokesmen of the Pelagian movement. Hostile contemporary sources credit these men with some essential Pelagian doctrines. Marius Mercator even attributed the origin of the heresy to Rufinus, "who not daring to promote it on his own, was clever enough to hoodwink a British monk named Pelagius into doing so, having given him a thorough grounding in the aforesaid unholy and foolish doctrine." Thus the seedbed of Pelagianism may have been Rome, Syria, or some other area apart from Britain. As R. A. Markus points out, there is no factual basis for supposing that the doctrines Pelagius taught in Rome were learned at his mother's knee in Britain.[135] Nor is there any evidence that Pelagius returned to his native Britain after arriving in Rome. The first act of the Pelagian drama may very well be set entirely in the Mediterranean. Only in the late 420s had the Pelagian heresy definitely reached Britain. In a *Life of Saint Germanus* written about 480 A.D., Constantius describes two anti-Pelagian missions to the island. In an earlier work written about 432, Prosper praised Pope Celestine's efforts to eradicate the heresy in Britain. Prosper later identified Agricola, son of the Bishop Severian, as one of the Pelagians who corrupted the British church. Prosper referred to "certain enemies of grace [Pelagians] who were occupying the soil of their native land." He dates the mission of Saint Germanus to 429 and seems to indicate that the heresy had first reached Britain about that time.[136] If so, the Pelagian heresy arrived in Britain two decades after the ending of Roman central authority there and cannot have directly affected the events of 406–11.

[134] B. R. Rees, "*Pelagius*," 111–24; Charles Thomas, *Christianity in Roman Britain*, 55–60; A. H. M. Jones, "Were Heresies?"
[135] B. R. Rees, *Pelagius*, 9. Marius Mercator *Book of the Footnotes on Words of Julian* Preface 2, *P.L.* 48:111, translated by B. R. Rees, *Pelagius*. Markus, "Pelagianism," 199.
[136] Constantius *Vita Germani* 12–27; Prosper *Against the Collator* 21.2, *P.L.* 51:271; Prosper *Chronicle*, year 429, *P.L.* 51:594–95.

Given the limitations of the evidence, scholarly debate over the chronology, origins, and social or political significance of Pelagianism for Roman Britain must be inconclusive. Pelagian rejection of extreme teachings on predestination and grace may really have undermined related conceptions of acceptance of Roman imperial and ecclesiastical authority and obedience to church and state. Certainly a prejudice against oath-taking and government or military service seems evident in some Pelagian writings. Without question Pelagians emphasized the need for individual moral reform and decried judicial corruption, oppression, luxury, and ostentation. The writings of the so-called "Sicilian Briton" and his stinging attacks on wealth, power, and injustice have already been discussed. The doctrinal enemies of the Pelagians accused them of preaching in the streets and proselytizing persons of the lower social orders. This may have been mere propaganda, but it was imperial concern over public order that led to the exile of the Pelagians from Rome in 418. Although it began as an ascetic reform movement, the developed Pelagian heresy may at least partially reflect latent class or regional hostility to the Roman church or state. As B. R. Rees concludes, "Thus the final defeat of Pelagius and his followers was not only a rejection of what the Church judged to be a heresy in theological terms but an elimination of what was identified as a potential source of schism in the body social and politic." The success of Pelagianism in Britain was sufficiently alarming to authorities in Gaul or Rome to prompt the intervention of counter-missions. The late Romano-British or immediate post-Roman church in Britain evidently found Pelagian teachings attractive. Once established in the island the heresy seems to have been particularly stubborn. Pelagian criticisms of wealth and participation in government service represent a particularly sharp, intense, and late strain of what Peter Brown calls the Christianity of discontinuity.[137] The tendency of certain elements of society to drop out of secular affairs, particularly the withdrawal of gifted and prominent men from public life, cannot have been welcomed by a Roman state under attack from without and desperate for men and loyalty. In this context it is perhaps worth noting that Christianity survived in Britain in a strongly monastic form until the arrival of the Roman mission of 597.

Gildas, writing in the post-Roman period, recalled the earlier Christian experience in Britain. His perspective and wording are jaundiced and suspect, but they provide a uniquely British view of Britain's Christian experience under Roman rule: "Christ's precepts were received by the inhabi-

---

[137] Peter Brown, *Religion and Society*, 195; B. R. Rees, *Pelagius*, 20. E. A. Thompson does not accept that Pelagianism was ever strongly established in Britain. See E. A. Thompson, *Saint Germanus*, 22–23; E. A. Thompson, "Gildas," 211. For a discussion of the strength and longevity of Pelagianism in Britain see B. R. Rees, *Pelagius*, 110–23.

tants [of Britain] without enthusiasm. . . ."[138] Nevertheless, the British Christians remained "more or less pure" and were strengthened in faith by martyrs such as Alban, victims of the persecution of Diocletian. Later, however: "This pleasant agreement [Christian concord] between the head and limbs of Christ endured until the Arian treason, like a savage snake, vomited its foreign poison upon us, and caused the fatal separation of brothers who had lived as one. And as though there were a set route across the ocean there came every kind of wild beast, brandishing in their horrid mouths the death-dealing venom of every heresy, and planting lethal bites in a country that always longed to hear some novelty—and never took firm hold of anything." Usurpation of tyrants followed closely on the heels of heresy. Gildas's concept of treason or treachery seems to include both spiritual and political aspects. Disaster culminated with the actions of Magnus Maximus, Gildas's arch-villain. "At length the tyrant thickets increased and were all but bursting into a savage forest. The island was still Roman in name, but not by law and custom. Rather, it cast forth a sprig of its own bitter planting, and sent Maximus to Gaul."[139] In fact, the career of Magnus Maximus ties Christianity and Britain to the ugly theme of state-enforced religious coercion. Using the British garrison, Magnus Maximus entered continental politics in an attempt to become emperor. He had the dubious distinction of first using the secular arm to execute heretics. In 384 Priscillianists were killed in Spain by his command, quite possibly by British troops.

Gildas exaggerated the Britons' propensity for heresy but recognized the vital link between Christian orthodoxy, religious unity, and political loyalty in the later Roman empire. In the 420s some Britons may well have given a warmer welcome to heretical notions than to St. Germanus and the representatives of fifth-century Roman orthodoxy. Their descendants certainly seem to have offered a chilly reception to a later Roman mission in 597 led by yet another Augustine. The Christian community in the immediate post-Roman period was thus itself divided and did not by any means unanimously support the established Roman social and cultural order. Moreover, the Christian element was only one portion of a diverse religious scene. At the ending of Roman Britain a divided religious community can have offered only negligible support to a Roman administration and *Romanitas* beset by foreign enemies without and internal factions within.

[138] Gildas *D.e.* 9.1.
[139] Gildas *D.e.* 12–13.

The Environment and the End of Roman Britain

THE POSSIBILITY EXISTS that the social and economic problems of later Roman Britain were worsened significantly by changes in the natural environment. Two factors in particular call for investigation—epidemic disease and climatic deterioration, the latter being potentially associated with the problems of harvest failure, famine, changes in settlement pattern, and migration.

The role assigned to environmental forces in the decline of Rome, like so much of the causal analysis associated with the demise of the empire, reflects a cyclic historical fashion. In the 1930s, geographical determinists (such as Ellsworth Huntington) elevated environmental factors and particularly climate into independent, even predominant, agents in the decline of civilizations. Rejection of such arguments led to their academic eclipse, but environmental factors such as disease are again being seriously considered as partially influencing the fortunes of civilizations. W. H. McNeill's *Plagues and Peoples* is a good example. Less heralded in popular historical debate are recent accomplishments in the study of historical climate.[1] Sophistication in methods of analysis and improved international cooperation among scholars have made possible a reconstruction of climate during the past two millennia. Three aspects of recent findings are particularly relevant for historians. First, the variability of climate during the historical period was far greater than has long been believed. Second,

[1] Huntington, *Civilization and Climate*; Huntington, "Climatic Change"; Tatham, "Environmentalism and Possibilism"; Manley, "Revival of Climatic Determinism." See also Lamb and Ingram, "Climate and History"; Rotberg and Rabb, eds., *Climate and History*.

climatic change was at times much more rapid than previously thought. Popular conceptions of climatic change as invariably part of a *longue durée*, the long duration of structural continuity including climate, the land, the sea, and vegetation, that alters so gradually over so long a time as to be virtually unnoticeable to a single human generation, underestimate the speed with which major climatic shifts can occur. As H. H. Lamb points out, climatic changes "extend to all time scales. . . . sometimes they are gradual but sometimes sharp." A stairstep pattern has been suggested, with periods of rapid change followed by long stable periods. This pattern, in contrast to earlier notions of slow, steady change, would have placed much greater stress during adverse conditions on the ability of human cultures to adapt successfully to changes in the environment. Third, although nothing like agreement exists among historians of past climate, recent analyses attempting to identify periods of globally synchronous, rapid climatic change suggest that the period circa 300–450 A.D. may mark an era of major change.[2] The coincidence in time of this suggested climatic deterioration and the political breakdown of Roman rule in Western Europe raises the possibility that the environment may have contributed to the Roman failure.

CLIMATE

The Roman era in Britain (A.D. 43–410) coincided with a generally favorable period of climate, conditions being warmer, drier, and less stormy than in the preceding "Belgic" Iron Age. Over a longer perspective, the climate of the Bronze Age had provided the climatic optimum, followed between 1000 and 750 B.C. by a sharp fall in temperatures along with increased rainfall. Two climatic factors, rainfall and temperature, exercise a controlling influence over British agriculture. A fall in yearly average temperature of even 1°C significantly reduces the growing season, while wetter than usual summers and falls are the most damaging circumstance for harvest yields. Changes in either temperature or rainfall are most destructive to western and northern regions. Although a thousand different microclimates lurk behind every generalization, in general, the higher the altitude or latitude the greater the effect of climatic change on British agriculture.

The climatic deterioration of the Iron Age produced an estimated fall in

[2] Parry, *Climatic Change*, 18–60; Bryson, "Cultural, Economic, and Climatic Records"; Wendland and Bryson, "Dating Climatic Episodes"; Frenzel, "Distribution Pattern"; Lamb, "Reconstruction," 11. See also Harding's comments in the same volume, Harding, ed., *Climatic Change*, 1–6.

average annual temperatures of 2°C in England, Ireland, Wales, and southern Scotland. This would have shortened the growing season by at least five weeks. At the peak of the cold episode (750–400 B.C.) areas of Britain experienced unmatched wetness. The growth rate for certain raised bogs dependent on surface water (rainfall and runoff) was 500 percent higher than for other times. This was also a stormy period resulting in coastal changes.[3] The increased wetness is reflected in the archaeological evidence. In the Somerset Levels, for example, traditional communications routes flooded in the changed climate and were topped with wooden causeways that also eventually flooded, to be replaced with boats (roughly 350 B.C.).[4] Lake villages were constructed in western areas (Glastonbury is a good example) in shallow lakes that have since disappeared. In western and southwestern British regions (Pennines, Dartmoor), the settlement pattern, tree line, and cultivation levels contracted from exposed high levels. These colder, wetter conditions in Britain were paralleled in central Europe and Scandinavia, where glacial advance and the rise of lake levels graphically recorded the climatic deterioration.

Climate in the Roman Period

The European climate began to moderate in the last two centuries B.C. Drier and warmer conditions prevailed, probably slightly superior to present climate (post-1950). About A.D. 400, however, a relatively sudden break occurred returning wetter and colder conditions.[5] The degree and timing of these changes are obviously crucial in interpreting the influence of environmental conditions in the affairs of later Roman Britain.

Temperature change. Long series of instrumentally recorded readings provide the best means of gauging changes in temperature trends. Such evidence is unavailable for the early historical period, however, and the scattered references surviving in the texts do not provide a sufficient or representative basis for estimating past changes in temperature.[6] Accordingly, reliance must be placed on proxy data—time series of non-meteorological events that sensitively reflect meteorological phenomena. For this purpose, studies have used the seasonal depositions in certain European lakes (varves); the correlation in some environments between tree-ring growth and temperature or rainfall (dendrochronology); the study of isotope ratios preserved in plant remains; and the long-term variations of the oxygen isotope ^{18}O preserved in the ice sheets of Greenland. The

[3] Lamb, "Climate from 1000 B.C. to 1000 A.D."
[4] Harding, ed., *Climatic Change.*
[5] Lamb, "Climate from 1000 B.C. to 1000 A.D.," 56ff.
[6] Bell and Olgilvie, "Weather Compilations."

margins of error in dating these various proxy records can be great, and estimates for decades and centuries rather than specific years or seasons are commonly produced.[7] The proxy records offer an important advantage, however: they are free of the subjective element associated with human records. They are objective and quantitative data that allow the separation of environmental from cultural influences.

For trends in temperature, the best sources of information for northwest Europe (including Britain) are recorded in the isotopic records of the Greenland ice sheets and in the movement of glaciers in Scandinavia and central Europe. The latter are dated by radiocarbon studies, tree-ring chronologies, and geomorphological techniques.[8] Neither glacier nor ice sheet can be found in Britain, of course, but the consistent, positive relationship between British climate and that of northwest Europe allows the application of information gained from the one to be applied to the other.[9] Speaking of the relationship between changes in temperature levels in Britain and the other areas of northwest Europe, Lamb remarks that "the timing in England is known to be representative for Europe north and west of the Alps as far as Iceland and the nearer sector of the Arctic."[10]

The ice sheets create a proxy record of temperature changes over time in the following fashion. The ice in the sheets is deposited seasonally layer by layer (just as the wood in tree-rings or the calcite in caves). Each layer chemically preserves a record of conditions at the time of its deposition.[11] Precipitation (snow) making up the ice in the sheets is composed of the two elements hydrogen and oxygen. There are three stable isotopes of oxygen (differing in mass) ^{16}O, ^{17}O, and ^{18}O. The lightest isotope (^{16}O) is the most abundant, but the ratios among the various isotopes vary over time. The concentration of ^{18}O in precipitation is determined mainly by the temperature at its formation. The lower the concentration in rain or snow, the lower the atmospheric temperature. Since precipitation falls as snow on the glaciers of Greenland and is preserved as a frozen layer (fossil

[7] Bryson and Padoch, "Climates of History." With the completion of the American Greenland Ice Sheet Project, it should soon be possible to compare yearly variations in ^{18}O by counting down from the surface and counting each summer maximum as a single year. The chronological precision should be roughly equivalent to a tree-ring chronology. Together with the ice core extracted by a European team in 1992, the recent cores will provide a useful check against the 1966 record from Camp Century and the GISP Ice Sheet Project of 1971–81.

[8] Alexander T. Wilson, "Isotope Evidence"; S. Porter, "Glaciological Evidence."

[9] "It has been shown that there is a strong similarity, firstly between the trends displayed by Manley's instrumental record [for central England] and those displayed by the movements of glaciers in northern and central Europe . . . and finally, between the records for Iceland, central England and the variation of ^{18}O in the Greenland ice cores. The convergent nature of this variety of evidence is clearly marked." Parry, *Climatic Change*, 57. See also Bryson, "Climates of History," 7 n. 6.

[10] Lamb, "Climate from 1000 B.C. to 1000 A.D.," 55.

[11] Alexander T. Wilson, "Isotopic Evidence," 215; Duplessy, "Isotope Studies."

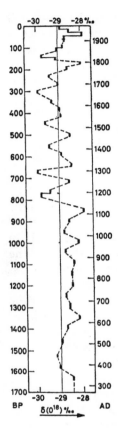

Figure 4. [18]O concentration from a depth-age nomograph for the 1390-meter-long Camp Century ice core. After Dansgaard et al., 1969. Copyright 1969 by AAAS. Reprinted from W. Dansgaard et al., "One Thousand Centuries of Climatic Record from Camp Century on the Greenland Ice Sheet," *Science* 166 (1969), 378.

ice), a vertical core cut through the ice sheet provides a record of temperature over time. The exact temperature cannot be reconstructed, but the trend of the temperature is preserved.[12] A series of such cores have been taken. The levels within the cores are dated by a variety of means—measurement of heavy isotopes by mass spectrometry, ^{14}C dating, and a third method that counts summer maxima in the [18]O content of each layer counting from the surface downwards.[13] Figure 4 illustrates the core taken from the ice sheet at Camp Century, Greenland.[14] Notice the movement between roughly 350 and 500 A.D., corresponding to a cold wave unmatched until the late twelfth century. Figure 5 compares the Camp

[12] Ten Brink and Werdick, "Greenland Ice Sheet History"; Dansgaard et al., "One Thousand Centuries."
[13] Dansgaard and Johnsen, "Flow Model."
[14] Ibid., 378, fig. 2.

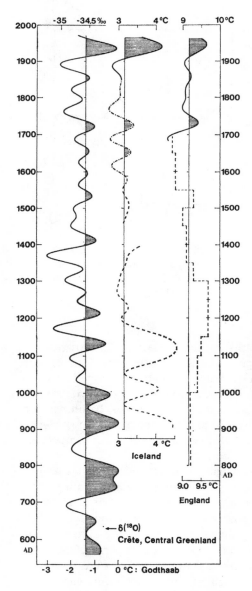

Figure 5. Comparison between the ¹⁸O concentration (left) in snow fallen at Crête, central Greenland (δ scale at top) and temperatures for Iceland and England. The curves are smoothed by a 60-year low-pass digital filter, except for England 800–1700 A.D. The solid curves are based on systematic, direct observations. The dashed curves rely on indirect evidence. After Dansgaard et al., (1975). Reprinted with permission from W. Dansgaard et al., "Climatic Changes, Norsemen and Modern Man," *Nature* 255 (1975), 25, fig. 2. Copyright 1979 Macmillan Magazines Limited.

Century record with the overlapping portion of the instrumentally recorded temperature series for central England.[15] The two are closely coin-

---

[15] Gribbin and Lamb, "Climatic Change," 72, fig. 4.1. Cf. Dansgaard et al., "New Greenland Deep Ice Core."

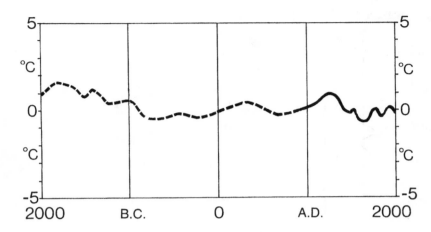

Figure 6. Estimated mean temperatures for the whole year in Central England expressed as departures from the modern all-year average. Based on H. H. Lamb, "Climate from 1000 B.C. to 1000 A.D.," *The Environment of Man,* edited by M. Jones and G. Dimbleby (Oxford, 1981), 54, fig. 3.1. Reproduced by permission of the author.

cident, particularly at extreme points of cold or warmth. The downturn in temperature for the later Roman period evident in the Camp Century core is also corroborated by botanical evidence for a sharp change in the climate of western Greenland in roughly A.D. 400.[16] Using a variety of evidence including isotopic, botanical, and literary sources, Lamb has constructed a graph of estimated changes in mean temperatures for the whole year in central England (Figure 6).[17] Notice the downturn in temperature for the period from roughly 350 to 600 A.D.

Studies of the Alpine and Norwegian glaciers indicate that a sharp cooling episode occurred about A.D. 400, followed by an advance of the glaciers lasting roughly until 750 A.D. The glaciers had been in retreat from approximately 300 B.C. to about 400 A.D. The great advances of the subsequent episode matched the glacial maxima of the sixteenth and nineteenth centuries, indicating a similarly severe cold period. The dating of the change from a relatively warm and dry climate to the colder winters and wetter summers associated with renewed glaciation can be approached through a variety of means including glaciological methods, radiocarbon dating, archaeological evidence, and tree-ring chronology.

[16] Cited by Lamb, *Climate Present, Past, and Future,* 427.
[17] Lamb, "Climate from 1000 B.C. to 1000 A.D.," 54, fig. 3.1.

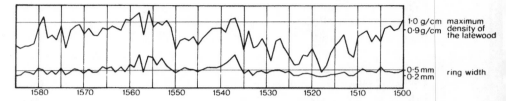

Figure 7. The ring widths (lower curve) and maximum density of the late-season's wood (upper curve) in larches that grew near Zermatt, Switzerland, from 1,585 to 1,500 years "before present" (1950)—i.e., from about A.D. 365 to 450. After F. Röthlisberger, "Gletscher und Klimaschwankungen im Raum Zematt, Ferpècle und Arolla," *Die Alpen,* Quartalshefte 3–4 (1976), 59–150, 114. Reproduced by permission of Club alpin suisse.

The results are consistent and point to a sudden change about A.D. 400. G. Delibrias has obtained radiocarbon dates from a number of trees uprooted by advancing glaciers near Grindelwald, Switzerland, which indicate that glacial advance began about 400 A.D.[18] W. Schneebeli's studies confirm this pattern.[19] F. Röthlisberger's researches provide a closer dating from a tree-ring record of the period A.D. 200 to 450. His results are reproduced in Figure 7.[20] The pattern reflects a build-up of warm temperatures in the fourth century with a sharp decline in approximately A.D. 414 prefaced by cold shocks in roughly the period 394–410. The fortunate combination of a glacier and a peat bog at Fernau in the Tyrol provides two additional dating methods for the initial advance of the Alpine glaciers, based on dated pollen layers and calculations from the growth rate of the peat. The results confirm the pattern of glacial retreat during the Roman period followed by an advance during the interval A.D. 400–750.[21] Archaeological confirmation of this pattern has been exposed recently by the now-retreating glaciers. Roman gold mines near Sonnblick, Austria, trackways, guard-posts, inscriptions, and a Roman-style stone bridge were all once disrupted by advancing glaciers. Speaking of the Col d'Herens route into Italy, Lamb concludes of the archaeological remains: "It seems clear that the route was interrupted by advancing glaciers before the Middle Ages, possibly soon after A.D. 400. A local legend of a King whose Kingdom was overwhelmed by ice is tentatively interpreted as referring to the experience of the local commander of one of the Roman guard posts."[22]

[18] Delibrias et al., "Le forêt fossil."
[19] Schneebeli, "Untersuchungen."
[20] Röthlisberger, "Gletscher und Klimaschwankungen."
[21] Le Roy Ladurie, *Times of Feast,* 244–62.
[22] Lamb, "Climate from 1000 B.C. to 1000 A.D.," 63.

The dating evidence for the onset of cold temperatures is varied but consistent. Even allowing for the imprecision inherent in most of the dating methods, and retaining some suspicion of a tendency to round numbers (for example, 400–750), the Camp Century dating is rather closely confirmed by radiocarbon dates and dendrochronology associated with the glaciers of Scandinavia and central Europe. The converging focus on the year 400 by various methods appears genuine, if startling. We may, with greater than usual confidence in such matters, conclude that the generally favorable climate of the Roman period became abruptly cooler in the first decade of the fifth century.

Moisture variation. One of the most sensitive records of changes in moisture (from rainfall and runoff) over time in northern Europe is preserved in the raised bogs (ombrotrophic mires).[23] The timing of major shifts in wetness of climate may be seen by comparing the peat-bog evidence of Germany, Scandinavia and Britain. Such general comparison reduces the danger of confusing some local topographical change in a particular bog (say through drainage or the action of man) with a change in climate. The plants which form the raised bogs, *Sphagnum* and *Eriophorum*, rely on rainfall or runoff rather than ground water. During dry climatic periods, bacteria can survive within the bog and their action breaks down the plant communities, forming highly humified (soil-like) layers within which the remains of individual plants cannot be recognized. During very dry conditions the bogs will be colonized by other plants such as ling, pine, and birch. Conversely, cold winters and summers with high rainfall and/or cool temperatures promote peat formation. If suitable conditions occur, the peat again begins to grow, bacteria fail to break down the remains of individual plants, and the upper layers of peat are unhumified. The transition between humified and unhumified peat is termed a recurrence surface (after Swedish *rekurrensytor*). Such surfaces may be dated through radiocarbon (organic content), tree ring chronology (tree stumps incorporated within the bog) and very rarely by archaeological finds of man-made artifacts.[24]

The study of recurrence surfaces (RYs) was pioneered in Germany and Scandinavia. Although the dating evidence and interpretation of the various recurrence surfaces was not consistent for all of northern Europe in these early studies, especially for the very early postglacial era, a number of major recurrence surfaces corresponding to major shifts from dry to

---

[23] See Godwin, *Archives of the Peat Bogs*; Barber, *Peat Stratigraphy*. For a recent review of the literature and a minimalist assessment of the potential of studies of recurrence surfaces see J. J. Blackford, "Peat Bogs."

[24] Barber, *Peat Stratigraphy*, 182.

wet climates were identified. In a classic study published in 1932, E. Granlund identified five "dry" eras in the stratigraphy of the Swedish bogs dated through archaeological association as ending respectively in about 2300 B.C. (RY V); 1200 B.C. (RY IV); 600 B.C. (RY III); 400 A.D. (RY II); and 1200 A.D. (RY I). These seemed to coincide generally with recurrence surfaces in Germany and Britain. The earliest were not an exact match, but RY II (roughly 400 A.D.) evidently marked a distinctive phase common to Sweden, Germany, and Britain.[25] Thus the chronological ending of Roman Britain in roughly 410 A.D. may have coincided with a marked deterioration to a wetter, colder climate. In Britain, the recurrence surfaces were linked with archaeological evidence as well as pollen studies to present a consistent picture. The evidence from the raised bogs dramatically illustrated the climatic deterioration between the late Bronze Age and the early Iron Age which I have already discussed. The British evidence seemed to confirm Granlund's hypothesis. Following after a drying phase beginning in the late Iron Age and lasting virtually throughout the Roman era in Britain, a climatic shift to wetter and colder conditions evidently began about 400 A.D.[26]

The later history of the study of recurrence surfaces is in many ways a good illustration of the controversies and disputes surrounding virtually all attempts to reconstruct past climates on the basis of proxy data. Later studies of pollen horizons and the application of radiocarbon dating to the recurrence surfaces of bogs shook the original assumption of synchroneity, the notion that the regeneration of different bogs and various areas within a single bog were common, simultaneous responses to a single climatic "event." Radiocarbon dates for what had been assumed was the same recurrence surface in different bogs produced widely scattered dates (asynchroneity). Subsequently, however, the sampling techniques of the radiocarbon studies were criticized in their turn and the argument has moved in a circle. Recent studies seem to confirm that a number of periods, corresponding in many cases to Granlund's original thesis, are evidently marked by wetter conditions promoting the formation of recurrence surfaces. The most recent studies, however, emphasize the difficulties of correlating these recurrence surfaces with climatic change. Local conditions related to changes in land use as well as general climate may influence significantly the growth cycles of individual raised

---

[25] Granlund, "De Svenska Hogmössarnas Geologi." F. Overbeck established RY II for Germany as dating from c. 400–700 A.D. His study is discussed in Le Roy Ladurie, *Times of Feast*, 256. For the British recurrence surfaces see Godwin, *History of British Flora*, 34 (RY II = c. 400 A.D.). For a table listing RYs see J. G. Evans, *Environment of Early Man*, 145.

[26] Judith Turner, "Contribution to the History"; Seddon, "Prehistoric Climate"; Hardy, "Studies of the Post-Glacial History," 364; J. G. Evans, *Environment of Early Man*, 145.

bogs. Various bogs are not equally sensitive to climatic fluctuation. In areas such as western Ireland, general conditions are so wet that only exceptional peaks of dryness seem to be recorded as changes in bog stratigraphy. Bogs in generally drier areas, such as central Germany, may only reflect large-scale shifts to greater wetness. "Threshold" theory suggests that there must be some necessary time lag between climatic change and the response of a particular bog. This time lag is influenced by local conditions of the location and circumstances of a particular bog. Antecedent conditions are also important. The climate of the Roman era, warmer and drier than our present climate, evidently so dried a number of bogs in Britain that they failed to regenerate even with the return of wetter, colder climate at the end of the Roman period. Presumably other bogs eventually regenerated only after considerable delays before their respective "thresholds" were attained.[27]

Other problems bedevil the accurate dating of recurrence surfaces. Radiocarbon dates from raised bogs are particularly liable to contamination because of rootlet penetration and related problems. The use of different calibrations in different studies complicates comparisons of radiocarbon dates, and of course, the dates are approximations. Using field characteristics it is difficult to locate precisely the beginning of a recurrence surface at a specific point within a particular bog. This problem creates dating uncertainty when samples are selected for radiocarbon dating. Given these various difficulties, emphasis in recent studies of the raised bogs has shifted away from comparisons of recurrence surfaces among different bogs to the construction of climatic curves illustrating more continuous trends within a single bog. A recent survey of work on recurrence surfaces gloomily concludes: "Studies of recurrence surfaces did not, however, provide precise or accurate proxy climatic data, being inaccurate in age, imprecise in timescale, and unspecific in meteorological implication."[28] Nevertheless, recent studies have confirmed the synchroneity of recurrence surfaces within individual bogs and even among different bogs and have also confirmed that the recurrence surfaces reflect genuine alterations in humification induced by climatic change, not merely variations in local conditions.[29]

Studies of individual British bogs have produced radiocarbon dates for recurrence surfaces of roughly 400 A.D. (1550 B.P.). W. Dickinson's study of Rusland Moss (Cumbria) is perhaps the most elegant. To locate the recurrence surface in each section of the bog he first measured the rate of peat

---

[27] For the discussion of modern studies of recurrence surfaces I have relied heavily on two works: Barber, "Peat-Bog Stratigraphy"; Judith Turner, "Iron Age," 250–261.
[28] Jeff Blackford, "Peat Bogs," 50.
[29] Barber, "Peat-Bog Stratigraphy," 104; Barber, *Peat Stratigraphy*, 194.

growth. The results confirmed the synchroneity of the recurrence surface throughout the bog. Radiocarbon dates of 439 ± 50; 415 ± 50; 398 ± 55; and 589 ± 55 (the last was judged anomalous because of the poor definition of the RY at that location) suggested a shift from the drier, warmer Roman era climate to wetter and colder conditions in about 400 A.D.[30] Certain other sites from Denmark, Sweden, Ireland, and elsewhere in Britain have produced a scatter of radiocarbon dates for a fifth-century recurrence surface, including approximately 400, 450, 475, and 500 A.D.[31] Given the limitations of radiocarbon dating for raised bogs and the probable effects of "threshold" considerations, this scattering of dates is not surprising. The results seem generally consistent with evidence discussed earlier. Thus the beginning of the fifth century probably marked the transition between an era of climate warmer and drier than the present and a climatic deterioration to wetter and colder conditions. This deterioration very probably intensified from about 450 A.D.

Another proxy record of periods of varying precipitation, the halogen (salt) content of lake sediments from the Lake District, corroborates the evidence of the raised bogs. The halogen content of bottom deposits in these lakes preserves a proxy record of the precipitation/evaporation ratios over time. Marked fluctuations of halogen content supposedly reflect increased oceanity of climate. Oceanity in its turn is chiefly characterized by increased rainfall and prevalence of offshore, westerly, rain-bearing winds.[32] The overall pattern reflected in the halogen record and a number of radiocarbon measurements taken from peat samples at a variety of locations in England and Scotland consistently points to increasing wetness within the period A.D. 400–600. Applebaum concluded this was evidence "of a steady worsening of the British climate in the direction of increased precipitation, which reached a maximum somewhere towards A.D. 500. . . ."[33]

If A.D. 400–500 marks a peak of sharply deteriorating climate, other evidence suggests a possible downturn toward wetter conditions beginning even earlier in the third century. This period saw major flooding in the southern Fens which forced a shift in settlement to higher ground.[34]

[30] W. Dickinson, "Recurrence Surfaces."

[31] For Sweden, RY c. 475 (Lundqvist, 1962) or c. 400 (Svensson, 1988); for Denmark, RY c. 450 (Aaby and Tauber, 1974–76); for Ireland, RY c. 500 (Mitchell, 1956). For a brief discussion and full references see Barber, "Peat-Bog Stratigraphy." Preliminary studies of blanket peats in Britain (not raised bogs) suggest a shift to wetter conditions c. 1400 B.P. (550 A.D.). J. J. Blackford and F. M. Chambers, "Proxy Records."

[32] For halogen values, see J. G. Evans, Environment of Early Man, 77; MacKereth, "Some Chemical Observations."

[33] Applebaum, "Roman Britain," 6.

[34] Ibid., 228; Hayes, "Roman to Saxon."

Flooding in the Fens probably resulted from a mixture of causes including marine inundation due to changes in relative sea level, waterlogging produced by inadequately maintained drainage schemes, and silt deposited by flooding rivers (alluviation). In general, the evidence of British alluvial sequences—sedimentation produced by river as distinct from marine flooding—is consistent with the suggested overall pattern of climate for the Roman era. Throughout most of the period there is little evidence for exceptional alluviation, but in Hertfordshire, Cumbria, and South Humberside evidence for late or post-Roman flooding and alluviation may be related to a deteriorating climate with increased rainfall, the eventual effects of human induced erosion caused by forest clearance, or both climatic and human influences acting together.[35] A possible increase in levels of rainfall during the fourth century may be indicated by a proliferation of "corn-drying" ovens in the archaeological levels of that period. The actual purpose of these ovens is contested, but they may reflect wet-cut crops and higher rainfall as well as possibly higher taxes paid in kind.[36] This change can be paired with the increasing cultivation of oats as a grain crop.[37] Oats, of course, do comparatively well in poorly drained soils and rainy conditions. Wetter conditions for the later Roman era are also indicated by the location of villas on the upper reaches of now dry streams. Most convincing, perhaps, as evidence of a higher water table are the numerous Roman wells. These are much shallower than those of later periods and remain dry when medieval and modern wells fill.[38] The overall evidence thus points persuasively to wetter conditions in the later Roman period.

Marine transgression and coastal change. The main effects of postglacial eustatic rise in sea levels caused by the melting of the ice sheets and the isostatic rise of land freed from the weight of the ice sheets occurred long before the Roman era. Over the last 4,000 years the rise in sea level has slowed and increases in relative sea levels have not been uniform, but alternated with sea-surface standstills and even downward movements. In Scandinavia, northwestern Britain, and northern Ireland, land uplift evidently outpaced rising sea levels to produce a net relative fall in sea levels in the period since about 4,000 B.C. In general, evidence of world-wide

[35] Martin Bell, "Effects of Land-Use," 132–34; Martin Bell, "Valley Sediments." For Hertfordshire see Potter, "Valleys and Settlement." For Cumbria see Potter, "Romans in North-West England."
[36] Goodchild, "Corn-Drying Ovens"; P. J. Reynolds and J. K. Langley, "Romano-British Corn-Drying Ovens." Another recent suggestion is that the corn-driers were used as malting floors. See C. J. Arnold, *Roman Britain to Saxon England,* 54–55.
[37] Applebaum, "Roman Britain," 120.
[38] Applebaum, "Roman Britain," 6, 120, 244–46.

changes in sea level accompanying climatic changes in the last 2,500 years must be considered tentative. Michael J. Tooley suggests that the present methodology of sea level investigation cannot produce age and altitude resolutions better than 100 radiocarbon years and 1 meter.[39] Within the Roman period, a considerable rise in sea levels has been suggested. Although some authors speak of a "Romano-British [Marine] Transgression" during the second to fourth centuries A.D., followed by a "Saxo-Norman Regression," it is probably more accurate to think in terms of a discontinuous, slowly rising sea level in the first through fifth centuries, A.D. with an upward tendency in which a series of inundations (transgressions) were interspersed with smaller regressions (downward movements) or standstills. The slowly rising sea level interacted with crustal movements including subsidence (southeastern Britain) and uplift (northwestern Britain). The trend toward rising sea levels varied spatially and had widely varying effects among the coastal margins of Britain and northwestern Europe, creating flooding in some areas and deposition of alluvium in others.[40] There are few closely dated index points for British sea levels in the Roman period, and these are unevenly distributed. Within the period about 50–400 A.D., recent studies suggest that the Fenland may have experienced negative tendencies of sea-level movement. In the period between roughly 120 and 400 A.D. (1830 ± 80 B.P. to 1550 ± 120 B.P.), however, in the Romney Marsh area of southeastern England, a positive tendency in sea-level movement seems indicated.[41] Roughly between 100 and 300 A.D., a phase of coastline building in some areas may have been associated with a possible standstill or relative fall in sea level together with variations in local sedimentation. Robert J. Devoy observes:

> The subsequent flooding and eventual marine inundation of coastal zones such as the Fenland and the Thames estuary in Britain, or the Netherlands and parts of northern Germany post A.D. 300 is frequently referred to in archaeological and early sea-level literature as the "Romano-British Transgression." This time of coastal retreat and flood-

[39] For an introduction see Tooley and Shennan, eds., *Sea Level Changes.* Cf. Shennan, "Problems of Correlating," 63.

[40] Helen Porter, "Environmental Change," 353–55; Devoy "Controls on Coastal and Sea-level Changes," 17–19; Burnham, "Coast of South-East England," 12–15. In the port of London, Highest Astronomical Tide (HAT) may have risen 0.4 m between 50 A.D. and the end of the first century. In the period between the construction of the first and second Roman quays at Dover, the contemporary waterline had risen .56 m. During the 200-year legionary occupation of Caerleon, the waterline evidently rose at least 1.43 m. See Waddelove and Waddelove, "Archaeology and Research," 263–66.

[41] "The present state of sea-level research prevents detailed correlation of sea level and climate." Shennan, "Problems of Correlating," 63. See also Lamb, "Climate from 1000 B.C. to 1000 A.D.," 57–63; Tooley, "Sea-level and Coastline Changes," 18.

ing may well have been facilitated by major storm events and it is probable that regional climate change had an important part to play in this pattern of sea-level behaviour.[42]

Flooding along the coasts of Britain and northwestern Europe in the fourth and fifth centuries evidently coincided with flooding in the Mediterranean.[43] During the same period the landlocked Caspian Sea's depth was much lower than in the modern era. If these various phenomena were related to the same causes, then the flooding may be taken as an aspect of world-wide climatic change.[44]

Some of the most dramatic evidence of flooding during the Roman period comes from Britain. The area of the Wash, the Fens, York, Somerset, and south Wales all present clear archaeological evidence of serious flooding. Indications of Roman-era marine transgressions have also been traced in the Thames estuary, the Norfolk Broads, the Solent, and the Arun Valley.[45] In the case of the Fens, warmer and drier conditions persisting in the early years of the Roman occupation, together with increased engineering skills and manpower, led to increased exploitation of rich silt lands about the time of Hadrian.[46] Probably because of changes in the relative level between sea and land, and because of river silting possibly related to deforestation, the subsequent history of the Fens' settlements was a blueprint for ecological disaster. Sea levels rose. Runoff from increased rainfall flooded the inland areas of the Fens even as the sea encroached along the coast. Drainage schemes, either ill-conceived or inadequately maintained, worsened the trouble by altering or destroying the natural drainage system. Within a short time from the initial settlement many of the new farms were abandoned.[47] Farming activity peaked in the

[42] Devoy, "Controls on Coastal and Sea-Level Changes," 18.
[43] Jelgersma et al., *Coastal Dunes*; W. Haarnagal, "Die Ergebnisse der Grabung"; Bantelmann, "Die Landschaftsentwicklung," 20. Waferbolk, "Landscape and Settlement Continuity"; Helen Porter, "Environmental Change," 353–55.
[44] Salway, *Roman Britain*, 555–57; Lamb, "Climate from 1000 B.C. to 1000 A.D.," 57; Lamb, *Climate Present, Past and Future*, 432.
[45] Helen Porter, "Environmental Change," 354–59; Salway, *Roman Britain*, 555–59. The Fens: Phillips, ed., *Fenland*; Godwin, *Fenland*; Potter, "Recent Work in the Roman Fens"; Hall and Chippendale, eds., "Survey, Environment, and Excavation." Roman sites had been dense along the Lincolnshire Fen Edge. These high-risk landscapes were mostly abandoned in the later third and fourth centuries (Hayes, "Roman to Saxon," 324). Hayes suggests that economic and political factors were the main short-term cause of settlement changes while environmental changes contributed to settlement discontinuity. East Anglia: Hallam, "Wash Coast-Levels"; Charles Green, "East Anglian Coast-Line." York: Ramm, "End of Roman York"; Addyman and Hood, "Palaeo-Climate." Somerset Levels and South Wales: Cunliffe, "Somerset Levels."
[46] Salway, *Roman Britain*, 189.
[47] Ibid., 267–69.

early second century, and by the middle of the third century much was deserted. A similar pattern appears in Somerset, where layers of silt covered second- and sometimes fourth-century levels of occupation. Still other areas with fourth-century Roman pottery were covered by peat bog growth. (As already mentioned, the raised bogs began to grow in Britain at the end of the Roman occupation.) East Anglia, Somerset, Cambridgeshire, Lincolnshire, Yorkshire, and south Wales were evidently affected either by coastal flooding or flooding from runoff.[48] In the Thames estuary, the north Kentish marshes, and the area around the Saxon Shore fort at Lympne, the deterioration caused by flooding and siltation evidently began about 300 and continued throughout the fourth century. In northwestern England a marine transgression (Lytham IX) affected the area between the Solway and the Mersey, possibly peaking in about 350 A.D. There may also have been flooding along the Humber in the same period.[49]

Widespread archaeological evidence suggests that the Roman-period coastlines in Britain were far from stable.[50] The early wharves and docks of Roman London were roughly four meters below present high-tide level. The Saxon waterfronts were both above (in altitude) and north of the earlier Roman waterfront, indicating a radical change similar to that established for the Frisian coasts during the fourth and fifth centuries.[51] The evidence for coastal change is not confined to eastern Britain. Pottery from the later third and early fourth century has come from a Dorset site now buried under four feet of silt.[52] The efforts of the Royal Geographical Society to map the Roman coastline have revealed how much the conditions of tide, river course, and coast had changed. In places the Roman coastline lay much further inland than expected, and some dense settlements on the Lincolnshire coast may actually have been located on offshore islands. The Goodwin Sands in the English Channel were first formed during stormy periods between A.D. 400 and 419, providing a British example to place with the extensive flooding which had pushed the Dutch coast further inland.[53] The general picture emerging from the study of marine transgression and coastal changes suggests that serious flooding

[48] Applebaum, "Roman Britain," 56.
[49] Judith Turner, "Iron Age," 262; Tooley, *Sea Level Changes*, 189–92; Cunliffe, "Excavations."
[50] F. H. Thompson, ed., *Archaeology and Coastal Change*. The two most important contributing factors were changes in sea levels and tectonic changes of the coast itself, the result of unstable crust. See Everand, "Southern Britain." See also Tooley, "Sea-Level and Coastline Changes," 5.
[51] Willcox, "Problems and Possible Conclusions."
[52] Salway, *Roman Britain*, 558.
[53] Lamb, "Climate from 1000 B.C. to 1000 A.D.," 61.

began early in the third century and persisted throughout the remainder of
the Roman era. In the North Sea and northeast Atlantic region the flooding may have worsened in the early fifth century.[54] The storm surges and
coastal changes affecting the southern British and Dutch coasts in the
fifth century would have been associated with changes in the storm tracks
of the upper-air circulation. This in turn would have resulted in less stable, less predictable weather.[55]

The effects of topographical changes in coastline and river courses
within the Roman period must have been significant.[56] Such changes
would have disrupted communications, drainage, and local economic organization. Even major defensive schemes suffered. Flooding would have
necessitated considerable movement of population. The loss of areas of
cultivation would have placed increased pressures on an already overstrained tax system.[57] The archaeological evidence from the flooded areas
of the Somerset Levels illustrates what must have been the case along
significant areas of the coast. A severe and lengthy inundation destroyed a
fertile agricultural region. Silts overlying Roman occupation levels measured five to twelve feet in depth. Some recolonization occurred during
the fourth century, but the economy had changed from agricultural to
industrial—pottery manufacture, salt-making, and metallurgy. Barry
Cunliffe, the excavator, concludes that "The alluvial levels of North
Somerset were deposited in the late Roman to post-Roman period as a
result of a gradual rise in sea level, beginning in the third century. More
than 100 square miles of inhabited land was inundated, giving rise to a
massive movement of population and an apparent reorientation of the
economy."[58] Landscape changes caused by deteriorating natural conditions, with consequent troubles in the Fens and the coasts of Yorkshire,
Kent, East Anglia, Lincolnshire, Somerset, and south Wales, presented a
very considerable potential for trouble in the form of disrupted communications, agricultural and fiscal systems, and defensive schemes, and
perhaps most important of all, the social unrest and hardships associated
with displaced population. Ironically, later Romano-British society may
have been partially a victim of the industriousness of its own farmers,
lumberjacks, and their predecessors. Erosion caused by the delayed but

54 Cunliffe, "Somerset Levels," 73; Lamb, "Climate and Its Variability." Notice the graph (29)
of severe sea floods per century.
55 Lamb, "Climate from 1000 B.C. to 1000 A.D.," 55ff., 61.
56 Salway, Roman Britain, 558.
57 Ibid., 548. The negative effects of flooding would have far outweighed gains from newly
created habitat for waterfowl and shellfish, and new areas for the collection of salt. Eventually,
of course, the silts deposited by flooding could be farmed by future inhabitants.
58 Cunliffe, "Somerset Levels," 73. Allen and Fulford, "Wentlooge Level," 91–93, reject the
idea of this Romano-British transgression.

cumulative effects of generations of forest clearance, grazing, and plowing probably intensified the natural environmental problems by contributing significantly to flooding and silting.

The Impact of Climatic Change

So far the catalogue of suggested climatic changes for later Roman Britain includes colder temperatures, greater wetness, and flooding. The aspect of society most affected by these changes would have been pastoral and arable agriculture. In Britain and elsewhere within the empire, land was the most important investment and agriculture the dominant element of the economy.[59] The impact of climatic change on agriculture would have depended on four interacting factors: (1) the magnitude or extent of the changes; (2) the time scale for the changes (their relative suddenness or gradualness); (3) the physical geography and distribution pattern of agrarian settlement in Roman Britain; and (4) the pressure exerted on the available food supply by dependent population, taxation, the army, export, and so forth. Each of these points will be discussed in turn.

The magnitude of climatic change. The most difficult part of the analysis is to estimate the magnitude of the climatic changes so far presented merely as trends. Any quantification must include a heavy element of subjective speculation and a number of imponderables. Modern records provide analogues, however, and certain natural phenomena such as renewed glaciation require observed environmental preconditions. Taking temperature first, in order to account for the suggested eustatic changes in sea level associated with the Roman era, an overall increase in annual mean temperatures of approximately .75°C above present normals (calculated 1900–1950) would be required.[60] At the other extreme, to initiate a Fernau-type cooling cycle with consequent glacial advance, such as occurred at the end of the Roman period, would require about a 1°C fall from current normal temperatures, perhaps a few tenths of a degree Celsius more. Temperature changes may have been more extreme at higher latitudes such as southern Norway (60–62°N) than in central England (52–55°N).[61] The suggested drop in annual temperatures for the later Roman era compared with the present would thus be more than 1°C. The relative overall change affecting Roman agriculture would have been more in-

[59] Rivet, "Rural Economy."
[60] Lamb, *Climate Present, Past, and Future,* 432.
[61] The glacial advance beginning c. 400 A.D. was quite similar to that of 1820. See Lamb, *Climate Present, Past, and Future,* 427 n. 1; Le Roy Ladurie, *Times of Feast,* 244, 255–56. A drop in temperature of 1°C and perhaps somewhat more would be required to initiate glaciation. Cf. Lamb, "Climate from 1000 B.C. to 1000 A.D.," 61.

tense, however, for the practical fall in temperatures would have been additive, from above present levels to below present levels, a drop of as much as approximately 1.75°C. Estimated changes in moisture related to rainfall are linked to the historical growth cycles of raised bogs. To trigger another recurrence phase in Britain today would require approximately a 10 percent increase above current annual average moisture.[62] The actual impact on the late Romano-British agricultural system would reflect the cumulative effect of change from a climate drier than the present to rainfall exceeding modern levels.

The time-scale for climatic change. The general chronology or time frame for the suggested climatic changes in Britain during the Roman era has been established by various dating methods including radiocarbon, dendrochronology, and pollen analysis. The chronology of change falls roughly into two unequal halves: (1) the first half (roughly 100 B.C. to A.D. 250) with optimal weather characterized by warmer than average temperatures, drier conditions, and less stormy climate; and (2) a deteriorating second half beginning in approximately A.D. 250 and lasting beyond A.D. 450. Within this second period, marine flooding began in the third century and continued throughout the remainder of the Roman era. Cooler temperatures and wetter conditions returned perhaps as early as A.D. 350, persisting into the early medieval era. Within this deteriorating period of climatic change, a sharply colder and wetter episode began in about A.D. 400.

The agrarian settlement pattern. The traditional geographical division of Britain into a Highland and a Lowland Zone, defined by a line drawn from the mouth of the River Exe in the southwest to the mouth of the River Tees in the northeast, is a useful oversimplification (see Figure 10). Modern classifications often split Britain into as many as five or six different agro-climatic regions. For all of the many topographical exceptions, however, the Highland-Lowland division retains an overall validity for essential differences of relief, soil, climate, agricultural economy, and communications.[63] The Highland Zone includes Dartmoor, Exmoor, much of Wales, the Lake District, Pennines, and much of Scotland. The distinction between the zones was created to a great extent by the climatic deterioration of the Iron Age, which brought greatly increased rainfall. Excessive

---

62 Parry, *Climatic Change,* 66ff.; J. L. Anderson, "Climate and the Historians," 313.
63 The classic exposition of the Highland and Lowland Zones is Cyril Fox, *Personality of Britain.* See also J. G. Evans, *Environment of Early Man,* 147–50; van der Veen, *Crop Husbandry,* 1–8; Salway, *Roman Britain,* 4–5.

rainfall rather than elevation is the chief limiting factor in the agriculture of the Highland Zone.

Although episodes of forest clearance among British regions were asynchronous, the great phase of Iron Age deforestation (from about 400 B.C. to 100 A.D.) meant that in much of Britain the Romans arrived to find a cleared and developed landscape. In southern England, both lowland and upland areas had been cleared to create agricultural lands and permanent grazing. On the whole, the pattern of land use from the late Iron Age was maintained and intensified in the Romano-British era. As Martin Jones observes: "It may be argued that the Roman period and preceding Iron Age make up a coherent subunit, characterized by a number of processes that gather momentum at an unprecedented scale at the outset, and maintain that momentum throughout the period represented by this subunit."[64] The pattern of agrarian settlement within the Roman period was not static, however. In northern Britain the Roman period marked a change of emphasis toward arable farming. In southern Britain cultivation of heavy loams and hard-to-drain clays was fully developed. Evidence for a proliferation in the number of settlements and the spread of settlements into previously uncultivated areas is recorded by aerial photography, archaeological field survey, the excavation of individual sites, and the analysis of pollen profiles. Pollen is seasonally deposited by the pollen "rain." Where surface bogs are found the pollen rain is preserved, season-by-season, forming a vertical stratigraphy. If a core is taken from one of these bogs, vegetational changes in the area surrounding the bog may be reconstructed. The first introduction of arable agriculture in a region alters the relative frequency of characteristic pollen types. If woodland is cleared for farming the subsequent pollen record will reflect an abrupt decline in tree pollen and a rise in grass pollens, or more conclusively, the pollen of domesticated grain will be found. Local conditions peculiar to particular bogs influence the pollen record, and distortion is possible in any given locality. A number of pollen studies taken from a variety of locations within a region, however, offset these potential difficulties. The pollen evidence for northwestern Britain indicates a major clearance phase with the introduction of cereal farming between roughly A.D. 250 and 450. The Lake District, the Yorkshire Dales, the Pennines, and areas of Wales, as well as the frontier area of southern Scotland, all show indications of clearance in the later Roman period. This finding is corroborated by increases in the number and size of upland settlements.[65] To a modest

---

[64] Martin Jones, "Crop Production," 98. For an overview of Iron Age development see Judith Turner, "Iron Age," 264–77.
[65] J. G. Evans, Environment of Early Man, 151, 164; Judith Turner, "Contribution to the History"; Pennington, History of British Vegetation, 83–98. For northern England as a whole

degree the expansion of agriculture was accompanied by improvements in the basic mixed-farming practices of Iron Age Britain. Native British strains of cattle may have been improved by the introduction of larger animals. In the third and fourth centuries, the farming of heavier soils was probably assisted by significant improvements in the technology of the plow. These included a coulter to cut the sod and an asymmetrical plowshare to undercut weeds and turn the soil.[66]

The explanation for the spread and intensification of rural settlement and land use in the Roman period is uncertain. It has been variously associated with increases in the native British population, changed consumer practices, urbanization, and the demands of the Roman garrison and government.[67] S. Applebaum interprets the evidence for arable expansion in northern and western Britain, particularly where it is closely associated with Roman military sites, as a response to the Roman tax levy. The changes forced by the requirements of the Roman economy ultimately destroyed the native rural order, even in the southern uplands. "It seems probable that Roman fiscal pressure ultimately destroyed the traditional native rural economy and thus caused the ultimate abandonment of the southern uplands as soon as the government that held the peasantry to its soil by coercion was removed."[68] The extent to which the Roman army concentrated in northern Britain depended on locally produced foodstuffs is disputed. Increasingly, however, the upland areas are viewed as a significant source of supplies, including grain.[69] Britain's long coastline and navigable rivers represented a considerable potential for moving foodstuffs over distances using water transport. This may have eased pressures

---

see Nick Higham, *Northern Counties*, 180ff. For a recent review of the evidence for the northeast see James D. Anderson, *Roman Military Supply.* Cf. Barber et al., "Climatic Change," 226–31. For Wales see M. J. C. Walker, "Holocene Vegetation Change," 181.

[66] Maltby, "Iron Age Animal Husbandry," 185–90; Sian E. Rees, *Agricultural Implements;* Martin Jones, "Development of Crop Husbandry."

[67] Applebaum, "Roman Britain," 223–49; Salway, *Roman Britain,* 618–30. Martin Jones suggests, in contrast, that by taking potential wealth to reinvest and expand, Roman taxation for a time may have slowed rather than stimulated British agriculture ("Crop Production," 105). For the influence of environmental factors, rather than social or political agencies, see Nick Higham, *Northern Counties,* 198. Higham cites improving environmental conditions as a possible factor, but in the major period of innovation in the early Iron Age, expansion of agriculture onto heavier soils may have been driven by climatic deterioration and soil exhaustion. This is a good cautionary example of the difficulty of disentangling social from environmental factors in explaining agricultural change. See Martin Jones, "Development of Crop Husbandry."

[68] Applebaum, "Roman Britain," 246.

[69] For a recent discussion see James D. Anderson, *Roman Military Supply.* Manning presents the argument for local supply ("Economic Influences"). Contrast his thesis with Selkirk, *Dramatic New View.* For an earlier view see Piggot, "Native Economies."

on local producers in Britain. Wastage involved in storage and transportation increased with distance, as did transportation costs. Losses due to theft and peculation were also factors. Given the detrimental effects of heavier burdens to taxpayers and losses to the state, there were obviously strong incentives to acquire needed supplies locally. Maintaining the army took precedence over local or regional civilian concerns. As Arther Ferrill remarks: "Normally military demands were high. In good years the army was simply a market in the regional economy, but in bad years, it was a terrible drain, particularly in those areas where purchase in the open market (or requisition and taxation) was a major source of supply."[70] Salway believes the north may have been more easily coerced than the more developed south and that the advantages of locally produced foodstuffs in terms of transportation and storage requirements led to a reordering of regional economies to suit the military. "There is good evidence for forest pastoralism and some arable, raising the possibility that troops continued to be stationed here in large numbers because they could be fed easily from a population less able to complain effectively than the villa-owners of the south. Either way, any economic or cultural advantages gained by the locals from Roman rule are likely to have been won against decidedly adverse circumstances."[71] The introduction or intensification of arable farming in areas of marginal or nearly marginal quality reflects a degree of insensitivity to the local environment on the part of Roman authorities whose actions and demands, backed by substantial resources and engineering skills or simply the power to coerce, seem to have had but little to do with the natural conditions and potentials of a particular locality. The Romano-Britons' own perceptions of marginality are difficult to reconstruct. Our concept of marginality is defined in terms of conditions for plant growth and risks of crop failure, particularly cereal yields. David Miles rightly refers to the Romano-British countryside as "a confusing and complex place where we are only beginning to find our way." Nevertheless, the accumulated evidence suggests an overall pattern for later Roman Britain of an unprecedented level of exploitation of all available land,

[70] Ferrill, *Fall of the Roman Empire*, 82. Lot estimates that under the Roman system of taxation in kind, two-thirds of the revenue was lost or wasted (*End of the Ancient World*, 57). For the relation between local agricultural production and army needs in areas away from the sea or navigable rivers see Finley, *Ancient Economy*, 128.

[71] Salway, *Roman Britain*, 613–14. The spread of agriculture in the Highland Zone and frontier districts may be related in the third and fourth centuries in some estates of southern Britain to the shift from traditional arable farming to stock ranching. This shift may have displaced large numbers of the rural poor. The evidence for such a change is suggestive rather than conclusive. Applebaum, "Roman Britain," 223–36. Salway does not wholly agree (*Roman Britain*, 281, 628). Cf. Collingwood and Myres, *Roman Britain and the English Settlements*, 223.

including soils only marginally appropriate for agriculture. The Romans not only continued and intensified the existing agricultural system in Britain, they also expanded agriculture into new areas and introduced new technologies and methods. As a consequence, the landscape became more vulnerable to environmental change. On this fully exploited landscape fell the weight of climatic deterioration.[72]

Pressure on available food supplies. Problems of supplying the population, government, and garrison of Roman Britain raise the question of demands on agricultural output. This involves a complicated equation with few constants but a great many uncertain or disputed variables, including rural and urban population, the extent of arable land and pasture, crop yields, rates of taxation, and rents. Grain was a medium of provincial taxation in Britain, as Tacitus recorded. Recent studies, while acknowledging all the uncertainties inherent in such numbers, estimate the population of Roman Britain in the period of the second through fourth centuries as approximately three and a half million people. This population density compares with the apex of medieval population in the fourteenth century, shortly before famine and plague radically reduced its numbers.[73] What is known of the agricultural techniques and crop yields of Roman farming and premodern British agriculture suggests that feeding a population of this magnitude would have placed considerable strain on a fully exploited countryside. Indeed, if the late Iron Age population and agriculture were as fully developed as has been suggested, then the additional requirements of Roman administration, garrison, and urbanization must have created significant additional stress. One aspect of this problem, the arable acreage theoretically needed to supply the grain eaten by the Roman army in Britain, has been the focus of considerable speculation. For example, A. L. F. Rivet calculates that about 53,000 acres of arable would have been a sufficient minimum to supply the grain rations required by the roughly 50,000 Roman soldiers stationed in Britain in the first century. Making a similar calculation but using somewhat different assumptions, Martin Millett estimated the required arable as approximately 61,000 acres (see Table 2). A Roman soldier probably consumed between .9 and 1.36 kilograms of grain each day. Roman and modern estimates of subsistence or working requirements seem roughly compar-

---

[72] Miles, "Romano-British Countryside," 115. For an overview of the impact of the Roman occupation on British agriculture see Martin Jones, "Agriculture in Roman Britain," 127–34. His categories of expansion, introduction, and exploitation are a useful framework for study. Salway, *Roman Britain,* 5, 190.
[73] Tacitus *Agricola* 19. For a recent discussion and estimate of population see Millett, *Romanization of Britain,* 181–86.

Table 2. Grain rations for the Roman army in Britain

	Army	Grain/man/year	Total grain required/ year	Agricultural yield	Total produce of acreage required
Rivet (1969)	c. 50,000 includes 24,000 legionaries plus auxiliaries and staffs of procurator and legate	11 bushels (693 lbs. of grain)	c. 530,000 bushels (33,390,000 lbs.)	10 bushels/acre (630 lbs./acre)	53,000 acres
Millett (1984)	c. 50,000	496.4 Kg. (1,092.08 lbs.) (3 lbs./day)	24,820 metric tonnes (54,604,000 lbs.)	1 metric tonne/hectare (894.3 lbs./acre)	24,820 hectares (61,057 acres)
Scott (1983) maximum	c. 63,000	1,095 lbs. (3 lbs./day)	68,985,000 lbs.	2.8 cwt./acre (313.6 lbs./acre)	219,978 acres
Scott (1983) minimum	c. 40,000	730 lbs. (2 lbs./day)	29,200,000 lbs.	3 long tons/acre (6,720 lbs./acre)	4,345 acres

Sources: A. L. F. Rivet, The Roman Villa in Britain (London, 1969); M. Millett, "Forts and the Origins of Towns: Cause or Effect?" in Military and Civilian in Roman Britain, edited by T. F. C. Blagg and A. C. King (Oxford, 1984), 65–74; Eleanor Scott, "Romano-British Wheat Yields," in Settlement in Northern Britain, edited by J. C. Chapman and H. C. Mytum (Oxford, 1983), 221–32.

Note: 1 bushel = 63 lbs. wheat; 1 cwt. = 112 lbs; 1 metric ton (tonne) = 2,200 lbs; 1 long ton = 2,240 lbs; 1 acre = 0.405 hectares.

able. Much more problematic is the question of the probable grain yields of Romano-British agriculture.[74]

Documentary sources seem to indicate that classical yields ranged between 11 and 20 bushels of grain per acre, but as J. K. Evans remarks, "the evidence with regard to wheat yields is at once meagre and plainly contradictory." The literary evidence for Roman agriculture has been variously interpreted to present a picture of perilously low average yields (yield:sown of 4.4:1) implying a rural peasantry living a precarious, hand-to-mouth existence, or a more robust condition with estimated yields of 8 or 10:1. Extrapolating from classical texts and prime cereal lands in Italy or Sicily to conditions in northern Europe and Britain is problematic. Mediterranean yields were probably higher because of the advantage of light, warm soils over the heavier, colder, germination-retarding soils in Britain.[75] Medieval grain yields in England evidently remained in the four-fold range or worse. Although these relatively low yields may have been in part tied to circumstances peculiar to the medieval era, to the extent that ancient-medieval comparisons of the same area are valid, this suggests that yields in Roman Britain might well have been on the low end rather than the high end of the suggested range for possible classical yields.[76] Rivet assumed a roughly five-fold yield for Roman Britain, producing about 10 bushels or 6 hundredweight of grain per acre (1 bushel = .56 hundredweight = 63 pounds). This is roughly equivalent to one-third of modern yields. Various attempts to reconstruct Romano-British farming systems have mostly suggested yields of 8 to 11 bushels per acre (4.5 to 6 hundredweight). At the extremes, George Boon estimates that the hinterlands of Silchester may have produced as little as 2.8 hundredweight per acre, while Applebaum suggests that the exceptionally fertile soils of the

---

[74] Rivet, *Roman Villa*, 189–98; Millett, "Forts and the Origins of Towns," 70–72. For the military diet see R. W. Davies, "Roman Military Diet," 123. For subsistence diet see Garnsey, "Grain for Rome"; the corn dole per day in Rome (118) was .54 Kg.

[75] J. K. Evans, "Wheat Production," 429. The key texts are Varro *Rust.* 1.44.1 (ten- to fifteen-fold yield: sown); Columella 3.3.4 (four-fold yield); Cicero *Verrines* 2.3.112 (eight- to ten-fold yield). Evans writes, "It may fairly be concluded that the spectre of starvation haunted the *imperium Romanum*, an imminent and frequently deadly pestilence." Cf. K. D. White, "Wheat Farming." In contrast, Garnsey and Saller conclude, "The upshot is that the ancient evidence, such as it is, does not support an argument of 'perilously low' average yields in wheat or other cereals. . . ." (*Roman Empire*, 82).

[76] For medieval yields in England see Postan, *Medieval Economy*, 61–71, 123–26. Medieval yields were three to four times the seed, or worse. Six to nine bushels per acre was the statistical mode of Postan's medieval evidence. Low medieval yields might be explained by (1) low quality of seed, (2) shallow ploughing, (3) lack of proper underdraining, (4) failure of fallowing to deal with weeds, and (5) insufficiency of manure. All of these factors might well apply to Romano-British agriculture. A final factor, decline of fertility in "anciently cultivated lands," is more difficult to apply to Roman Britain. Given late Iron Age clearance, lands continuously farmed into the third or fourth century A.D. might well reflect this problem.

Bignor villa estate may have produced 20 bushels (11.2 hundredweight) per acre. Naturally any theoretical average implies a range of yields depending on farming methods, workforce, soils, location, and so forth.[77]

In contrast to the evidence of classical, medieval, and early modern yields, the Butser experimental Iron Age farm has produced surprisingly high yields in excess of 2.5 tonnes per hectare and average yields of about 2 metric tonnes per hectare (about 16 hundredweight or 28 bushels per acre), without the use of manure. Because of a number of variables in the Butser experiment including modern climate, seed-bed preparation, density of planting, and weed control, the experimental yields represent no more than a boundary of potential for ancient farming. The soil at Butser had been under grass for two hundred years and was at peak fertility. Accordingly, during the first decade of cultivation at Butser, yields had not yet suffered from the potentially dramatic decline associated with prolonged cereal cropping and the progressive mining out of accumulated nutrients in the soil. In the Rothampstead experiment, the Broadbalk field plot was farmed over 125 years. In this period yields dropped from an initially high average yield of about 30 bushels to level out at about 12 bushels. The quality of soil at Broadbalk was intrinsically high and the ploughs and seed used there were modern. For all of these reasons, Butser's experimental yields may not readily apply to Roman Britain. As Martin Jones remarks, the results from Butser "do not necessarily show that prehistoric productivity was high, but they do demonstrate that contemporary agricultural techniques and cereal strains were in principle capable of high yields."[78]

Given the great range of theoretical yields and related questions such as the quantity of seed grain necessarily reserved from the harvest, estimates of the land required to feed the army in Britain can and do vary enormously (see Table 2). All such theoretical calculations, however, no doubt seriously underassess the actual impact of the presence of the Roman army on the agricultural society of Britain. Not only must such estimates of the grain required specifically as food rations be adjusted upwards to allow for the significant effects of loss, wastage, and peculation, but the Roman army's requirements of course extended far beyond basic grain rations. The host countryside had also to supply fodder for thousands of military animals. Great quantities of iron, wood, and leather were also required. To equip a single legion with tents probably required 54,000

[77] Scott, "Romano-British Wheat Yields"; Rivet, *Roman Villa,* 196; Boon, *Silchester,* 247; Applebaum, "Some Observations," 121–30.
[78] Peter J. Reynolds, *Iron Age Farm,* 59–61. For a discussion of some of these variables see P. J. Fowler, *Farming of Prehistoric Britain,* 14–16; Martin Jones, "Development of Crop Husbandry," 115. For the Rothampstead experiment begun in 1843 see Postan, *Medieval Economy,* 69–70.

calfhides. David Breeze rightly described the needs of the army as a seemingly "endless catalogue." Land requirements must be adjusted to include not only arable but also the associated acres of woodland, meadow, pasture, and wasteland required by working farms. Arable acreage does not exist in an agricultural vacuum. Provision must also be made for areas left fallow in a system of field rotation. The vital requirement of seed grain, perhaps as much as a third of the total harvest, must also somehow be factored into calculations of the arable required to feed the army. To this list must be added the grain consumed by the agricultural workforce. Perhaps most significantly, the calculations discussed above do not include provision for the profits in rents and services required from the land by private owners. Beyond official taxes and payments, it was the level of rents in the compulsory outgoings that was most important in determining the precariousness or stability of the lives of the rural peasantry. Heavy burdens may also adversely affect yields.[79]

Estimates of the overall cost of the army in terms of its pay provide a fuller idea of its impact than do estimates confined to required grain rations. Using the limited literary evidence, Anthony R. Birley calculates that the entire Roman army throughout the empire in 150 A.D. cost about 210 million denarii. At a strength of about 50,000, the army stationed in Britain represented probably 11 to 12.5 percent of this total. Millett adjusts Birley's estimate and calculates the pay of the army in Britain in the late first century A.D. as roughly 11.55 to 13.125 million denarii. To translate the impact of such an expense on Romano-British agricultural society, this monetary figure may be expressed as a grain equivalent. The underlying assumption is that the price of gold and the price of grain remained in a stable relationship. In the late first century A.D., if 1 *modius* of grain = 3 HS (*sestertii*), as Keith Hopkins has suggested, then the pay of the army in Britain corresponded to the grain equivalent of 102,400 to 116,700 metric tonnes. Recall that this is an equivalent expressed in a measure of grain rather than a figure for the amount of grain actually consumed by the army. Millett uses a very high estimated yield of 1 metric tonne per hectare and calculates that this quantity of grain represented the product of 102,400 to 116,700 hectares of arable (251,904 to 287,082 acres). Substituting a more traditional estimated classical yield of 10 bushels per acre

---

[79] Rivet attempted to allow for some of these factors and adjusted his base figure of 53,000 acres to 106,000 acres to account for the needs of seed corn, fallow every third year, and rations for the agricultural workers and oxen. The figure still appears much too low. Rivet, *Roman Villa*, 196–97. Millett halved the two metric tonnes/hectare recorded as an average yield from Butser, partly to allow for the needed seed corn ("Forts and the Origins of Towns," 71–72). For private rents and services and their effects on yields and the condition of the rural peasants, see Postan, *Medieval Economy*, 131. For the demands of the Roman army see Breeze, "Demand and Supply," 272.

produces a figure of roughly 357,587 to 407,524 acres. Taking these figures one step farther, if we assume with Hopkins that the rate of taxation in this period was about 10 percent of the gross product, then the theoretical tax base of arable land required to produce the grain equivalent of the pay of the Roman army in late first-century Britain ranges between 2.5 and 4 million acres.[80]

One final theoretical calculation provides a useful comparison for the figures discussed above. Basing his estimate on the work of Hopkins, Michael Fulford estimates the cost of the army in Britain in the late first century at approximately 63.6 million HS, or roughly 16 million denarii. Hopkins has suggested that the annual tax extracted from the total Roman imperial population was about 15 HS per head, the equivalent of 33 kilograms of wheat per person. Given the difficulties inherent in estimating population, tax rates, and the total state budget, this is obviously a highly speculative estimate. Nevertheless, if Hopkins' estimate is approximately correct, then the cost of the Roman army in Britain may be said to represent the tax-revenue equivalent of 4.24 million people. Even if we substitute Millett's smaller estimated costs for the army, the result still represents the average tax revenues of a population of 3 to 3.5 million people.[81] If the Romano-British population reached a maximum of three and a half or four million, then these theoretical calculations suggest that a fully exploited Romano-British population would have been hard pressed or even insufficient to pay the cost of the Roman army and government in Britain.

In fact, despite evidently significant expansion of agriculture, particularly in northern and western Britain, there are archaeological indications that the army in northern Britain imported grain and other basic materials by sea over long distances during the first and second century, and again from the Severan period onwards. Evidence of the construction of granaries and the presence of exotic pests and grain species or unusual grain assemblages cannot demonstrate the amount or frequency of such imports. Probably the bulk of imported grain was supplied over middle distances from lowland Britain, but some of the material possibly originated on the continent, probably in the Netherlands. Given the Roman preference for local production and the expense and difficulty of importation over middle and long distance, the presence of imports suggests that regional production was insufficient to meet the demands of the army and

[80] Cassius Dio 78.36; Herodian 4.4.7. Anthony R. Birley estimates the strength of the entire Roman army at 405,500 to 433,500, with a British garrison of 50,180 to 53,180 ("Economic Effects," 40–42). For money and grain see A. H. M. Jones, *Later Roman Empire*, 1:27; Reece, "Wages and Prices," 241; Hopkins, "Taxes and Trade," 120; Millett, "Forts and the Origins of Towns," 70–72.
[81] Fulford, "Demonstrating Dependence," 130–31.

that the combined output of Roman Britain may not have been sufficient to satisfy the simultaneous needs of the army, civil government, and ongoing Romanization.[82]

Over three centuries of occupation, the size of the Roman army in Britain and its socioeconomic impact fluctuated considerably. The documentary and archaeological evidence for the strength of the army permit a wide range of estimates. Breeze reckons the total strengths for a series of rough dates as follows:

120 A.D.	45,000 to 53,000
210 A.D.	47,000 to 55,000
300 A.D.	21,000 to 25,000
400 A.D.	28,000 to 33,000

Much depends on assumptions concerning the strength of the units of the late Roman army. As Simon James has pointed out, at the extremes the evidence may be interpreted to represent a British diocese "swarming with troops" through most of the fourth century, or, using a deliberately extreme minimalist approach, the army may be numbered under 20,000, perhaps even under 15,000 from the late third century through the fourth century.[83]

The requirements of the army in Britain, of course, did not exist in isolation from the needs of the agricultural population or the demands of the civilian government and urban population. It is impossible to quantify the requirements of the civil bureaucracy in Britain. The inhabitants of twenty cities and numerous towns, conservatively estimated, probably represented roughly 5 percent of the total population. Peter Brown characterizes Late Antiquity as a world continuously on the edge of starvation,

[82] For an overview of the problem of supply see Garnsey and Saller, *Roman Empire*, 88–95. For a study of the capacity of military granaries see Gentry, *Stone-Built Granaries*, 23–34. For the archaeological argument that Roman Britain was not self-sufficient in the first and second centuries see Fulford, "Demonstrating Dependence," 129–39. Fulford also suggests that in the third century, with the reduction of the army in Britain, production may have exceeded the demands of defense and administration. The third-century granary at South Shields, however, contained seed assemblages suggesting the possibility of long-distance importation of grain. The presence of the bones of the garden dormouse, a species not native to Britain, strengthens the speculation. James D. Anderson concludes that during the third century and after, bread-wheat was imported by ship to South Shields, probably from the Netherlands. He also concludes that only in the period c. 100–200 A.D. could the army of northeastern Britain have been supplied locally. James D. Anderson, *Roman Military Supply*, 60–63, 81, 101–2. Van der Veen determines that the evidence from South Shields for long-distance importation of grain is inconclusive (*Crop Husbandry Regimes*, 154–55). *Sitophilus granarius* is an example of a grain pest unknown in Iron Age contexts and presumed to be an import into Roman Britain. See Buckland, "Cereal Production," 43–45.

[83] For a discussion and references see Breeze, "Demand and Supply," 268; Simon T. James, "Britain and the Late Roman Army," 164.

with an urban population of 10 percent extracting a small agricultural surplus from the remaining 90 percent of the rural population. How far his vision may be extended from the Mediterranean to the world beyond the Alps and to Britain may be debated. We have no secure way to estimate the total burdens on the Romano-British farmer, but a reasonable guess is that he lost from half to two-thirds of his net yields to nonproducers.[84] Some have suggested that innovations in Romano-British agriculture in the late third and fourth century, together with significant reduction in the size of the Roman army in Britain, may have created an agricultural surplus. An improvement in agricultural productivity is speculative and must be balanced against environmental factors, possibly including less favorable climate and declining fertility in deteriorating soils. Reduction in the size of the army in Britain must be balanced against possibly higher tax rates and increased demands that may have been associated with a shift from cash payments to subsidies paid in kind (annona militaris). Even allowing for the significant reduction of the army in Britain from perhaps 50,000 soldiers in the second century to 20,000 at the end of the fourth century, the army and its dependents would have represented perhaps 80,000 to 100,000 mouths.[85] Together with the nonfood producing civilian population these must have posed a considerable drain on the agricultural population, even under optimal conditions. Demands on late Romano-British food production included one other significant element. In the fourth century, Britain exported grain to the Rhine frontier and acted as an emergency reserve in case of disaster in Gaul or Germany. These exports of grain are sometimes cited as evidence of Romano-British prosperity and productivity, a reversal of the earlier need to import grain into Britain. In fact, the exports from Britain are more probably an indication of the devastation inflicted on continental agriculture by the barbarian invasions rather than a sign of changed British production. In Ammianus, the main literary source recording the shipments, the grain exports do not seem to be part of a regular commercial trade, but are levies in kind. As such the shipments reflect the Roman government's ability to coerce and collect in Britain but say nothing about agricultural development. In one example, the emperor Julian arbitrarily increased the exported grain by 600 extra shiploads.[86] Clearly the cumulative demands of urban and rural populations, the army, the bureaucracy and export requirements must

[84] Peter Brown, World of Late Antiquity, 12; Nick Higham, "Roman Impact," 105–6.
[85] Simon T. James, "Britain and the Late Roman Army," 173–79; Martin Jones, "Development of Crop Husbandry," 119. For the annona militaris see Rickman, Roman Granaries, 278–83. Millett estimates that an army of 10,000 to 20,000 plus dependents numbered 50,000 to 200,000 (Romanization of Britain, 185).
[86] Ammianus 18.2.3; Eunapius Fr. 12; Julian Ep. ad Ath. 280A, C; Zosimus 3.5.

have severely taxed and quite possibly overstrained the potential of Romano-British agriculture.

We are now in a position to draw together the various threads of analysis and evaluate the impact of climatic change on Roman Britain's food supply. Although it is often difficult to isolate the process by which climatic changes induce economic changes, environmental factors significantly determine the suitability of different areas for the cultivation of particular plants, for pasturage, and for animal husbandry. The impact of climatic change varies among different regions and areas depending on factors such as latitude, exposure, elevation, and soils. Even small-scale differences can be significant. As Gordon Manley observes: "Experience indeed shows that the climate of Britain is marginal in very many respects. So much so that the diversity of the land surface arising from small-scale local relief, from soil, from proximity to waterbodies, and from many local modifications that can be ascribed to the work of man, plays an unusually large part."[87] Climatic change and local topography interact in various and complex ways, but a glance at Figures 8–10 reveals the major consequence of climatic change to agriculture in late Roman Britain. Much of the area taken in for arable by the expansion into the Highland Zone—the Lake District, Peak District, Pennines, Wales, and southern Scotland—lies within a region defined even by modern standards as marginal for agriculture.[88] Within these areas the yield for sown is relatively poor, and changes in weather conditions can create absolute harvest failure. In comparison to the more fertile areas of the southern Lowland Zone, the Highland Zone has longer winters, heavier rainfall, and lower average temperatures. Summer wetness, summer warmth, and exposure are the key weather factors affecting yield and harvest failure.[89] An additional factor, great variability of weather, exacerbates the sensitivity of marginal areas. The variability of weather increases with higher altitudes, as in the British uplands. One important aspect of harvest failure in the marginal regions is simply the inability of farmers to anticipate weather conditions and choose an appropriate crop, soil preparation, planting time, and so forth.[90] Marginal areas suffer from any increase in "continentality" of climate which combines wider ranges of temperature and rainfall with reduced reliability.[91] Finally, a historical problem of agriculture in the marginal

[87] Manley, "Climate of the British Isles," 82.
[88] Parry, *Climatic Change*, 85, figs. 19 and 20. See also Thran and Broekhuizen, *Agro-Ecological Atlas*, maps 374 and 506.
[89] J. G. Evans, *Environment of Early Man*, 147–51; Parry, "Upland Settlement," 38.
[90] Parry, *Climatic Change*, 69ff.
[91] J. L. Anderson, "Climate and the Historians," 314; Utterström, "Climatic Fluctuations."

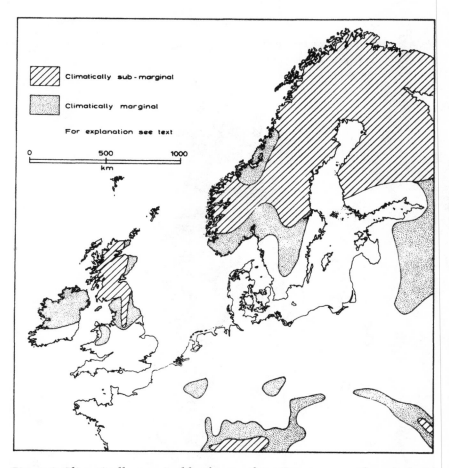

Figure 8. Climatically marginal land in northern Europe mapped on the basis of the number of growing months with a mean temperature above 10° C, and the amount of increase in average annual precipitation deficits during the months July–September. After M. L. Parry, *Climatic Change, Agriculture, and Settlement* (Folkestone, Kent, 1978), 85, fig. 20. Reproduced by permission of the author.

areas has been the absence of a buffer against bad times. The slim return of yield to sown even in good years tended to preclude stored surplus. This problem intensified the already low tolerance to climatic change in an agricultural system poorly adapted to its natural environment.[92]

[92] Parry, *Climatic Change,* 69ff.

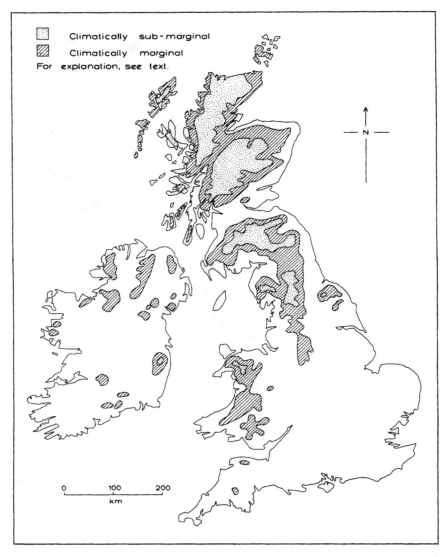

Figure 9. Climatically marginal land in the British Isles mapped on the basis of accumulated temperature alone. After M. L. Parry, *Climatic Change, Agriculture, and Settlement* (Folkestone, Kent, 1978), 83, fig. 19. Reproduced by permission of the author.

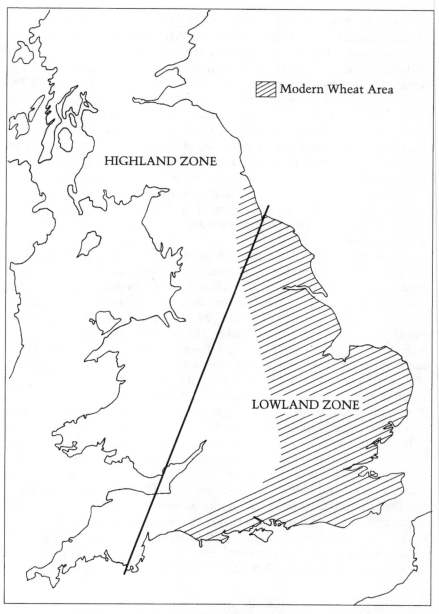

Figure 10. Division of Britain into Highland and a Lowland Zone. Modern wheat-growing areas of England. After H. H. Lamb, *The Biological Significance of Climatic Changes in Britain* (London, 1965).

Rainfall plays an essential role in the productivity or marginality of British agriculture. As Manley observes: "The rainfall-evaporation ratio, in these islands lying on the margin of the principal track of so many Atlantic depressions, and beset by so many others . . . can be regarded as a fundamental variable upon which agricultural prosperity depends."[93] Too much moisture is the greatest problem. Drought is rarely catastrophic. Even in the more favorable conditions of lowland Britain, 45 percent of observed variation in harvest size is related to summer rainfall.[94] Autumn rainfall is crucial in the marginal areas of the Highland Zone, where an inverse ratio between rainfall and the harvest of autumn sown crops can be plotted. Heavier than normal rainfall affects the lodging of the harvested grain, can cause grain to sprout on the ear, prolongs the harvest while it delays autumnal preparation of the land, mildews the grain, and makes a heavier, wetter soil more difficult to prepare and plant with winter crops.[95]

The Romans recognized that drainage and excessive moisture were serious agricultural problems in Britain even in favored lowland conditions during the relatively optimal climatic conditions of the first century A.D. "The climate is unpleasant, with frequent rain and mist, but it does not suffer from extreme cold. The day is longer than elsewhere in the empire and the night is clear and in the north short, with only a brief interval between nightfall and first light. . . . The soil is fertile and is suitable for all crops except the vine, olive, and other plants requiring warmer climates. Crops grow quickly but ripen slowly. This is due to the high rainfall and dampness of the soil."[96] In the later Roman period in Britain, the evidence discussed suggests that at least a 10 percent increase in wetness (rainfall) occurred. The effects on the marginal upland regions in Britain must have been extremely deleterious. In the lowlands, on the heavy and intractable clay soils developed for cereal production, already formidable problems of drainage and tillage must have become even more acute. Increased rainfall would have adversely affected a number of upland and lowland soils. By accelerating the processes of soil erosion and soil degradation (soil structural changes), increased rainfall would have further lessened soil fertility and significantly reduced agricultural output and potential. These processes resulted from an interaction between ongoing human interference in the landscape and recent climatic deterioration.[97]

[93] Manley, "Climate of the British Isles," 88.
[94] Ibid., 71. Cf. E. L. Jones, *Seasons and Prices.*
[95] Parry, *Climatic Change,* 69.
[96] Tacitus *Agricola* 12. The other classical sources mentioning British climate are not particularly helpful: Diodorus Siculus 5.21.6; Strabo 4.5.2; Caesar *B.G.* 5.12.7.
[97] For the relative importance of human agency and climatic causes in erosion and alluviation

The progressive deforestation of the Iron Age and Roman eras in Britain, associated with expanded agriculture and grazing, promoted soil erosion by reducing transpiration and exposing the soil. More rainfall would have added to this problem by increasing runoff, promoting flooding and alluviation, and accelerating the erosion of topsoil. Winter rains would have been particularly damaging. The flooding and drainage problems created by increased rainfall on the Romano-British wetlands, including the Fens, Somerset Levels, and Wentlooge Levels, have already been discussed. The social, economic, and demographic consequences must have been significant. The area of the Wentlooge Levels of southeastern Wales alone was about 325 square kilometers.

The lightest and heaviest soils would have been most affected by increased rainfall. On thin and hungry sandy soils or shallow overlays, increased rainfall would have accelerated the progressive leaching of minerals and denudation of accumulated soil nutrients associated with the spread of agriculture onto marginal soils. The resulting fall in chemical fertility would significantly have affected crop yields. On the damp and intractable heavy clay soils, increased rainfall would have accelerated the breakdown of soil structure caused by continuous ploughing and the cultivation of grain. With these soils drainage is the key problem. Ploughing promotes the creation of "plough pans" underneath the tilled surface, dense horizons relatively impermeable to water. These pans increase soil wetness and waterlogged conditions. Indeed, ploughing and the cultivation of grain can destroy the very composition of clay soils, creating "a pasty mass impervious to moisture and air and hard to reduce to a sowable tilth."[98] Both the spread of agriculture onto thin, marginal soils and the cultivation of heavy clays for cereals were characteristics of late Romano-British agriculture. To some degree, the effects of overcropping, erosion, and climatic deterioration could be countered on lighter soils by marling, manuring, and crop rotation. Worsening problems of tillage and drainage on the heavy clay loams of the lowlands might be partially remedied by continued intensive investment of manpower, animal power, and metals. The expense and scarcity of these resources, however, limited Romano-British agriculture's ability to respond to change. High rainfall would also have promoted podsolization and contributed to the spread of heath and blanket peat. Podsols are agriculturally unproductive and difficult to reclaim for agriculture. Expansion of heath and bog represent an overall loss

---

see Potter, *Changing Landscape,* 24–26. Cf. Martin Bell, "Valley Sediments," 87; Martin Bell, "Effects of Land-Use."
[98] Postan, *Medieval Economy,* 24, 71.

in ecological productivity.[99] The combined effects of significant erosion of topsoil and substantial acceleration of soil deterioration would not only have reduced grazing and agricultural production, they would have reduced absolutely the very basis of the rural economy.

Returning to the influence of temperature over British agriculture, about 6°C is generally accepted as a minimum mean air temperature needed to begin and sustain plant growth. In Scotland and parts of northern England a drop in annual average temperatures of 1°C jeopardizes cereal cultivation. Upland areas are particularly sensitive to changes in summer temperature because lowered temperatures oscillate across the 6°C growth threshold. The frequency of harvest failure increases with elevation in an S-shaped curve. Modern observation indicates that mean temperatures in Britain decrease at a crude rate of 1°C for each 154 to 165 meters of height above sea level. In northern England and Scotland, the growing season for grass decreases about fourteen days for each 100 meters of altitude. Climatic changes that lowered annual average temperatures would also have lowered the altitudinal limits of plant growth and cultivation, shortened the growing season, and reduced the "accumulated temperature" within the growing season. The accumulated temperature for any day is the amount in degrees by which the mean temperature exceeds that required to begin and maintain plant growth. Extrapolating from modern figures, the postulated drop of 1.5°C in average temperature associated with the climatic deterioration in later Roman Britain would have lowered the altitudinal threshold of agriculture by perhaps 200 meters in the uplands and reduced the growing season by about thirty days. A. C. Whittle has pointed out the limitations of such general calculations. Reductions in growing season vary spatially, seasonally, and according to steepness of slope.[100] Nevertheless, these figures provide a useful rough yardstick for assessing the fate of later Romano-British agriculture in the marginal areas. In the lowlands where agricultural activities were not so near critical environmental thresholds, lower average temperature associ-

99 For a discussion of the processes of soil degradation see Askew et al., "Upland Soils." For maintenance of soil quality and Roman Britain see Martin Jones, "Development of Crop Husbandry," 112-20; Martin Jones, "Crop Production," 99. For rainfall and podsolization see Judith Turner, "Iron Age," 279-81. For grazing, heath, and bog see Whittle, "Climate, Grazing, and Man." As Nick Higham concludes, "In total, the Romano-British community had lost parts of the habitat of their distant ancestors . . . largely the result of the pauperization of soils" (Northern Counties, 183).
100 Appleby, "Epidemics and Famine," 78. A drop of 1°C in temperature is equivalent to raising the level of the surface by five hundred feet. The chances of successive harvest failures are greatly increased. See Alexander T. Wilson, "Isotope Evidence." For the significance of temperature see Manley, "Climate of the British Isles," 93, 112-13; Parry, "Upland Settlement," 38. For Britain, the adopted value for accumulated temperature is 42°F (5.6°C). Whittle, "Climate, Grazing, and Man," 196-99.

ated with climatic deterioration would have worsened the problem of ripening crops and added to troubles connected with frost and the length of frost-free periods. For cereal crops, delays in the onset of the growing season rather than its overall length might have posed problems. Moreover, small variations in annual temperatures (smaller even than 1°C) may disguise briefer periods of much more extreme temperature change. In this sense annual average figures may be deceptive.[101] Over a long period of time, average figures tend to cancel out yearly or seasonal extremes. The seasonal variability experienced within the average, however, particularly if combined with untimely precipitation, could have proved fatal to agriculture. In Genesis the seven lean cows of Joseph's friend Pharaoh consumed the seven fat cows. Evidence suggests that the overall drop in yearly average temperatures during the later Roman period in England, Ireland, Wales, and southern Scotland possibly exceeded 1.5°C. This would presumably have reduced the average growing season by almost four weeks and lowered the upper limit of productive cultivation in England by almost 200 meters.[102]

Falling temperatures and increased rainfall would also have affected pasturage and animal husbandry, the other leg of Romano-British mixed farming. In the lowlands increased rainfall might have improved pasture, although cooler temperatures would have delayed early growth and slowed or reduced the hay crop. In the uplands the climatic changes would have had a strongly adverse effect on the economy. Longer winters, delayed springs, and shorter, colder summers would have reduced hay crops and necessitated greater slaughter of animals when hay and fodder ran out. Winter husbandry would have become more difficult, with fewer animals carried through the winter, and those with lower body weight and poorer chances of breeding and survival. Because of the relation between soil and pasture, the increased leaching and podsolization associated with increased rainfall would probably have caused changes in pasture type and decreased pasture value. Higher rainfall would also have promoted the spread of blanket peat at the expense of grassland. These shifts to rougher pasture would have reduced the carrying capacity of the land for sheep and cattle. Finally, colder and wetter conditions might have increased animal mortality caused by disease or parasite.[103]

[101] Gribbin and Lamb, "Climatic Change," 75.
[102] Lamb, "Approach to the Study," 303. See also Burgess, "Population, Climate, and Upland Settlement," 125; Lamb, "Climate from 1000 B.C. to 1000 A.D.," 55.
[103] Whittle, "Climate, Grazing and Man," 196–98. Parry suggests that severe losses of sheep and cattle from animal diseases in the fourteenth century may have been due to increased virulence associated with weather. Rinderpest and liver-fluke are possibilities. Parry, "Upland Settlement," 47. Hoof-and-mouth disease is another possibility. Harding, "Introduction: Climatic Change and Archaeology," 3.

Modern analogues, based on the observed climatic effects during periods of instrumentally recorded weather conditions, combined with the suggested climatic conditions in later Roman Britain, indicate that the climate of that period would have proved catastrophic for agriculture within the marginal Highland Zone.[104] A terrible combination of colder temperatures, excessive moisture, greater storminess, and unpredictability would have destroyed crops in the field and precluded adequate drainage and preparation of the soil.[105] Similar conditions in the fourteenth, sixteenth, and seventeenth centuries led to widespread harvest failure and famine in the north, associated at times with political violence and instability.[106] Although southern lowland areas were not subject to similar degrees of risk in the face of changing climate, any significant shortfall in northern harvests and animal products affected local supplies for the army and must have increased demands for exportation and taxation in the south. Uplands and lowlands must have been linked in misery when the fine balance between production and consumption within the British diocese was significantly disturbed. Areas within the Lowland Zone first cultivated during the Roman agricultural expansion also would have experienced reduced harvests and occasional harvest failure.[107] Rich and influential landowners in the south were perhaps prompted by wetter and colder condtions to change from arable farming to less vulnerable ranching, even as cultivation was driven onto lighter soils and higher elevations to escape problems of drainage and a rising water table (as in Surrey and East Anglia). The extent and pattern of the changes in the later Roman period long fooled historians, who mistook field remains located at altitudes and on soils never again farmed as the usual Roman practice. In fact, these outliers were aberrant examples, the evidence for more characteristic Roman arable in the richer lowlands having long since been destroyed by subsequent deep plowing.

The Romans thus fell into an ecological and climatic trap in Britain. Pushed by the demands of a growing population, urbanization, Romanization, and the needs of the army and government, pulled by logistical convenience, successful coercion, and the siren song of abnormally favorable climate, arable and grazing intensified in developed areas and spread into previously undeveloped areas and soils. During this climatic "op-

---

[104] C. G. Johnson and L. P. Smith, eds., *Biological Significance*; Parry, "Secular Climatic Change"; Catherine D. Smith and M. L. Parry, *Consequences of Climatic Change*. Some of the scanty evidence is conveniently assembled by Stratton and Brown, *Agricultural Records*.
[105] J. A. Taylor, ed., *Hill Climates*; J. A. Taylor, ed., *Climatic Change*.
[106] For example, unrest in 1315, 1597, and 1623. Walton, "Climate and Famines"; Appleby, "Epidemics and Famine," 77.
[107] Brandon, "Agriculture and Effects of Floods"; Brandon, "Late-Medieval Weather."

timum," marginal lands became temporarily supramarginal. Within a century and a half, however, climatic deterioration transformed perhaps several million hectares of upland from climatically viable for cereal cultivation to submarginal.[108] Climatic change gravely altered conditions of agriculture. Finally, the sharp deterioration occurring in roughly 400 A.D. must have triggered a severe crisis.

It is notoriously difficult to connect climatic change with specific historical events—in the case of the ending of Roman Britain, to link directly the hurly-burly of political, economic, and social changes with the silent evidence of pollen profiles, bog stratigraphies, and ice cores. As J. A. Taylor has remarked, "climatic change and culture change may be conceived on two separate but complementary wavelengths."[109] Although the influence of environmental change on food supply is undeniable, agricultural change is inherently complex. Premodern agricultural societies on some level were accustomed to coping with environmental fluctuation. As a consequence, they had some capacity to absorb a degree of environmental change. The impact of climatic change is transmuted within a complex and oscillating interaction of environmental, socioeconomic, cultural, and demographic causalities. The course of historical change in environmental crisis is influenced by ideology and social values, the existing system of resource utilization, and the elements of the social order directly linked to the peculiar environment. Within a crisis, a number of solutions might be conceivable. As Carl Moneyhon writes, "We do not, as yet, fully understand the precise way in which society and nature interrelate. . . . Shifts in resource bases can spark a variety of structural responses in one society."[110] Conceivable solutions might include: (1) an attempt to maintain the status quo by more vigorous exploitation of the environment (running faster to stay in place); (2) reorganization through a change of institutions; (3) radical alteration of the pattern of rural settlement and economy, possibly including abandonment or severe reduction of activity; and (4) simultaneous pursuit of a number of responses, some evidently contradictory. As we shall see, Roman Britain does not disappoint in the complexity of its responses to climatic change. The difficult

[108] Parry, "Upland Settlement," 38, 45. The situation for later Roman Britain must have been roughly analogous to the transition from the medieval warm epoch into the harsher climate of the later Middle Ages. Parry suggests that 12 percent of the British mainland, c. 2.75 million hectares, is represented by uplands marginal for cereal cultivation. Probably roughly 15 percent of the mainland is submarginal. At least 2 million hectares of unimproved moorland would have been climatically viable for cereal production during the warm period of the early Middle Ages.
[109] J. A. Taylor, "Role of Climatic Factors," 18.
[110] Moneyhon, "Introduction." Cf. Whittle, "Climate, Grazing, and Man," 199, with van der Veen, Crop Husbandry Regimes, 2, 159.

problem of tracing those responses is compounded by a paucity of literary evidence and by the archaeological elusiveness of post-Roman settlement. As Colin Burgess remarks: "Archaeology generally in the post-Roman period is full of voids and imponderables, no aspect more so than settlement archaeology. . . . Throughout Britain it has proved singularly difficult to determine what was going on in the uplands in the post-Roman period. In many regions it has proved impossible to find any settlements at all, let alone establish the extent and nature of upland settlement."[111] Our ignorance permits a variety of interpretations. The evident overall reduction in settlements may reflect a severe dislocation and absolute decline in population. Alternatively, archaeologists may simply be unable to identify sites occupied in the post-Roman period by people producing few distinctive objects. Or perhaps settlement changed in form, with greater nucleation resulting in fewer settlement sites but not necessarily a dramatic reduction in overall levels of population.

Given the suggested climatic changes and their projected effect on the rural economy, we might expect to find in response to increased submarginality in the Romano-British uplands both a retreat of cultivation and reforestation. We might also expect to find at the close of Roman Britain or in the immediate post-Roman period a demographic crisis and intense competition for scarce resources. Shortage of food and outright famine might be linked to rural rebellion or regional and civil wars. Maintaining trade, a level of urbanization, armies, and government ought to have become significantly harder in a world suffering environmental change and reduced production in the countryside.

In fact, the palaeobotanical evidence suggests that the great asynchronous process of woodland clearance in Britain, stretching back to 400 B.C. and continuing on an unprecedented scale in the Roman era, was substantially ended by 400 A.D.. There is limited evidence for forest regeneration in some upland areas. Elsewhere, Roman field systems seem to have been abandoned in a number of areas including the Pennines, Yorkshire, the east Midlands, and the Downs.[112] We lack any reliable chronology to date the abandonment of fields and settlements and the regional variations seem complex. Nevertheless, it is tempting to connect the evident contraction of settlement in the marginal areas and the reordering and possible reduction of the intensity of farming and settlement in some areas of lowland Britain to environmental change. Significantly, however,

---

[111] Burgess, "Population, Climate, and Upland Settlement," 199.
[112] G. Davies and J. Turner, "Pollen Diagrams," 801–3. For reversion to woodland see Burgess, "Population, Climate, and Upland Settlement," 199. Cf. Judith Turner, "Environment of Northeast England." For a recent review see Higham, *Rome, Britain, and the Anglo-Saxons,* 77–80, 108–36.

there is no palaeobotanical evidence for simultaneous, widespread, massive regeneration of forest in the immediate post-Roman period in either the uplands or lowlands. Indeed, in northwest England clearance begun in the late Roman period perhaps accelerated in the post-Roman period. In northwest England and southwest Scotland there are limited indications of clearance phases begun in the post-Roman era.[113] The degree of sensitivity of pollen diagrams to changes of population occurring within fully exploited and densely populated areas is problematic. The absence of a massive return to secondary forest invading long-cleared arable or pasture probably implies at least a significant degree of continuity of rural population and economy. The events of 406–10 A.D. have left no dramatic mark on the landscape.

Evidently then, adjustment rather than widespread, immediate abandonment seems to characterize late and post-Roman Britain's response to environmental change. Some have seen the absence of wholesale reforestation as evidence of continuing political and economic stability in the post-Roman north. Others have suggested that post-Roman clearance may indicate a continuation of exceptionally favorable weather. More probably the pattern reflects attempts by the native population to exploit the environment more vigorously in response to shrinking agricultural output. This need not imply tranquility or stability. An influx of refugees from invasion is another possible factor in explaining maintenance or sporadic expansion in the northern landscapes. It is worth recalling that land clearance, cultivation of heavier soils, and changed crop regimes all occurred in the late Iron Age against a background of deteriorating environment and possibly increased insecurity. That the "push" of continued population pressure rather than the "pull" of opportunity or stability underlies post-Roman clearance is suggested by the pollen diagrams

[113] For a discussion of post-Roman clearance with references see Judith Turner, "Iron Age," 272–75. For a review of pollen diagrams from the northeast see P. A. G. Clack, "Northern Frontier." Most of the pollen diagrams from Teesdale show expansion of grassland at the expense of woodland continuing from the Iron Age into the Roman era. Of nine dated diagrams, two indicate clearance phases confined entirely within the Roman period. Only Moss Mire shows a clearance beginning after the Roman occupation ended. From this site a substantial episode of clearance ended c. A.D. 400 ± 90 followed by a smaller post-Roman clearance in A.D. 520 ± 90. Cereal cultivation is indicated at the end of the first (Roman-era) clearance. The pollen diagram from Hallowell Moss indicates that maximum clearance occurred after the Roman withdrawal. In southwestern Westmorland, three pollen diagrams indicate a phase of clearance dated to about A.D. 436, coinciding with wetter conditions in the mires. See A. G. Smith, "Two Lacustrine Deposits." D. Walker, "Late-Quaternary History," suggests that clearance in the Cumberland lowlands occurred only after the Roman departure. At Bolton Fell Moss, however, Barber found "no evidence for the major clearances claimed to date from the fifth century by other authors" (Peat Stratigraphy, 115). The diagram from Bloak Moss in Ayrshire, Scotland, indicates extensive clearances dated c. A.D. 415. The phase was short lived, however, and forest regeneration resumed c. A.D. 580.

from the Lake District. Here the clearance phase of roughly 436 coincided with distinctly wetter, unfavorable weather.[114]

The regional variety and the complex interweaving of adjustment and abandonment in the landscape of later Roman Britain are illustrated by local regional studies. In the Upper Thames region, Romano-British settlements located along the flood plain and dependent on labor-intensive drainage schemes were abandoned by the mid-fifth century. The heavier valley soils were marginal because of their damp and intractable nature, and problems with drainage and tillage were overcome only by intensive labor. Retreat from such soils at the end of the Roman period occurred elsewhere in the Thames valley. The valley bottoms did not go completely out of use, however, but shifted from production of bread-wheat and flax to grazing. Occupation continued on the lighter soils of the gravel terraces above the floodplain. Barton Court Farm, for example, located on the second terrace, evinced a pattern of expansion during the Roman period with the development of valley-bottom crops. The villa or farmstead was demolished sometime during the first half of the fifth century, but people using Anglo-Saxon pottery occupied the site. They used the land less intensively. The Roman crop of spelt-wheat disappeared as did garden cultivation of exotic plants, but flax and barley continued to be grown. Grazing declined and shrub pollen increased. Cattle and horses declined in numbers while sheep increased.[115] All of these changes are consistent with adaptation to wetter conditions. The example illustrates the difficulty of isolating particular causes for changes in the landscape. Was the drainage of the valley soils ruined by alluviation created by intensive farming of the nearby Cotswold slopes, or the result of increased rainfall, or both factors in combination? Does the lower intensity of land use stem from lessened demands of a reduced population, changes in social groups and tastes, or climatic deterioration? There is no obvious way to disentangle anthropogenic from climatic influence, but the changes in the landscape including preference for lighter soils, abandonment or changed use of the heavier, hard-to-drain soils, a shift in emphasis away from arable

[114] For the idea of continued political and economic stability see G. Davies and J. Turner, "Pollen Diagrams," 802. For the notion of continued favorable weather see Higham, *Northern Counties*, 244. For the idea of refugees see Rackham, *Trees and Woodland*, 52. For the Lake District see A. G. Smith, "Two Lacustrine Deposits." For the Iron Age see van der Veen, *Crop Husbandry Regimes*, 146.
[115] For an introduction to the study of the Upper Thames region see Miles, "Confusion in the Countryside." For details of the Roman and post-Roman landscape see Mark Robinson, "Iron Age to Early Saxon Environment." Robinson finds no evidence for climatic change and attributes the various alterations within the region to "human activity, intentional or otherwise" (270). Compare the conclusions of Miles, "Romano-British Countryside," 126, with those of Martin Jones, "Agriculture in Roman Britain," 132.

farming to stock rearing, and a retreat of settlement from marginal areas form a pattern consistent with expected response to deteriorating climate.

In the Romano-British southwest the pattern of desertion in the late Roman settlement varies among different areas. In the Somerset Levels, as in other Romano-British wetlands, flooding and drainage difficulties evidently drove many inhabitants from the land. West of the River Parrett, there seems to have been comparatively little disruption, possibly because the basic density of population and subsistence agriculture of the pre-Roman order had been so little affected by the Roman presence. East of the River Parrett, considerable abandonment of settlement occurred, confined to discrete areas. To a significant extent this may have been related to problems with drainage. Roger Leech has tentatively suggested that the changes in the southwest resulted first from the imposition of an alien administrative system and an increase in the area of cultivation, followed by the collapse of that system and its demands with a consequent contraction of the cultivated area.[116] Here as elsewhere, chronological uncertainties stalk the analysis. A large number of settlements were deserted after the end of the fourth century, but the desertion may have occurred early in the fifth century or decades later. The fifth century evidently saw significant mobility of settlement throughout Britain. Dating is often uncertain, but desertion of Roman settlement sites occurred throughout the various regions and involved both marginal areas and areas of intensive land use. Summarizing three decades of research on the Romano-British countryside, David Miles concludes: "There is no doubt, however, that the fifth century witnessed, in the more Romanized South at least, a substantial economic and probably demographic collapse."[117]

The timing of the suggested demographic crisis is controversial. As we have seen, palaeobotanical evidence is not easily reconciled with a demographic catastrophe in the fifth century. Socioeconomic adjustments which themselves produced serious stress and dislocation perhaps postponed the population crisis. Sooner or later, however, a numerous and harvest-sensitive population, afflicted with declining agricultural production from a fully exploited landscape exposed to climatic deterioration, must have faced severe demographic crisis. As Burgess observes: "The state of overpopulation may itself be triggered by climatic change. A level of population that may comfortably be supported in one period may become unsupportable when the environment becomes less favourable. It is then that disease, famine, and war exert their influence. These may be

[116] Leech, "Roman Interlude." Leech holds open the possibility of environmental change as an alternate explanation (251).
[117] Miles, "Romano-British Countryside," 126. Cf. Higham, *Rome, Britain, and the Anglo-Saxons*, 108-21.

undetectable in the archaeological record. . . ."[118] Overt historical symptoms of a crisis of relative overpopulation might include famine, brigandage, social revolt, raiding, and civil war. These must be sought within the
meager and problematic literacy evidence.

Gildas is our essential literary source. He evidently wrote in a period of
relative quiet and sufficiency amidst a generation who "had experienced
only the calm of the present." (D.e. 26.3) There is no indication that he had
personal experience of famine. He referred to Britain's potential for "vigorous" agriculture in lowland and upland and also alluded to transhu-
mance and animal husbandry (D.e. 3.3). In contrast to this contemporary
image, Gildas's vision of the more distant Romano-British past and immediate post-Roman period is dominated by images of scarcity and stamped
with the memory of famine. For Gildas, Rome's political relation with
Britain was defined by a series of departures and returns, an imperialistic
revolving door. To explain the periodic departures, Gildas inferred scarcity. For example, "The conquerors soon went back to Rome—allegedly
for want of land—and had no suspicion of [British] rebellion" (D.e. 6). In
the next episode, "the country [Britain] now being empty of wine and oil,
they made for Italy" (D.e. 7). This portion of Gildas's narrative is historically inaccurate and impressionistic, but the retrospective impression of
scarcity forcing Roman withdrawal from Britain seems to be independent
of Gildas's own experience and may be a significant reflection of popular
memory.

Eventually the Romans leave never to return. The Britons alone face
the Picts and Scots and the defense is ineffectual. Fleeing from the invaders, the Britons are driven by hunger to prey upon one another. "For
they resorted to looting each other, there being only a tiny amount of food
to give brief sustenance to the wretched people; and the disasters from
abroad were increased by internal disorders, for as a result of constant
devastations of this kind the whole region came to lack the staff of any
food. . . ." (D.e. 19.4). Here we have civil war, or at least brigandage,
caused by hunger. Following a final unsuccessful appeal for Roman aid,
the Britons suffered from a full-scale famine (fames dira). "Meanwhile, as
the Britons feebly wandered, a dreadful and notorious famine gripped
them, forcing many of them to give in without delay to their bloody
plunderers, merely to get a scrap of food to revive them" (D.e. 20.2). The
final reference to famine in Gildas is metaphorical. "But a new and more
virulent famine was quietly sprouting. In the respite from devastation, the

---

[118] Burgess, "Population, Climate, and Upland Settlement," 196. See the implications
discussed by Michael E. Jones, "Climate, Nutrition, and Disease." Cf. Parry, "Upland Settlement and Climatic Change," 38.

island was so flooded with abundance of goods that no previous age had known the like of it." (Fame alia virulentiore tacitus pullulante. Quiescente autem vastitate tantis abundantiarum copiis insula affluebat ut nulla habere tales retro aetas meminisset, cum quibus omnimodis et luxuria crescit.) (*D.e.* 21.2). Hugh Williams translates *fame virulentiore* as "poisonous hunger" and interprets *nulla . . . retro aetas* as "no age remembered the possession of such [resources of affluence] afterwards." This last variation is an acceptable translation and the nuance may be significant.[119]

Typically, Gildas provides no particulars for the date or the location of the notorious famine within Britain. As early as the eighth century historians attempted to remedy the missing chronology by assimilating the British famine into famines recorded elsewhere. The famine and plague at Constantinople about 446 A.D. recorded by Marcellinus Comes has been a popular choice. While it is possible that the British famine was a component of a greater crisis spreading even to Constantinople and the east, it is also possible that it was part of a regional episode affecting only the western provinces, or confined to Britain and neighboring Gaul. Famines were relatively rare in Gaul. A fifth-century chronicle recorded a great famine in roughly 414 A.D. A number of Gallic sources recorded a great famine in about 470 A.D.[120] Britain's location on the periphery of the temperate zone, with greater marginality of agriculture and sensitivity to climatic change, make it quite possible that the famine in Gildas was entirely confined to Britain or even peculiar to some region within Britain. Attempts to date the British famine by association with other areas are only guesswork. On the basis of internal relative chronology, Gildas's famine

---

[119] Gildas, *Gildas,* trans. Williams, p. 49. See Winterbottom's comment, Gildas, *Ruin of Britain,* p. 149.

[120] For what it is worth, Jerome recorded a famine in Palestine c. 405 A.D. (*Ep.* 114.1). Under the consular entry for Valentinan vii and Aetius iii, Marcellinus Comes records a famine followed by plague. The relation in Bede between the British famine and the famine in Constantinople is problematic (*H.e.* 1.12–14). Bede concludes *H.e.* 1.13 with the famine in Constantinople, which he knew from Marcellinus Comes and immediately follows in *H.e.* 1.14 with the famine he knew from Gildas. Colgrave and Mynors translate Bede so as to link the two famines as one. Sims-Williams draws attention to the omission of *sua* in the critical phrase *fames sua praefata* in one group of manuscripts ("C2") and suggests that Bede meant to distinguish the British famine from the one in Constantinople but that eighth-century editors blurred the two famines together ("Settlement of England," 19 n. 77). Bede may have been merely drawing a parallel, but the location of the two famines immediately adjacent in Bede's narrative suggests that he flirted with the identification of the two famines as a single event. For famines in Gaul, I am grateful to Ralph W. Mathisen for allowing me to read his paper "Nature or Nurture?" prior to publication. Under the 20th regnal year of Arcadius and Honorius, the Gallic Chronicle of 452 gives: "Ingens in Gallis fames." If located correctly, the date is 414 A.D. The chronological red herring provided by the appeal of the Britons to "Aetius three times consul" is discussed above.

occurred fairly soon after the final Roman withdrawal and before the arrival of the Saxons. This should locate the famine early within the period between roughly 410 and 442 A.D.

At first glance, the sequence in Gildas of famine followed immediately by abundance (*D.e.* 20.2; 21.2) seems nonsensical or at least incompatible with a pattern of climatic deterioration. In fact, instability in the weather with wild variation in harvests is typically associated with the initial phase of a climatic downturn.[121] Other aspects of the story presented by Gildas take on significance in a context of shortages and famine. The Saxon revolt in Britain began when supplies fell short. "The barbarians who had been admitted to the island asked to be given supplies [*impetrant sibi annonas dari*] falsely representing themselves as soldiers ready to undergo extreme dangers for their excellent hosts. The supplies were granted, and for a long time 'shut the dogs mouth.' Then they again complained that their monthly allowance [*epimenia*] was insufficient, purposely giving a false colour to individual incidents, and swore that they would break their agreement and plunder the whole island unless more lavish payment were heaped on them. There was no delay: they put their threats into immediate effect" (*D.e.* 23.5). This is a crucial event, but curiously Gildas provides no reason for the Britons' fatal refusal to provide the Saxons with the promised supplies. The Britons may have been playing their own version of the dangerous Roman game of using subsidy and blockade to make food supplies a strategic weapon with which to control barbarians. Alternatively, generalized food shortages related to climatic change and agricultural decline would provide a satisfactory explanation.[122] The Britons may have been caught on the horns of a dilemma, with subsistence needs of the population on one side and security needs and rations for the mercenary Saxons on the other. Once the Saxon revolt spread successfully, hunger forced Britons to surrender. "Others, their spirit broken by hunger, went to surrender to the enemy; they were fated

---

[121] Burgess, "Population, Climate, and Upland Settlement," 198. Alternatively, such extreme fluctuation of harvests may simply reflect chance variations of weather within a climatic period. In Gaul, for example, the famine in the early 470s followed a good harvest year and was itself followed by a good harvest. Mathisen, "Nature or Nurture?" speculates that this famine in Gaul may be related to an eruption of Mt. Vesuvius or even more local volcanic activity in the Auvergne.

[122] Gildas may have felt that the Britons were actually at fault. The parallel with the Old Testament example of the Gibeonites was in his mind when he wrote the preface to *De excidio.* The Gibeonites tricked the Israelites, just as the Saxons tricked the Britons. The Gibeonites and Israelites make an agreement (*foedus*), just as the Britons and Saxons agree over *annonae* and *epimenia* (*D.e.* 1.4; 23.5). The Israelites break the treaty and are punished by God with famine. The Britons fail to supply the required rations and also suffer from starvation. Cf. Sims-Williams, "Gildas and the Anglo-Saxons," 27–28.

to be slaves for ever. . . ." (*D.e.* 25.1) It may be significant in this context that the pivotal battle of Mount Badon was a siege.

Other aspects of Gildas's narrative may also be significant in the context of suggested climatic change, harvest failure, and hunger. Gildas described the Scots and Picts raiding Britain as "like greedy wolves, rabid with extreme hunger" (*D.e.* 16). This may be mere bombast, but the Saxon raiders were evidently hungry for rations. The intensification of barbarian raiding in Britain in the first half of the fifth century is suggestive, for it coincides with the chronology of postulated climatic change. The raids follow a period of relative quiet up to the mid-fourth century. Because of the effects of latitude, the movement of ocean polar currents, and other considerations, the suggested climatic changes would possibly have been roughly twice as severe north of Hadrian's Wall as to the south. The gradients of climatic change and environmental deterioration run roughly north-south and west-east. Accordingly, the Picts north of the frontier and the Scots west of Britain in Ireland would have been early and severely affected. Their impetus to raiding would have been sharpened by the socioeconomic effects of climatic change. Climatic change and continued flooding along the North Sea littoral must have been one factor sending Germanic *comitatenses* raiding into the empire and Britain. Warrior elites possibly compensated for reduced agricultural and pastoral productivity at home by raiding abroad for precious metals and perishable goods needed to maintain their wealth and status. Slaves such as Saint Patrick were no doubt a significant part of perishable booty. Settlement within some richer imperial area, moving to the wealth rather than moving the wealth home, was another option. The "push" of scarcity and change in the tribal homelands must have added to the "pull" of easy pickings in a Britain no longer effectively defended by the Roman army and fleet. The relation between climatic changes and settlement patterns along the North Sea and Channel coasts is a complicated problem. It is too simple to suggest that deteriorating environments at the end of the Roman era led necessarily or directly to massive migration into Britain. As we have seen, evidence for key factors in flooding and coastal change such as rising sea levels and changing patterns of storm intensity is thin and unevenly distributed for this period. The chronology of flooding is poorly established and within the dominant pattern of rising sea levels there are significant regional and local anomalies. A possible period of standstill or relative fall in sea level may date to roughly 150–300 A.D. Tooley suggests that sea levels may have peaked about 150 A.D., with levels possibly falling thereafter, perhaps over the next five hundred years. Sea level and coastal data for the North Sea and Channel coasts indicate a complex and various pattern with inundation in many areas but local and widespread coastal advance elsewhere. In the Netherlands, for example, tidal flats may have expanded between roughly 1700 and 1250 B.P. (250 and 700 A.D.). The terpen mounds of Friesland, however, and the Flanders coast show evidence of marine transgression in this same period. The "Dunkerque II" transgression has been dated from the first century to a peak in the mid-fourth century. The fate of settlements in the fifth century such as Wijster, Gristede, and Feddersen Wierde must be viewed against a long, complex, and changing pattern of coastal settlement. Given the interaction among crustal movement, sea level, climatic change, siltation, and erosion as well as human actions, we may reasonably infer that environmental influences played a role in changing settlement and migration during the fourth and fifth centuries and after, but so too did political change and shifting trade networks. In any case, however, genuine mass movements of agricultural communities across the North Sea to Britain were not logistically feasible.[123]

Gildas gives few indications of the direct causes of the hunger and famine suffered by the Britons. Famine and starvation are loosely connected to barbarian depredations of the Picts, Scots, and later the Saxons. Civil war among the Britons creates hunger. The ultimate cause of famine and attendant suffering is moral. In Gildas's calculus God creates famine and hunger to punish and instruct the Britons just as God uses the barbarian invaders. The moral significance of famine is made evident by Gildas's use of *fames* as a metaphor, ironically for the sins that grow with plenty. The connection between famine and God's actions with his chosen people was in Gildas's thoughts when he composed the preface to De excidio. He relates the cautionary tale of the Gibeonites in the Old Testament (D.e. 1.4). These people trick the Israelites into a treaty (*foedus*), just as the Saxons trick the Britons. When the Israelites break the treaty God punishes them with famine, just as the Britons suffer starvation during the Saxon revolt after they fail to deliver the supplies (*annonae, epimenia*)

---

123 For the north-south gradient see Lamb, "Climate from 1000 B.C. to 1000 A.D.," 55. Cf. Manley, "Effective Rate." For sea levels see Tooley, *Sea Level Changes*, 182–92; Tooley, "Sea-Level and Coastline Changes," 1. Cf. Devoy, "Controls on Coastal and Sea-Level Change," 18. For flooding see Porter, "Environmental Change," 354–55, 359. Lamb uses the obviously inadequate literary evidence to plot severe flooding in the North Sea and Channel coasts century by century ("Climate and Its Variability," 29, Fig. 3). For economic changes see Hodges, *Anglo-Saxon Achievement*, 15, 24. For the view that environmental compulsion drove peasants overseas to Britain see Whittock, *Origins of England*, 15–19. Sonia Hawkes concludes that Britain may have faced a major refugee problem ("South-East after the Romans," 85). The Roman Netherlands provides an interesting case. Roman occupation ended abruptly toward the end of the third century, a casualty of political unrest, economic changes, and a rising water table. The native population seems to have disappeared from the western Netherlands at this time. There is no evidence that they migrated to Britain. See TeBrake, *Medieval Frontier*, 100–102.

promised to the Saxons. Given the strong link between morality and famine in Gildas's paradigm, it is perhaps unsurprising to find there no connection with environmental change. In a study of the literary evidence for
famine in the Graeco-Roman world, Peter Garnsey concludes that while
food shortage due to variability in the weather was endemic, mortal famine was rare. J. K. Evans is more pessimistic: "So delicately balanced was
the relationship between production and consumption in the Roman
world. Any interruption of the mechanism might provoke a crisis. . . . It
may fairly be concluded that the spectre of starvation haunted the *imperium Romanum*, an imminent and frequently deadly pestilence."[124] Modern theories of famine causation include climatic and environmental factors but shy away from simple climatic determinism. Overpopulation in
its neo-Malthusian forms is still an influential theory. Critics, however,
suggest that the simple equation of "too many stomachs and too little
food equals famine" confuses causes and effects. Hoarding, speculation,
burden of debt, and unequal entitlements in highly stratified agricultural
societies combine to produce long-term socioeconomic factors making a
society vulnerable or fragile. Roman society of course was no stranger to
distributional inequalities or the dominance of a wealthy class. For the
ending of Roman Britain and the immediate post-Roman period, climate
seems to play a primary role in creating a subsistence crisis. It is, however,
a multidimensional crisis and social inequalities and outside invasion no
doubt played significant roles.[125] Within the limited compass of Gildas's
narrative we seem to find the usual suspects of famine, brigandage, civil
war, and raiding that serve to link the hypothetical effects of an environmental crisis to specific historical events. If we follow E. A. Thompson's
controversial interpretation of Zosimus, even social revolt may be added
to the list: "And the barbarians from across the Rhine, who now attacked
in force, reduced the inhabitants of Britain and some of the Celtic tribes to
the point of throwing off Roman rule and living independently, without
further submission to Roman laws. So the Britons took up arms and facing
danger for their own safety they freed their cities from the barbarians who
threatened them; and all Armorica and the other provinces of Gaul followed the British example and freed themselves in the same way, expelling their Roman governors and setting up their own administrations as
best they could" (Zosimus 6.5.2–3, trans. *Literary Sources*, 53).
Thompson argues that the aim of the rebellion was to separate from the
empire. He further suggests that the motive was social as well as political.
The Armorican imitation of the British rebellion, according to Thompson,

---

[124] J. K. Evans, "Wheat Production," 441–42. Cf. Garnsey, *Famine and Food Supply.*
[125] For a good discussion of famine theory see David Arnold, *Famine,* 1–72.

was a revolt of the poorer classes in the countryside against the Roman government and the landed aristocracy.[126] Certainly in later periods wetter, colder weather led to famine and rural revolt in Scotland and northern England. Describing the often tumultuous early modern countryside, J. P. Kenyon argues that the lower classes, helpless victims to the least climatic fluctuation and a ready prey to famine or disease, were receptive to rabble-rousing and prone to revolt.[127] Recent studies of early-modern revolution and rebellion have stressed the role of subsistence crises in which population pressure on limited resources overwhelmed inflexible institutions. Later Roman Britain shared with early modern and medieval analogues all the major ingredients for rural rebellion and political disorder: population pressure, inflation, climatic fluctuation, and even the religious ferment of spreading heresy. It would be surprising in the extreme if these common ingredients failed to produce a similar cake of troubles for the end of the Roman era.

DISEASE

Epidemic disease is a possible by-product of climatic change and consequent agricultural failure. The lessened production of basic grains and the movement of a population closer to subsistence creates the Malthusian possibility of harvest failure, famine, and the spread of epidemics through a weakened population.[128] A. H. M. Jones believes that the rural peasantry in general during the Roman period were hard pressed by the tax collector and near subsistence even in times not afflicted with climatic deterioration.[129] Galen's famous description of hungry peasants of the second century afflicted by famine can be matched with similar accounts in both East and West during the fourth and fifth centuries.[130] "The famine prevalent for many successive years in many provinces has clearly displayed . . . the effect of malnutrition in generating illness. The city dwellers, as it was

---

[126] E. A. Thompson, "Zosimus on the End," 163–67.

[127] Kenyon, Stuart England, 16. For general introductions see Post, Last Great Subsistence Crisis; Lucas, "Great European Famine"; Appleby, Famine in Tudor and Stuart England; Clarkson, Death, Disease, and Famine; Goldstone, Revolution and Rebellion.

[128] Segraves, "Malthusian Proposition"; Parry, Climatic Change, 140ff., especially 143: "The suggestion is that the relationship between climate and settlement is sometimes expressed in a complicated fashion through harvest size, food supply, epidemic disease, mortality rates (including infant mortality) and population size."

[129] A. H. M. Jones, Later Roman Empire, 2:810, 1043.

[130] Ambrose: "If so many cultivators are starved and so many farmers die, our corn supply will be ruined for good. . . . " Libanius: "Famine had filled our city with beggars, some of whom had abandoned their fields, since they had not even grass to eat. . . . " These passages are quoted in A. H. M. Jones, Later Roman Empire, 2:810. Ambrose Off. 3.45–47; Libanius Or. 27.6, 14.

their custom to collect and store enough corn for the whole of the next year immediately after the harvest, carried off all the wheat, barley, beans, and lentils, and left to the peasants various kinds of pulse. . . . After consuming what was left in the course of the winter, the country people had to resort to unhealthy foods in the spring; they ate twigs and shoots of trees and bushes and bulbs and roots of inedible plants. . . ."[131] The effects of the suggested climatic deterioration and consequent agricultural failure on a peasantry such as existed in late Roman Britain must have been terrible.

The second component of the Malthusian model, disease, is elusive in Roman Britain. Gildas gives prominence to a great plague in Britain: "For a deadly plague swooped brutally on the stupid people, [*Pestifera namque lues feraliter insipienti populo incumbit*] and in a short period laid low so many people, with no sword, that the living could not bury all the dead" (*D.e.* 22.2). The same epidemic evidently is referred to earlier in the *De excidio* as *famosa pestis*.[132] This "memorable plague" has periodically appeared in the historical analysis of the end of Roman Britain. Edward Foord links the undated plague mentioned in Gildas with the events of the mid-fifth century (about 454).[133] He was followed in this by Stevens, who specifically matches Gildas's account with entries in the *Chronicles* of Hydatius and Marcellinus Comes.[134] Hydatius observed a plague that in Spanish eyes "spread almost throughout the whole world." Britain, however, is never mentioned in Hydatius's *Chronicle*, so his phrasing carries no compelling implication that the epidemic of roughly 443 A.D. reached there. Marcellinus Comes gave no details of the geographic extent of the epidemic troubling Constantinople in approximately 446 A.D. There is no strong argument to link events in Constantinople and Britain in these years. Attempts to date the plague in Gildas by association with other sources are as problematic as similar attempts to date the famine in Gildas discussed above.

Several problems preclude the inclusion of plague or epidemic disease as a significant contributor to the end of Roman authority in Britain. The deliberate historical parallels drawn by Gildas for Britain with the Old Testament (both being examples of God's chastisement of a guilty people) raise the outside possibility that the British epidemic is "Egyptian," a

---

[131] Galen *De probis pravisque alimentorum succis* 1; translation by Fergus Millar, quoted in Salway, *Roman Britain*, 234.

[132] Gildas *D.e.* 2.

[133] Foord, *Last Age*, 199.

[134] Hydatius *Chron.* 126; Marcellinus Comes *Chronicon* 13. The chronological conjunction outlined by Stevens is seductive ("Gildas Sapiens," 363). For cogent criticism of his argument see Myres, "Adventus Saxonum," 228–29; Harrison, *Framework*, 25–26.

rhetorical device rather than an actual disease. Gildas is the only source for the British epidemic, and his account is not only undated, it includes no description of medical symptoms.[135] If the British plague is in fact an extension of one of the various pestilences affecting parts of the empire in the mid-fifth century and after (from about 442 to 540), it is still too late to have influenced the Roman political failure in Britain. As will be shown, this can be securely dated to roughly A.D. 410. The only clue to the date of the British epidemic is its relative position within Gildas's narrative. The plague falls after the final departure of the Romans, within the period of prosperity associated with a lull in Pictish and Scottish raiding, but before the ill-advised invitation to the Saxons extended by the "proud tyrant" and his council (D.e. 21.1–3; 23). Connecting this internal chronology with the dates for the Saxon *adventus* derived from Constantius, the Gallic Chronicle of 452, and the *Historia Brittonum* suggests that the British plague dated after 410 but probably before 442 and quite possibly before 428 A.D.[136]

Infectious disease certainly played an important role in the high mortality rates associated with life in the ancient world. Even the incomplete and discontinuous literary record marks a number of destructive epidemics in the Roman period. The plague of Galen (Antonine plague) and the bubonic pandemic of Justinian's reign are merely the best known of a series of epidemics to strike the empire.[137] Ironically, however, for all of their other troubles, the late fourth and early fifth centuries are noteworthy for the relative absence of epidemics in contemporary sources. Apart from Hydatius and Marcellinus Comes, we have only reference to disease in Italy (roughly 452) at the time of Attila's invasion and an epidemic in the east recorded by Evagrius and dated to about 455 A.D. This last may not have affected the western provinces. This relative paucity of records stands in marked contrast to the frequency with which epidemics are cited in sixth-century evidence. The conclusion that epidemics were relatively rare in the fourth and early fifth centuries is in a sense an argument from silence. A number of fourth- and fifth-century authors, however, viewed their world through an apocalyptic lens and it would be remarkable and inexplicable had they chosen not to include contemporary experience of epidemics in their catalogues of problems. In fact, Ammianus,

---

135 As Foord states, Gildas's description is "rhetorical and destitute of chronology" (*Last Age*, 199).
136 For a discussion of Gildas and sixth-century plague see O'Sullivan, *Authenticity and Date*, 22, 79–85.
137 Gilliam, "Plague under Marcus Aurelius," provides a good review of epidemics and their significance in the Roman empire. For a more lurid treatment see Cartwright, *Disease and History*, 8–28. There were serious epidemics in A.D. 79, 125, 165/66–89 and 250–71. Then, apart from localized epidemics, comes a relative hiatus lasting until the mid-fifth century.

Eutropius, Jerome, and Orosius all refer to earlier historical epidemics. In this particular case, the dog that does not bark seems significant. John Wacher argues that epidemic diseases partially explain the collapse of both church and urban life in Britain in the fifth century and after. His views have been severely criticized by Malcolm Todd.[138]

The lack of definitive symptoms of the various fifth-century "pests" highlights a final problem of associating epidemic disease with the end of Roman Britain. Without specific knowledge of a disease, the Malthusian link between malnutrition related to harvest failure and the spread of epidemics becomes tenuous. Mortality associated with famine should not be underestimated, but Andrew Appleby's work has revealed the lack of any obvious connection between malnutrition and epidemics of bubonic plague, typhus, or smallpox.[139] Thus the suggested climatic deterioration and consequent subsistence problems associated with the end of Roman Britain need not imply the presence of significant epidemics. Because of these various circumstances, epidemic disease, however important it may have been in changing the population and settlement patterns of post-Roman Britain, must be largely discounted as a contributory force in the destruction of Roman rule.

Owen Lattimore once remarked acidly that the fall of Rome should not be attributed to a joggle of the barometer.[140] In the ending of Roman Britain, were climatic and related environmental influences significant causative agents or merely contributory woes? A study of climate and the environment in later Roman Britain reveals far more than a joggle. Instead, the suggested pattern of climatic deterioration, economic decline, relative overpopulation, and social stress must have prepared the ground for the extreme political instability of the first decade of the fifth century—the final decade of Roman Britain. Did environmental changes act as long-term causes or as triggers? The polarity of choice between

---

[138] Wacher, *Towns*, 414ff.; Todd, "Famosa Pestis." An ironic effect of the events of 410 and the separation of Britain from Roman government and from the Roman army would have been the attenuation of links along which epidemics might have passed. Todd argues that no means of transmitting the plague from Spain to Britain existed in the fifth century. This is perhaps overstated, since the British army and pretenders were active in Spain c. 410. E. A. Thompson draws attention to evidence of British settlement on the north coast of Spain in the sixth century. These Britons might have emigrated in the fifth or sixth century, and such contacts furnished potential links for transmission of disease from Spain back to Britain. See E. A. Thompson, "Britonia." Todd's other arguments relating specifically to Wacher's treatment of plague and cities are better founded. In contrast, Salway argues (in keeping with McNeill) that Britain would have been opened to disease introduced into a previously uncontaminated or unexposed population by her inclusion in the Roman network of trade and communications. If this were the case, Britain might have suffered acutely. Salway, *Roman Britain*, 552.

[139] Flinn, "Relationship of Climatology to Medicine"; Appleby, "Epidemics and Famine."

[140] Repeated by Gordon Manley in the foreword to Le Roy Ladurie, *Times of Feast*, xv.

"straightforward muddy catastrophe" and "significant tipping of the scales" is too simple.[141] Using temperature as an example, the sharply colder episode beginning in about 400 A.D. directly affected only the final decade of nearly four centuries of Roman occupation in Britain. The episode might well be described as a "trigger." The years 388–410 seem important, however, out of all proportion to chronological length. Perhaps "detonator" is a better metaphor for the role of environmental change at this critical juncture of events. Or, considering temperature more generally, favorable temperatures were an important ingredient in the agricultural and demographic development of Roman Britain. Taken together, the influences of warmer-than-present conditions and the late-striking cold episode suggest that temperature was not a trigger but a long-term cause. Increased rainfall influenced a longer span of the late Romano-British period than did colder temperatures. Flooding and drainage problems, erosion and soil deterioration are products of the interaction of anthropogenic and climatic influences. "Trigger" does not seem an adequate description of their causal role and influence in a number of regions of later Roman Britain. For the wetlands and marginal areas of the uplands, temperature and rainfall probably acted as long-term causes. In better-sheltered lowland areas climatic deterioration probably produced significant but short-term reversions in the agricultural landscape. In geographical terms the generalized model suggested by M. L. Parry for the medieval period has good application for later and post-Roman Britain. Parry indicates that in the lowlands agricultural changes were a product of long-term changes in economic, social, and institutional bases, sometimes triggered by short-term variations in climate affecting harvest yields. For the uplands, the relative roles were reversed. In the uplands environmental changes acted on land climatically marginal for cereal cultivation as a long-term influence creating an agricultural resource base sensitive to "proximate social, economic and political factors."[142]

Climatic changes and related environmental deterioration coincided fully with the immediate post-Roman era, and for this period must be considered as long-term causes. Communities faced with serious environmental challenge confront a "Catch 22." As Moneyhon concludes: "The nature of a community's action will be conditioned by the ideology informing its behavior. Since an ideology includes a particular set of social values, which, in turn, are predicated on a particular mode of interaction with the society's environment, a change in any part of this mode of

141 Whittle, "Climate, Grazing, and Man," 192.
142 Parry, "Upland Settlement," 47–48.

interaction might well present a challenge to the continued existence of the society as such. Refusing to change the complex of rules and values of a society will limit its members' capacity to respond to environmental crisis conditions; change, however, opens the door to social and political chaos."[143] In the fifth and sixth centuries the degree of survival of aspects of *Romanitas* was affected by political and socioeconomic change but also by the changing environment. We have traced connections between environmental change and declining food supplies affecting famine, civil war, barbarian raiding, and relative overpopulation. Sometime between the fourth and eleventh centuries, probably between the mid-sixth and late-seventh centuries, a full-blown demographic catastrophe occurred that possibly halved Britain's population. To a great extent this loss resulted from the epidemics of the sixth century and after. Demographic catastrophe theory posits a grim tripod of warfare, mortal epidemic, and climatic deterioration. The third leg, climatic change and increased agricultural marginality, can be traced back to the late Roman period in Britain.[144] This is not to advocate crude environmental determinism. Obviously environmental change alone neither created nor destroyed the socioeconomic orders of late Roman and tribal societies. Environmental change did play a full-fledged role, interacting with man-made problems, in accelerating and exacerbating the process of decline. The two elements combined to produce a multidimensional crisis at the ending of Roman Britain, a crisis extending into the Balkanized post-Roman period of the Anglo-Saxon expansion.

The terrible events triggering the end of the empire in the West began on the last day of A.D. 406, when Alans, Sueves, Vandals, and other agents of destruction moved into Roman territory. The frontier was betrayed by weather, for the Rhine had frozen and no longer impeded invasion. The crisis on the Rhine frontier spread into Gaul, evoking a British response which led directly to the end of Roman political and military authority in Britain. The image of the frozen Rhine raises one final question concerning the role of environmental change in the ending of Roman Britain. How can climatic change, a phenomenon that was world-wide, explain the peculiar fate of Roman Britain and its post-Roman aftermath? It freezes and rains on the just and the unjust, on the inhabitants of the eastern

---

[143] Moneyhon, "Introduction," 4.
[144] See Burgess, "Population, Climate, and Upland Settlement." Burgess suggests that the population disaster of the post-Roman period was related to natural factors, especially marginality and climatic change, and had more to do with those natural factors than with prevailing political and socioeconomic systems. According to Burgess, the major loss of population probably occurred between the 540s and the late seventh century.

empire, on Gallo-Romans and Hispano-Romans as well as on Romano-Britons. Of course, in an empire extending over more than twenty degrees of latitude and thirty degrees of longitude there was significant climatic difference among regions. As Kevin Greene notes, "It would be a mistake to try to apply any single climatic model to the whole empire." In fact, wetter and cooler conditions detrimental in Britain would probably have benefited the "dry farming" of much of the Mediterranean region, including parts of Spain and Gaul. Jan Bouzek observes that "the peaks of prosperity in central (and northern) Europe and in the Mediterranean are complementary to each other, the optima in the north meant usually pessima in the south and vice-versa."[145] The gradients of climatic change run generally north-south and west-east. Britain's location at the extreme northwest of the empire meant that climatic deterioration was felt comparatively early and intensely there. Thus geographical position parallels Britain's cultural and socioeconomic position on the extreme periphery of the Mediterranean core of the empire. Apart from Scandinavia, Britain's closest overall parallels are with the other fringes of imperial territory at the higher latitudes, not with Spain and Gaul. Burgess writes: "Britain with so much of its land agriculturally marginal, was particularly sensitive to the pressures which lead to population disasters, especially climatic deterioration. . . . This observation might be seen as obvious by some, as simplistic by others, but nevertheless it expresses a crude truth for an island which occupies a marginal position for cultivating the main crops of prehistory, wheat and barley."[146] We have discussed the uplands and lowlands and the effects of local topography on the sensitivity of agriculture to climatic change within Britain.[147] Overall, because of Britain's latitude and altitude, its extensive marginal agriculture, and the interaction of weather, yield, and harvest failure, Britain's population and crops

---

[145] Kevin Greene, *Archaeology of the Roman Economy*, 86; Bouzek, "Climatic Changes," 189.

[146] Burgess, "Population, Climate, and Upland Settlement," 197. Cf. Groenman-van Waateringe, "Disastrous Effect." For the west-east gradient, including the unequal effects of storminess, decreased temperature, and increased rainfall, see Whittle, "Climate, Grazing, and Man," 192. Differences related to latitude include declining altitude of the sun, higher winds, increased cloud, higher rainfall, instability of surface air, shorter duration of bright sunshine, and increased proximity to Arctic ice. Manley, "Climate of the British Isles," 109. Due to the last factor, there was probably an unequal degree of cooling owing to the southward shift of cold polar water in the north Atlantic. As a consequence, temperature was reduced more in Scotland than in England and more in England than in France. Parry, "Upland Settlement," 42. For Britain's cultural and environmental location on the periphery of the Mediterranean core areas see Chapman and Mytum's introduction to their *Settlement in North Britain*, ii.

[147] N. J. Higham points out that some areas in the east-coast districts of England may have suffered from summer droughts during the Roman period and may have found that increased rainfall aided productivity (*Rome, Britain, and the Anglo-Saxons*, 133).

were more harvest-sensitive than those of her provincial neighbors. The effects of the environmental crisis were correspondingly severe. This is an important distinction. If in the ending of Roman Britain some fail to note the joggle of a barometer, we may detect a splash in the bog and a slip on the ice.

CHAPTER SEVEN

Epilogue and Conclusion:
The Fall, A.D. 406–410

THE LITERARY SOURCES dealing with the final years of Roman Britain's political history are relatively rich compared with the usually thin Romano-British evidence.[1] They offer a rare counterpoint of specific events and personalities to complement the sometimes necessarily diffuse analysis of population, society, and environment.

BACKGROUND TO THE CRISIS, A.D. 340–401

Britain enjoyed the fruits of Constantine the Great's successful usurpation.[2] He proved to be the only winner among all the tyrants supported by Britain. Constantine's death in 337 triggered a return to military revolt and political violence. The empire was shared among his sons, but the arrangement was unstable. Constantine II controlled Britain, Gaul, and Spain. In 340 he invaded Italy and was defeated and killed by his brother Constans. The composition of the heavily defeated army is unknown, but it may well have included units drawn from Britain. With the death of Constantine II Britannia returned to its accustomed historical role as participant in the losing faction. Trouble struck directly in Britain late in the year 342. The crisis brought the emperor Constans in person, hurrying unseasonably across the Channel in the first months of 343. The particu-

---

[1] The sources include Zosimus, Orosius, Prosper, Olympiodorus, the Gallic Chronicles, Merobaudes, Sozomen, Ammianus, and Marcellinus Comes.
[2] There are a number of standard accounts providing full references to the primary sources. I am indebted to Frere, *Britannia*, 326–77; Salway, *Roman Britain*, 348–426.

lar elements of the crisis are vague.[3] Sketchy records suggest a mixture of troubles, possibly including a threat of rebellion by advocates of the murdered Constantine II; a northern frontier emergency involving Picts and perhaps Scots with the mutinous *areani* (frontier scouts); and hints of a threatened crisis in the area of the possibly newly christened *litus Saxonicum*.[4] Conditions in Britain and elsewhere in the West evidently deteriorated beyond Constans's ability to control. He lost popularity and in 350 was displaced by Magnentius, a usurper described as a *laetus* of barbarian ancestry, possibly sired by a British father.[5] Typically of Romano-British politics, the diocese backed this ultimate loser and was visited with the ravages of Paulus Catena, "The Chain."

Beginning in 360, the frontier problems in Britain seem to have become increasingly serious. The Picts and Scots renewed their raiding, forcing the move from Gaul to Britain of Julian's *magister militum* with elements of the field army. The tempo of crisis quickened. In 364–65 attacks by Picts, Scots, and Attacotti harassed Britain. An extraordinary conspiracy of barbarians acting in concert overwhelmed the Roman defenses in Britain in 367.[6] Two years elapsed before Roman control could be restored over Scots, Picts, *areani*, Roman military deserters, and perhaps also escaped slaves and *coloni*.[7] Some historians suggest that the subsequent reconstruction of the British diocese by Theodosius the elder may have marked the beginning of the end of Roman rule in the far north, where British tribal leaders were perhaps entrusted with the security of territories now denuded of Roman garrisons.[8] Theodosius's actions proved to be the last full Roman restoration. Rebellion broke out again in 383 when the usurper Magnus Maximus took portions of the British garrison with him to the continent, where he and much of his army were eventually destroyed.[9] Following his death the Scots and Picts returned to their plundering. Probably not until 396–399 did the Roman authorities again fully address the problem of military security in Britain. At the direction of Stilicho, the Vandal general commanding for the young and incompetent

---

[3] The relevant books of Ammianus are lost.
[4] For *areani*, see Ammianus 28.3.8.
[5] Frere, *Britannia*, 338. See Jones, Martindale, and Morris, *Prosopography*, 1:532.
[6] Tomlin, "Date of the Conspiracy."
[7] Frere, *Britannia*, 340. Frere writes: "Almost certainly escaped slaves and coloni also took advantage of the general disorder to flee their masters and enrich themselves with plunder." I have already discussed the question of possible *Bagaudae* in Britain.
[8] Frere, *Britannia*, 341–44. For a different view see Salway, *Roman Britain*, 374–86.
[9] Frere, *Britannia*, 353–55. For a less traditional and more positive view of the effects of Maximus's actions on Britain's security see Casey, "Magnus Maximus in Britain." On the basis of coin evidence Casey suggests that Maximus returned to Britain from Gaul during his usurpation, probably in 384, and won a substantial victory over the Picts and Scots. Compare Salway, *Roman Britain*, 401–5.

emperor Honorius, a Roman military expedition sent to Britain achieved success against the Picts, Scots, and Saxons before events in Italy forced its premature withdrawal. In 401 Stilicho not only recalled the reinforcements dispatched to Britain, but if Claudian can be trusted, also withdrew one of Britain's long-established "legions" from an already inadequate garrison.[10]

The events of 340–401 have been discussed often and thoroughly. I have briefly sketched them only to draw conclusions from specific details which confirm the previously discussed problems of Britain's security. Four important lessons can be isolated. (1) The northern frontier was never permanently pacified. Both Picts and Scots seem to have prospered rather than otherwise, despite Rome's military efforts. This external problem was exacerbated by the participation of the Saxons, the Attacotti (and possibly the Franks), the increased maritime mobility of the raiders, and the enhanced abilities of the barbarians to coordinate their movements (the barbarian conspiracy). (2) The Roman garrison in Britain, despite its cost and numbers, proved inadequate. Casualties lost in civil Roman conflicts involving the various British-spawned usurpers may have contributed to the problem. (3) Internal security in Britain was inadequate. This is most graphically shown by the number of usurpers associated with Britain. The problem was not confined to usurpation at the top command levels—the twice-treacherous *areani*, the disbanded *exploratores*, and the numerous army deserters of Theodosius's troubles all attest to this. (4) In the final analysis, just as in Julius Caesar's preliminary involvement, Britain represented for Rome an overextension. The periodic commitment of forces from the *comitatenses* to the "British ulcer" and the occasional presence of the emperor during emergencies only highlight this fact. At the last, Stilicho left Britain with its defense problems unresolved, its garrison reduced, and its security subordinated to Italian interests.

THE FALL: A.D. 406–410

Roman Britain's death throes began on the last day of December 406, when Alans, Vandals, and Sueves crossed the Rhine and began the invasion of Gaul.[11] About this same time a certain Marcus, the first of the last series of British usurpers, had been proclaimed emperor in Britain. Marcus was a soldier; nothing else is known about him, not even the reason for his

---

[10] Claudian *De bello Gothico* 416–18; *De consulatu Stilichonis* 2.250–55; *In Eutropium* 1.391–93. M. Miller, "Stilicho's Pictish War."

[11] For the fall, see E. A. Thompson, "Britain, A.D. 406–410"; Bartholomew, "Fifth-Century Facts"; Stevens, "Marcus, Gratian, and Constantine"; Freeman, *Western Europe in the Fifth Century*, 1–170.

elevation.[12] Failing to please the army in Britain, he was murdered and replaced by Gratian, a native of Britain and a member of the urban aristocracy. Zosimus records that the British garrison was worried that the barbarians ravaging in Gaul would next cross the Channel.[13] Whatever the truth of this statement, Gratian made no move toward Gaul and was murdered by the army after a four-month reign.[14] A common soldier with a lucky name, Constantine (Constantine III), became the third tyrant. He crossed with British forces into Gaul, secured the Channel coast, and first fought but then seemingly cohabited with the barbarians. Constantine extended his control into Spain in about 408. The barbarians continued to plunder Gaul and the hard-pressed Honorius (the legitimate Augustus) granted Constantine official if unloving recognition.

A number of different motives have been attributed to the soldiers in Britain to explain their successive elevation of three usurpers. Zosimus's suggestion that the army desired to intervene in Gaul in order to forestall a barbarian invasion of Britain is at least plausible. It would not be the last time that British security was associated with friendly control of the French Channel coast. Discontent with the rule of Stilicho and his weakening of the army in Britain for operations in Italy, combined with continuing fear of the Picts, Scots, and Saxons and concern over a brewing threat to the Rhine frontier, would have been potent sources of anger, insecurity, and revolt.

Sozomen, a lawyer and church historian working in Constantinople in the 440s, records a different motive. He states that Constantine III was elevated "on account of his name." The implied association between this usurper and the memory of Constantine the Great gains credibility in the context of the year 406, the centenary of the latter's elevation to emperor at York in 306. Moreover, archaeological evidence indicates that the coinage necessary to pay the soldiers in Britain had not been imported since about 402. Unpaid or short-changed since then, with newly refurbished fancies of the booty and promotions associated with the successful usurpation of Constantine the Great, the army in Britain understandably may have decided to raise another local candidate to the purple. Although Marcus, Gratian, and Constantine seem to have ridden the tiger of usurpation rather than controlled it, personal ambition must have played some role in their calculations. Constantine III may have imitated Magnus Maximus. There are some important similarities in the patterns of their respective operations. Magnus Maximus provides another possible exam-

[12] Zosimus 6.2; Olympiodorus fr. 12; Sozomen 9.11.
[13] Zosimus 6.3.1. E. A. Thompson, "Zosimus 6.10.2.," evaluates the British passages in Zosimus.
[14] Olympiodorus fr. 12.

ple of a name with powerful and attractive historical associations for the army in Britain. When Gerontius, Constantine III's general, rebelled against his master and created his own emperor, the new tyrant was named Maximus. Both Zosimus and Sozomen based much of their accounts for this period on the reliable contemporary history of Olympiodorus of Thebes, whose twenty-two books describing the events of 407–25 survive only as fragments quoted in other works. Unfortunately, these fragments do not explain the reasons behind the usurpations in Britain. Perhaps the least credible of all the various explanations for the actions of the army and usurpers in Britain is the idea that they were motivated by a spirit of sacrifice and a sense of their ultimate responsibility, abandoning their local homes and connections in Britain, and intervening in Gaul to save the Roman empire in the West.[15] There is in fact no evidence for this view. The provincial sources from Gaul and Spain make clear that Constantine failed to check the barbarians' destructive plundering.[16] Indeed, as will be seen, Constantine leagued himself with the invaders the better to pursue his war against fellow Romans. His lieutenants were responsible for opening the Pyrennean passes, hitherto invulnerable, and allowing the barbarians to enter Spain.

Like so many of his predecessors, Constantine succeeded in Gaul with the forces of Britain, but failed in his attempt to win supreme power by a conquest of Italy. Betrayed by his British-born *magister militum* (Gerontius), inadequately supported by barbarian allies recruited from the Rhine, Constantine's ambitions collapsed.[17] This time, however, the ebb and flow of British rebellion's usual pattern—initial success followed by ultimate failure and repression—was forever broken. The aftermath of Constantine's failure in 409–411 marks the final end of Roman authority in Britain. Denuded of troops, betrayed even by their own usurpers, the Britons successfully and permanently rejected Roman government. In the words of Zosimus: "The barbarians from across the Rhine, who now attacked in force, reduced the inhabitants of Britain and some of the Celtic tribes to the point of throwing off Roman rule and living independently, without further submission to Roman laws. So the Britons took up arms and facing danger for their own safety they freed their cities from the barbarians who threatened them; and all Armorica and the other provinces of Gaul followed the British example and freed themselves in the same way, expelling their Roman governors and setting up their own

---

[15] Sozomen 9.11–13; Zosimus 6.1–5; Olympiodorus fr. 12, 16; Orosius 7.40. Compare the discussions of motives in Frere, *Britannia*, 356–58; Bury, *Later Roman Empire*, 1:185–211; Matthews, *Western Aristocracies*, 308–20.
[16] Freeman, *Western Europe in the Fifth Century*, 52–53.
[17] He was executed by Honorius in 411.

administrations as best they could." As Salway notes, Zosimus had the imperial administrative experience to understand fully the legal and political implications of this description.[18]

Despite their evidently extraordinary actions and intentions, the rebels must have expected imperial retaliation and an attempt to reoccupy Britain. Factions within Britain no doubt remained loyal to the empire. The boot of imperial retaliation did not immediately drop because the legitimate government of Honorius was beset by uncontrolled barbarians, rivalry with the eastern court, and a financial crisis. The usurpations begun in Britain had proved to be contagious examples, and local tyrants were active in 410–13 in Gaul, Spain, Italy, and Africa. In about 410 the emperor Honorius wrote to the British cities and bid them look to their own defense.[19] This letter is usually taken to be an official handwashing in response to the pleas of still-loyal factions for imperial help. The noteworthy aspect of the letter is that the emperor directed his reply to the cities—presumably because no duly constituted Roman authority any longer existed in Britain. By the end of 413, however, the usurpers had been plucked down like caterpillars by a variety of unlikely hands. This was as satisfying as it was surprising to the legitimate imperial government. Contemporaries saw the hand of God rewarding the piety of Honorius. Even the surviving soldiers of Constantine III and Gerontius in Gaul returned their allegiance to Honorius.[20] The fall of the usurpers and the unexpected recovery of Honorius's government provided an opportunity for the Britons to return to the imperial fold, had they wished to do so. The permanent rejection of Roman government and law in Britain (and Armorica) was exceptional even in the disturbed context of the early fifth

[18] Zosimus 6.5.2, translation from *Literary Sources*, edited by Mann and Penman. Salway, *Roman Britain*, 434 n.1.

[19] Zosimus 6.10.2, translation from *Literary Sources*, edited by Mann and Penman: "Honorius sent letters to the British cities telling them to look after their own defense." Some scholars have argued that the passage is corrupt and should read "Bruttium" (Italy) instead of Britain. Bartholomew, "Fifth-Century Facts," has most recently supported this idea. In my opinion, E. A. Thompson, "Zosimus 6.10.2," has destroyed this particular argument and shown that Zosimus intended the passage to refer to Britain. My personal belief is that in keeping with Zosimus's often topsy-turvy chronology, the passage may precede in time the rebellion in Britain, and reflects an attempt by Britons to gain help from Honorius to end the barbarian threat. Failing to receive anything but letters, the Britons acted in their own defense and then expelled the Roman government. A second question is whose governors—the usurper Constantine's or all the Roman administration legitimate and otherwise? I believe the latter to be the case. For a discussion of Zosimus and the events of 410 see Michael E. Jones and John Casey, "Gallic Chronicle Restored," 379–92.

[20] In addition to Constantine III, Constans, and Maximus, the list of usurpers includes Attalus, Jovinus, Sebastian, and Heraclian. Only Attalus survived, maimed but pardoned. See Bury, *Later Roman Empire*, 1:192–95. For the hand of God see Sozomen 9.11, 9.16; Orosius 7.42. For the soldiers of Constantine III and Gerontius see Sozomen 9.14–15.

century. In the aftermath of the defeat of Constantine III, the Britons used their chance not merely to oust the government of a failed usurper, but to break with the empire altogether. This is the true significance of Zosimus's account. Referring to the year 411, Procopius writes, "The army of the Visigoths under Adaulphus marched on Gaul, and Constantine was defeated in battle and died with his sons. Nonetheless, the Romans were no longer able to recover Britain, which from that time on continued to be ruled by tyrants."[21] Another Roman source groups the loss of Britain with other disasters befalling the Roman state in 410: "Britaniae [sic] Romano nomini in perpetuum sublatae."[22]

The British traditions are consistent with the Roman sources. A passage in Gildas seems to link up with the letter of Honorius mentioned by Zosimus.[23] The *Historia Brittonum* reads: "Hitherto the Romans had ruled the British for 409 years. But the British overthrew the rule of the Romans, and paid them no taxes, and did not accept their kings to reign over them, and the Romans did not dare to come to Britain to rule anymore, for the British had killed their generals." This may be a somewhat garbled confirmation of the rebellion of 410 recorded in Zosimus.[24] Bede associates the end of Roman rule in Britain with the Gothic sack of Rome (410): "Fracta est autem Roma a Gothis anno millesimo CLXIIII suae conditionis, ex quo tempore Romani in Britannia regnare cesserunt."[25]

I have belabored the discussion of the British revolt of 410 with primary source quotations for several reasons. A variety of evidence and perspectives—Roman, Greek, Gallic, British, even Saxon—securely dates the end of Roman authority in Britain to that year. The usurpers and their military forces were gone (and presumably were mostly dead) and the remaining Roman governors, administration, tax apparatus, and law were forcibly expelled from the island by the Britons themselves. The succeeding era of British history is no longer Roman. The rejection of Roman

---

[21] Procopius *De bello vandalico* 1.2.38. Stevens argued that Procopius was using a contemporary source ("Marcus, Gratian, and Constantine," 340).

[22] *Narratio de imperatoribis:* "Britain was forever removed from the Roman name." For this translation and a discussion see Muhlberger, *Fifth-Century Chronicles*, 152–57. Compare Thompson, "Zosimus 6.10.2," 461. The relation between *Narratio de imperatoribis* and the "Gallic Chronicle of 452" is disputed.

[23] Gildas *D.e.* 18.

[24] *H.B.* 28. The dating structure of the *Historia Brittonum*, if there is a structure, has defied generations of scholars. In places A.D. dating is used, however, and the passage fits with the rebellion dated in classical sources to c. 410. The Romans, of course, did not actually begin their rule in Britain in A.D. 1. The translation is from Nennius, *British History and Welsh Annals*.

[25] Bede *H.e.* 1.11: "Rome fell to the Goths in the 1164th year after its foundation. At the same time Roman rule came to an end in Britain." I do not weigh Bede's date very heavily. It may simply be guesswork, associating disaster in Britain with the greater event of the fall of Rome in 410, which Bede elsewhere incorrectly dates as 409. Cf. *H.e.* 5.24.

authority was sudden and final. The incidental details of the last Romano-British political crisis are particularly revealing. The usurper Marcus was an unknown. Gratian, however, was a native Briton, the last of a numerous line of urban aristocrats either caught up with or willingly abetting the cause of treason.[26] His murder by the army could symbolize the fate of Romanization in a politically unstable diocese. Constantine III and his officers are the most interesting of the personalities. Possibly chosen to rule as a lucky namesake (Constantine the Great was the only successful British-sponsored usurper in Roman political history), he reinforced the association by renaming his sons Julian and Constans, two more imperial names from the house of Constantine the Great. The underlying reason for this propaganda seems clear—there was an important reservoir of loyalty to be tapped in Britain, not an abstract loyalty to Rome but to the family representing successful British sponsored pretension. A probable analogue is provided by the puppet emperor Maximus, raised up by the British general Gerontius. As noted, this seems to be a political invocation of the memory of Magnus Maximus, the usurper elevated in Britain. Interestingly, both Magnus Maximus and Gerontius pass into medieval British legend and folklore.[27] Finally, Gerontius himself provides graphic insight into the conditions within later Roman Britain.[28] He was evidently a British provincial, a successful general who rebelled against Constantine III and his son Constans. Moving from Spain either late in 409 or early in 410, Gerontius leagued himself with the barbarian invaders (the story is reminiscent of Vortigern's later adventures) and pursued Constans to the city of Vienne.[29] In some undisclosed fashion Gerontius captured and murdered Constans, then besieged Constantine III in Arles. The siege became a double siege, however, when an army sent by Honorius (the legitimate emperor) from Italy to remove his competitor, Constantine III, found him already attacked by Gerontius. To attack Constantine III, Honorius's forces had first to destroy Gerontius. The latter found himself sandwiched between two hostile forces and his army deserted to the army of Honorius. Gerontius escaped back to Spain with a small party. The troops left behind in Spain abandoned his cause after hearing of his defeat in Gaul and attacked him in his fortified house. Gerontius was trapped with his wife Nunchia, a handful of slaves, and a faithful Alan companion. Assaulted at night, Gerontius's household successfully repelled the en-

[26] Orosius 7.40.4.
[27] See Freeman's comments (*Western Europe in the Fifth Century*, 100). Lukman, "The British General Gerontius."
[28] Freeman, *Western Europe in the Fifth Century*, 99–115, 123–27.
[29] The chronology of Gerontius's movements can only be approximated. See Roger Collins, *Early Medieval Spain*, 14–19.

emy. As the attack ceased the slaves escaped from the house in the dark-
ness. Gerontius refused to leave his wife. The Alan, like a true *thegn* or
gesith, refused to leave his lord.[30] Sozomen records the death scene:

> The Spanish soldiery conceived an utter contempt against Gerontius, on
> account of his cowardly retreat, and took counsel to slay him. They
> attacked his house during the night, but he, with one Alanus his friend,
> and a few slaves, ascended to the top of the house, and did such execu-
> tion with their arrows, that no less than three hundred of the soldiers
> fell. When the stock of arrows was exhausted, the slaves made their
> escape from the house; and Gerontius might easily have followed their
> example, had not his devotion for Nunchia, his wife, detained him by
> her side. At day-break the next day, the soldiers deprived him of all hope
> of saving his life, by setting fire to the house; and he cut off the head of
> Alanus, in compliance with his entreaties. His wife then besought him,
> with groans and tears, to perform the same office for her rather than
> permit her to fall into the hands of another; and he complied with her
> last request. Thus died one who manifested a degree of courage worthy
> of her religion; for she was a Christian: and her death deserves to be held
> in remembrance. Gerontius then struck himself thrice with his sword;
> but, not succeeding in wounding himself mortally, he drew forth his
> poignard, which he wore at his side, and plunged it into his heart.[31]

This scene is better suited to *The Saga of Burnt Njal* than to a staid
ecclesiastical history. Gerontius and Gratian are a good symbolic pair to
represent the fate of Roman Britain. Gerontius clearly has one leg already
anchored in the heroic society of the Dark Ages. Gratian, a Romanized
urban provincial, is murdered by the army that also betrays Gerontius—
both men live and die in a society and political era already blurring into
the age of the tyrant and the warband.

THE ANGLO-SAXON INVASIONS
AND THE END OF ROMAN BRITAIN

The circumstances surrounding the events of 406–410 confirm the major
findings of the preceding chapters. An examination of the probable scale
and nature of the Anglo-Saxon invasions led to the rejection of the Anglo-

---

[30] Freeman describes the Alan as a *thegn* (*Western Europe in the Fifth Century,* 124).

[31] Sozomen *Ecclesiastical History* 9.13. As with all such death scenes, one wonders who told
the tale. Presumably like losers at the Alamo and Thermopylae, Gerontius had his messenger
of defeat. I do not think the wounds of Gerontius are a deliberate Christian conceit. Other
accounts of Gerontius's death are Zosimus 6.5; Orosius 7.42; Olympiodorus fr. 12.

Saxons as a primary agent in the destruction of Roman culture. A chronological argument supports this conclusion. Roman rule in Britain ended in a whirl of rebellion and betrayal climaxing in the British revolt of 410. According to Zosimus, the revolt against the Roman empire was triggered by unrestricted incursions by barbarians from across the Rhine. Their way into Britain had been opened by the internecine struggle between Constantine III and Gerontius. That these barbarian attacks were exceptional seems confirmed by the "Gallic Chronicle of 452." In a rare mention of Britain this source records a devastation of the British provinces in the sixteenth regnal year of Honorius (410) and identifies the invaders as Saxons. Although Britain had long been plagued by raiding Saxons and invading Scots and Picts, this devastation of 410 is the first attested great independent Saxon threat.[32] On this occasion, however, the Britons were evidently victorious. Only thereafter began the decades-long and bitter struggle between the independent Britons and the Anglo-Saxon invaders. The semilegendary figures of Ambrosius, Vortigern, and Hengest and the rebellion, defeat, and ultimate triumph of the Anglo-Saxons lie in the darker age of the later fifth and sixth centuries. In this sense the Roman occupation of almost four hundred years and the long-drawn Anglo-Saxon conquest overlap by but a single year. The story of this conquest is not strictly part of the history of Roman Britain at all. The Anglo-Saxons and the destruction of Roman Britain are in the same relation as lobsters and Lewis Carroll's "Lobster Quadrille"—the figure may be danced without them.

A review of the conclusions from Chapters 4 through 6 establishes several salient points. The early medieval British vision of the Roman past was heavily colored by memories of insecurity, taxation, oppression, a hatred of Roman law, and the rebellion of usurpers. This medieval vision is largely confirmed by the classical sources which present the same themes. The investigations of conditions within the Romano-British diocese in the later fourth century help to explain why this was the case. They present a generally grim picture. Problems of the economy and hints of social unrest are alike confirmed by the political history, which reveals a fundamental or structural instability. Britain was destabilized by unre-

---

[32] Zosimus 6.4; "Chronicle of 452," *s.a.* Honorius xvi: "Hac tempestate praevaletudine Romanorum vires funditus attenuatae. Britanniae Saxonum incursione devastatae." (In the sixteenth regnal year of Honorius the multitude of the enemy so prevailed that the strength of the Romans was diminished. The Britains [the British provinces] were devastated by an invasion of Saxons.) The date of the Saxon invasion and the British rebellion is much disputed. A 408/9 date has been suggested by E. A. Thompson based on an interpretation of Zosimus. The date derived from Zosimus must be inferred from an inexact and confused context, while the date of the Gallic Chronicle is explicit. The sixteenth regnal year of Honorius is the equivalent of 410. See Michael E. Jones and John Casey, "Gallic Chronicle Restored," 379–92.

solved frontier problems in the north and by recurring actions of usurpers who periodically dragged the provinces into rebellion, defeat, and repression at the hands of the central authorities. This monotonous litany of political adventurism and barbarian invasion appears again and again in the Roman era. Denied the fruits of high political office, culturally snubbed and insecure, Britons sought their place within Roman civilization through the sword of the usurper. Economically, Britain's treason may have represented a rational self-interest. Periods of prosperity in Roman Britain sometimes seem to have been associated with the government of usurpers rather than the duly constituted empire. Rebellion rested on a foundation of misgovernment, insecurity, and social and economic crisis heightened by a rapidly deteriorating environment. This proved to be a fatal combination.

To speak euphemistically as so many historians have done of a Roman "withdrawal" from Britain, to write of a tenacious British loyalty to Rome, and to speak of the Anglo-Saxons as external destroyers of Romano-British civilization, all these descriptions are alike inaccurate. Many of Roman Britain's mortal wounds were internal. This conclusion does not fit easily within the mold of the subject's traditional historiography. The field of Roman-British studies was for long defined by two basic tenets. The first of these suggested that Britain was effectively Romanized. The second observed that Roman civilization in the island perished primarily from external shocks delivered by various barbarians, particularly the Anglo-Saxons.[33] I should perhaps say that these tenets confined as well as defined, for they loomed like great iron-bound bookends constricting and directing thought and research. In a review article written in 1984, Barry Cunliffe observed: "The overall impression one gets reading the books and papers on Roman Britain published in the late 1970s and early 1980s is of Britannia as an aged, corseted old lady, sitting immobile in an airless room reeking of stale scent, fawned on by a bevy of tireless, dedicated servants. Can we not at the very least open a window or two?"[34] Since Cunliffe made these deliberately provocative statements, a

---

[33] For example, compare Haverfield, *Romanization*, with Collingwood and Myres, *Roman Britain and the English Settlements*. The latter has been replaced in the Oxford History of England with Salway, *Roman Britain*. Salway's book is an excellent study, more narrowly conceived in terms of the Anglo-Saxon invasions than its predecessor, but some of the same basic tenets may still be found. On the Romanization of Britain, for example: "There is no reason to suppose the traditions and attitudes of the Romano-British were any different from those of the Gallo-Romans. . . ." Salway, *Roman Britain*, 441. On the Saxons: "The prospects for the Romano-British upper class may have appeared bright in 409 . . . had the relations between Roman and barbarian in fifth century Gaul been paralleled in Britain. But the Saxons were to prove very different from the Visigoths, the Franks, or even the Huns." Salway, *Roman Britain*, 663.
[34] Cunliffe, "Images of Britannia," 178.

number of stimulating revisionist studies have prized open the window to the currents of conflicting interpretation.[35] Differing explanations for the end of Roman Britain parallel in many ways more general debates concerning the decline or transformation of the Roman west. In polar terms, was the collapse incidental, the product of contingency and coincidence, or was the result deterministic, the inevitable culmination of long-term processes? In the case of Britain, what relative causal weight should be given to insular and indigenous factors as opposed to general forces acting simultaneously throughout the empire? Is the question better defined in material terms of related social, political, economic, and military problems or in terms of morality, intellect, and spirit? Roman Britain provides a purely Western parallel to what is sometimes called the Byzantine *non sequitur*—why was it that the Roman empire failed to survive in Western Europe but lasted for an additional thousand years in the East? Many of the same significant forces were at work in both regions. In a British-Western context, why was the collapse of *Romanitas* in Britain so much more complete than in Gaul or elsewhere in the West? What necessary and sufficient causes operated unequally on Britain and her Western neighbors? As is universally acknowledged, the vast geographical expanse of the Roman empire encompassed a great regional and local variety. Theoretical and comparative studies of the structures of Roman society and economy, however, tend to focus on general rather than particular conditions. In a recent influential theory the fall of the Roman empire has been assimilated into a generalized explanation for the collapse of complex societies. According to this model, the larger a society grows, the more complicated and socially differentiated it becomes. Maintenance costs increase accordingly. Eventually, however, expansion provides a diminishing return while continued stresses and unexpected costs create ever growing demands for resources. At some point crisis leads to collapse unless some significant new factors intervene. Such crisis often results in the tipping of a precarious balance between center and periphery.[36] Britain's position on the extreme northwestern periphery of a Mediterranean empire makes it a prime candidate for this scenario. The hyphen in "Romano-British" represents an enormous administrative, cultural, and strategic distance between Britain and the Roman imperial core. This distance made Britain

[35] For examples dealing with the end of Roman Britain see C. J. Arnold, *Roman Britain to Saxon England*; R. M. Reece, *My Roman Britain*, 109–37; Esmonde Cleary, *Ending of Roman Britain*; Higham, *Rome, Britain, and the Saxons*. Jeremy Evans, "From the End of Roman Britain."

[36] Averil Cameron, *Later Roman Empire*, 190–94; Tainter, *Collapse of Complex Societies*, 128–52; Champion, ed., *Centre and Periphery*. Such theories come close in spirit to Gibbon's thesis that the decline of Rome "was the natural and inevitable effect of immoderate greatness" (*Decline and Fall*, 4:160–63).

particularly vulnerable to changes affecting the center. In a thorough and well-argued study of the end of Roman Britain based heavily on archaeological evidence, Simon Esmonde Cleary concludes that the collapse of Roman Britain "is entirely comprehensible within the framework of the ending of the western empire." Roman culture collapsed in Britain because changes elsewhere in the empire removed the necessary economic system. Cleary states that "the causes of the end of Roman Britain lay outside the island and not within it."[37]

External and general causes undoubtedly played a significant role in the ending of Roman Britain. They should not, however, obscure the significance of local variables and insular factors. Roman Britain was a more peculiar place in the context of the later Roman empire than many scholars have allowed. We have noted distinctive elements in Britain's security problems and exceptionally restive garrison, in the religious development of the diocese, in the reputation and attitudes of the Romano-Britons, and in the environmental sensitivity of Britain's economy and population. To these we can add the significant absence of a Romano-British elite integrated into the governing circles of the empire. Collectively these represent potent insular causes that help to explain rebellion, usurpation, and finally the ejection of Roman governance from Britain. One peculiarity of British history is the hiatus of a generation or so between the end of effective Roman occupation and successful barbarian conquest (roughly 410–40). The fate of *Romanitas* during this hiatus was in the hands of the Britons themselves. Barbarian invasion and raiding played an important role. Conditions elsewhere in the empire that prevented Roman reoccupation were also a key element in the pattern of events, but to see the fate of *Romanitas* in Britain as determined exclusively or overwhelmingly by general and external forces is misguided. From the standpoint of Anglo-Saxon studies, the role played by the Anglo-Saxon invaders in the destruction of the Roman order and the scale and nature of their migration are hotly debated. The Germanist view emphasizing large-scale migration with consequent discontinuity and cultural change still finds scholarly supporters and strongly influences popular perceptions of the origins of England.[38]

---

[37] Esmonde Cleary, *Ending of Roman Britain*, x, 159. Cf. Jeremy Evans, "From the End of Roman Britain," 98, 101, who suggests that Roman Britain imploded under its own weight.
[38] Higham provides a good discussion of the historiography. He notes, "The Germanist view of the English settlment remains entrenched. It dominates the popular view of England's origins and has a surprisingly influential following among scholars. Adapted a little and couched in a new language, this interpretation remains fundamentally intact" (*Rome, Britain, and the Anglo-Saxons*, 8).

Neither the notion that Britain was fully and effectively Romanized nor the belief that the Anglo-Saxons destroyed an older order while creating a new one may be confidently maintained. It should no longer be credible to conceive of a Hengest figure who, Atropos-like, cuts a convenient beginning for an English history segregated from the Roman or Celtic or even Iron Age British past. The garment of British history is indeed seamless. Whatever the ultimate historical explanation for the distinctive elements and qualities of later "English" history, the roots of this evolution must lie in significant part with the Britons, who were but partially Romanized, and their resurgent Celtic and tribal society. We may speculate on the reasons for the extraordinary cultural vitality of the British isles in the early medieval period, but in some fashion it must be seen as an extension of the events and forces which led the Britons (uniquely among the western Roman provincials) to create a successful, final severance with Rome. The Britons' break with Rome and their exceptional resistance to the barbarian invaders would alone be remarkable. Coupled with these achievements, however, was the successful Christian mission to the pagan Irish supported by the fifth-century British church. Such a provincial mission was the first of its kind in Western Europe, directed beyond the bounds of the empire.[39] From it eventually stemmed the curious blending of tribal society, monasticism, and classical learning of the Hiberno-Saxon culture. Men of this composite background galvanized the society and learning of the early Middle Ages from Scandinavia to Italy. Mommsen once wrote that "it was not Britain that gave up Rome, but Rome that gave up Britain."[40] We may turn this axiom on its head. The Britons rejected political Rome, and the implications of that action for the development of western civilization were profound.

[39] In contrast to the evidently abortive Papal mission to Ireland led by Palladius. But see now Charles-Edwards, "Palladius, Prosper, and Leo."
[40] Mommsen, *Provinces,* 1:194.

Chronological List
of Selected Events

55 B.C.	Julius Caesar's first expedition to Britain marks the beginning of direct Roman involvement.
A.D. 43	Claudian invasion creates a Roman province in Britain.
60	Boudicca's revolt.
78–84	Agricola promotes urbanization and Romanization.
c. 87	The northern frontier contracts to the Clyde-Forth line.
c. 118	Revolt in Brigantian territory.
122	Hardrian tours Britain. Romanization is encouraged and a fixed fortified frontier is begun in the north.
139	Antonine frontier expands to include southern Scotland.
c. 150–160	Revolt in northern Britain.
c. 163	Renewed revolt in northern Britain. Antonine frontier abandoned for Hadrianic frontier line.
180	Northern tribes overrun Hadrian's (?) Wall.
184	Ulpius Marcellus crushes northern invasion and reestablishes the frontier.
193	Clodius Albinus usurps the imperial title.
196	C. Albinus campaigns in Gaul. Northern tribes raid into the British province.
197–202	Septimius Severus successfully eliminates all competition and becomes sole emperor. He dispatches Virius Lupus to restore order in Britain.
211	Septimius Severus dies at York after campaigning in north Britain.
259–273	Britain forms a component of the breakaway "Gallic" empire.
c. 275	Saxon (?) raids prompt intensified fortification along the southeast British coast.
286–287	Carausius uses his naval command of the Channel to create an independent rule in Britain and northern Gaul.

296	Constantius restores Britain to the empire.
305–306	Constantius, now an emperor, campaigns against the Picts but dies at York. His son Constantine is proclaimed emperor in Britain.
314	British bishops attend the Council at Arles.
343	Constans, western Augustus, campaigns in Britain.
350	Magnentius usurps the imperial title. He fails and Britain suffers reprisals led by Paul "the Chain."
360	Raiding by Picts and Scots.
365	Picts, Scots, Attacotti, and Saxons threaten Britain.
367	The barbarian conspiracy.
383	Magnus Maximus is elevated to the purple by the garrison in Britain.
c. 398	Stilicho's forces campaign in Britain.
c. 401	Britain loses troops to the defense of Italy.
406	Marcus usurps the imperium in Britain. Suebi, Vandals, and Alans invade Gaul.
407	Gratian replaces Marcus in Britain. Constantine III replaces the murdered Gratian and crosses to Gaul with forces from Britain.
410	A Saxon invasion devastates Britain. The Honorian rescript (?); the Britons expel the Roman officials.
429	Saint Germanus visits Britain to combat the Pelagian heresy.
441/42	The Saxons win control over some portion of Britain.

Population of the Roman Empire

THE MOST RECENT demographic survey of the Roman empire is Salmon's, *Population et dépopulation*. The standard reference remains Beloch's, *Die Bevölkerung*. Beloch's figures are now treated as underestimates or minimums. He later substantially raised his own calculations of the populations of Italy and Gaul.[1] Beloch's calculations reflect now outdated views on the productivity of agriculture and the density of rural settlement within the empire. The table gives a historiographic summary of population estimates for the Roman empire. Beloch's influence is readily apparent.

Earlier historical perceptions of the population of the Roman empire provide insight into how historians viewed their own societies, even as they illuminate the question of population.[2] In the sixteenth and seventeenth centuries writers such as J. Lipsius and Isaac Vossius presented greatly inflated figures of the size of Roman population, in accordance with their own veneration of the classical past. Montesquieu believed his own eighteenth-century Europe possessed only a tenth of the earlier population of the Roman empire. The more self-confident authors of the Enlightenment, for example Gibbon and Hume, reduced estimates of the Roman population, although Gibbon calculated the inhabitants of the empire at 120 millions. In the nineteenth century writers such as Dureau de la Malle and Moreau de Jonnès, confident in the industrial wealth and

---

[1] See Drinkwater, *Roman Gaul*, 169ff.; Brunt, *Italian Manpower*, 121–30.
[2] Lot has a good discussion of this idea (*End of the Ancient World*, 65–71).

Population of the Roman Empire in millions

Author	Publication date	1st century (Augustus)	2d century (Antonine)	3rd/4th centuries
Chambers	1987	54 to 80		
Boren	1986	50 to 100		
Duncan-Jones	1982	50		
Hopkins	1978	50 to 60		
McEvedy & Jones	1978			46
Grant	1974		70	
Africa	1974	50	100	
Pounds	1974		50 to 70	
Finley	1973	50 to 60		
Katz	1955		50 to 60	
Stein	1949–51	70		(1928) 50
Lot	1931	60 to 65		
Bury	1923	54		(1928) 70
Delbrück	1921			90
Beloch	1886	54		

Sources: Mortimer Chambers et al. *The Western Experience,* 4th ed. (New York, 1987), 1: 163; Henry C. Boren, *The Ancient World,* 2d ed. (Englewood Cliffs, N.J., 1986), 305; R. P. Duncan-Jones, *The Economy of the Roman Empire,* 2d ed. (Cambridge, 1982), 2; Keith Hopkins, *Conquerors and Slaves,* (Cambridge, 1978), 1; Colin McEvedy and Richard Jones, *Atlas of World Population History* (Harmondsworth, 1978), 21; Michael Grant, *The Climax of Rome,* (London, 1974), 86; Thomas W. Africa *The Immense Majesty: A History of Rome and the Roman Empire* (Arlington Heights, Ill., 1974), 224, 250; N. J. G. Pounds, *An Economic History of Medieval Europe* (London, 1974), 6; Moses I. Finley, *The Ancient Economy* (Berkeley, 1973), 30; Solomon Katz, *The Decline of Rome and the Rise of Medieval Europe* (Ithaca, 1955), 7; E. Stein, *Geschichte des spätrömischen Reiches* (Vienna, 1928), 1:3; E. Stein, "Introduction à l'histoire et aux institutions byzantines," *Traditio* 7 (1949–51), 154; Ferdinand Lot, *The End of the Ancient World and the Beginnings of the Middle Ages,* trans. Philip and Mariette Leon (New York, 1961), 65–71; J. B. Bury, *The Invasion of Europe by the Barbarians* (London, 1928), 38; J. B. Bury, *History of the Later Roman Empire,* (London, 1923), 1:62; Hans Delbrück, *Geschichte des Kriegskunst* (Berlin, 1921), 2:237–38; K. Julius Beloch, *Die Bevölkerung der griechisch-römischen welt* (Leipzig, 1886), 507.

power of Europe, reacted against earlier inflated perceptions of Roman population.[3]

In fact, notions of serious depopulation and manpower shortages have been urged as major or even dominant causes in explaining the collapse of the Roman West.[4] It seems likely, however, that the manpower shortages facing the Roman authorities in the areas of the military and economy of the fifth century were at least as much social as demographic.[5]

[3] Montesquieu, *Persian Letters,* 112; Gibbon, *Decline and Fall,* 1:46; Hume, "Populousness of Ancient Nations"; de la Malle, *Économie politique;* de Jonnès, *Statistique des peuples.*
[4] Boak, *Manpower Shortage;* Hodges and Whitehouse, *Mohammed,* 28–53; A. H. M. Jones, *Later Roman Empire,* 2:1040–43.
[5] Finley, review of *Manpower Shortage;* Salmon, *Population et dépopulation,* 114ff. Downey remarks that "for one of the most important problems, the question whether there was a real decline in population, no really satisfactory evidence exists" (*Late Roman Empire,* 97).

Because we lack statistical evidence from the Roman and early medieval periods, estimates of population must rest on dubious bases such as food payments, occasional observations of numbers in the primary sources, the rare census, military contingents and topographical calculations of surface areas and the density of rural settlements. Even this evidence is often scattered and fragmentary. Estimates must necessarily be extremely conjectural.[6] Some would say impossible. Marc Bloch writes: "Toute évaluation de la population du monde romain, sous l'Empire, ou de ses différentes parties, est impossible."[7] For studies of social, economic and military questions, however, some estimate of population is indispensable.[8] We are forced either to argue our historical interpretations without the vital consideration of population or make the best estimate possible and risk the retribution of critics who justifiably denounce dubious methods and evidence. This second choice seems better to me.

[6] Salmon, *Population et dépopulation*, 7–10. Russell, *Late Ancient and Medieval Population*, provides a useful introduction to the study of ancient population.
[7] Marc Bloch, "Les invasions," part 2, 18.
[8] Brunt, *Italian Manpower*, 3.

Roman Provincial Population in Europe

Roman provincial population in Europe (excluding Britain and Dacia) in millions

	Beloch (1886) 1st century A.D.	Russell (1958) 1st century A.D.	Russell (1958) A.D. 350	Russell (1972) A.D. 500	Russell (1972) A.D. 650
Italy	6.0 [revised 7 to 8]	7.4	4.0	4.0	2.5
Sicily	.6				
Sardinia	.5				
Spain	6.0	6.0	4.0	4.0	3.5
Narbonese Gaul	1.5				
The Three Gauls	3.4 [revised 4.5]				
Gaul		6.6	5.0		
France and the Low Countries				5.0	3.0
Danubian provinces	2.0				
Balkans		2.0	3.0		
Greece	3.0	3.0	2.0		
Greece and the Balkans				5.0	3.0
Total	23.0 [25.1 to 26.1]	25.0	18.0	18.0	12.0

Beloch estimates the population in the European provinces in the first century A.D. (excluding Britain and Dacia) at 23 million of a total of 54 million for the entire empire.[1] He later selectively increased his esti-

[1] Beloch, *Die Bevölkerung*, 507; Beloch, "Die Bevölkerung Galliens"; Beloch, "Die Bevölkerung Italiens."

imperial population of 54 million.[2] Russell's estimate is comparable, a first-century European provincial population of 25 million.[3] McEvedy and Jones suggest that the European provincial population in 200 A.D. stood at 28 million of a 46 million imperial total.[4] All of these figures are conservative, at the lower end of the spectrum of estimates of provincial population. The figures quoted in the table deliberately understate the great disparity between the populations of the invading Germans and the provincials. For example, Bennett estimates the European provincial population of the first century A.D. at 37 million, growing to 67 million by A.D. 200.[5] Stein estimates the European provincial population of the fourth century A.D. as 24 million of the imperial total of 50 million.[6] Contrast these figures with Russell's 18 million in the table. The range of high-end figures for individual provinces is even greater: Augustan Italy 10 to 14 million;[7] late Roman Gaul 12 to 20 million;[8] late Roman Spain 9 to 12 million.[9]

---

[2] Bury, *History of the Later Roman Empire*, 1:62.
[3] Russell, *Late Ancient and Medieval Population*, 148. Compare his estimate from 1972 ("Population in Europe," 36).
[4] McEvedy and Jones, *Atlas of World Population History*, 21.
[5] Cited in Slicher van Bath, *Agrarian History*, 78.
[6] E. Stein, "Introduction à l'histoire," 7.
[7] Duncan-Jones, *Economy*, 274 n. 2.
[8] Salmon, *Population et dépopulation*, 33; Drinkwater, *Roman Gaul*, 169–70.
[9] Russell, *Late Ancient and Medieval Population*, 74 n. 23.

Barbarian Tribal Population

HANS DELBRÜCK PIONEERED the modern study of barbarian tribal populations. His commentary on the primary textual evidence is still worth
reading.[1] Delbrück suggested that tribal populations at the time of the
invasions numbered between 50,000 for the larger tribes and 25,000 or less
for the smaller.[2] Subsequent studies by J. B. Bury, Ludwig Schmidt, A. H.
M. Jones, and Walter Goffart stress the difficulty and subjectivity of any
estimates but generally confirm the scale of Delbrück's calculations.[3] The
largest tribal confederations might have numbered as many as 100,000
persons and the smaller tribes fewer than 25,000 people.

The Ostrogoths, Visigoths, Burgundians, and Vandals have all received
particular attention. Ostrogothic population has been estimated by three
different authors in recent studies. The results illustrate the potentials
and limits of such attempts. Each estimate rests on the same body of
textual evidence. Primary sources give the numbers of people or of warriors in various migrating Gothic hosts. There may be some confusion

---

[1] Delbrück, Numbers in History; Geschichte der Kriegskunst, vol. 2.
[2] See the English translation of Delbrück's study, History of the Art of War, 2: 285–99.
[3] Bury, Invasion of Europe, 42; Bury, History of the Later Roman Empire, 1: 100, 104–5;
Schmidt, Geschichte der deutschen Stämme 1: 29ff.; A. H. M. Jones, Later Roman Empire, 1:
194–96; Goffart, Barbarians and Romans, 231–34. See also Pounds, Economic History, 43,
and Russell, "Population in Europe," 63. An exception to the above consensus is Arther
Ferrill, Fall of the Roman Empire. Ferrill is interested in upgrading our perceptions of the
military threat the barbarians posed to the empire. His higher estimates of barbarian numbers
(for example, 200,000 Visigoths) are not critically discussed and hark back to the days of
Hodgkin and Dahn. See Hodgkin, Italy and Her Invaders, 3: 201–2.

between military population and total population, but this is the starting point for modern calculations. In addition, surviving details of treaties between Romans and Goths record that rations were to be provided for specific numbers of men, or that a given weight of gold was to be paid to a particular host. These figures provide a check for the consistency and credibility of the other written evidence. Total population is calculated from military population through the use of a multiplier. A ratio of 1:5 (warriors to total population) is generally assumed for a migrating population. However, this multiplier (five) may well be too high. Adult males were probably more than 20 percent of a migratory tribal population. Recent studies of the Roman population suggest that adult males were possibly 28 percent, 35 percent, or even 51.7 percent of the total population. If so, the adjusted multiplier used to convert numbers of warriors into total populations should be a factor of two or three rather than five. Probably most of the adult men of a migrating tribe would have been warriors. The adjusted multiplier would, of course, greatly reduce the estimated tribal populations.[4]

The credibility of the derived figures for total population is checked against incidental evidence, such as the sheltering of a barbarian host within the walls of a Roman town whose area can be calculated. On this basis Peter Heather and Herwig Wolfram estimate the combined forces of the Ostrogoths and allies settling in Italy as numbering about 20,000 warriors with a total population of roughly 100,000. Thomas Burns calculates the Ostrogothic population settling in Italy as approximately 40,000. These estimates differ substantially but represent the same order of magnitude, particularly in relation to the Roman provincial population.[5] The Visigoths were perhaps approximately the same size, numbering as many as 70,000 to 80,000 when they settled in Spain.[6] Lot, however, estimated that the Gothic army at Adrianople numbered 10,000 warriors, implying a smaller figure for total population of perhaps 40,000 to 50,000.[7] Smaller tribes settling within the empire such as the Suevi and Heruli may have numbered only 25,000 to 35,000 souls.[8] By the time they were finally

---

[4] For a discussion with references see Hodges and Whitehouse, *Mohammed*, 50.
[5] Schmidt, *Geschichte der deutschen Stämme*, 293; Wolfram, *Geschichte der Goten*, 374ff.; Burns, "Calculating Ostrogothic Army," 187–90; Burns, "Calculating Ostrogothic Population," 457–63; Heather, *Goths and Romans*, 248–56, 280–302. The details recorded in Procopius concerning the Ostrogoths in Italy are discussed in Hannestad, "Les forces militaires"; Teall, "Barbarians"; E. A. Thompson, *Romans and Barbarians*, 278 n. 15, 280 n. 61, 282 n. 28.
[6] Latouche, "Aspects démographiques," 686; Schmidt, *Geschichte der deutschen Stämme*, 403–4; Reinhart, "Sobre el asentamiento de los Visigodos."
[7] Lot, *End of the Ancient World*, 229.
[8] E. A. Thompson, *Romans and Barbarians*, 158–59, 295 n. 98.

settled in Gaul, the ill-fated Burgundians may have been reduced to similarly small numbers.[9]

The evidence for the Vandal population on the eve of their move from Spain to North Africa is generally treated as the most reliable figure in the texts.[10] Goffart has recently cast doubt on even this evidence. The figure of 80,000 for the total population of the Vandals, their allies and dependents is probably exaggerated but roughly credible.[11]

A number of difficulties bedevils the demographic interpretation of the textual evidence. The references are few and scattered. The numeracy of the ancient authors is questionable, and in general they probably exaggerated barbarian numbers. Population within tribes and confederations must have fluctuated significantly. Even setting these problems aside, the figures given are not cold-blooded censuses but impressionistic indexes of the authors' credulity, fears, admirations, and even apocalyptic visions. Hollingsworth, writing a general guide to historical demography, drew up a list of circumstances in which figures should be treated as possibly (probably) unreliable. The list includes: boasting of one's own strength, exultation over the numbers of a defeated enemy, requests for relief from natural or man-inflicted disasters, and revelling in the extremes of epidemic mortality recently survived.[12] Unfortunately, practically all of the contemporary estimates of tribal populations (or armies) during the migrations can be slotted into one of these suspicious categories. A few figures possibly associated with official pay-lists or rosters may be more reliable, and these figures along with studies of place-names, genealogies, military details, law codes, and archaeology, particularly cemetery evidence, provide the raw material for estimates of barbarian population.[13]

[9] Schmidt, *Geschichte der deutschen Stämme*, 168; Guichard, *Essai sur l'histoire*, 338ff.; Ebersolt, *Les cimetières burgondes*; Coville, *Recherches sur l'histoire de Lyon*, 153–58.
[10] Courtois, *Les Vandales et l'Afrique*, 215–18; Courtois, *Victor de Vita*, 23ff.; Schmidt,"Zur Frage nach der Volkzahl"; E. A. Thompson, *Romans and Barbarians*, 155–56; Randers-Pehrson, *Barbarians and Romans*, 153.
[11] Goffart, *Barbarians and Romans*, 231–34.
[12] Hollingsworth, *Historical Demography*, 47.
[13] Musset thought these difficulties made the numerical aspect of the migrations "insoluble" but concluded that the invading armies were certainly not large (*Germanic Invasions*, 171). Some of the key texts are Jerome *Chron.* 2389; Victor Vitensis *Historia persecutionis Vandalicae* 1.1; Procopius *Bell. Vandal.* 1.5.18; Procopius *Anecdota* 18.6; Orosius 7.32.11; Ammianus 28.5.8–11, 31.10.5; Jordanes *Romana* 309; Dexippus *Fr.* 6.4; *Cod. Theod.* 7.8.5; Eunapius *Fr.* 6.

The *Historia Brittonum*

THE *Historia* survives in some forty manuscripts. Nine different Latin recensions and a Middle Irish translation are represented. Successive editions vary in content, including both additions and omissions. The earliest surviving full text is Harleian MS 3859. The content of the *Historia* breaks down as follows:[1]

Chapters

1–6	computistical six ages of the world
7–18	British, Irish, and Pictish origins, early history, geography of Britain
19–30	Roman Britain
31–50	Saxon *adventus*, story of Vortigern, Hengest, St. Germanus
50–55	St. Patrick
56	Arthur
57–61	genealogies of Anglo-Saxon kings
62–65	"Northern History," regnal lists, events in north Britain
66	chronological calculations, list of British cities
67–76	marvels and wonders of Britain and Ireland

For Chapters 1–30, the *Historia* is derivative, based largely on Gildas, Jerome, Orosius, Prosper, and antiquarian speculations and popular traditions of doubtful value. Chapters 31–50 are the crucial section for the fifth-century invasions. Chapters 51–55 are drawn from Prosper and later, worthless, medieval hagiography.[2] A British "catalogue" or listing poem

---

[1] See W. Davies, *Wales*, 205–6; Alcock, *Arthur's Britain*, 29–41.
[2] R. P. C. Hanson, *Saint Patrick*, 82.

giving Arthur's battles is the most likely source for Chapter 56.[3] Chapters 56–65 are based on a lost British chronicle of about the mid-eighth century, itself derived from material perhaps as early as the sixth century.[4] The Anglian genealogies are probably derived from a lost Mercian eighth-century source. Chapter 66 is a list of cities probably invented in the ninth century.[5] Additionally, in Harley 3859, the earliest full version of the *Historia*, is included the *Annales Cambriae* and a set of Welsh genealogies. The development of the *Annales Cambriae* seems in some ways to parallel that of the *Historia*. The annals are a St. David's record contemporary for the eighth century and derived for the earlier period from a set of northern British annals and entries made in Irish sources, with material as early perhaps as the late sixth century.[6]

One of the basic issues in dispute is how the author-compiler of the *Historia* used his sources. The "Nennian" preface states, "I, Nennius, pupil of the holy Elvodug, have undertaken to write down some extracts that the stupidity of the British cast out. . . . I have therefore made a heap of all that I have found. . . . I ask every reader . . . to pardon me for daring to write . . . like a chattering bird or an incompetent judge."[7] This preface is found only in some of the later manuscripts and Dumville has shown that it has no authority prior to the eleventh century. He thinks the preface has exercised an unfortunate influence over scholars who have accepted a medieval modesty topos at face value and concluded therefrom that the *Historia* is something of an inadvertent sourcebook, "Nennius" being too clumsy to alter or adulterate his materials.[8]

Dumville is correct not to underestimate the intellectual power of the original compiler of the *Historia* and to caution against the possibility of ninth-century synchronism and invention. Even without the disputed preface, however, it seems clear that in various parts of the *Historia* "heaping" accurately describes the compiler's method in treating distinct and sometimes contradictory origin stories, chronology, and even the narratives of specific events (for example, compare *H.B.* 36 with 37).

Unlike the case of the Anglo-Saxons, pagan and illiterate until after c. 597 A.D., there is no comparable chronological horizon for written accounts by post-Roman Britons who were Christian and literate. This makes the question of whether or not earlier intermediate or lost British

---

[3] Dumville, "Sub-Roman Britain," 177.
[4] Jackson, "Northern British Section." For the opposite view, see Dumville, "North British Section," 348.
[5] Jackson, "Twenty-Eight Cities."
[6] Hughes, "Welsh Latin Chronicles"; Hughes, "A-Text."
[7] *H.B.* preface.
[8] Dumville, "'Nennius' and the *Historia*," 78–95. See the comments of John Morris, *Nennius: British History and Welsh Annals*, 1–8; Alcock, *Arthur's Britain*, 29–41; Gransden, *Historical Writing*, 8; Liebermann, "Nennius," 32–33.

sources were incorporated into the *Historia* very difficult. The account of the invasions in the *Historia* must be tested by the plausibility of its circumstantial detail; its relation to earlier sources such as Gildas or Bede, and its compatibility with archaeological evidence. On this last count the *Historia* poses no difficulty. In terms of plausibility the account of the *Historia*, like that of Procopius, "combines the probable, the possible and the fabulous in proportions which so far have defied the skill of any editor to untangle."[9] Stripped of the most obviously fantastic elements, however, the account of the invasions is generally plausible in its intrinsic circumstantial detail.

The relation between the *Historia* and Bede is a difficult question. Their accounts of the invasion of Kent are compatible but probably not entirely independent. A close comparison of the relevant sections suggests that the *Historia* drew on some of the materials used by Bede but not on Bede directly. If this interpretation is correct, it tends to validate the reliability of the account in the *Historia* but also undercuts its value as an independent source. The problem is a good example of the dense undergrowth of scholarly debate. Mommsen thought Bede borrowed his account from an early version of the *Historia*. Lot thought the *Historia* borrowed from Bede. Liebermann concluded that both used common material.[10]

The author of the *Historia* relied heavily on Gildas. In the account of Vortigern and the Saxons (*H.B.* 31, 36–38, 43–46), however, there are so many differences and additions of detail that the *Historia* clearly used other sources. In addition to Gildas, details seem to be drawn from a Book of Saint Germanus, as well as material from Anglo-Saxon sources, either oral or written. The various strands are not well integrated and the result is a diploid account reflecting British and Anglo-Saxon traditions of the same events. Much of this material is obviously of a fantastic nature. There is no scholarly consensus concerning the historical value of the additional plausible detail.[11]

---

[9] Fisher, *Anglo-Saxon Age*, 10.
[10] See Mommsen, *MGH AA* 13:115–32; Lot, *Nennius*, 72; Liebermann, "Nennius," 25–28; Jackson, "Northern British Section," 26, 49–52; Dumville, "Historical Value," 11–13; Zimmer, *Nennius Vindicatus*, 61; Gransden, *Historical Writing*, 7; Fletcher, *Arthurian Material*, 24.
[11] See Fletcher, *Arthurian Material*, 18–30; Dumville, "Historical Value," 11–14; H. M. Chadwick, *Origin of the English Nation*, 38–53. On the possible date for the Book of Saint Germanus see Lot, *Nennius*, 80–86 (written by Nennius himself); Dumville, "Sub-Roman Britain," 177 (late eighth century); Fletcher, *Arthurian Material*, 9 (seventh or eighth century); Liebermann, "Nennius," 37 n. 139 (not much earlier than the *Historia*); N. K. Chadwick, "Early Culture and Learning," 113 (not later than the seventh century). Ifor Williams and N. K. Chadwick think the entries regarding Germanus were derived from oral saga tradition, not monkish hagiography. See N. K. Chadwick, "Note on the Name Vortigern."

A crux in the belief held by many scholars that the *Historia* preserves genuine fifth-century details is chronology. The *Historia* offers a traditional insular date for the *adventus* (428 A.D.), in contrast to the mid-fifth century or later dates inferred from Gildas and created by Bede.[12] The 428 date is only one among several for the *adventus* in the "heap" of the *Historia*'s chronology. It is calculated in several ways, however, and must have originated as an A.P. date, a form misunderstood and garbled before it was used in the *Historia*. The compiler of the *Historia* incorrectly linked this date through intercalculation with A.D. dates contemporary with the ninth century. Most importantly, the 428 date is the only one for the *adventus* which can be reconciled with the continental evidence and the revised archaeological dating for the arrival of the Anglo-Saxons in Britain. It is an argument for the genuineness of some early tradition within the *Historia*.[13]

In his overall conclusion regarding the historical value of the *Historia* Dumville states "I, at least, am not prepared to write fifth-century British history on the basis of legends retold from Anglo-Saxon sources by a Welshman in the ninth century." In contrast (speaking of the same source!) Morris writes that the *Historia*'s account of the conquest "is a rational straightforward narrative of the campaign of Vortigern and his sons against the English of Hengest and Horsa in Kent."[14] Dumville is a highly critical minimalist and Morris is overly sanguine. Considerations of plausibility, the *Historia*'s relation to earlier sources, its chronology and compatibility with the archaeological evidence—all these combine to suggest that the *Historia* does contain genuine early information, albeit in a very adulterated form. As H. M. Chadwick concludes, "The story itself is not intrinsically improbable, nor does it really conflict with the few indications regarding the invasion given by the British historian Gildas."[15]

[12] See *H. B.* 16, 31, 66. *H. B.* 66, a computus section, is found only in the Harley recension and its derivative.
[13] Alcock, *Arthur's Britain*, 39; Myres, *English Settlements*, 18; Liebermann, "Nennius," 40; Michael E. Jones, "Saint Germanus."
[14] Dumville, "Sub-Roman Britain," 185. Dumville, "Historical Value," 14. Morris in Nennius, *British History and Welsh Annals*, 4.
[15] H. M. Chadwick, *Origin of the English Nation*, 47.

Bibliography

COLLECTIONS OF ANCIENT AUTHORS

Caspari, C. P. *Briefe Abhandlungen und Predigten aus den zwei letzen Jahrhunderten des kirchlichen Altertums und dem Anfang des Mittelalters.* Christiania, 1890.

Chambers, R. W. *England before the Norman Conquest.* London, 1926.

Corpus Scriptorum Ecclesiasticorum Latinorum (CSEL). Vienna, 1866– .

Councils and Ecclesiastical Documents Relating to Great Britain and Ireland. Edited by A. W. Haddan and W. Stubbs. 3 vols. Oxford, 1859–71.

Ecclesiae Occidentalis Monumenta Iuris Antiquissima. Edited by E. Schwartz. Leipzig, 1939.

Liebermann, F. *Die Gesetze der Angelsachsen.* 3 vols. Halle, 1903–16.

The Laws of the Earliest English Kings. Edited and translated by F. L. Attenborough. London, 1922.

Literary Sources for Roman Britain. Edited by J. C. Mann and R. G. Penman. LACTOR 11. London, 1977.

Monumenta Germaniae Historica (MGH). Berlin, various dates. (*AA* = *Auctores Antiquissimi.*)

Monumenta Historica Britannica. Edited by Henry Petrie. Vol. 1. London, 1848.

The Northern Frontier in Britain from Hadrian to Honorius: Literary and Epigraphic Sources. Edited by J. C. Mann. Newcastle, 1971.

Patrologiae Cursus Completus, Series Latina (PL). Edited by Jacques Paul Migne. 221 vols. Paris, 1844–80.

Pelagius. *The Letters of Pelagius and His Followers.* Translated by B. R. Rees. Woodbridge, 1991.

Rivet, A. L. F., and Colin Smith. *The Place-Names of Roman Britain.* London, 1979.

Sacrorum Conciliorum Nova et Amplissima Collectio. Edited by J. D. Mansi et al. New edition and continuation. Paris, 1901- .

Select Library of Nicene and Post-Nicene Fathers of the Christian Church. Edited by P. Schaff. 28 vols. New York, 1886–1900.

Whitelock, D., ed. *English Historical Documents.* Vol. 1. London, 1955.

INDIVIDUAL ANCIENT AUTHORS

Adomnan. *Life of Columba.* Translated by A. O. and M. O. Anderson. London, 1961.

Ammianus Marcellinus. *Historiae.* Edited by J. C. Rolfe. 3 vols. Loeb ed. Cambridge, Mass., 1935–39.

Aneirin. *Gododdin.* Translated by K. H. Jackson. In *The Gododdin: The Oldest Scottish Poem.* Edinburgh, 1961.

The Anglo-Saxon Chronicle. Edited by Benjamin Thorpe. 2 vols. Rolls series. London, 1861. Translated by G. N. Garmonsway. London, 1953.

The Anglo-Saxon Chronicle. Edited by Dorothy Whitelock, David C. Douglas, and Susie I. Tucker. 2d ed. London, 1965.

Antonine Itinerary. Edited by Otto Cuntz. *Itineraria Romana.* Vol. 1, *Itineraria Antonini et Burdigalense.* Leipzig, 1929.

Appian. *Appian's Roman History.* Edited by Horace White. 4 vols. Loeb ed. Cambridge, Mass., 1912–13.

Aurelius Victor. *De caesaribus.* Edited by F. Pinchlmayr. Teubner ed. Leipzig, 1911.

Ausonius. Edited by Hugh G. Evelyn White. 2 vols. Loeb ed. Cambridge, Mass., 1919.

Avienus. *Ora Maritima.* Edited by A. Schulten. Barcelona, 1922.

Bede. *Chronica Maiora* and *Chronica Minora.* Edited by T. Mommsen. *MGH (AA)* 13, 223–354.

——. *Ecclesiastical History of the English People.* Edited by Bertram Colgrave and R. A. B. Mynors. Oxford, 1969. Also edited by C. Plummer. In *Venerabilis Baedae Opera Historica.* Oxford, 1956. Translated by Leo Sherley-Price. *A History of the English Church and People.* Revised ed. Harmondsworth, 1968.

Caesar. *The Gallic War.* Edited by H. J. Edwards. Loeb ed. Cambridge, Mass., 1917.

Cassius Dio. *Roman History.* Edited by E. W. Cary. 9 vols. Loeb ed. Cambridge, Mass., 1914–27.

"Chronicle of 452." Edited by T. Mommsen. *MGH (AA),* vol. 9. Berlin, 1892.

Claudian. Edited and translated by M. Platnauer. 2 vols. Loeb ed. Cambridge, Mass., 1922.

Constantius. *Vita Sancti Germani.* Edited by W. Levison. *MGH, Scriptores Rerum Merovingicarum,* vol. 7. Berlin, 1920. Translated by F. R. Hoare. *The Western Fathers.* New York, 1954.

De rebus bellicis. Edited by E. A. Thompson. In *A Roman Reformer and Inventor: Being a New Text of the Treatise "De rebus bellicis."* Oxford, 1952.

Diodorus Siculus. *Bibliotheca historica.* Edited by F. Vogel and C. T. Fischer. Teubner ed. Leipzig, 1888–1906.

Early Welsh Genealogical Tracts. Edited by P. C. Bartrum. Cardiff, 1966.

Eutropius. *Breviarium ab urbe condita.* Edited by F. Ruhl. Teubner ed. Leipzig, 1887. Translated by H. W. Bird. *Eutropius Breviarium.* Liverpool, 1993.

Felix. *Vita S. Guthlaci.* In *Felix's Life of St. Guthlac,* edited by B. Colgrave. Cambridge, 1956.

Geoffrey of Monmouth. *Historia regnum Britanniae.* In *La légende arthurienne, études et documents,* edited by Edmond Faral. 3 vols. Paris, 1929. Translated by Lewis Thorpe. *The History of the Kings of Britain.* Harmondsworth, 1966.

Gildas. *De excidio et conquestu Britanniae.* Edited by T. Mommsen. *MGH (AA),* vol. 13. Berlin, 1898. Edited and translated by Hugh Williams. *Gildas.* 2 parts. Cymmrodorion Record Series 3. London, 1899 and 1901. Also translated by Michael Winterbottom. *Gildas: The Ruin of Britain and Other Works.* London, 1978.

Herodian. *Ab excessu divi Marci.* Edited by K. Stavenhagen. Teubner ed. Leipzig, 1922. Translated by E. C. Echols. *History of the Roman Empire from the Death of Marcus Aurelius to the Accession of Gordian III.* Berkeley, 1961.

Historia Brittonum. See Nennius.

Hydatius. *Chronicle.* Edited by T. Mommsen. *MGH (AA)* 11. Berlin, 1894. Edited and translated by R. W. Burgess. *The Chronicle of Hydatius and the Consularia Constantinopolitana: Two Contemporary Accounts of the Final Years of the Roman Empire.* Oxford, 1993.

Jerome. *Principal Works of Jerome.* Translated by W. H. Fremantle. A Select Library of Nicene and Post-Nicene Fathers. 2d series, vol. 6. Grand Rapids, Mich., reprinted 1979.

Jordanes. *De origine actibusque Getarum.* Edited by C. A. Closs. Stuttgart, 1866. Translated by C. C. Mierow. *Getica.* Princeton, 1915.

Julian. Edited and translated by Wilmer C. Wright. 3 vols. Loeb ed. Cambridge, Mass., 1913–23.

Libanius. *Selected Works.* Edited and translated by A. F. Norman. 2 vols. Loeb ed. Cambridge, Mass., 1969.

Mann, J. C., and R. G. Penman, eds. *The Literary Sources for Roman Britain.* LACTOR 11. London, 1977.

Marcellinus Comes. *Chronicle.* Edited by T. Mommsen. *MGH (AA),* vol. 11. Berlin, 1894.

Narratio de imperatoribus domus Valentinianae et Theodosianae. Edited by T. Mommsen. *MGH (AA),* vol. 9. Berlin, 1892.

Nennius. *Historia Brittonum.* Edited by T. Mommsen. *MGH (AA),* vol. 13. Berlin, 1898. Translated by John Morris. *Nennius: British History and the Welsh Annals.* London, 1980.

Notitia dignitatum. Edited by O. Seeck. Berlin, 1876.

Olympiodorus. *Fragmenta.* Translated by C. D. Gordon. In *The Age of Attila.* Ann Arbor, 1966.

Orosius. *Historiarum adversum paganos libri septem.* Edited by Karl Zangemeister. Teubner ed. Leipzig, 1889. Translated by Roy J. Defarrari. *Seven Books of History against the Pagans.* Washington, D.C., 1964.

Panegyrici Latini Veteres. Edited by R. A. B. Mynors. Oxford, 1964.

Saint Patrick. "Liber epistolarum sancti patricii episcopi: Introduction, Text, and Commentary." Edited by L. Bieler. *Classica et Mediaevalia* 11 (1950), 1–150; 12 (1951), 81–214. Translated by A. B. E. Hood. *Saint Patrick: His Writings and Muirchu's Life.* London, 1978.

Pausanias. *Description of Greece.* Edited by W. H. S. Jones and R. E. Wycherley. 4 vols. Loeb ed. Cambridge, Mass., 1918–35.

Pliny the Elder. *Naturalis historia.* Edited by H. Rackham, W. H. S. Jones, and D.E. Eichholz. 10 vols. Loeb ed. Cambridge, Mass., 1938–64.

Pliny the Younger. *The Letters of the Younger Pliny.* Translated by B. Radice. Harmondsworth, 1963.

Priscus. Translated by C. D. Gordon. In *The Age of Attila.* Ann Arbor, 1966.

Procopius. *History of the Wars.* Edited and translated by H. B. Dewing. 7 vols. Loeb ed. Cambridge, Mass., 1914–40.

Prosper Tiro. *Chronicle.* Edited by T. Mommsen. *MGH,* vol. 9. Berlin, 1892.

Ptolemy. *Geographia.* Translated by Edward L. Stevenson. New York, 1932.

Ravennatis anonymi cosmographia. Edited by Joseph Schnetz. Leipzig, 1939–40.

Rutilius Namatianus. *De reditu suo.* Edited by C. H. Keene and translated by George F. Savage-Armstrong. In *The Homecoming of Rutilius Claudius Namatianus from Rome to Gaul in the Year 416.* London, 1907.

Salvian. *De gubernatione Dei.* Translated by J. F. O'Sullivan. In *The Writings of Salvian the Presbyter.* Washington, D.C., 1947.

Scriptores historiae augustae. Edited and translated by David Magie. 3 vols. Loeb ed. Cambridge, Mass., 1922–32.

Senchus Fer nAlban. Translated by J. Bannerman. In *Studies in the History of Dalriada.* Edinburgh, 1974.

Sidonius Apollinaris. *The Letters of Sidonius.* Edited and translated by O. M. Dalton. 2 vols. Oxford, 1915.

———. *Poems and Letters.* Edited and translated by W. B. A. Anderson. 2 vols. Loeb ed. Cambridge, Mass., 1965.

Socrates. *Historia ecclesiastica.* Translated by A. C. Zenos. In *The Nicene and Post-Nicene Fathers.* Second series. Vol. 2. Grand Rapids, Mi., 1957.

Sozomen. *Ecclesiastical History.* Translated by E. Walford. London, 1855.

Strabo. *Geographica.* Edited by H. L. Jones and J. R. S. Sterrett. 8 vols. Loeb ed. Cambridge, Mass., 1917–49.

Suetonius. *De vita caesarum.* Edited by J. C. Rolfe. Loeb ed. Cambridge, Mass., 1914.

Tabula itineraria Peutingeriana. Edited by Conrad Mannert. Leipzig, 1824.

Tacitus. *Annales.* Edited by J. Jackson. Loeb ed. Cambridge, Mass., 1931–37; 1951–52. Translated by Donald R. Dudley. London, 1966.

———. *De vita Agricolae.* Edited by R. M. Ogilvie and Sir Ian Richmond. Oxford, 1967. Translated by H. Mattingly. Revised by S. A. Handford. *The "Agricola" and the "Germania."* Harmondsworth, 1970.

———. *Historiae.* Edited by C. H. Moore. Loeb ed. Cambridge, Mass., 1931–37; 1951–52. Translated by Kenneth Wellesley. Harmondsworth, 1964.

Theodosian Code. Translated by C. Pharr. Princeton, 1952.

Vegetius. *Epitoma rei militaris.* In *Vegetius: Epitome of Military Science,* Translated by N. P. Milner. Liverpool, 1993.

Victor Vitensis. *Historia persecutionis Vandalicae.* Edited by C. Halm. *MGH (AA),* vol. 3. Berlin, 1879. Translated by John Moorhead. *Victor of Vita: History of the Vandal Persecution.* Liverpool, 1992.

Vita sancti Gildae. Edited by T. Mommsen. *MGH (AA)* 13:91–110. Berlin, 1898. Edited by F. Lot. "Gildae vita et translatio." *Annales Bretagne* 25 (1909–10), 346–65, 493–516.
Vita St. Melania Junioris. Analecta Bollandiana 8 (1889), 19–63.
Zosimus. *Historia nova.* Edited by Ludwig Mendelssohn. Teubner ed. Leipzig, 1887. Translated by James J. Buchanan and Harold T. Davis. San Antonio, Tex., 1967. Translated by Ronald T. Ridley. *New History.* Sidney, 1982.

INSCRIPTIONS

Burn, A. R., ed. *The Romans in Britain: An Anthology of Inscriptions.* Rev. ed. Oxford, 1969.
Collingwood, R. G., and R. P. Wright, eds. *Roman Inscriptions of Britain.* Vol. 1. Oxford, 1965.
Corpus Inscriptionum Latinarum (C.I.L.). Berlin, 1863– .
Greenstock, M. C., ed. *Some Inscriptions from Roman Britain.* LACTOR 4. London, 1971.
Moore, R. W., ed. *The Romans in Britain.* 3d ed. London, 1954.

UNPUBLISHED MANUSCRIPTS

London. British Museum. Cotton Nero E. 1.
London. British Museum. Cotton Vitellius A. vi.
London. British Museum. Harley 3859.

SECONDARY SOURCES

Abbot, F. F., and A. C. Johnson. *Municipal Administration in the Roman Empire.* Princeton, 1926.
Abels, Richard P. *Lordship and Military Obligation in Anglo-Saxon England.* Berkeley, 1988.
Åberg, N. *The Orient and the Occident in the Art of the Seventh Century.* 3 vols. Stockholm, 1947.
Acsádi, G., and J. Nemeskéri. *A History of Human Life Span and Mortality.* Translated by K. Balas. Budapest, 1970.
Adams, William Y., Dennis P. Van Gerven, and Richard S. Levy. "The Retreat from Migrationism." *Annual Review of Anthropology* 7 (1978), 483–532.
Addyman, P. V., and J. S. R. Hood. "Palaeoclimate in Urban Environmental Archaeology at York, England: Problems and Potential." *World Archaeology* 8 (1976), 220–33.
Africa, Thomas W. *The Immense Majesty: A History of Rome and the Roman Empire.* Arlington Heights, Ill., 1974.
Åkerlund, H. *Nydamskeppen: En studie i tidig skandinavisk skeppsbyggnadskont.* Göteborg, 1963.
Alcock, Leslie. *Arthur's Britain.* Harmondsworth, 1989.
——. *Economy, Society, and Warfare among the Britons and Saxons.* Cardiff, 1987.
——. "Quantity or Quality: The Anglian Graves of Bernicia." In *Angles, Saxons, and Jutes,* edited by Vera I. Evison, 168–86. Oxford, 1981.

Allen, J. R. L., and M. G. Fulford. "The Wentlooge Level: A Romano-British Salt-marsh Reclamation in Southeast Wales." *Britannia* 17 (1986), 91–117.

Alonso-Núñez, J. M. "Jordanes on Britain." *Oxford Journal of Archaeology* 6 (1987), 127–29.

Amulree, Lord. "Hygiene Conditions in Ancient Rome and Modern London." *Medical History* 17 (1973), 244–55.

Anderson, A. O. "Gildas and Arthur." *Celtic Review: Proceedings of the Symposium of the Faculty of Arts of Uppsala University* 8 (1912–13), 149–65.

Anderson, J. L. "Climate and the Historians." In *Climatic Change and Variability: A Southern Perspective*, edited by A. B. Pittock et al., 310–16. Cambridge, 1978.

Anderson, James D. *Roman Military Supply in North-East England*. British Archaeological Reports BS 224. Oxford, 1992.

Andersson, T., and K.I. Sandred, eds. *The Vikings*. Uppsala, 1978.

Applebaum, S. "Roman Britain." In *The Agrarian History of England and Wales*, edited by H. P. R. Finberg, 1.2:3–277. Cambridge, 1972.

———. "Some Observations on the Economy of the Roman Villa at Bignor, Sussex." *Britannia* 6 (1975), 118–32.

Appleby, Andrew B. "Disease or Famine? Mortality in Cumberland and Westmorland 1586–1640." *Economic History Review* 26 (1973), 403–31.

———. "Epidemics and Famine in the Little Ice Age." In *Climate and History: Studies in Interdisciplinary History*, edited by R. I. Rotberg and T. K. Rabb, 63–83. Princeton, 1981.

———. *Famine in Tudor and Stuart England*. Stanford, 1978.

———. "Nutrition and Disease: The Case of London, 1550–1750." *Journal of Interdisciplinary History* 6 (1975), 1–22.

Arenhold, L. "The Nydam Ship at Kiel." *Mariner's Mirror* 4 (1914), 182–85.

Arnold, C. J. *An Archaeology of the Early Anglo-Saxon Kingdoms*. London, 1988.

———. "The End of Roman Britain." In *The Romano-British Countryside: Studies in Rural Settlement and Economy*, edited by David Miles, pt. 2, 451–59. Oxford, 1982.

———. *Roman Britain to Saxon England*. London, 1984.

Arnold, David. *Famine: Social Crisis and Historical Change*. Oxford, 1988.

Arnold, W. T. *Roman Provincial Administration*. Salem, N.H., 1974.

Askew, G. P., R. W. Payton, and R. S. Shiel. "Upland Soils and Land Clearance in Britain during the Second Millenium B.C." In *Upland Settlement in Britain: The Second Millenium B.C. and After*, edited by Don Spratt and Colin Burgess, 5–33. Oxford, 1985.

Association bourguignonne. *Saint Germain d'Auxerre et son temps: communications présentées à l'occasion du xixᵉ congrès de l'Association bourguignonne des sociétés savantes réuni à Auxerre (29 juillet–2 août 1948)*. Auxerre, 1950.

Bachrach, Bernard S. *Merovingian Military Organization, 481–751*. Minneapolis, 1972.

Baker, Derek, ed. *The Church in Town and Countryside: Papers Read at the Seventeenth Summer Meeting and Eighteenth Winter Meeting of the Ecclesiastical Historical Society*. Oxford, 1979.

Baldwin, Barry. "Peasant Revolt in Africa in the Later Roman Empire." *Nottingham Medieval Studies* 6 (1962), 3–11.

Bammesberger, Alfred, and Alfred Wollman, eds. *Britain 400–600: Language and History.* Heidelberg, 1990.

Bang-Anderson, Arne, Basil Greenhill, and Egil Harald Grude, eds. *The North Sea.* Oslo, 1985.

Bantelmann, Albert. *Die Landschaftsentwicklung an der schleswig-hosteinischen Westküste dargestellt am Beispiel Nordfriesland; bëine Funktionschronik durch fünf Jahrtausende.* Neumunster, 1967.

Barber, K. E. *Peat Stratigraphy and Climatic Change: A Palaeoecological Test of the Theory of Cyclic Peat Bog Regeneration.* Cambridge, 1981.

———. "Peat-Bog Stratigraphy as a Proxy Climate Record." In *Climatic Change in Later Prehistory,* edited by A. F. Harding, 103–13. Edinburgh, 1982.

Barber, K. E., Lisa Dumayne, and Rob Stoneman. "Climatic Change and Human Impact during the Late Holocene in Northern Britain." In *Climate Change and Human Impact on the Landscape,* edited by F. M. Chambers, 225–36. London, 1993.

Barley, M. W., and R. P. C. Hanson, eds. *Christianity in Britain 300–700: Papers Presented to the Conference on Christianity in Roman and Sub-Roman Britain.* Leicester, 1968.

Barnes, T. D. "The Beginnings of Donatism." *Journal of Theological Studies* 26 (1975), 13–22.

Barrow, G. W. S. "Northern English Society in the Early Middle Ages," *Northern History* 4 (1969), 1–28.

Barrow, R. H. *The Romans.* Harmondsworth, 1949.

Bartholomew, P. "Fifth-Century Facts." *Britannia* 13 (1982), 261–70.

———. "Fourth-Century Saxons." *Britannia* 15 (1984), 169–85.

Bartholomew, P., and R. Goodburn, eds. *Aspects of the "Notitia Dignitatum":Papers Presented to the Conference in Oxford (December 13–15, 1974).* British Archaeological Reports S 15. Oxford, 1976.

Bartlett, J. N. "The Expansion and Decline of York in the Later Middle Ages." *Economic History Review* 12 (1959–60), 17–33.

Bartley, D. D. "Palaeobotanical Evidence." In *English Medieval Settlement,* edited by P. H. Sawyer, 133–42. London, 1979.

Bartley, D. D., C. Chambers, and B. Hart-Jones. "The Vegetational History of Parts of South and East Durham." *New Phytologist* 77 (1976), 437–68.

Basch, L. "On the Reliability of Ancient Writers in Matters Maritime." *Mariner's Mirror* 66 (1980), 366–69.

———. "One Aspect of the Problems Which Arise from the Interpretation of Representations of Ancient Ships." *Mariner's Mirror* 62 (1976), 231–33.

Bass, George F., ed. *A History of Seafaring Based on Underwater Archaeology.* London, 1972.

Basset, Steven, ed. *The Origins of Anglo-Saxon Kingdoms.* Leicester, 1989.

———. "In Search of the Origins of Anglo-Saxon Kingdoms." In *The Origins of Anglo-Saxon Kingdoms,* edited by Steven Basset, 3–27. Leicester, 1989.

Bately, J. "Bede and the Anglo-Saxon Chronicle." In *Saints, Scholars, and Heroes: Studies in Medieval Culture,* edited by M. H. King and W. M. Stevens, 1:233–54. Collegeville, Minn., 1979.

Bell, Martin. "The Effects of Land-Use and Climate on Valley Sedimentation." In

Climatic Change in Later Prehistory, edited by A. F. Harding, 127–42. Edinburgh, 1982.

——. "Valley Sediments and Environmental Change." In *The Environment of Man: The Iron Age to the Anglo-Saxon Period*, edited by M. Jones and G. Dimbleby, Oxford, 1981.

Bell, W. T., and A. E. J. Olgilvie, "Weather Compilations as a Source of Data for the Reconstruction of European Climate during the Medieval Period." *Climatic Change* 1 (1978), 331–48.

Beloch, K. Julius. *Die Bevölkerung der griechisch-römischen Welt*. Leipzig, 1886.

——. "Die Bevölkerung Galliens zur Zeit Caesars." *Rheinisches Museum* 54 (1899), 414–38.

——. "Die Bevölkerung Italiens in Altertum." *Klio* 3 (1903), 471–90.

Berlin, Isaiah. *The Hedgehog and the Fox*. New York, 1986.

Bessinger, J. B. "The Sutton Hoo Ship Burial: A Chronological Bibliography." *Speculum* 33 (1958), 515–22.

Biddick, Kathleen. "Field Edge, Forest Edge: Early Medieval Social Change and Resource Allocation." In *Archaeological Approaches to Medieval Europe*, edited by Kathleen Biddick, 105–18. Kalamazoo, Mich., 1984

——, ed. *Archaeological Approaches to Medieval Europe*. Kalamazoo, Mich., 1984.

Biddle, Martin, Alan Binns, J. M. Cameron, D. M. Metcalf, R. I. Page, Charles Sparrow, and F. L. Warren. "Sutton Hoo Published: A Review." *Anglo-Saxon England* 6 (1977), 249–65.

Bilsky, Lester J., ed. *Historical Ecology: Essays on Environment and Social Change*. Port Washington, N.Y., 1980.

Binns, Alan. *Viking Voyagers*. London, 1980.

Birley, Anthony R. "The Assimilation of Britain." *Times Literary Supplement*. 6 November 1981, 1305.

——. "The Economic Effects of Roman Frontier Policy." In *The Roman West in the Third Century*, edited by Anthony King and Martin Henig, 39–53. Oxford, 1981.

——. *The Fasti of Roman Britain*. Oxford, 1981.

——. *Life in Roman Britain*. London, 1981.

——. *The People of Roman Britain*. Berkeley, 1980.

——. "The Roman Governors of Britain." *Epigraphische Studien* 4 (1967), 63–102.

——. *Septimius Severus the African Emperor*. Rev. ed. New Haven, 1988.

Birley, Eric. "Septimius Severus and the Roman Army." *Epigraphische Studien* 8 (1969), 61–82.

Blackford, J. J. "Peat Bogs as Sources of Proxy Climatic Data: Past Approaches and Future Research." In *Climate Change and Human Impact on the Landscape*, edited by F. M. Chambers, 47–56. London, 1993.

Blackford, J. J., and F. M. Chambers. "Proxy Records of Climate from Blanket Mires: Evidence for a Dark Age (1400 BP) Climatic Deterioration in the British Isles." *The Holocene* 1 (1991), 63–67.

Blagg, T. F. C., and A. C. King, eds. *Military and Civilian in Roman Britain: Cultural Relationships in a Frontier Province*. British Archaeological Reports BS 136. Oxford, 1984.

Bloch, H. "The Pagan Revival in the West at the End of the Fourth Century." In *The Conflict between Paganism and Christianity in the Fourth Century*, edited by A. Momigliano, 193–218. Oxford, 1963.

Bloch, Marc. "Les invasions." *Annales d'histoire sociale* (1945), part i. 33–46 and ii. 13–28.

Boak, A. E. R. *Manpower Shortage and the Fall of the Roman Empire in the West.* Ann Arbor, 1955.

Böhme, H. W. "Das Ende der Römerherrschaft in Brittanien und die angelsächsische Besiedlung Englands im 5. Jahrhundert." *Jahrbuch des Römisch-Germanischen Zentralmuseums* 33 (1986), 469–574.

——. *Germanische Grabfunde des 4. bis 5. Jahrhunderts zwischen unterer Elbe und Loire.* Munich, 1974.

——. "Das Land zwischen Elbe- und Wesermündung vom 4. bis 6. Jahrhunderts." *Führer zu Vor- und Frühgeschichtlichen Denkmälern* 29 (1976), 205–25.

Bolton, W. F. *A History of Anglo-Latin Literature 597–1066.* Vol. 1. Princeton, 1967.

Bonney, D. J. "Early Boundaries and Estates in Southern England." In *Medieval Settlement: Continuity and Change,* edited by P. H. Sawyer, 72–82. London, 1976.

——. "Pagan Saxon Burials and Boundaries in Wiltshire." *Wiltshire Archaeological and Natural History Magazine* 61 (1960), 25–30.

Bonser, W. *The Medical Background of Anglo-Saxon England: A Study in History, Psychology, and Folklore.* London, 1963.

Boon, G. C. *Roman Silchester.* 2d ed. London, 1974.

Boren, Henry C. *The Ancient World.* 2d ed. Englewood Cliffs, N. J., 1986.

Boserup, Ester. *The Conditions of Agricultural Growth: The Economics of Agrarian Change Under Population Pressure.* Foreword by Nicholas Kaldor. London, 1965.

——. "The Impact of Population Growth on Agricultural Output." *Quarterly Journal of Economics* 89 (1975), 257–70.

——. *Population and Technological Change.* Chicago, 1981.

Boulding, K. E. "The Malthusian Model as a General System." *Social and Economic Studies* 4 (1955), 195–205.

Bouzek, Jan. "Climatic Changes and Central European Prehistory." In *Climatic Change in Later Prehistory,* edited by A. F. Harding, 179–91. Edinburgh, 1982.

Bowen, E. G. *Britain and the Western Seaways.* London, 1972.

Bradley, Richard. "Anglo-Saxon Cemeteries: Some Suggestions for Research." In *Anglo-Saxon Cemeteries, 1979,* edited by P. Rahtz, T. Dickinson, and L. Watts, 171–76. Oxford, 1980.

Branden, P. F. "Agriculture and the Effects of Floods and Weather at Barnhorne, Sussex during the Late Middle Ages." *Sussex Archaeological Collections* 109 (1971), 69–93.

——. "Late-Medieval Weather in Sussex and Its Agricultural Significance." *Transactions of the Institute of British Geographers* 54 (1971), 1–17.

——, ed. *The South Saxons.* London, 1978.

Brandt, Roel, and Jan Slofstra, eds. *Roman and Native in the Low Countries: Spheres of Interaction.* British Archaeological Reports S 184. Oxford, 1983.

Branigan, K. *The Roman Villa in South-West England.* Bradford-on-Avon, 1977.

Brass, W., ed. *Biological Aspects of Demography.* London, 1971.

Breeze, David. "Demand and Supply on the Northern Frontier." In *Between and Beyond the Walls: Essays on the Prehistory and History of North Britain in*

Honor of George Jobey, edited by Roger Miket and Colin Burgess, 264–86. Edinburgh, 1984.

——. *The Northern Frontiers of Roman Britain*. London, 1982.

Bremmer, Rolf H., Jr. "The Nature of the Evidence for a Frisian Participation in the *Adventus Saxonum*." In *Britain 400–600: Language and History*, edited by Alfred Bammesberger and Alfred Wollman, 355–71. Heidelberg, 1990.

Brøgger, A. W., and Haakon Shetelig. *The Viking Ships: Their Ancestry and Evolution*. Translated by Katherine John. Oslo, 1951.

Bronson, Bennet. "The Role of Barbarians in the Fall of States." In *The Collapse of Ancient States and Civilizations*, edited by Norman Yoffe and George L. Cowgill, 196–218. Tucson, 1988.

Brooks, Dodie A. "Gildas' *De Excidio*: Its Revolutionary Meaning and Purpose." *Studia Celtica* 18–19 (1983–84), 1–10.

Brothwell, D. "Palaeodemography and Earlier British Populations." *World Archaeology* 4 (1972–73), 75–87.

——. "Stones, Pots, and People: A Plea for Statistical Caution." In *Science in Archaeology: A Survey of Progress and Research*, edited by D. Brothwell and E. Higgs, 669–79. Rev. ed. London, 1969.

Brothwell, D., and P. Brothwell. *Food in Antiquity: A Survey of the Diet of Early Peoples*. London, 1969.

Brothwell, D., and E. Higgs, eds. *Science in Archaeology: A Survey of Progress and Research*. Foreword by Grahame Clark. London, 1969.

Brothwell, D., A. T. Sandison, and C. Thomas, eds. *Diseases in Antiquity: A Survey of the Diseases, Injuries, and Surgery of Early Populations*. Springfield, Ill., 1967.

Brown, A. E., ed. "Archaeology in Northamptonshire 1982." *Northamptonshire Archaeology* 18 (1983), 171–83.

Brown, D. *Anglo-Saxon England*. London, 1978.

Brown, Peter. *Augustine of Hippo*. Berkeley, 1967.

——. "The Later Roman Empire." *Economic History Review*, 2d ser., 20 (1967), 327–43.

——. "Pelagius and His Supporters: Aims and Environment." *Journal of Theological Studies*, n.s., 19 (1968), 93–114.

——. *Power and Persuasion in Late Antiquity*. Madison, 1992.

——. *Religion and Society in the Age of Saint Augustine*. London, 1972.

——. "Religious Dissent in the Later Roman Empire." *History* 44 (1961), 83–101.

——. *The World of Late Antiquity: A.D. 150–750*. London, 1971.

Bruce-Chwatt, L. J. "A Medieval Glorification of Disease and Death." *Medical History* 16 (1972), 76–77.

Bruce-Mitford, Rupert. "The Snape Boat Grave." *Proceedings of the Suffolk Institute of Archaeology* 26 (1952), 1–26.

——. *The Sutton Hoo Ship Burial: A Handbook*. London, 1979.

Bruce-Mitford, Rupert, et al. *The Sutton Hoo Ship Burial I: Excavations, Background, the Ship, Dating, and Inventory*. London, 1975.

Brunt, P. A. "Charges of Provincial Maladministration under the Early Principate." *Historia* 10 (1961), 189–227.

——. *Italian Manpower 225 B.C.–A.D. 14*. 1971. Reprint Oxford, 1987.

Bryson, R. A. "Cultural, Economic, and Climatic Records: A Global View of Cultural Change from the Climatic Perspective." In *Climatic Change and Variability: A Southern Perspective*, edited by A. B. Pittock et al., 316–27. Cambridge, 1978.

Bryson, R. A., and C. Padoch. "On the Climates of History." In *Climate and History: Studies in Interdisciplinary History*, edited by R. I. Rotberg and T. K. Rabb, 3–17. Princeton, 1981.

Buckland, P. C. "Cereal Production, Storage, and Population." In *The Effect of Man on the Landscape: The Lowland Zone*, edited by Susan Limbrey and J. G. Evans, 43–45. London, 1978.

Burgess, Colin. "Population, Climate, and Upland Settlement." In *Upland Settlement in Britain: The Second Millenium B.C. and After*, edited by Don Spratt and Colin Burgess, 195–229. Oxford, 1985.

——. "The Prehistoric Settlement of Northumbria: A Speculative Survey." In *Between and Beyond the Walls: Essays on the Prehistory and History of North Britain in Honour of George Jobey*, edited by Roger Miket and Colin Burgess, 126–75. Edinburgh, 1984.

Burkitt, F. C. "The Bible of Gildas." *Revue Bénédictine* 46 (1934), 206–15.

Burn, A. R. "Procopius and the Island of Ghosts." *English Historical Review* 70 (1955), 258–61.

Burnham, Barry, and John Wacher. *The Small Towns of Roman Britain*. Berkeley, 1990.

Burnham, C. P. "The Coast of South-East England in Roman Times." In *The Saxon Shore: A Handbook*, edited by Valerie A. Maxfield, 12–17. Exeter, 1989.

Burns, Thomas S. "Calculating Ostrogothic Army and Population." *Ancient World* 1 (1978), 187–90.

——. "Calculating Ostrogothic Population." *Acta Antiqua Academiae Scientarum Hungaricae* 26 (1978), 457–63.

Bury, J. B. *History of the Later Roman Empire: From the Death of Theodosius I to the Death of Justinian*. 2 vols. London, 1923.

——. *The Invasion of Europe by the Barbarians*. London, 1928.

——. *The Life of Saint Patrick*. London, 1905.

Butler, R. M., ed. *Soldier and Civilian in Roman Yorkshire*. Leicester, 1971.

Buxton, L. H. D. "The Racial Affinities of the Romano-Britons." *Journal of Roman Studies* 25 (1935), 35–50.

Cameron, Alan. *Claudian: Poetry and Propoganda at the Court of Honorius*. Oxford, 1970.

——. "Rutilius Namatianus, St. Augustine, and the Date of the *De Reditu*." *Journal of Roman Studies* 57 (1967), 31–39.

Cameron, Averil. *The Later Roman Empire*. Cambridge, Mass., 1993.

——. *Procopius and the Sixth Century*. London, 1985.

Campbell, James, ed. *The Anglo-Saxons*. Ithaca, 1982.

——. "Bede's 'Reges' and 'Principes.'" Jarrow Lecture, 1979.

——. "The End of Roman Britain." In *The Anglo-Saxons*, edited by James Campbell, 8–19. Ithaca, 1982.

——. "The Lost Centuries 400–600." In *The Anglo-Saxons*, edited by James Campbell, 20–44. Ithaca, 1982.

——. "The Scandinavian Viking-Age Burials of England—Some Problems of Interpretation." In *Anglo-Saxon Cemeteries, 1979*, edited by P. Rahtz. To Dickinson, and L. Watts, 379–82. Oxford, 1980.

Cartwright, Frederick F. *Disease and History*. New York, 1972.

Carver, M. O. H., ed. *The Age of Sutton Hoo*. Woodbridge, 1992.

——. "Pre-Viking Traffic in the North Sea." In *Maritime Celts, Frisians, and Saxons*, edited by Séan McGrail, 117–25. London, 1990.

Casey, P. J., ed. *The End of Roman Britain*. British Archaeological Report 71. Oxford, 1979.

——. "Magnus Maximus in Britain." In *The End of Roman Britain*, edited by P. J. Casey, 66–79. Oxford, 1979.

Castiglioni, A. *A History of Medicine*. Translated by E. B. Krumbhaar. London, 1947.

Chadwick, H. M. *The Heroic Age*. Cambridge, 1912.

——. *The Origin of the English Nation*. Cambridge, 1907.

——. *Studies on Anglo-Saxon Institutions*. Cambridge, 1905. Reprint, New York, 1963.

Chadwick, H. M., and N. K. Chadwick. *The Growth of Literature*. Vol. 1. Cambridge, 1932.

Chadwick, N. K., ed. *Celt and Saxon: Studies in the Early British Border*. Cambridge, 1964.

——. "Early Culture and Learning in North Wales." In *Studies in the Early British Church*, edited by N. K. Chadwick, 29–120. Cambridge, 1958.

——. "Intellectual Contacts between Britain and Gaul in the Fifth Century." In *Studies in Early British History*, edited by N. K. Chadwick, 189–263. Cambridge, 1954.

——. "A Note on the Name Vortigern." In *Studies in Early British History*, edited by N. K. Chadwick, 34–38. Cambridge, 1954.

——. *Poetry and Letters in Early Christian Gaul*. London, 1955.

——, ed. *Studies in Early British History*. Cambridge, 1954.

——, ed. *Studies in the Early British Church*. Cambridge, 1958.

Chadwick, Owen. "Gildas and the Monastic Order." *Journal of Theological Studies*, n.s., 5 (1974), 78–80.

Chamberlin, Thomas C. "The Method of Multiple Working Hypothesis." *Science* 148 (1965), 754–59.

Chambers, F. M., ed. *Climate Change and Human Impact on the Landscape*. London, 1993.

Chambers, J. D. *Population, Economy, and Society in Pre-Industrial England*. Edited by W. A. Armstrong. Oxford, 1972.

Chambers, Mortimer, Raymond Grew, David Herlihy, Theodore K. Rabb, and Isser Woloch. *The Western Experience*. 4th ed. New York, 1987.

Chambers, R. A. "A Further Quantitative Approach to the Analysis of Burial Practice in Roman Britain." In *Temples, Churches, and Religion: Recent Research in Roman Britain, with a Gazeteer of Romano-Celtic Temples in Continental Europe*, edited by Warwick Rodwell, 165–74. Oxford, 1980.

Champion, Timothy C., ed. *Centre and Periphery: Comparative Studies in Archaeology*. London, 1989.

Chapman, J. C., and H. C. Mytum, eds. *Settlement in North Britain 1000 B.C.–A.D. 1000.* British Archaeological Reports BS 118. Oxford, 1983.

Charles-Edwards, T. M. "Kinship, Status, and the Origins of the Hide." *Past and Present* 56 (1972), 3–33.

——. "Palladius, Prosper, and Leo the Great: Mission and Primatial Authority." In *Saint Patrick A.D. 493–1993,* edited by David N. Dumville et al., 1–12. Woodbridge, 1993.

——. Review of *Gildas: New Approaches* edited by M. Lapidge and D. Dumville. *Cambridge Medieval Celtic Studies* 12 (1986), 114–20.

Cherf, W. J. Review of *Procopius. American Historical Review* 91 (1986), 894.

Christensen, Arne Emil. "Scandinavian Ships from the Earliest Times to the Vikings." In *A History of Seafaring Based on Underwater Archaeology,* edited by George F. Bass, 159–80. London, 1972.

Cicotti, E. "Indivizzie metodi negli studi de demografia antica." *Bibliotheca di storica economica* 4 (1909), 7–103.

Cipolla, C. M. *The Economic History of World Population.* 7th ed. Harmondsworth, 1978.

——, ed. *The Middle Ages.* Vol. 1. London, 1972.

Clack, P. A. G. "The Northern Frontier: Farmers in the Military Zone." In *The Romano-British Countryside: Studies in Rural Settlement and Economy,* edited by David Miles, 377–402. Oxford, 1982.

Clack, P. A. G., and Susanne Haselgrove, eds. *Rural Settlement in the Roman North.* Durham, 1982.

Clarke, G. "The Invasion Hypothesis in British Prehistory." *Antiquity* 40 (1966), 172–89.

Clarkson, Leslie. *Death, Disease, and Famine in Pre-Industrial England.* New York, 1976.

Cockburn, T. A. "Infectious Diseases in Ancient Populations." *Current Anthropology* 12 (1971), 45–62.

Collingwood, R. G. "Town and Country in Roman Britain." *Antiquity* 3 (1929), 261–76.

Collingwood, R. G., and J. N. L. Myres. *Roman Britain and the English Settlements.* 2d ed. Oxford, 1937.

Collins, D., ed. *The Origins of Europe.* New York, 1976.

Collins, R. *Early Medieval Spain: Unity in Diversity.* London, 1983.

——. "Theodebert I, *Rex Magnus Francorum.*" In *Ideal and Reality in Frankish and Anglo-Saxon Society: Studies Presented to J. M. Wallace-Hadrill,* edited by Patrick Wormald, Donald Bullough, and Roger Collins, 7–33. Oxford, 1983.

Collis, J. R., ed. *The Iron Age in Britain—A Review.* Sheffield, 1977.

Copley, Gordon. *Archaeology and Place-Names in the Fifth and Sixth Centuries.* British Archaeological Report 147. Oxford, 1986.

Cornwall, J. "English Country Towns in the Fifteen-Twenties." *Economic History Review,* 2d ser., 15 (1962–63), 54–69.

Coster, C. H. *Late Roman Studies.* Cambridge, Mass., 1968.

Courtois, C. *Les Vandales et l'Afrique.* Paris, 1955.

——. *Victor de Vita et son oeuvre.* Algiers, 1954.

Coville, Alfred. *Recherches sur l'histoire de Lyon du Ve au IXe siècle.* Paris, 1928.

Crawford, O. G. S. *Air Photography for Archaeologists.* London, 1929.

Crumlin-Pedersen, Ole. "Boats and Ships of the Angles and Jutes." In *Maritime Celts, Frisians, and Saxons*, edited by Séan McGrail, 98–116. London, 1990.
——. "Gredstedbroskibet." In *Mark og Montre, fra Sydvestjyske Museum*, 11–15. Århus, Denmark, 1967.
——. "The Viking Ships of Roskilde." *Maritime Monographs and Reports* 1 (1970), 7–23.
Cunliffe, Barry. "Excavations at the Roman Fort at Lympne." *Britannia* 11 (1980), 37–54.
——. "Images of Britannia." *Antiquity* 58 (1984), 175–78.
——. "Settlement and Population in the British Iron Age: Some Facts, Figures, and Fantasies." In *Lowland Iron Age Communities in Europe*, edited by Barry Cunliffe and T. Rowley, 3–24. Oxford, 1978.
——. "The Somerset Levels in the Roman Period." In *Rural Settlement in Roman Britain*, edited by Charles Thomas, 68–73. London, 1966.
Cunliffe, Barry, and T. Rowley, eds. *Lowland Iron Age Communities in Europe*. British Archaeological Reports S 48. Oxford, 1978.
Dahn, F. *Die Könige der Germanen*. Vol. 6. Leipzig, 1885.
Dansgaard, W., H. B. Clausen, N. Gundestrup, C. U. Hammer, S. F. Johnsen, P. M. Kristinsdottir, and N. Reeh. "A New Greenland Deep Ice Core," *Science* 218 (1982), 1273–77.
Dansgaard, W., and S. J. Johnsen. "A Flow Model and a Time Scale for the Ice Core from Camp Century, Greenland." *Journal of Glaciology* 8 (1969), 215–23.
Dansgaard, W., S. J. Johnsen, J. Moller, and C. C. Langway. "One Thousand Centuries of Climatic Record from Camp Century on the Greenland Ice Sheet." *Science* 166 (1969), 377–81.
Dansgaard, W., S. J. Johnsen, N. Reeh, N. Gundestrup, H. B. Clausen, and C. U. Hammer. "Climatic Changes, Norsemen, and Modern Man." *Nature* 255 (1975), 24–28.
Dark, K. R. "A Sub-Roman Re-Defence of Hadrian's Wall?" *Britannia* 23 (1992), 111–20.
Davies, G., and J. Turner. "Pollen Diagrams from Northumberland." *New Phytologist* 82 (1979), 783–804.
Davies, R. W. "The Roman Military Diet." *Britannia* 2 (1971), 122–42.
Davies, W. "Roman Settlements and Post-Roman Estates in South-east Wales." In *The End of Roman Britain*, edited by P. J. Casey, 153–73. Oxford, 1979.
——. *Wales in the Early Middle Ages*. Leicester, 1982.
Davies, W., and H. Vierck. "The Contexts of the Tribal Hidage: Social Aggregates and Settlement Patterns." *Frühmittelalterliche Studien* 8 (1974), 223–93.
Davis, K. R. *Britons and Saxons: The Chiltern Region, A.D. 400–700*. Chichester, 1982.
Davis, R. H. C. "Did the Anglo-Saxons Have Warhorses?" In *Weapons and Warfare in Anglo-Saxon England*, edited by Sonia C. Hawkes, 141–44. Oxford, 1989.
Davis, R. W. "Some Roman Medicine." *Medical History* 14 (1970), 101–6.
de Jonnès, Moreau. *Statistique des peuples de l'antiquité*. Paris, 1851.
de la Malle, Dureau. *Économie politique de Romains*. 2 vols. Paris, 1840.
Delbrück, Hans. *Geschichte der Kriegskunst im Rahmen der politischen Geschichte*. 3 vols. 3d ed. Berlin, 1921. Translated by Walter J. Renfroe, Jr. *History of the Art of War*. Westport, 1980.

——. *Numbers in History.* London, 1914.
Deleage, A. *La capitation du Bas-Empire.* Paris, 1945.
Delibrias, G., M. Ladurie, and E. L. Ladurie. "Le forêt fossil de Grindelwald: nouvelles datations." *Annales: Économies, sociétés, civilisations,* n.s., 30 (1975), 137–47.
de Plinval, Georges. "Les campagnes de Saint-Germain en Bretagne contre les Pélagiens." In *Saint-Germain et son temps, XVe centenaire de la mort de Saint-Germain.* Association bourguignonne, 135–49. Auxerre, 1950.
DeVoy, Robert J. N. "Controls on Coastal and Sea-Level Changes and the Application of Archaeological-Historical Records to Understanding Recent Patterns of Sea-Level Movement." In *Maritime Celts, Frisians, and Saxons,* edited by Seán McGrail, 17–26. London, 1990.
Dickinson, Tania. "The Present State of Anglo-Saxon Cemetery Studies." In *Anglo-Saxon Cemeteries, 1979,* edited by P. Rahtz, T. Dickinson, and L. Watts, 11–33. Oxford, 1980.
Dickinson, W. "Recurrence Surfaces in Rusland Moss, Cumbria (Formerly North Lancashire)." *Journal of Ecology* 63 (1975), 913–35.
Dill, S. *Roman Society from Nero to Marcus Aurelius.* London, 1926.
——. *Roman Society in Gaul in the Merovingian Age.* London, 1904.
——. *Roman Society in the Last Century of the Western Empire.* London, 1926.
Dimbleby, G. *Plants and Archaeology.* 2d ed. London, 1979.
Dixon, Philip. *Barbarian Europe.* Oxford, 1976.
——. "A Continent in Ferment." In *The Making of Britain: The Dark Ages,* edited by Lesley M. Smith, 7–20. London, 1984.
——. "How Saxon Is the Saxon House?" In *Structural Reconstruction,* ed. P. J. Drury, 275–88. Oxford, 1982.
Dockès, P. "Révoltes bagaudes et ensauvagement." In *Sauvages et ensauvagés,* edited by P. Dockès and J. M. Servet, 143–262. Lyon, 1980.
Dockès, P., and J. M. Servet. *Sauvages et ensauvagés.* Lyon, 1980.
Dodgshon, R. A. *The Origin of British Field Systems: An Interpretation.* London, 1980.
Donat, P., and H. Ullrich. "Einwohnerzahlen und Siedlungsgrösse der Merovingerzeit." *Zeitschrift für Archäologie* 5 (1971), 234ff.
Downey, Glanville. *The Late Roman Empire.* New York, 1969.
Drew, Katherine F. "Another Look at the Origins of the Middle Ages: A Reassessment of the Role of the Germanic Kingdoms." *Speculum* 62 (1987), 803–12.
——, ed. *The Barbarian Invasions: A Catalyst of a New Order.* 1970. Reprint, Huntington, N.Y., 1977.
Drinkwater, John F. "The Bacaudae of Fifth-Century Gaul." In *Fifth-Century Gaul: A Crisis of Identity?* edited by John F. Drinkwater and Hugh Elton, 208–17. Cambridge, 1992.
——. *The Gallic Empire: Separation and Continuity in the North-Western Provinces of the Roman Empire.* Stuttgart, 1987.
——. *Roman Gaul.* London, 1983.
Drinkwater, John F., and Hugh Elton, eds. *Fifth-Century Gaul: A Crisis of Identity?* Cambridge, 1992.
Driscoll, Stephen T., and Margaret R. Nieke, eds. *Power and Politics in Early Medieval Britain and Ireland.* Edinburgh, 1988.

Drummond, J. C., and A. Wilbraham. *The Englishman's Food: A History of Five Centuries of English Diet.* London, 1958.

Drury, P. J., ed. *Structural Reconstruction: Approaches to the Interpretation of the Excavated Remains of Buildings.* BAR BS 110. Oxford, 1982.

Dumville, David. "The Chronology of *De Excidio*, Book I." In *Gildas: New Approaches,* edited by M. Lapidge and D. Dumville, 61–84. Woodbridge, 1984.

——. "Gildas and Maelgwn: Problems of Dating." In *Gildas: New Approaches,* edited by M. Lapidge and D. Dumville, 51–59. Woodbridge, 1984.

——. *The "Historia Brittonum": The Vatican Recension.* Cambridge, 1985.

——. "The Historical Value of the *Historia Brittonum*" *Arthurian Literature* 6 (1986), 1–26.

——. "'Nennius' and the *Historia Brittonum.*" *Studia Celtica* 10–11 (1975–76), 78–95.

——. "On the North British Section of the *Historia Brittonum.*" *Welsh History Review* 8 (1977), 345–54.

——. "Sub-Roman Britain: History and Legend." *History,* n.s., 62 (1977), 173–92.

——. "The Tribal Hidage: An Introduction to Its Texts and Their History." In *The Origins of Anglo-Saxon Kingdoms,* edited by Steven Basset, 225–30. Leicester, 1989.

——. "The West-Saxon Genealogical Regnal List and the Chronology of Early Wessex." *Peritia* 4 (1985), 21–66.

Dumville, David N., et al. *Saint Patrick A.D. 493–1993.* Woodbridge, 1993.

Duncan-Jones, R. P. "City Population in Roman Africa." *Journal of Roman Studies* 53 (1963), 85–100.

——. *The Economy of the Roman Empire.* 2d ed. Cambridge, 1982.

Duplessy, Jean-Claude. "Isotope Studies." In *Climatic Change,* edited by John Gribbin, 46–67. Cambridge, 1978.

Dyson, S. L. "Native Revolts in the Roman Empire." *Historia* 20 (1971), 239–74.

Eagles, Bruce. "Anglo-Saxons in Lindsey and the East Riding of Yorkshire in the Fifth Century." In *Anglo-Saxon Cemeteries, 1979,* edited by P. Rahtz, T. Dickinson, and L. Watts, 285–87. Oxford, 1980.

Ebersolt, J. *Les cimetières burgondes du Doubs et du Jura à l'époque barbare.* Besançon, 1950.

Ellmers, Detlev. "The Frisian Monopoly of Coastal Transport in the 6th–8th Centuries A.D." In *Maritime Celts, Frisians, and Saxons,* edited by Séan McGrail, 91–92. London, 1990.

——. *Frühmittelalterliche Handelsschiffahrt in Mittel und Nordeuropa.* Neumünster, 1972.

——. "Die Schiffe der Angelsachsen." *Sachsen und Angelsachsen, Veröffenlichungen des Helms-Museums* 32 (1978), 495–509.

Engelhardt, Conrad. *Nydam Mosefund.* Copenhagen, 1865.

Esmonde Cleary, A. S. *The Ending of Roman Britain.* London, 1989.

Evans, Angela C. "The Clinker-Built Boats of the North Sea, 300–1000 A.D." In *The North Sea,* edited by Arne Bang-Andersen, Basil Greenhill, and Egil Harald Grude, 63–78. Oslo, 1985.

Evans, Angela C., and Rupert Bruce-Mitford. "The Ship." In *The Sutton Hoo Ship Burial,* edited by Rupert Bruce-Mitford, 1:345–435. London, 1975.

Evans, Jeremy. "From the End of Roman Britain to the 'Celtic West.'" *Oxford Journal of Archaeology* 9 (1990), 91–103.

Evans, J. G. *The Environment of Early Man in the British Isles.* London, 1975.

Evans, J. G., Susan Limbrey, and Henry Cleere, eds. *The Effect of Man on the Landscape: The Highland Zone.* CBA Research Report 11. London, 1975.

Evans, J. K. "Wheat Production and Its Social Consequences in the Roman World." *Classical Quarterly,* n.s., 31 (1981), 428–42.

Everand, C. E. "Southern Britain: An Unstable Crust and Changing Sea Level." Paper presented in October 1977 at a Society of Antiquaries conference on "Archaeology and Coastal Change in Southern Britain." London, 1977.

Everitt, Alan. *Continuity and Colonization: The Evolution of Kentish Settlement.* Leicester, 1987.

Evison, Vera I. "Distribution Maps and England in the First Two Phases." In *Angles, Saxons, and Jutes,* edited by Vera I. Evison, 126–67. Oxford, 1981.

——. *Dover: The Buckland and Anglo-Saxon Cemetery.* London, 1987.

——, ed. *Angles, Saxons, and Jutes.* Oxford, 1981.

Faral, Edmond. *La légende arthurienne: Études et documents.* Vol. 3. Paris, 1929.

Farrell, A. W. "Mast and Sail in Scandinavia in the Bronze Age." *Mariner's Mirror* 63 (1977), 190; 65 (1979), 83.

Faull, M. L. "British Survival in Anglo-Saxon Northumbria." In *Studies in Celtic Survival,* edited by L. Laing, 1–55. Oxford, 1977.

——. "Roman and Anglian Settlement Patterns in Yorkshire." *Northern History* 9 (1974), 6–25.

——. "The Semantic Development of Old English *Wealh.*" *Leeds Studies in English* 8 (1975), 20–37.

——, ed. *Studies in Late Anglo-Saxon Settlement.* Oxford, 1984.

Fenwick, V. *The Graveney Boat.* British Archaeological Report 53. Prepared for publication by Ann Morlen. Oxford, 1978.

Ferrill, Arther. *The Fall of the Roman Empire: The Military Explanation.* New York, 1986.

Filmer-Sankey, W. "A New Boat Burial from the Snape Anglo-Saxon Cemetery, Suffolk." In *Maritime Celts, Frisians, and Saxons,* edited by Séan McGrail, 126–34. London, 1990.

Finberg, H. P. R. "English Society in the Seventh Century." In *The Agrarian History of England and Wales,* edited by H. P. R. Finberg, vol. 1, pt. 2, 430–48. Cambridge, 1972.

——. *Roman and Saxon Withington: A Study in Continuity.* Leicester, 1955.

——, ed. *The Agrarian History of England and Wales.* Vol. 1, Pt. 2. Cambridge, 1972.

Finley, Moses I. *The Ancient Economy.* Berkeley, 1973.

——. Review of *Manpower Shortage and the Fall of the Roman Empire in the West,* by A. E. R. Boak. *Journal of Roman Studies* 48 (1958), 156–64.

Fisher, D. J. V. *The Anglo-Saxon Age c. 400–1042.* London, 1973.

Fitzgerald, C. P. "A New Estimate of the Chinese Population under the T'ang Dynasty in 618 A.D." *The China Journal* 16 (1932), 5–14.

Fletcher, R. H. *The Arthurian Material in the Chronicles.* Ed. R. S. Loomis. 2d ed. New York, 1966.

Flinn, L. B. "Reflections on the Relationship of Climatology to Medicine." *Transactions of the American Clinical and Climatological Association* 79 (1968), 146–56.

Foard, G. "The Administrative Organization of Northhamptonshire in the Saxon Period." *Anglo-Saxon Studies in Archaeology and History* 4 (1985), 185–222.

Food and Agriculture Organization. *Production Year Books.* Vols. 5–27. Rome, 1951–73.

Foord, Edward. *The Last Age of Roman Britain.* London, 1925.

Foote, Peter. "Wrecks and Rhymes." In *The Vikings*, edited by T. Andersson and K. I. Sandred, 57–66. Uppsala, 1978.

Forster, R., and P. Ranum, eds. *The Biology of Man in History: Selections from the Annals, Economies, Societies, Civilizations.* Baltimore, 1975.

Fowler, Elizabeth, ed. *Field Survey in British Archaeology.* London, 1971.

Fowler, P. J. *The Farming of Prehistoric Britain.* Cambridge, 1983.

——, ed. *Recent Work in Rural Archaeology.* Bradford-on-Avon, 1975.

Fox, Cyril. *The Personality of Britain: Its Influence on Inhabitant and Invader in Prehistoric and Early Historic Times.* 4th ed. Cardiff, 1943.

Frank, Tenney. *Roman Imperialism.* New York, 1914.

Freeman, E. A. "The Tyrants of Britain, Gaul, and Spain, A.D. 406–411." *English Historical Review* 1 (1886), 53–85.

——. *Western Europe in the Fifth Century.* London, 1904.

Frend, W. H. C. "Ecclesia Britannica: Prelude or Dead End?" *Journal of Ecclesiastical History* 30 (1979), 129–44.

——. "Pagans, Christians, and 'the Barbarian Conspiracy' of A.D. 367 in Roman Britain." *Britannia* 23 (1992), 121–31.

——. "Religion in Roman Britain in the Fourth Century." *Journal of the British Archaeological Association*, 3d ser., 18 (1955), 1–18.

——. "Romano-British Christianity: Comparison and Contrast." In *The Early Church in Western Britain and Ireland*, edited by S. M. Pearce, 5–16. Oxford, 1982.

Frenzel, B. "The Distribution Pattern of Holocene Climatic Change in the Northern Hemisphere." In *World Meteorological Organization Symposium on Long-Term Climatic Fluctuations*, 105–18. Geneva, 1975.

Frere, Sheppard. *Britannia: A History of Roman Britain.* 3d ed. London, 1987.

——. "Civitas—A Myth?" *Antiquity* 35 (1961), 29–36.

Fries, Udo, and Martin Heusser, eds. *Meaning and Beyond: Ernst Leisi zum 70. Geburtstag.* Tübingen, 1989.

Fulford, Michael. "Demonstrating Britannia's Economic Dependence in the First and Second Centuries." In *Military and Civilian in Roman Britain: Cultural Relationships in a Frontier Province*, edited by T. F. C. Blagg and A. C. King, 129–42. Oxford, 1984.

Garnsey, Peter. "Aspects of the Decline of the Urban Aristocracy in the Empire." *Aufstieg und Niedergang der römischen Welt, Part II: Principat, vol. 1* (1974), 229–51.

——. *Famine and Food Supply in the Graeco-Roman World.* Cambridge, 1988.

——. "Grain for Rome." In *Trade in the Ancient Economy*, edited by Peter Garnsey et al., 118–30. London, 1983.

Garnsey, Peter, K. Hopkins, and G. R. Whittaker, eds. *Trade in the Ancient Economy*. London, 1983.

Garnsey, Peter, and R. Saller. *The Roman Empire: Economy, Society, and Culture*. London, 1987.

Geary, Patrick J. *Before France and Germany*. Oxford, 1988.

Gelling, Margaret. "Towards a Chronology for English Place-Names." In *Anglo-Saxon Settlement*, edited by Della Hooke, 59–76. Oxford, 1988.

Gentry, Anne P. *Roman Military Stone-Built Granaries in Britain*. British Archaeological Report 32. Oxford, 1976.

Genzmer, F. *Germanische Seefahrt und Seegeltung*. Munich, 1944.

Gibbon, Edward. *The History of the Decline and Fall of the Roman Empire*. Edited by J. B. Bury. 7 vols. London, 1909–14.

Gillam, J. P. "Romano-Saxon Pottery: An Alternative Interpretation." In *The End of Roman Britain*, edited by P. J. Casey, 103–18. Oxford, 1979.

Gilliam, J. F. "The Plague under Marcus Aurelius." *American Journal of Philology* 82 (1961), 225–51.

Glare, P. W., ed. *Oxford Latin Dictionary*. Oxford, 1982.

Glass, D. V. and D. E. C. Eversley, eds. *Population in History*. London, 1965.

Glob, P. V. *Rock Carvings in Denmark*. Jutland Archaeological Society Publication 7. Copenhagen, 1969.

Glover, T. R. *Life and Letters in the Fourth Century*. Cambridge, 1901.

Godwin, Sir Harry. *The Archives of the Peat Bogs*. Cambridge, 1981.

——. *Fenland: Its Ancient Past and Uncertain Future*. Cambridge, 1978.

——. *The History of British Flora*. Cambridge, 1956.

Goffart, Walter. *Barbarians and Romans, A.D. 418–584: The Techniques of Accommodation*. Princeton, 1980.

Goldstone, Jack A. *Revolution and Rebellion in the Early Modern World*. Berkeley, 1991.

Goodburn, R., and P. Bartholomew, eds. *Aspects of the "Notitia Dignitatum."* British Archaeological Report S 15. Oxford, 1976.

Goodchild, R. G. "T-Shaped Corn-Drying Ovens in Roman Britain." *Antiquaries Journal* 23 (1943), 148–53.

Granlund, E. "De Svenska hogmössarnas geologi." *Sveriges Geologiska Undersoekning* 26 (1932), 1–193.

Gransden, Antonia. *Historical Writing in England c. 550–c. 1307*. Ithaca, 1974.

Grant, Michael. *The Climax of Rome*. London, 1974.

——. *The Fall of the Roman Empire*. rev. ed. New York, 1990.

——. *The Roman Emperors*. New York, 1985.

Green, C. S. *Excavations at Poundbury*. Vol. 1, *The Settlement*. Dorchester, 1988.

Green, Charles. "East Anglian Coast-Line Levels since Roman Times." *Antiquity* 35 (1961), 21–27.

——. *Sutton Hoo: The Excavation of a Royal Ship Burial*. London, 1963.

Green, M. J. *A Corpus of Religious Material from the Civilian Areas of Roman Britain*. British Archaeological Report 24. Oxford, 1976.

Greene, Kevin. *The Archaeology of the Roman Economy*. Berkeley, 1986.

Greene, L. S., ed. *Malnutrition, Behavior, and Social Organization*. New York, 1977.

Greenhill, Basil. *Archaeology of the Boat: A New Introductory Study.* London, 1976.

Gregory, T. E. *Vox Populi: Popular Opinion and Violence in the Religious Controversies of the Fifth Century* A.D. Columbus, Ohio, 1979.

Gribbin, John, ed. *Climatic Change.* Cambridge, 1978.

Gribbin, John, and H. H. Lamb. "Climatic Change in Historical Times." In *Climatic Change,* edited by John Gribbin, 68–82. Cambridge, 1978.

Grigg, D. B. "Ester Boserup's Theory of Agrarian Change." *Progress in Human Geography* 3 (1979), 64–84.

——. "Population Pressure and Agricultural Change." *Progress in Geography* 8 (1976), 133–76.

Grimes, W. F., ed. *Aspects of Archaeology in Britain and Beyond: Essays Presented to O. G. S. Crawford.* London, 1951.

Groenman-van Waateringe, W. "The Disastrous Effect of the Roman Occupation." In *Roman and Native in the Low Countries: Spheres of Interaction,* edited by Roel Brandt and Jan Slofstra, 147–57. Oxford, 1983.

Grosjean, P. "La bible de 'Gildas.'" *Analecta Bollandiana* 75 (1957), 203–6.

——. "Dominicati Rhetorici." *Archivum Latinitatis Medii Aevi* 25 (1955), 41–46.

——. "Les Pictes apostats dans l'épître de S. Patrice." *Analecta Bollandiana* 76 (1958), 354–78.

Guichard, R. *Essai sur l'histoire du peuple burgonde.* Paris, 1965.

Gwynn, E. J. *The Book of Armagh: The Patrician Documents.* Dublin, 1937.

Haarnagel, Werner. "Die Ergebnisse der Grabung Feddersen Wierde im Jahre 1961." *Germania* 41 (1963), 280ff.

Hachmann, Rolf. *The Germanic Peoples.* Translated by J. Hogarth. London, 1971.

Hall, A. "Population of Roman Britain." *Notes and Queries,* ser. 8, 8 (1895), 148.

Hall, Roberta L. "A Test of Palaeodemographic Models." *American Antiquity* 43 (1978), 715–29.

Hallam, S. "Wash Coast-Levels since Roman Times." *Antiquity* 35 (1961), 152–56.

Halpen, L. *Les Barbares, de grandes invasions aux conquêtes Turques du XI siècle.* Paris, 1930.

Hammond, N. G. L., and H. H. Scullard, eds. *The Oxford Classical Dictionary.* 2d ed. Oxford, 1970.

Hannestad, Knud. "Les forces militaires d'après la guerre gothique de Procope." *Classica et Mediaevalia* 21 (1960), 136–83.

Hanning, R. W. *The Vision of History in Early Britain: From Gildas to Geoffrey of Monmouth.* New York, 1966.

Hanson, R. P. C. "The Date of St. Patrick." *Bulletin of the John Rylands University Library* 61 (1978), 60–77.

——. *The Life and Writings of the Historical Saint Patrick.* New York, 1983.

——. "The Reaction of the Church to the Collapse of the Western Roman Empire in the Fifth Century." *Vigiliae Christianae* 26 (1972), 272–87.

——. *Saint Patrick, His Origins and Career.* Oxford, 1968.

Hanson, W. S., and L. J. F. Keppie, eds. *Roman Frontier Studies 1979.* British Archaeological Report S 71. Oxford, 1980.

Harding, A. F., ed. *Climatic Change in Later Prehistory.* Edinburgh, 1982.

——. "Introduction: Climatic Change and Archaeology." In *Climatic Change in Later Prehistory,* edited by A. F. Harding, 1–10. Edinburgh, 1982.

Hardy, E. M. "Studies of the Post-Glacial History of Vegetation v: The Shropshire and Flint Maelor Mosses." *New Phytologist* 38 (1939), 364–96.

Härke, Heinrich. "Changing Symbols in a Changing Society: The Anglo-Saxon Weapon Burial Rite in the Seventh Century." In *The Age of Sutton Hoo*, edited by M. O. H. Carver, 149–65. Woodbridge, 1992.

———. "Early Saxon Weapon Burials: Frequencies, Distributions, and Weapon Combinations." In *Weapons and Warfare in Anglo-Saxon England*, edited by Sonia C. Hawkes, 49–61. Oxford, 1989.

———. " 'Warrior Graves'? The Background of the Anglo-Saxon Weapon Burial Rite." *Past and Present* 26 (1990), 22–43.

Harris, E., and J. R. Harris. *The Oriental Cults in Roman Britain*. Leiden, 1965.

Harrison, Kenneth. *Framework of Anglo-Saxon History to A.D. 900.* Cambridge, 1976.

Hartley, Brian, and John Wacher, eds. *Rome and Her Northern Provinces.* London, 1983.

Hassal, M. W. C., and Robert Ireland, eds. *De Rebus Bellicis.* British Archaeological Report S 63. Oxford, 1979.

Haverfield, F. J. *The Romanization of Roman Britain.* 4th ed. Oxford, 1923.

Hawkes, C. F. C. *Britain and Julius Caesar.* London, 1978.

Hawkes, C. F. C., and G. C. Dunning. "The Belgae of Gaul and Britain." *Archaeological Journal* 87 (1930), 150–335.

Hawkes, Sonia C. "Some Recent Finds of Late Roman Buckles." *Britannia* 5 (1974), 386–93.

———. "The South-East after the Romans: The Saxon Settlement." In *The Saxon Shore*, edited by Valerie A. Maxfield, 78–95. Exeter, 1989.

———. *Weapons and Warfare in Anglo-Saxon England.* Oxford, 1989.

Hawkes, Sonia C., and G. C. Dunning. "Soldiers and Settlers in Britain, Fourth to Fifth Century." *Medieval Archaeology* 5 (1961), 1–70.

Hayes, P. P. "Roman to Saxon in the South Lincolnshire Fens." *Antiquity* 62 (1988), 321–26.

Haywood, John. *Dark Age Naval Power.* London, 1991.

Heather, Peter. *Goths and Romans, 332–489.* Oxford, 1991.

Hedeager, Lotte. "Kingdoms, Ethnicity, and Material Culture: Denmark in a European Perspective." In *The Age of Sutton Hoo*, edited by M. O. H. Carver, 279–300. Woodbridge, 1992.

Henig, Martin. "Religion in Roman Britain." In *Research on Roman Britain*, edited by Malcolm Todd, 219–34. London, 1989

Herren, Michael W. "Gildas and Early British Monasticism." In *Britain 400–600: Language and History*, edited by Alfred Bammesberger and Alfred Wollman, 65–78. Heidelberg, 1990.

Higham, N. J. "Continuity Studies in the First Millenium A.D. in North Cumbria." *Northern History* 14 (1978), 1–18.

———. *The Northern Counties to A.D. 1000.* London, 1986.

———. "The Roman Impact upon Rural Settlement in Cumbria." In *Rural Settlement in the Roman North*, edited by Peter Clack and Susanne Haselgrove, 105–22. Durham, 1982.

———. *Rome, Britain, and the Anglo-Saxons.* London, 1992.

Higham, N. J., and G. D. B. Jones. "Frontiers, Forts, and Farmers: Cumbrian Aerial Survey 1974–75." *Archaeological Journal* 132 (1975), 16–53.

Hills, Catherine. "Anglo-Saxon Cremation Cemeteries, with Particular Reference to Spong Hill, Norfolk." In *Anglo-Saxon Cemeteries, 1979*, edited by P. Rahtz, T. Dickinson, and L. Watts, 197–207. Oxford, 1980.

——. "The Archaeology of Anglo-Saxon England in the Pagan Period: A Review." *Anglo-Saxon England* 8 (1979), 297–329.

——. "Roman Britain to Anglo-Saxon England." *History Today* 40 (1990), 46–52.

——. *Spong Hill: Part III: Catalogue of Inhumations.* East Anglian Archaeology 21. Gressenhall, 1984.

Hills, Catherine, K. Penn, and R. Rickett. *The Anglo-Saxon Cemetery at Spong Hill, North Elmham: Part IV: Catalogue of Cremations.* East Anglian Archaeology 34. Gressenhall, 1987.

Hind, J. G. F. "The British Province of Valentia and Orcades." *Historia* 24 (1975), 101–11.

——. "Litus Saxonicum—The Meaning of 'Saxon Shore'." In *Roman Frontier Studies 1979*, edited by W. S. Hanson and L. J. F. Keppie, 317–24. Oxford, 1980.

——. "Who Betrayed Britain to the Barbarians in A.D. 367?" *Northern History* 19 (1983), 1–7.

Hines, John. "The Military Context of the *Adventus Saxonum:* Some Continental Evidence." In *Weapons and Warfare in Anglo-Saxon England*, edited by Sonia C. Hawkes, 25–48. Oxford, 1989.

——. "Philology, Archaeology, and the *Adventus Saxonum vel Anglorum.*" In *Britain 400–600: Language and History*, edited by Alfred Bammesberger and Alfred Wollman, 17–36. Heidelberg, 1990.

——. *The Scandinavian Character of Anglian England in the Pre-Viking Period.* British Archaeological Report 124. Oxford, 1984.

Hinton, David A. *Archaeology, Economy, and Society: England from the Fifth to the Fifteenth Century.* London, 1990.

Hirst, Susan. "Some aspects of the Analysis and Publication of an Inhumation Cemetery." In *Anglo-Saxon Cemeteries, 1979*, edited by P. Rahtz, T. Dickinson, and L. Watts, 239–52. Oxford, 1980.

Hoare, F. R., trans. *The Western Fathers.* New York, 1954.

Hodder, I., and M. Hassall. "The Non-Random Spacing of Romano-British Walled Towns." *Man* 6 (1971), 391–407.

Hodges, Richard. *The Anglo-Saxon Achievement.* Ithaca, 1989.

——. *Dark Age Economics: The Origins of Towns and Trade, A.D. 600–1000.* New York, 1982.

Hodges, Richard, and David Whitehouse. *Mohammed, Charlemagne, and the Origins of Europe.* London, 1983.

Hodgkin, Thomas. *Italy and Her Invaders.* New York, 1885.

Hollingsworth, T. H. *Historical Demography.* Cambridge, 1976.

Hope-Taylor, Brian. *Yeavering: An Anglo-British Centre of Early Northumbria.* London, 1977.

Hopkins, Keith. *Conquerors and Slaves.* Cambridge, 1978.

——. "Taxes and Trade in the Roman Empire (200 B.C.–A.D. 400)." *Journal of Roman Studies* 70 (1980), 101–25.

Hornus, J. *It Is Not Lawful for Me to Fight: Early Christian Attitudes toward War, Violence, and the State.* Scottdale, Pa., 1980.

Howe, Nicholas. *Migration and Mythmaking in Anglo-Saxon England.* New Haven, 1989.

Howells, William W. "Estimating Population Numbers through Archaeological and Skeletal Remains." In *The Applications of Quantitative Methods in Archaeology,* edited by R. F. Heizer and S. F. Cook, 158–76. Viking Fund Publication in Anthropology 28. New York, 1960,

Hughes, Kathleen. "The A-Text of *Annales Cambriae.*" In *Celtic Britain in the Early Middle Ages,* 86–100. Woodbridge, 1980.

———. *Celtic Britain in the Early Middle Ages: Studies in Scottish and Welsh Sources.* Woodbridge, 1980.

———. "The Welsh Latin Chronicles: *Annales Cambriae* and Related Texts." In *Celtic Britain in the Early Middle Ages,* 67–85. Woodbridge, 1980.

Hume, D. "Of the Populousness of Ancient Nations." In *Essays: Moral, Political, and Literary,* edited by T. H. Green, 381–443. London, 1875.

Huntington, Ellsworth. *Civilization and Climate.* London, 1915.

———. "Climatic Change and Agricultural Exhaustion as Elements in the Fall of Rome." *Quarterly Journal of Economics* 31 (1917), 173–208.

Ilkjaer, J. and V. Lønstrup, V. "Interpretation of the Great Votive Deposits of Iron Age Weapons." *Journal of Danish Archaeology* 1 (1982), 95–103.

Jackson, Kenneth H. *Language and History in Early Britain: A Chronological Survey of the Brittonic Languages.* Edinburgh, 1953.

———. "Nennius and the Twenty-Eight Cities of Britain." *Antiquity* 12 (1938), 44–55.

———. "On the Northern British Section in Nennius." In *Celt and Saxon: Studies in the Early British Border,* edited by N. K. Chadwick, 20–62. Cambridge, 1964.

James, Edward. "Cemeteries and the Problem of Frankish Settlement in Gaul." In *Names, Words, and Graves: Early Medieval Settlement,* edited by P. H. Sawyer, 55–89. Leeds, 1979.

———. "Interpreting Gildas." *Nottingham Medieval Studies* 12 (1986), 101–5.

———. *The Merovingian Archaeology of Southwest Gaul.* 2 vols. British Archaeological Report S 25. Oxford, 1977.

———. "Merovingian Cemetery Studies, and some Implications for Anglo-Saxon England." In *Anglo-Saxon Cemeteries, 1979,* edited by P. Rahtz, T. Dickinson, and L. Watts, 35–55. Oxford, 1980.

———. "The Origins of Barbarian Kingdoms: The Continental Evidence." In *The Origin of Anglo-Saxon Kingdoms,* edited by S. Basset, 40–52. Leicester, 1989.

James, S., A. Marshall, and M. Millet. "An Early Medieval Building Tradition." *Archaeological Journal* 141 (1984), 182–215.

James, Simon T. "Britain and the Late Roman Army." In *Military and Civilian in Roman Britain: Cultural Relationships in a Frontier Province,* edited by T. F. C. Blagg and A. C. King, 161–86. Oxford, 1984.

Jarrett, Michael G. "Magnus Maximus and the End of Roman Britain." *Transactions of the Honourable Society of Cymmrodorion* (1983), 422–35.

Jarrett, Michael G., and Brian Dobson, eds. *Britain and Rome: Studies Presented to Eric Birley.* Kendal, 1966.

Jelgersma, S., J. De Jong, W. H. Zagwin, and J. F. van Regteren Altena. *The Coastal Dunes of the Western Netherlands: Geology, Vegetational History, and Archaeology.* Meddedelingen Rijks Geologische Dienst n.s. no. 21. Maastricht, 1970.

Jobey, George. "Homesteads and Settlements of the Frontier Area." In *Rural Settlement in Roman Britain,* edited by Charles Thomas, 1–14. London, 1966.

———. "Notes on Some Population Problems in the Area between the Two Walls." *Archaeologia Aeliana,* 5th ser., 2 (1974), 17–26.

Johnson, C. G., and L. P. Smith, eds. *The Biological Significance of Climatic Changes in Britain.* London, 1965.

Johnson, Stephen. *Hadrian's Wall.* London, 1989.

———. *Later Roman Britain.* London, 1980.

———. *The Roman Forts of the Saxon Shore.* London, 1976.

Johnston, C. "Ausonius, Fourth-Century Poet." *History Today* 25 (1975), 390–400.

Johnston, D. E. *The Saxon Shore.* London, 1977.

Johnstone, Paul. *The Sea-Craft of Prehistory.* London, 1980.

Jolliffe, J. E. A. "Northumbrian Institutions." *English Historical Review* 41 (1926), 1–42.

———. *Pre-Feudal England: The Jutes.* Oxford, 1933.

Jones, A. H. M. "The Date and Value of the Verona List." *Journal of Roman Studies* 44 (1954), 21–29.

———. *The Decline of the Ancient World.* London, 1966.

———. "Inflation under the Roman Empire." *Economic History Review* 5 (1953), 293–318.

———. *The Later Roman Empire.* 2 vols. Norman, Okla., 1964.

———. *The Roman Economy.* Oxford, 1974.

———. "Were Ancient Heresies National or Social Movements in Disguise?" *Journal of Theological Studies* 10 (1959), 280–98.

Jones, A. H. M., J. R. Martindale, and J. Morris, eds. *The Prosopography of the Later Roman Empire.* 2 vols. Cambridge, 1971–80.

Jones, E. L. *Seasons and Prices: The Role of Weather in English Agricultural History.* London, 1964.

Jones, G. D. B., and J. Walker. "Either Side of the Solway: Towards a Minimalist View of Romano-British Agricultural Settlement in the North-West." In *Settlement in North Britain 1000 B.C. to 1000 A.D.,* edited by J. Chapman and H. Mytum, 185–204. Oxford, 1983.

Jones, G. R. J. "Multiple Estates and Early Settlement." In *Medieval Settlement: Continuity and Change,* edited by P. H. Sawyer, 15–40. London, 1976.

Jones, M., and G. Dimbleby, eds. *The Environment of Man: The Iron Age to the Anglo-Saxon Period.* British Archaeological Reports BS 87. Oxford, 1981.

Jones, Martin. "Agriculture in Roman Britain: The Dynamics of Change." In *Research on Roman Britain 1960–89,* edited by Malcolm Todd, 127–34. London, 1989.

———. "Crop Production in Roman Britain." In *The Romano-British Countryside: Studies in Rural Settlement and Economy,* edited by David Miles, 97–107. Oxford, 1982.

———. "The Development of Crop Husbandry." In *The Environment of Man: The Iron Age to the Anglo-Saxon Period,* edited by M. Jones and G. Dimbleby, 95–127. Oxford, 1981.

Jones, Michael E. "The Appeal to Aetius in Gildas." *Nottingham Medieval Studies* 32 (1988), 141–55.

——. "Climate, Nutrition, and Disease: An Hypothesis of Romano-British Population." In *The End of Roman Britain*, edited by P. J. Casey, 231–51. British Archaeological Report 71. Oxford, 1979.

——. "The Failure of Romanization in Celtic Britain." *Proceedings of the Harvard Celtic Colloquium* 7 (1989), 126–45.

——. "The Historicity of the Alleluja Victory." *Albion* 18 (1986), 363–73.

——. "The Literary Evidence for Mast and Sail during the Anglo-Saxon Invasions." *Studies in Medieval and Renaissance History*, n.s., 13 (1992), 33–67.

——. Review of *Who Was Saint Patrick?* by E. A. Thompson. *Albion* 19 (1987), 209–10.

——. "Saint Germanus and the *Adventus Saxonum*." *Haskins Society Journal: Studies in Medieval History* 2 (1990), 1–11.

Jones, Michael E., and John Casey. "The Gallic Chronicle Restored: A Chronology for the Anglo-Saxon Invasions and the End of Roman Britain." *Britannia* 19 (1988), 367–98.

Jones, R. F. J. "A Quantitative Approach to Roman Burial." In *Burial in the Roman World*, edited by Richard Reece, 20–25. London, 1977.

Katz, Solomon. *The Decline of Rome and the Rise of Medieval Europe*. Ithaca, 1955.

Kemble, J. M. *The Saxons in England*. 2 vols. London, 1876.

Kenyon, J. P. *Stuart England*. Harmondsworth, 1978.

Kerlouégan, François. *Le "De Excidio Britanniae" de Gildas: Les destinées de la culture latine dans l'île de Bretagne au VIe siècle*. Paris, 1987.

——. "Le latin du *De Excidio Britanniae* de Gildas." In *Christianity in Britain, 300–700*, edited by M. W. Barley and R. P. C. Hanson, 151–76. Leicester, 1968.

Kershaw, I. "The Great Famine and Agrarian Crisis in England 1315–1322." *Past and Present* 59 (1973), 3–50.

Keys, A. B. *The Biology of Human Starvation*. Vol. 2. Minneapolis, 1950.

Keyser, Erich. *Bevölkerungsgeschichte Deutschlands*. 2d ed. Leipzig, 1941.

Kidd, D. S. W. "Some Questions of Method in the Study of Migration Period Pottery." In *Archäologische Beiträge zur Chronologie der Völkerwanderungszeit Antiquitas*, edited by G. Kossack and J. Reichstein, ser. 3, pt. 4, vol. 20, 93–102. Bonn, 1977.

King, Anthony, and Martin Henig, eds. *The Roman West in the Third Century*. British Archaeological Report S 109. Oxford, 1981.

King, M. H., and W. M. Stevens, eds. *Saints, Scholars, and Heroes: Studies in Medieval Culture*. 2 vols. Collegeville, Minn., 1979.

King, N. Q. "The Theodosian Code as a Source for the Religious Policies of the First Byzantine Emperors." *Nottingham Medieval Studies* 6 (1962), 12–17.

Kirby, D. P. "Bede's Native Sources for the *Historia Ecclesiastica*." *Bulletin of the John Rylands Library* 48 (1966), 341–71.

——. *The Earliest English Kings*. London, 1991.

——. "Problems of Early West Saxon History." *English Historical Review* 80 (1965), 10–29.

Kirsten, Ernst. *Raum und Bevölkerung in der Weltgeschichte*. Würzburg, 1968.

Knight, D. *Late Bronze Age and Iron Age Settlement in the Nene and Great Ouse Basins*. British Archaeological Report 130. Oxford, 1984.

Kolb, Eduard. "Schiff und Seefahrt im Beowulf und im Andreas." In *Meaning and Beyond: Ernst Leisi zum 70. Geburtstag*, edited by Udo Fries and Martin Heusser, 237–52. Tübingen, 1989.

Kossack, G., and J. Reichstein. *Archäologische Beiträge zur Chronologie der Völkerwanderungszeit Antiquitas*. Bonn, 1977.

Krause, J. T. "Some Implications of Recent Work in Historical Demography." *Comparative Studies in Society and History* 1 (1959), 114–18.

Laing, Lloyd, ed. *Studies in Celtic Survival*. British Archaeological Report 37. Oxford, 1977.

Laing, Lloyd, and Jennifer Laing. *Anglo-Saxon England*. Granada ed. London, 1982.

———. *Celtic Britain and Ireland 200–800: The Myth of the Dark Ages*. New York, 1990.

Laistner, M. L. W. *Thought and Letters in Western Europe, A.D. 500–900*. London, 1957.

Lamb, H. H. "An Approach to the Study of the Development of Climate and Its Impact in Human Affairs." In *Climate and History*, edited by T. M. L. Wigley, M. J. Ingram, and G. Farmer, 291–309. Cambridge, 1981.

———. *The Biological Significance of Climatic Changes in Britain*. London, 1965.

———. "Climate and Its Variability in the North Sea-Northeast Atlantic Region." In *The North Sea*, edited by Arne Bang-Anderson et al., 27–38. Oslo, 1985.

———. "Climate from 1000 B.C. to 1000 A.D." In *The Environment of Man: The Iron Age to the Anglo-Saxon Period*, edited by M. Jones and G. Dimbleby, 53–65. Oxford, 1981.

———. *Climate Present, Past, and Future*. London, 1977.

———. "Reconstruction of the Course of Postglacial Climate over the World." In *Climatic Change in Later Prehistory*, edited by A. F. Harding, 11–32. Edinburgh, 1982.

Lamb, H. H., and M. J. Ingram. "Climate and History." *Past and Present* 88 (1980), 136–41.

Landsberger, H. A., ed. *Rural Protest: Peasant Movements and Social Change*. London, 1974.

Lane Fox, R. *Pagans and Christians*. Harmondsworth, 1986.

Lapidge, Michael. "Gildas's Education and the Latin Culture of Sub-Roman Britain." In *Gildas: New Approaches*, edited by Michael Lapidge and David Dumville, 27–50. Woodbridge, 1984.

Lapidge, Michael, and D. Dumville, eds. *Gildas: New Approaches*. Woodbridge, 1984.

Lassen, A. "The Population of Denmark in 1660." *Scandinavian Economic History Review* 13 (1965), 1–30.

Latouche, R. "Aspects démographiques de la crise des grandes invasions." *Population* 2 (1947), 681–90.

Lebecq, Stéphane. *Marchands et navigateurs frisons du haut Moyen Age*. Vol. 1. Lille, 1983.

Leday, A. *La campagne à l'époque romaine dans le centre de la Gaule: Villas, vici et sanctuaires dans la cité des Bituriges Cubi*. British Archaeological Report S 73. Oxford, 1980.

Lee, N. E. "The Sutton Hoo Ship Burial in Sweden?" *Antiquity* 31 (1957), 40–41.

Lee, R. "Population in Pre-Industrial England: An Econometric Analysis." *Quarterly Journal of Economics* 87 (1973), 581–607.

Leech, Roger. "The Roman Interlude in the South-West: The Dynamics of Economics and Social Change in Romano-British South Somerset and North Dorset." In *The Romano-British Countryside: Studies in Rural Settlement and Economy*, edited by David Miles, 209–67. Oxford, 1982.

Leeds, E. T. *The Archaeology of the Anglo-Saxon Settlements*. Oxford, 1913.

Lennard, R. V. "The Character of the Anglo-Saxon Conquests: A Disputed Point." *History*, n.s., 18 (1933–34), 204–15.

Le Roy Ladurie, Emmanuel. *Times of Feast, Times of Famine: A History of Climate since the Year 1000*. Translated by B. Bray. London, 1972.

Levison, W. "Bede as Historian." In *Bede: His Life, Times, and Writing*, edited by A. Hamilton Thompson, 111–51. New York, 1966.

Lewis, Archibald R. *The Northern Seas: Shipping and Commerce in Northern Europe*. Princeton, 1958.

Lewis, Archibald R., and Timothy Runyan. *European Naval and Maritime History, 300–1500*. Bloomington, 1985.

Lewis, M. J. T. *Temples in Roman Britain*. Cambridge, 1966.

Lewis, N., and M. Reinhold, eds. *Roman Civilization Sourcebook. Vol. 2, The Empire*. New York, 1966.

Liebermann, F. *Die Gesetze der Angelsachsen*. 3 vols. Halle, 1903–16.

——. "Nennius the Author of the 'Historia Brittonum.'" In *Essays in Medieval History Presented to Thomas Frederick Tout*, edited by A. G. Little and F. M. Powicke, 25–44. Manchester, 1925.

Liebschuetz, W. "Did the Pelagian Movement Have Social Aims?" *Historia* 12 (1963), 227–41.

——. "Pelagian Evidence in the Last Period of Roman Britain." *Latomus* 26 (1967), 436–47.

Limbrey, Susan, and J. G. Evans, eds. *The Effect of Man on the Landscape: The Lowland Zone*. CBA Research Report 21. London, 1978.

Lindqvist, Sune. *Gotlands Bildsteine*. 2 vols. Stockholm, 1941–42.

Lindsay, W. M. *The Corpus, Épinal, Erfurt and Leyden Glossaries*. Oxford, 1921.

Liversidge, J. *Britain in the Roman Empire*. London, 1973.

Longley, D. "Hanging Bowls." In *Hanging Bowls, Penannular Brooches, and the Anglo-Saxon Connexion*, edited by D. Longley, 15–31. Oxford, 1975.

——, ed. *Hanging-Bowls, Penannular Brooches, and the Anglo-Saxon Connexion*. British Archaeological Reports 22. Oxford, 1975.

Lopez, R. S. "Le problème des relations anglo-byzantines du septième au dixième siècle." *Byzantion* 18 (1948), 139–62.

Lorren, Claude. "Early Medieval Cemeteries: Reflections of the Society of the Living?" Paper delivered at the 25th International Congress on Medieval Studies, May 10–13, 1990. Kalamazoo, Mich., 1990.

Losco-Bradley, S., and H. M. Wheeler. "Anglo-Saxon Settlement in the Trent Valley." In *Studies in Late Anglo-Saxon Settlement*, edited by M. Faull, 101–14. Oxford, 1984.

Lot, Ferdinand. "Bretons et Anglais aux Vᵉ et VIᵉ siècles." *Proceedings of the British Academy* 16 (1930), 327–44.

——. *The End of the Ancient World and the Beginnings of the Middle Ages.* Translated by Philip and Mariette Leon. New York, 1961.

——. "Nennius et Gildas." *Le Moyen Âge* 7 (1894), 1–5, 26–31; 8 (1895), 177–84; 9 (1896), 1–13, 25–32.

——. *Nennius et l' "Historia Brittonum."* Paris, 1934.

Loyn, H. R. *Anglo-Saxon England and the Norman Conquest.* London, 1962.

——. "Anglo-Saxon England: Reflections and Insights." *History* 64 (1979), 171–81.

——. *The Governance of Anglo-Saxon England 500–1087.* London, 1984.

Lucas, H. S. "The Great European Famine of 1315, 1316, 1317." *Speculum* 5 (1930), 343–77.

Luck, Kenneth. Untitled description of the Ashby Dell finds. *Yarmouth Mercury*, 8 January 1927.

Lukman, N. "The British General Gerontius (410) in Medieval Epics." *Classica et Mediaevalia* 12 (1951), 215–35.

Luttwak, Edward N. *The Grand Strategy of the Roman Empire: From the First Century A.D. to the Third.* Baltimore, 1976.

MacDougall, Hugh A. *Racial Myth in English History: Trojans, Teutons, and Anglo-Saxons.* Hanover, N.H., 1982.

Macinnes, Lesley. "Settlement and Economy: East Lothian and the Tyne-Forth Province." In *Between and Beyond the Walls: Essays on the Prehistory and History of North Britain in Honour of George Jobey,* edited by Roger Miket and Colin Burgess, 176–98. Edinburgh, 1984.

Mackereth, F. J. H. "Some Chemical Observations on Post-Glacial Lake Sediments." *Royal Society of London Philosophical Transactions* B.250 (1966), 165–213.

MacMullen, Ramsay. *Christianizing the Roman Empire.* New Haven, 1984.

——. *Corruption and the Decline of Rome.* New Haven, 1988.

——. *Enemies of the Roman Order: Treason, Unrest, and Alienation in the Empire.* Cambridge, Mass., 1967.

——. "How Big Was the Roman Imperial Army?" *Klio* 62 (1980), 451–60.

Maltby, M. "Iron Age, Romano-British, and Anglo-Saxon Animal Husbandry." In *The Environment of Man: The Iron Age to the Anglo-Saxon Period,* edited by M. Jones and G. Dimbleby, 155–203. Oxford, 1981.

Malthus, T. R. *First Essay on Population.* Royal Economic Society Reprint. London, 1926.

Manley, Gordon. "The Climate of the British Isles." In *Climates of Northern and Western Europe,* edited by C. C. Wallén, 81–133. Amsterdam, 1970.

——. "The Effective Rate of Altitudinal Change in Temperate Atlantic Climates." *Geographical Review* 35 (1945), 408–17.

——. "The Revival of Climatic Determinism." *Geographical Review* 48 (1958), 98–105.

Mann, J. C. "The Administration of Roman Britain." *Antiquity* 35 (1961), 316–20.

——. "The Historical Development of the Saxon Shore." In *The Saxon Shore: A Handbook,* edited by Valerie A. Maxfield, 1–11. Exeter, 1989.

——. "The Northern Frontier after A.D. 369." *Journal of the Glasgow Archaeological Society* 3 (1974), 34–42.

Manning, W. H. "Economic Influences on Land Use in the Military Areas of the

Highland Zone during the Roman Period." In *The Effect of Man on the Landscape: The Highland Zone*, edited by J. G. Evans, 112–16. London, 1975.

Marcus, G. J. "The Evolution of the Knörr." *Mariner's Mirror* 41 (1955), 115–22.

———. "The Nydam Craft and the Anglo-Saxon Invasions." *Mariner's Mirror* 41 (1955), 66.

Markus, R. A. "Pelagianism: Britain and the Continent." *Journal of Ecclesiastical History* 37 (1986), 191–204.

Marsden, G. J. "The Mast and Sail in the North." *Mariner's Mirror* 39 (1953), 140–41.

Marsh, Henry. *Dark Age Britain: Some Sources of History.* Newton Abbot, 1970.

Mathisen, Ralph W. " 'Nature or Nurture?'—Some Perspectives on the Gallic Famine of Circa A.D. 470." Unpublished paper.

Matthews, John F. "Macsen, Maximus, and Constantine." *Welsh History Review* 11 (1983) 431–48.

———. *Western Aristocracies and Imperial Court.* Oxford, 1975.

Maxfield, Valerie A., ed. *The Saxon Shore: A Handbook.* Exeter, 1989.

Mayr-Harting, Henry. *The Coming of Christianity to Anglo-Saxon England.* London, 1972.

McCormick, Michael. *Eternal Victory: Triumphal Rulership in Late Antiquity, Byzantium, and the Early Medieval West.* Cambridge, 1986.

McEvedy, Colin, and Richard Jones. *Atlas of World Population History.* Harmondsworth, 1978.

McGinn, Bernard. *Visions of the End: The Apocalyptic Traditions in the Middle Ages.* New York, 1979.

McGrail, Seán. *Ancient Boats in N.W. Europe: The Archaeology of Water Transport to A.D. 500.* London, 1987.

———. *The Ship: Rafts, Boats, and Ships from Prehistoric Times to the Medieval Era.* London, 1981.

———, ed. *Maritime Celts, Frisians, and Saxons.* CBA Research Report 71. London, 1990. 98–116.

McGregor, I. "Health and Communicable Disease in a Rural African Environment." *Oikos* 27 (1976), 180–92.

McKeown, T. *The Modern Rise of Population.* New York, 1976.

McNeill, W. H. *Plagues and Peoples.* New York, 1976.

McWhirr, A., L. Viner, and C. Wells. *Romano-British Cemeteries at Cirencester.* Cirencester, 1982.

Meany, Audrey. *A Gazetteer of Early Anglo-Saxon Burial Sites.* London, 1964.

Merrifield, Ralph. *London: City of the Romans.* London, 1983.

Miket, Roger. "A Restatement of Evidence from Bernician Anglo-Saxon Burials." In *Anglo-Saxon Cemeteries, 1979*, edited by P. Rahtz, T. Dickinson, and L. Watts, 289–305. Oxford, 1980.

Miket, Roger, and Colin Burgess, eds. *Between and Beyond the Walls: Essays on the Prehistory and History of North Britain in Honour of George Jobey.* Edinburgh, 1984.

Mildenberger, Gerhard. Review of *Germanische Grabfunde des 4. bis 5. Jahrhunderts zwischen unterer Elbe und Loire.* *Germania* 53 (1975), 256–63.

———. *Sozial- und Kulturgeschichte der Germanen.* Stuttgart, 1972.

Miles, David. "Confusion in the Countryside: Some Comments from the Upper

Thames Region." In *The Romano-British Countryside: Studies in Rural Settlement and Economy*, edited by David Miles, 53–79. Oxford, 1982.

——. "The Romano-British Countryside." In *Research on Roman Britain 1960–89*, edited by Malcolm Todd, 115–26. London, 1989.

——, ed. *The Romano-British Countryside: Studies in Rural Settlement and Economy*. British Archaeological Report 103. Oxford, 1982.

Millar, F. G. B. *A Study of Cassius Dio*. Oxford, 1964.

Miller, Daniel, and Christopher Tilley, eds. *Ideology, Power, and Prehistory*. Cambridge, 1984.

Miller, M. "Bede's Use of Gildas." *English Historical Review* 90 (1975), 241–61.

——. "Historicity and the Pedigrees of the Northcountrymen." *Bulletin of the Board of Celtic Studies* 26 (1975), 255–80.

——. "The Last British Entry in the 'Gallic Chronicles.'" *Britannia* 9 (1978), 315–18.

——. "Relative and Absolute Publication Dates of Gildas's *De Excidio* in Medieval Scholarship." *Bulletin of the Board of Celtic Studies* 26 (1974–76), 169–74.

——. "Starting to Write History: Gildas, Bede, and 'Nennius.'" *Welsh History Review* 8 (1976–77), 456–65.

——. "Stilicho's Pictish War." *Britannia* 6 (1975), 141–45.

Millett, M. "Forts and the Origins of Towns: Cause or Effect?" In *Military and Civilian in Roman Britain: Cultural Relationships in a Frontier Province*, edited by T. F. C. Blagg and A. C. King, 65–74. Oxford, 1984.

——. *The Romanization of Britain*. Cambridge, 1990.

Millett, M., and S. James. "Excavations at Cowdery's Down, Basingstoke, Hants, 1978–81." *Archaeological Journal* 140 (1983), 151–279.

Minor, Clifford E. "'Bagaudae' or 'Bacaudae'?" *Traditio* 31 (1975), 318–22.

Mohrmann, C. *The Latin of Saint Patrick*. Dublin, 1961.

Momigliano, A., ed. *The Conflict between Paganism and Christianity in the Fourth Century*. Oxford, 1963.

——. "Introduction: Christianity and the Decline and Fall of the Roman Empire." In *The Conflict between Paganism and Christianity in the Fourth Century*, edited by A. Momigliano, 1–16. Oxford, 1963.

Mommsen, T. *The Provinces of the Roman Empire*. 2 vols. London, 1909.

Moneyhon, Carl H. "Introduction." In *Historical Ecology: Essays on Environment and Social Change*, edited by Lester J. Bilsky, 3–5. Port Washington, N.Y., 1980.

Montesquieu. *Persian Letters*. Translated by C. J. Betts. Harmondsworth, 1973.

Morgan, Kenneth O., ed. *The Oxford Illustrated History of Britain*. Oxford, 1984.

Morris, John R. *The Age of Arthur*. London, 1973.

——. "Dark Age Dates." In *Britain and Rome: Studies Presented to Eric Birley*, edited by M. G. Jarrett and Brian Dobson, 145–85. Kendal, 1966.

——. "The Dates of the Celtic Saints." *Journal of Theological Studies*, n.s., 17 (1966), 358–75.

——. "The Literary Evidence." In *Christianity in Britain*, edited by M. W. Barley and R. P. C. Hanson, 53–73. Leicester, 1968.

——. "Pelagian Literature." *Journal of Theological Studies*, n.s., 16 (1965), 26–60.

Muhlberger, Steven. *The Fifth-Century Chroniclers*. Leeds, 1990.

———. "The Gallic Chronicle of 452 and Its Authority for British Events." *Britannia* 14 (1983), 23–33.

Mullet, C. F. *The Bubonic Plague in England.* Lexington, Ky., 1956.

Musset, Lucien. *The Germanic Invasions: The Making of Europe A.D. 400–600.* Translated by Edward James and Columba James. London, 1975. Originally published as *Les invasions: Les vagues Germaniques* (Paris, 1965).

Myres, J. N. L. "Adventus Saxonum." In *Aspects of Archaeology in Britain and Beyond,* edited by W. F. Grimes, 221–41. London, 1951.

———. *Anglo-Saxon Pottery and the Settlement of England.* Oxford, 1969.

———. *A Corpus of Anglo-Saxon Pottery in the Pagan Period.* Cambridge, 1977.

———. *The English Settlements.* Oxford, 1986.

———. "Introduction." In *Christianity in Britain,* edited by M. W. Barley and R. P. C. Hanson, 1–8. Leicester, 1968.

———. "Pelagius and the End of Roman Rule in Britain." *Journal of Roman Studies* 50 (1960), 21–36.

———. Review of *Sutton Hoo,* by Charles Green. *English Historical Review* 80 (1965), 572–73.

Myres, J. N. L., and B. Green. *The Anglo-Saxon Cemeteries of Caistor-by-Norwich and Markshall, Norfolk.* London, 1973.

Naroll, R. "Floor Area and Settlement Population." *American Antiquity* 27 (1962), 587–89.

Nouhuys, Van. "Some Doubtful Points with Regard to the Nydam Ship." *Mariner's Mirror* 22 (1936), 476–79.

Nutton, V. "Medicine and the Roman Army: A Further Reconsideration." *Medical History* 13 (1969), 260–70.

Nyberg, Tore, ed. *History and Heroic Tale.* Odense, 1985.

Nylén, Erik. *Stones, Ships, and Symbols.* Stockholm, 1988.

O'Donnell Lectures. *Angles and Britons.* Cardiff, 1963.

Onions, C. T. *The Oxford Dictionary of English Etymology.* Oxford, 1966.

O'Rahilly, T. F. *The Two Patricks: A Lecture on the History of Christianity in Fifth Century Ireland.* Dublin, 1942.

Ordnance Survey. *Field Archaeology in Great Britain.* 5th ed. Southampton, 1973.

Orlandi, Giovanni. "*Clausulae* in Gildas's De Excidio Britanniae." In *Gildas: New Approaches,* edited by M. Lapidge and D. Dumville, 127–49. Woodbridge, 1984.

O'Sullivan, Thomas D. *The "De Excidio" of Gildas: Its Authenticity and Date.* Leiden, 1978.

Painter, K. S. "Villa and Christianity in Roman Britain." *British Museum Quarterly* 35 (1971), 157–75.

Palanque, J. R., and P. de Labriolle. *The Church in the Christian Roman Empire.* London, 1952.

Parry, M. L. *Climatic Change, Agriculture, and Settlement.* Folkestone, Kent, 1978.

———. "Secular Climatic Change and Marginal Agriculture." *Transactions of the Institute of British Geographers* 64 (1975), 1–13.

———. "The Significance of the Variability of Summer Warmth in Upland Britain." *Weather* 31 (1976), 212–17.

———. "Upland Settlement and Climatic Change: The Medieval Evidence." In *Upland Settlement in Britain: The Second Millennium B.C. and After,* edited by Don Spratt and Colin Burgess, 35–49. Oxford, 1985.

Paschoud, François. *Roma aeterna: Études sur le patriotisme romain dans l'Occident latin à l'époque des grandes invasions*. Rome, 1967.

Paton, Lucy. "The Story of Vortigern's Tower: An Analysis." In *Studies in English and Comparative Literature*, Radcliffe College Monograph 15, 13–23. Boston, 1910.

Pearce, S. M. ed. *The Early Church in Western Britain and Ireland*. British Archaeological Report BS 102. Oxford, 1982.

Pearson, Michael Parker. "Economic and Ideological Change: Cyclical Growth in the Pre-State Societies of Jutland." In *Ideology, Power, and Prehistory*, ed. Daniel Miller and Christopher Tilley, 69–90. Cambridge, 1984.

Pennington, W. *The History of British Vegetation*. London, 1974.

Percival, John. *The Roman Villa: A Historical Introduction*. London, 1976.

——. "Seigneurial Aspects of Late Roman Estate Management." *English Historical Review* 84 (1969), 449–73.

Petersen, W. "A Demographer's View of Prehistoric Demography." *Current Anthropology* 16 (1975), 227–45.

Pflaum, H. G. *Le Marbre de Thorigny*. Paris, 1948.

Phillips, C. W., ed. *The Fenland in Roman Times*. Royal Geographical Society Research Series 5. London, 1970.

Philpott, Robert. *Burial Practices in Roman Britain*. British Archaeological Report 219. Oxford, 1991.

Piggot, S. "Native Economies and the Roman Occupation of North Britain." In *Roman and Native in North Britain*, edited by I. A. Richmond, 1–27. Edinburgh, 1958.

Pirenne, H. *Mohammed and Charlemagne*. Translated by Bernard Miall. 1939. Reprint, New York, 1957.

Pittock, A. B., L. A. Frakes, D. Jensen, J. A. Peterson, and J. W. Zillman, eds. *Climatic Change and Variability: A Southern Perspective*. Cambridge, 1978.

Platt, C. *The English Medieval Town*. London, 1979.

Porter, Helen. "Environmental Change in the Third Century." In *The Roman West in the Third Century*, edited by Anthony King and Martin Henig, 353–62. Oxford, 1981.

Porter, S. "Glaciological Evidence of Holocene Climatic Change." In *Climate and History*, edited by T. M. L. Wigley et al., 82–110. Cambridge, 1981.

Post, John D. *The Last Great Subsistence Crisis in the Western World*. London, 1977.

Postan, M. M. *The Medieval Economy and Society*. London, 1972.

——. "Some Economic Evidence of Declining Population in the Later Middle Ages." *Economic History Review*, 2d ser., 2 (1950), 221–46.

Potter, T. W. *The Changing Landscape of South Etruria*. London, 1979.

——. "Recent Work in the Roman Fens of Eastern England and the Question of Imperial Estates." *Journal of Roman Archaeology* 2 (1989), 267–74.

——. *Romans in North-West England*. Kendal, 1979.

——. "Valleys and Settlement: Some New Evidence." *World Archaeology* 8.2 (1976), 207–19.

Potts, W. T. W. "History and Blood Groups in the British Isles." In *Medieval Settlement: Continuity and Change*, edited by P. H. Sawyer, 236–61. London, 1976.

Pounds, N. J. G. *An Economic History of Medieval Europe*. London, 1974.

Pujol, E. Perez. *Historia de las instituciones sociales de la España Goda.* Vol. 4. Valencia, 1896.

Rackham, Oliver. *Trees and Woodland in the British Landscape.* London, 1981.

Radford, C. A. Ralegh. "Christian Origins in Britain." *Medieval Archaeology* 15 (1971), 1–12.

Rahtz, P. "Buildings and Rural Settlement." In *The Archaeology of Anglo-Saxon England,* edited by D. M. Wilson, 49–98. London, 1976.

Rahtz, P., T. Dickinson, and L. Watts, eds. *Anglo-Saxon Cemeteries, 1979.* British Archaeological Report 82. Oxford, 1980.

Ramm, H. G. "The End of Roman York." In *Soldier and Civilian in Roman Yorkshire,* edited by R. M. Butler, 179–99. Leicester, 1971.

Randall, H. J. "Population and Agriculture in Roman Britain: A Reply." *Antiquity* 4 (1930), 80–90.

Randers-Pehrson, Justine Davis. *Barbarians and Romans: The Birth Struggle of Europe, A.D. 400–600.* London, 1983.

Randsborg, Klavs. *The Viking Age in Denmark: The Formation of a State.* New York, 1980.

Ravetz, A. "Fourth Century Inflation and Romano-British Coin Finds." *Numismatic Chronicle,* 7th ser., 4 (1964), 201–31.

Razzell, P. E. "An Interpretation of the Modern Rise of Population in Europe: A Critique." *Population Studies* 28 (1974), 5–17.

Reece, Richard. *My Roman Britain.* Cotswold Studies. Cirencester, 1988.

——. "Town and Country: The End of Roman Britain." *World Archaeology* 12 (1980), 77–92.

——. "Wages and Prices." In *Archaeological Theory and Practice,* edited by D. E. Strong, 239–45. London, 1973.

——, ed. *Burial in the Roman World.* CBA Research Report 22. London, 1977.

Rees, B. R. *Pelagius: A Reluctant Heretic.* Woodbridge, 1988.

Rees, Sian E. *Agricultural Implements in Prehistoric and Roman Britain.* British Archaeological Report 69. Oxford, 1979.

Rees, W. "Survival of Ancient Celtic Custom in Medieval England." In *Angles and Britons,* 148–68. O'Donnell Lectures. Cardiff, 1963.

Reinhart, W. "Sobre el asentamiento de los Visigodos en la Peninsula." *Archivo Español de Arqueologia* 18 (1945), 124–39.

Renbourn, E. T. *Materials and Clothing in Health and Disease: History, Physiology, and Hygiene: Medical and Psychological Aspects.* London, 1972.

Reynolds, Peter J. *Iron Age Farm: The Butser Experiment.* London, 1979.

Reynolds, Peter J., and J. K. Langley. "Romano-British Corn-Drying Ovens: An Experiment." *Archaeological Journal* 136 (1979), 27–42.

Richards, M. "The Irish Settlements in South-West Wales: A Topographical Approach." *Journal of the Royal Society of Antiquaries of Ireland* 90 (1960), 133–52.

Riche, P. "Problems de démographie historique du haut moyen age (V-VIII) siècles." *Annales de démographie historique* (1966), 37–55.

Richmond, I. A. "The Four *Coloniae* of Roman Britain." *Archaeological Journal* 103 (1947), 57–84.

——. "The Sarmatae, Bremetannacum Veteranorum, and the Regio Bremetannacensis." *Journal of Roman Studies* 35 (1945), 15–29.

———, ed. *Roman and Native in North Britain*. Edinburgh, 1958.

Rickman, G. *Roman Granaries and Store Buildings*. Cambridge, 1971.

Rivet, A. L. F. *The Roman Villa in Britain*. London, 1969.

———. "The Rural Economy of Roman Britain." *Aufstieg und Niedergang der römischen Welt: Principat* 2.3 (1975):328–63.

———. *Town and Country in Roman Britain*. 2d ed. London, 1964.

Roberts, B. F. "Geoffrey of Monmouth and Welsh Historical Tradition." *Nottingham Medieval Studies* 20 (1976), 29–40.

Roberts, Brian K. *Rural Settlement in Britain*. London, 1977.

Roberts, Clayton, and David Roberts. *A History of England*. Vol. 1. Englewood Cliffs, N.J., 1985.

Roberts, W. I. *Romano-Saxon Pottery*. British Archaeological Report 106. Oxford, 1982.

Robinson, Mark. "The Iron Age to Early Saxon Environment of the Upper Thames Terraces." In *The Environment of Man: The Iron Age to the Anglo-Saxon Period*, edited by M. Jones and G. Dimbleby, 251–86. Oxford, 1981.

Robinson, T. H. *Prophecy and the Prophets in Ancient Israel*. London, 1979.

Rodwell, Warwick, ed. *Temples, Churches, and Religion: Recent Research in Roman Britain, with a Gazetteer of Romano-Celtic Temples in Continental Europe*. British Archaeological Report 77. Oxford, 1980.

Rodwell, Warwick, and K. A. Rodwell. *Rivenhall: Investigation of a Villa, Church, and Village, 1950–1977*. CBA Research Report 55. London, 1985.

Roesdahl, Else. *Viking Age Denmark*. London, 1982.

Roos, A. G. "Herodian's Method of Composition." *Journal of Roman Studies* 5 (1915), 191–202.

Rosenthal, Joel T. *Anglo-Saxon History: An Annotated Bibliography, A.D. 450–1066*. New York, 1985.

Rotberg, R. I., and T. K. Rabb, eds. *Climate and History: Studies in Interdisciplinary History*. Princeton, 1981.

Röthlisberger, F. "Gletscher und Klimaschwankungen im Raum Zermatt, Ferpècle, und Arolla." *Die Alpen* 52 (1976), 59–150.

Rouse, Irving. *Migrations in Prehistory: Inferring Population Movements from Cultural Remains*. New Haven, 1986.

Rubin, S. *Medieval English Medicine A.D. 500–1300*. New York, 1974.

Russell, J. C. *Late Ancient and Medieval Population*. Philadelphia, 1958.

———. *Medieval Regions and Their Cities*. Bloomington, 1972.

———. "Population in Europe 500–1500." In *The Middle Ages*, vol. 1 of *The Fontana Economic History of Europe*, edited by C. M. Cipolla, 25–70. 7th ed. Harmondsworth, 1978.

———. "The Preplague Population of England." *Journal of British Studies* 5 (1961), 1–20.

———. "Recent Advances in Mediaeval Demography." *Speculum* 40 (1965), 84–101.

———. "The Tribal Hidage." *Traditio* 5 (1947), 192–209.

Said, Edward W. *Orientalism*. New York, 1979.

Salmon, Pierre. *Population et dépopulation dans l'Empire romain*. Collection Latomus 137. Brussels, 1974.

Salway, Peter. *The Frontier People of Roman Britain*. Cambridge, 1965.

———. *The Oxford Illustrated History of Roman Britain*. Oxford, 1993.

——. *Roman Britain*. Oxford, 1981.

Sawyer, P. H. *The Age of the Vikings*. London, 1971.

——. *From Roman Britain to Norman England*. London, 1978.

——, ed. *English Medieval Settlement*. London, 1979.

——, ed. *Medieval Settlement: Continuity and Change*. London, 1976.

——, ed. *Names, Words, and Graves: Early Medieval Settlement*. Leeds, 1979.

Scarborough, J. *Roman Medicine*. London, 1969.

——. "Roman Medicine and the Legions: A Reconsideration." *Medical History* 12 (1968), 254–61.

Schmidt, Ludwig. *Geschichte der deutschen Stämme bis zum Ausgang der Völkerwanderung: Die Ostgermanen*. 2d ed. Munich, 1934.

——. "Die Ursachen der Völkerwanderung." *Neue Jahrbücher für das Klassische Altertum: Geschichte und deutsche Literatur* 11 (1903), 340ff.

——. "Zur Frage nach der Volkzahl der Wandalen." *Byzantinische Zeitschrift* (15) 1906, 620–21.

Schneebeli, W. "Untersuchungen von Gletscherschwankungen im Val de Bagnes." *Die Alpen* 52 (1976), 5–57.

Schutz, Herbert. *The Prehistory of Germanic Europe*. New Haven, 1983.

Scott, Eleanor. "Romano-British Wheat Yields." In *Settlement in North Britain 1000 B.C. to A.D. 1000*, edited by J. C. Chapman and H. C. Mytum, 221–32. Oxford, 1983.

Scrimshaw, N., and V. Young. "The Requirements of Human Nutrition." *Scientific American* 253 (1976), 50–64.

Scullard, H. H. *Roman Britain: Outpost of the Empire*. London, 1979.

Seddon, B. "Prehistoric Climate and Agriculture: A Review of Recent Paleo-Ecological Investigations." In *Weather and Agriculture*, edited by J. A. Taylor, 173–85. Oxford, 1967.

Segraves, B. A. "The Malthusian Proposition and Nutritional Stress: Differing Implications for Man and for Society." In *Malnutrition, Behavior, and Social Organization*, edited by L. S. Greene, 173–218. New York, 1977.

Selkirk, R. *A Dramatic New View of Roman History: The Piercebridge Formula*. Cambridge, 1983.

Setton, K. M. *The Christian Attitude towards the Emperor in the Fourth Century*. New York, 1941.

Shennan, Ian. "Problems of Correlating Flandrian Sea-Level Changes and Climate." In *Climatic Change in Later Prehistory*, edited by A. F. H. Harding, 52–67. Edinburgh, 1982.

Sherwin-White, A. N. *Racial Prejudice in Imperial Rome*. Cambridge, 1970.

Shetelig, H., and F. Johannessen. "Das Nydamschiff." *Acta Archaeologica* 1 (1930), 1–30.

Shiel, Norman, ed. *The Episode of Carausius and Allectus: The Literary and Numismatic Evidence*. British Archaeoloical Reports 40. Oxford, 1977.

Sieveking, G. de G., ed. *Prehistoric and Roman Studies*. London, 1971.

Simmons, I. G., and M. J. Tooley, eds. *The Environment in British Prehistory*. Ithaca, 1981.

Simpson, C. J. "Belt-Buckles and Strap-Ends of the Later Roman Empire: A Preliminary Survey of Several New Groups." *Britannia* 7 (1976), 192–223.

Simpson, W. Douglas. "Stilicho in Britain." *Journal of the British Archaeological Association* 7 (1942), 50–51.

Sims-Williams, Patrick. "Gildas and the Anglo-Saxons." *Cambridge Medieval Celtic Studies* 6 (1983), 1–30.

——. "Gildas and Vernacular Poetry." In *Gildas: New Approaches*, edited by M. Lapidge and D. Dumville, 169–92. Woodbridge, 1984.

——. "The Settlement of England in Bede and the *Chronicle*." *Anglo-Saxon England* 12 (1983), 1–41.

——. "Some Functions of Origin Stories in Early Medieval Wales." In *History and Heroic Tale*, edited by Tore Nyberg, 97–131. Odense, 1985.

Sisam, K. "Anglo-Saxon Genealogies." *Proceedings of the British Academy* 39 (1953), 287–343.

Slicher van Bath, B. H. *The Agrarian History of Western Europe*. London, 1963.

Smith, A. G. "Two Lacustrine Deposits in the South of the English Lake District." *New Phytologist* 57 (1958), 363–86.

Smith, Catherine D., and M. L. Parry. *Consequences of Climatic Change*. Nottingham, 1981.

Smith, Christopher. "The Valleys of the Tame and the Middle Trent—Their Populations and Ecology." In *The Iron Age: A Review*, edited by J. R. Collis, 51–61. Sheffield, 1977.

Smith, Leslie M., ed. *The Making of Britain: The Dark Ages*. London, 1984.

Smith, Roger. "Ships and the Dating of *Beowulf*." *Answers, Notes and Queries*, n.s., 3 (1990), 99–103.

Smyth, Alfred P. *Warlords and Holy Men: Scotland A.D. 80–1000*. London, 1984.

Spratt, Don, and Colin Burgess, eds. *Upland Settlement in Britain: The Second Millenium B.C. and After*. British Archaeological Reports BS 143. Oxford, 1985.

Starr, Chester G. *A History of the Ancient World*. 3d ed. Oxford, 1983.

——. *The Roman Empire 27 B.C.–A.D. 476: A Study in Survival*. Oxford, 1982.

Stein, E. *Geschichte des spätrömischen Reichs*. Vienna, 1928.

——. "Introduction à l'histoire et aux institutions byzantines." *Traditio* 7 (1949–51), 95–168.

Stein, F. "Franken und Romanen in Lotharingen." In *Studien zur vor- und frühgeschichtlichen Archäologie: Festschrift für J. Warner*, ed. Georg Kossack and Günter Ulbert, 2:579–89. 2 vols. Munich, 1974.

Stein, Z., M. Susse, G. Saenger, and F. Marolla. *Famine and Human Development: The Dutch Hunger Winter of 1944–45*. New York, 1975.

Stenton, Sir Frank Merry. *Anglo-Saxon England*. 3d. ed. Oxford, 1971.

——. "The Foundations of English History." In *Preparatory to Anglo-Saxon England*, 116–26. Oxford, 1970.

——. *Preparatory to Anglo-Saxon England: Being the Collected Papers of Frank Merry Stenton*. Edited by D. M. Stenton. Oxford, 1970.

Stevens, C. E. "The British Sections of the 'Notitia Dignitatum.'" *Archaeological Journal* 97 (1940), 125–54.

——. "Gildas Sapiens." *English Historical Review* 56 (1941), 353–73.

——. "Marcus, Gratian, and Constantine." *Athenaeum* 35 (1957), 316–47.

——. "A Possible Conflict of Laws in Roman Britain." *Journal of Roman Studies* 37 (1947), 132–34.

——. "A Roman Author in North-West Britain." *Transactions of the Cumberland and Westmorland Antiquarian and Archaeological Society*, n.s., 5 (1951), 70–79.

——. *Sidonius Apollinaris and His Age.* Oxford, 1933.

Stevenson, G. H. *Roman Provincial Administration till the Age of the Antonines.* Oxford, 1939.

Stevenson, W. H. "The Beginnings of Wessex." *English Historical Review* 14 (1899), 32–46.

Stratton, John M., and John Houghton Brown. *Agricultural Records in Britain A.D. 220–1977.* 2d ed. Edited by Ralph Whitlock. Hamden, Conn., 1979.

Strong, D. E., ed. *Archaeological Theory and Practice.* London, 1973.

Sutherland, A. C. "The Imagery of Gildas's *De Excidio Britanniae.*" In *Gildas: New Approaches*, edited by Michael Lapidge and David Dumville, 157–68. Woodbridge, 1984.

Swedlund, A. C., and G. J. Armelagos. *Demographic Anthropology.* Dubuque, Iowa, 1976.

Syme, R. *Ammianus and the "Historia Augusta."* Oxford, 1968.

——. *Tacitus.* 2 vols. Oxford, 1958.

Szilagyi, J. "Beiträge zur Statistik der Sterblichkeit in der west-europäischen Provinzen des römischen Imperium." *Acta Archaeologica Academiae Scientiarum Hungaricae* 13 (1961), 126–56.

Tainter, Joseph A. *The Collapse of Complex Societies.* Cambridge, 1988.

Talbot, C. H. *Medicine in Medieval England.* London, 1967.

Tatham, G. "Environmentalism and Possibilism." In *Geography in the Twentieth Century*, edited by G. Taylor, 128–62. New York, 1957.

Taylor, Christopher. "Roman Settlements in the Nene Valley: The Impact of Recent Archaeology." In *Recent Work in Rural Archaeology*, edited by P. J. Fowler, 107–20. Bradford-on-Avon, 1975.

——. *Village and Farmstead: A History of Rural Settlement in England.* London, 1983.

Taylor, G., ed. *Geography in the Twentieth Century.* 3d ed. New York, 1957.

Taylor, J. A. "Environmental Changes in Wales during the Holocene Period." In *Culture and Environment in Prehistoric Wales*, edited by J. A. Taylor, 101–30. Oxford, 1980.

——. "The Role of Climatic Factors in Environmental and Cultural Changes in Prehistoric Times." In *The Effect of Man on the Landscape: The Highland Zone*, edited by J. G. Evans, 6–19. London, 1975.

——, ed. *Climatic Change with Special Reference to Wales and Its Agriculture.* Aberystwyth, 1965.

——, ed. *Culture and Environment in Prehistoric Wales.* British Archaeological Reports 76. Oxford, 1980.

——, ed. *Hill Climates and Land Useages with Special Reference to the Highland Zone of Britain.* Aberystwyth, 1960.

——, ed. *Weather and Agriculture.* Oxford, 1967.

Teall, J. L. "The Barbarians in Justinian's Armies." *Speculum* 40 (1965), 294–322.

TeBrake, William H. *Medieval Frontier: Culture and Ecology in Rijnland.* College Station, Texas, 1985.

Temporini, H., ed. *Aufstieg und Niedergang der römischen Welt: Geschichte und Kultur Roms im Spiegel der neueren Forschung.* Berlin, 1975– .

Ten Brink, N. W., and A. Werdick. "Greenland Ice Sheet History since the Last Glaciation." *Quarternary Research* 4 (1974), 429–40.

Thirsk, J. "The Common Fields." *Past and Present* 29 (1964), 3–25; 33 (1966), 412–17.

Thomas, Charles. *Celtic Britain.* London, 1986.

———. *Christianity in Roman Britain to A.D. 500.* London, 1981.

———. "Churches in Late Roman Britain." In *Temples, Churches, and Religion: Recent Research in Roman Britain, with a Gazetteer of Romano-Celtic Temples in Continental Europe,* edited by Warwick Rodwell, 129–64. Oxford, 1980.

———. "Irish Colonists in South-West Britain." *World Archaeology* 5 (1973), 5–13.

———. "The Irish Settlements in Post-Roman Western Britain: A Survey of the Evidence." *Journal of the Royal Institute of Cornwall,* n.s., 6 (1972), 251–74.

———, ed. *Rural Settlement in Roman Britain.* CBA Research Report 7. London, 1966.

———. "Saint Patrick and Fifth Century Britain: An Historical Model Explored." In *The End of Roman Britain,* edited by P. J. Casey, 81–101. Oxford, 1979.

Thomas, D. H. "The Awful Truth about Statistics in Archaeology." *American Antiquity* 43 (1978), 231–44.

Thompson, A. Hamilton, ed. *Bede: His Life, Times, and Writing.* Oxford, 1935. Reprint, New York, 1966.

Thompson, E. A. "Britain, A.D. 406–410." *Britannia* 8 (1977), 303–18.

———. "Britonia." In *Christianity in Britain 300–700: Papers Presented to the Conference on Christianity in Roman and Sub-Roman Britain,* edited by M. W. Barley and R. P. C. Hanson, 201–5. Leicester, 1968.

———. "Gildas and the History of Britain." *Britannia* 10 (1979), 203–26; 11 (1980), 344.

———. *The Historical Work of Ammianus Marcellinus.* Cambridge, 1947.

———. "Peasant Revolts in Late Roman Gaul and Spain." *Past and Present* 2 (1952), 11–23.

———. "Procopius on Brittia and Britannia." *Classical Quarterly* 30 (1980), 498–507.

———. *Romans and Barbarians: The Decline of the Western Empire.* Madison, Wis., 1982.

———. *Saint Germanus of Auxerre and the End of Roman Britain.* Woodbridge, 1984.

———. "St. Patrick and Coroticus." *Journal of Theological Studies,* n.s., 31 (1980), 12–27.

———. *Who Was Saint Patrick?* New York, 1985.

———. "Zosimus 6.10.2 and the Letters of Honorius." *Classical Quarterly* 32 (1982), 445–62.

———. "Zosimus on the End of Roman Britain." *Antiquity* 30 (1956), 163–67.

Thompson, F. H., ed. *Archaeology and Coastal Change.* Being the Papers presented at meetings in London and Manchester on October 27 and November 5, 1977. London, 1980.

Thorpe, B. *Ancient Laws and Institutes of England.* London, 1840.

Thran, P., and S. Broekhuizen. *Agro-Ecological Atlas of Cereal Growing in Europe.* Amsterdam, 1965.

Tinsley, H. "Cultural Influences on Pennine Vegetation with Particular Reference to North Yorkshire." *Institute of British Geographers* 1 (1976), 310–22.

Tischler, F. "The Continental Background." *Medieval Archaeology* 3 (1959), 1–7.

Todd, Malcolm. "Famosa Pestis and Britain in the Fifth Century." *Britannia* 8 (1977), 319–25.

——. *The Northern Barbarians.* Rev. ed. New York, 1987.

——. *Roman Britain: 55 B.C.–A.D. 400.* London, 1981.

——. *Studies in the Romano-British Villa.* Leicester, 1978.

——, ed. *Research on Roman Britain.* London, 1989.

Tolstoy, N. "Who Was Coroticus?" *Irish Ecclesiastical Record,* 5th ser., 97 (1962), 137–47.

Tomlin, R. "The Date of the 'Barbarian Conspiracy.'" *Britannia* 5 (1974), 303–9.

Tooley, Michael J. "Sea-Level and Coastline Changes during the Last 5000 Years." In *Maritime Celts, Frisians, and Saxons,* edited by Seán McGrail, 1–16. London, 1990.

——. *Sea Level Changes in North-West England during the Flandrian Stage.* Oxford, 1978.

Tooley, Michael J., and Ian Shennan, eds. *Sea Level Changes.* Oxford, 1987.

Turner, C. H. *Ecclesiae Occidentalis Monumenta Iuris Antiquissima.* Leipzig, 1939.

Turner, Judith. "A Contribution to the History of Forest Clearance." *Proceedings of the Royal Society* B.161 (1965), 343–53.

——. "The Environment of Northeast England during Roman Times as Shown by Pollen Analysis." *Journal of Archaeological Science* 6 (1979), 285–90.

——. "The Evidence for Land Use by Prehistoric Farming Communities: The Use of Three-Dimensional Pollen Diagrams." In *The Effect of Man on the Landscape: The Highland Zone,* edited by J. G. Evans, Susan Limbrey, and Henry Cleere, 86–95. London, 1975.

——. "The Iron Age." In *The Environment in British Prehistory,* edited by I. G. Simmons and M. J. Tooley, 250–81. Ithaca, 1981.

Turville-Petre, J. E. "Hengest and Horsa." *Saga Book of the Viking Society* 14 (1957), 273–90.

Ucko, Peter J. "Ethnography and Archaeological Interpretation of Funerary Remains." *World Archaeology* 1 (1969), 262–80.

Ullmann, W. "On the Use of the Term 'Romani' in the Sources of the Earlier Middle Ages." *Studia Patristica* 2 (1957), 155–63.

Usher, A. P. "A New Estimate of the Population of Britain in Roman Times." *The Geographical Review* 20 (1930), 674–76.

Utterström, G. "Climatic Fluctuations and Population Problems in Early Modern History." *Scandinavian Economic History Review* 3 (1955), 1–47.

——. "Some Population Problems in Pre-Industrial Sweden." *Scandinavian Economic History Review* 2 (1954) 103–65.

Van Dam, Raymond. *Leadership and Community in Late Antique Gaul.* Berkeley, 1985.

van der Veen, Marijke. *Crop Husbandry Regimes: An Archaeobotanical Study of Farming in Northern England.* Sheffield, 1992.

van Es, W. A. "Introduction." In *Roman and Native in the Low Countries: Spheres of Interaction,* edited by Roel Brandt and Jan Slofstra, 1–9. Oxford, 1983.

Van Sickel, C. E. "Diocletian and the Decline of the Roman Municipalities." *Journal of Roman Studies* 28 (1938), 9–18.

Vives, J. V. *An Economic History of Spain*. Princeton, 1969.

Wacher, J. S. *The Civitas Capitals of Roman Britain*. Leicester, 1975.

———. *The Coming of Rome*. London, 1979.

———. *The Towns of Roman Britain*. London, 1974.

Waddelove, A. C., and E. Waddelove. "Archaeology and Research into Sea Level during the Roman Era: Toward a Methodology Based on Highest Astronomical Tide." *Britannia* 21 (1990), 252–66.

Wade-Evans, A. W. *Nennius's "History of the Britons"; together with, "The Annals of the Britons"; and, "Court Pedigrees of Hywell the Good"; also, "The Story of the Loss of Britain."* London, 1938.

———. "Some Insular Sources of the *Excidio Britanniae*." *Y Cymmrodor* 27 (1917), 37–69.

Waterbolk, H. T. "Landscape and Settlement Continuity in Northern Holland." Paper presented January 15, 1982 at a conference on "The North Sea Province." Oxford, 1982.

Walbank, F. W. *The Awful Revolution: The Decline of the Roman Empire in the West*. Liverpool, 1969.

Walker, D. "The Late-Quaternary History of the Cumberland Lowland." *Philosophical Transactions of the Royal Society of London* B.251 (1966), 2–210.

Walker, D., and R. G. West, eds. *Studies in the Vegetational History of the British Isles*. Cambridge, 1970.

Walker, M. J. C. "Holocene (Flandrian) Vegetation Change and Human Activity in the Carneddau Area of Upland Mid-Wales." In *Climate Change and Human Impact on the Landscape*, edited by F. M. Chambers, 169–84. London, 1993.

Wallace-Hadrill, Andrew, ed. *Patronage in Roman Society*. London, 1989.

Wallace-Hadrill, J. M. *The Barbarian West, 400–1000*. Rev. ed. Oxford, 1985.

———. *Bede's Ecclesiastical History of the English People: A Historical Commentary*. Oxford, 1988.

———. *The Long Haired Kings*. London, 1962.

Wallén, C. C., ed. *Climates of Northern and Western Europe*. Amsterdam, 1970.

Walton, K. "Climate and Famines in Northeast Scotland." *Scottish Geographical Magazine* 68 (1952), 13–22.

Ward, J. O. "Procopius, *Bellum Gothicum* II.6.28: The Problem of Contacts between Justinian I and Britain." *Byzantion* 38 (1968), 460–71.

Wardman, A. *Religion and Statecraft among the Romans*. Leiden, 1982.

Webster, G., and B. Hobley. "Aerial Reconnaissance over the Warwickshire Avon." *Archaeological Journal* 121 (1964), 1–22.

Webster, Graham. "The Possible Effects on Britain of the Fall of Magnentius." In *Rome and Her Northern Provinces*, edited by B. Hartley and J. Wacher, 240–54. London, 1983.

———. *The Roman Invasion of Britain*. London, 1980.

Welch, Martin G. *Discovering Anglo-Saxon England*. London, 1992.

———. "Late Romans and Saxons in Sussex." *Britannia* 2 (1971), 232–37.

———. "Reflections on the Archaeological Connections between Scandinavia and Eastern England in the Migration Period." *Studien zur Sachsen-forschung* 6 (1987), 251–59.

———. "Rural Settlement Patterns in the Early and Middle Anglo-Saxon Periods."
   Landscape History 7 (1985), 13–25.
———. "The Saxon Cemeteries of Sussex." In *Anglo-Saxon Cemeteries, 1979*, edited
   by P. Rahtz, T. Dickinson, and L. Watts, 255–83. Oxford, 1980.
Wellcome, H. S. *Anglo-Saxon Leechcraft*. London, 1912.
Wells, Calvin. *Bones, Bodies, and Disease: Evidence of Disease and Abnormality
   in Early Man*. London, 1964.
Welsby, Derek A. *The Roman Military Defence of the British Provinces in Its Later
   Phases*. British Archaeological Report 101. Oxford, 1982.
Wendland, W. M., and R. A. Bryson. "Dating Climatic Episodes of the Holocene."
   Quaternary Research 4 (1974), 9–24.
Werner, J. "Zur Zeitstellung des Bootgrabes von Snape." In *Actes du vii congrés
   internationale des sciences préhistoriques et protohistoriques, Prague, 1966*,
   997–98. Prague, 1970.
Wheeler, G. H. "The Genealogy of the Early West Saxon Kings." *English Historical
   Review* 36 (1921), 161–71.
———. "Gildas *de Excidio Britanniae*, Chapter 26." *English Historical Review* 41
   (1926), 497–503.
Wheeler, R. E. M. "Mr. Collingwood and Mr. Randall: A Note." *Antiquity* 4 (1930),
   91–95.
———. *Report on the Excavations of the Prehistoric, Roman, and Post-Roman Site
   of Lydney Park, Gloucester*. London, 1932.
White, Donald A. "Changing Views of the *Adventus Saxonum* in Nineteenth and
   Twentieth Century English Scholarship." *Journal of the History of Ideas* 32
   (1971), 585–94.
———. *Litus Saxonicum: The British Saxon Shore in Scholarship and History*.
   Madison, Wis., 1961.
White, K. D. "Wheat Farming in Roman Times." *Antiquity* 37 (1963) 207–12.
Whitelock, D., D. C. Douglas, and S. I. Tucker. *The Anglo-Saxon Chronicle*. Lon-
   don, 1965.
Whittle, Alasdair. "Climate, Grazing, and Man." In *Climatic Change in Later
   Prehistory*, edited by A. F. Harding, 192–203. Edinburgh, 1982.
Whittock, Martyn. *The Origins of England 410–600*. Totowa, N.J., 1986.
Widmer, Edward. "Dating Saint Patrick." *Harvard Magazine* 91 (1989), 4–5.
Wightman, E. M. "Peasants and Potentates: An Investigation of Social Structure
   and Land Tenure in Roman Gaul." *American Journal of Ancient History* 3
   (1978), 97–128.
———. "Rural Settlement in Roman Gaul." *Aufstieg und Niedergang der römischen
   Welt* 3.4 (1975), 584–657.
Wigley, T. M. L., M. J. Igram, and G. Farmer, eds. *Climate and History*. Cambridge,
   1981.
Willcox, G. H. "Problems and Possible Conclusions Related to the History and
   Archaeology of the Thames in the London Region." *Transactions of the London
   and Middlesex Archaeological Society* 26 (1975), 285–92.
Williams, Ifor. "Mommsen and the Vatican Nennius." *Bulletin of the Board of
   Celtic Studies* 11–12 (1941), 43–48.
———. "Notes on Nennius." *Bulletin of the Board of Celtic Studies* 7 (1933–35),
   380–89.

Willigan, J. Dennis, and Katherine A. Lynch, eds. *Sources and Methods of Historical Demography*. New York, 1982.

Wilson, Alexander T. "Isotope Evidence from Past Climatic and Environmental Change." In *Climate and History: Studies in Interdisciplinary History*, edited by R. I. Rotberg and T. K. Rabb, 215–32. Princeton, 1981.

Wilson, D. M. "Introduction." In *The Archaeology of Anglo-Saxon England*, edited by D. M. Wilson, 1–22. Cambridge, 1976.

——. "The Scandinavians in England." In *The Archaeology of Anglo-Saxon England*, edited by D. M. Wilson, 393–403. London, 1976.

——, ed. *The Archaeology of Anglo-Saxon England*. Cambridge, 1976.

——, ed. *The Northern World: The History of Northern Europe, A.D. 400–1100*. New York, 1980.

Wilson, P. A. "St. Patrick and Irish Christian Origins." *Studia Celtica* 14–15 (1979–80), 344–79.

Winterbottom, M. "The Preface of Gildas's *De Excidio*." *Transactions of the Cymmrodorion Society* (1974–75), 277–87.

Witney, K. P. *The Kingdom of Kent*. London, 1982.

Wolf, D. J. "A Population Model for the Analysis of Osteological Materials." Ph.D. diss., University of Arizona, 1976.

Wolfram, Herwig. *Geschichte der Goten*. Munich, 1979. Translated by Thomas J. Dulap. *History of the Goths*. Berkeley, 1988.

——. "The Shaping of the Early Medieval Kingdom." *Viator* 1 (1970), 1–20.

Wood, Ian. "The Channel from the 4th to the 7th Centuries A.D." In *Maritime Celts, Frisians, and Saxons*, edited by Seán McGrail, 93–97. London, 1990.

——. "The Fall of the Western Empire and the End of Roman Britain." *Britannia* 18 (1987), 251–62.

——. "The End of Roman Britain: Continental Evidence and Parallels." In *Gildas: New Approaches*, edited by M. Lapidge and D. Dumville, 1–25. Woodbridge, 1984.

——. *The Merovingian North Sea*. Alingsås, 1983.

Wooding, Jonathan. "Saxons Who Furrow the British Sea with Hides." *The Great Circle* 10 (1988), 33–36.

Woolf, R. "The Idea of Men Dying with Their Lord in the *Germania* and in *The Battle of Maldon*." *Anglo-Saxon England* 5 (1976), 63–81.

Wormald, Patrick, Donald Bullough, and Roger Collins, eds. *Ideal and Reality in Frankish and Anglo-Saxon Society: Studies Presented to J. M. Wallace-Hadrill*. Oxford, 1983.

Wright, Neil. "Did Gildas Read Orosius?" *Cambridge Medieval Celtic Studies* 9 (1985), 31–42.

——. "Gildas's Geographical Perspective: Some Problems." In *Gildas: New Approaches*, edited by Michael Lapidge and David Dumville, 85–105. Woodbridge, 1984.

——. "Gildas's Prose Style and Its Origins." In *Gildas: New Approaches*, edited by M. Lapidge and D. Dumville, 107–28. Woodbridge, 1984.

Wrigley, E. A. *Population and History*. New York, 1969.

Yorke, Barbara. *Kings and Kingdoms of Early Anglo-Saxon England*. London, 1990.

Young, Bailey. "The Barbarian Funerary Tradition in Gaul in the Light of the Archaeological Record: Considerations and Reconsiderations." Paper delivered April 4, 1992 at the Sewanee Medieval Colloquium. Sewanee, 1992.

Zimmer, H. *Nennius Vindicatus: Über Enstehung, Geschichte, und Quellen der "Historia Brittonum."* Berlin, 1893.

Zubrow, Ezra B. W., ed. *Demographic Anthropology: Quantitative Approaches.* Albuquerque, 1976.

Index

CPSIA information can be obtained
at www.ICGtesting.com
Printed in the USA
BVHW032226010921
615884BV00006B/37